# TRAJECTORIES IN THE DEVELOPMENT OF MODERN SCHOOL SYSTEMS

> "This book really comes together. What it shows—time and time again, in a variety of national contexts and time periods—is that efforts to import school policies and curricula and practices from elsewhere always experience an intense interaction with national policies and curricula and practices. It's not that globalization efforts have no impact; it's that this impact is nonlinear and not at all necessarily in the intended direction. National systems of schooling use international initiatives for their own purposes, just as globalizers try to use national vulnerabilities to advance their own agendas."
>
> *David F. Labaree, Stanford University, USA*

As contemporary education becomes increasingly tied to global economic power, national school systems attempting to influence one another inevitably confront significant tensions caused by differences in heritage, politics, and formal structures. *Trajectories in the Development of Modern School Systems* provides a comprehensive theoretical and empirical critique of the reform movements that seek to homogenize schooling around the world. Informed by historical and sociological insight into a variety of nations and eras, these in-depth case studies reveal how and why sweeping, convergent reform agendas clash with specific institutional policies, practices, and curricula. Countering current theoretical models that fail to address the potential pressures born from these challenging isomorphic developments, this book illuminates the cultural idiosyncrasies that both produce and problematize global reform efforts and offers a new way of understanding curriculum as a manifestation of national identity.

**Daniel Tröhler** is professor of education and director of the Doctoral School in Educational Sciences at the University of Luxembourg and visiting professor of comparative education at the University of Granada, Spain.

**Thomas Lenz** is a postdoctoral research associate at the Research Unit for Education, Culture, Cognition and Society (ECCS) at the University of Luxembourg. He was a scientific collaborator at the University of Trier, Germany, and has taught courses at Hamline University, United States, and at the Babes-Bolyai University, Romania.

# STUDIES IN CURRICULUM THEORY
William F. Pinar, Series Editor

| | |
|---|---|
| Tröhler/Lenz (Eds.) | Trajectories in the Development of Modern School Systems: Between the National and the Global |
| Popkewitz (Ed.) | The "Reason" of Schooling: Historicizing Curriculum Studies, Pedagogy, and Teacher Education |
| Henderson (Ed.) | Reconceptualizing Curriculum Development: Inspiring and Informing Action |
| Magrini | Social Efficiency and Instrumentalism in Education: Critical Essays in Ontology, Phenomenology, and Philosophical Hermeneutics |
| Wang | Nonviolence and Education: Cross-Cultural Pathways |
| Hurren/Hasebe-Ludt (Eds.) | Contemplating Curriculum: Genealogies/Times/Places |
| Pinar (Ed.) | International Handbook of Curriculum Research, Second Edition |
| Latta | Curricular Conversations: Play Is the (Missing) Thing |
| Doll | Pragmatism, Post-Modernism, and Complexity Theory: The "Fascinating Imaginative Realm" of William E. Doll, Jr. Edited by Donna Trueit |
| Carlson | The Education of Eros: A History of Education and the Problem of Adolescent Sexuality Since 1950 |
| Taubman | Disavowed Knowledge: Psychoanalysis, Education, and Teaching |
| Pinar | What Is Curriculum Theory? Second Edition |
| Tröhler | Languages of Education: Protestant Legacies, National Identities, and Global Aspirations |
| Hendry | Engendering Curriculum History |
| Handa | What Does Understanding Mathematics Mean for Teachers? Relationship as a Metaphor for Knowing |
| Joseph (Ed.) | Cultures of Curriculum, Second Edition |

| | |
|---|---|
| Sandlin/Schultz/Burdick (Eds.) | Handbook of Public Pedagogy: Education and Learning Beyond Schooling |
| Malewski (Ed.) | Curriculum Studies Handbook—The Next Moment |
| Pinar | The Wordliness of a Cosmopolitan Education: Passionate Lives in Public Service |
| Taubman | Teaching by Numbers: Deconstructing the Discourse of Standards and Accountability in Education |
| Appelbaum | Children's Books for Grown-Up Teachers: Reading and Writing Curriculum Theory |
| Eppert/Wang (Eds.) | Cross-Cultural Studies in Curriculum: Eastern Thought, Educational Insights |
| Jardine/Friesen/Clifford | Curriculum in Abundance |
| Autio | Subjectivity, Curriculum, and Society: Between and Beyond German Didaktik and Anglo-American Curriculum Studies |
| Brantlinger (Ed.) | Who Benefits from Special Education?: Remediating (Fixing) Other People's Children |
| Pinar/Irwin (Eds.) | Curriculum in a New Key: The Collected Works of Ted T. Aoki |
| Reynolds/Webber (Eds.) | Expanding Curriculum Theory: Dis/Positions and Lines of Flight |
| McKnight | Schooling, the Puritan Imperative, and the Molding of an American National Identity: Education's "Errand Into the Wilderness" |
| Pinar (Ed.) | International Handbook of Curriculum Research |
| Morris | Curriculum and the Holocaust: Competing Sites of Memory and Representation |
| Doll | Like Letters in Running Water: A Mythopoetics of Curriculum |
| Westbury/Hopmann/Riquarts (Eds.) | Teaching as a Reflective Practice: The German Didaktic Tradition |
| Reid | Curriculum as Institution and Practice: Essays in the Deliberative Tradition |
| Pinar (Ed.) | Queer Theory in Education |
| Huebner | The Lure of the Transcendent: Collected Essays by Dwayne E. Huebner. Edited by Vikki Hillis. Collected and Introduced by William F. Pinar |

For additional information on titles in the Studies in Curriculum Theory series visit **www.routledge.com/education**

# TRAJECTORIES IN THE DEVELOPMENT OF MODERN SCHOOL SYSTEMS

## Between the National and the Global

*Edited by Daniel Tröhler and Thomas Lenz*

First published 2015
by Routledge
711 Third Avenue, New York, NY 10017

and by Routledge
2 Park Square, Milton Park, Abingdon, Oxon, OX14 4RN

*Routledge is an imprint of the Taylor & Francis Group, an informa business*

© 2015 Taylor & Francis

The right of the editors to be identified as the authors of the editorial material, and of the authors for their individual chapters, has been asserted in accordance with sections 77 and 78 of the Copyright, Designs and Patents Act 1988.

All rights reserved. No part of this book may be reprinted or reproduced or utilised in any form or by any electronic, mechanical, or other means, now known or hereafter invented, including photocopying and recording, or in any information storage or retrieval system, without permission in writing from the publishers.

*Trademark notice*: Product or corporate names may be trademarks or registered trademarks, and are used only for identification and explanation without intent to infringe.

*Library of Congress Cataloging-in-Publication Data*
Trajectories in the development of modern school systems : between the
 national and the global / edited by Daniel Tröhler and Thomas Lenz.
 1. Education and state—Europe—History. 2. School management and organization—Europe—History. 3. Education and globalization—Europe. I. Tröhler, Daniel, editor of compilation.
  LC93.A2T73 2015
  379.4—dc23
  2014045723

ISBN: 978-1-138-90348-7 (hbk)
ISBN: 978-1-315-69689-8 (ebk)

Typeset in Bembo
by Apex CoVantage, LLC

Printed and bound in the United States of America by Publishers Graphics, LLC on sustainably sourced paper.

# CONTENTS

**PART I**
**The Global and the Local in the History of Education**  1

1 Between the National and the Global: Introduction  3
 *Daniel Tröhler and Thomas Lenz*

2 Practical Knowledge and School Reform: The Impracticality
 of Local Knowledge in Strategies of Change  10
 *Thomas S. Popkewitz, Yanmei Wu, and Catarina Silva Martins*

**PART II**
**Fabricating the Nation: National and International
Impacts on Schooling in the Long 19th Century**  25

3 People, Citizens, Nations: Organizing Modern Schooling
 in Western Europe in the 19th Century: The Cases of
 Luxembourg and Zurich  27
 *Daniel Tröhler*

4 Educating the Catholic Citizen: The Institutionalization
 of Primary Education in Luxembourg in the 19th Century
 and Beyond  46
 *Ragnhild Barbu*

5　Early School Evaluation and Competency Conflicts
　　Between Primary and Secondary Schools in Luxembourg
　　Around 1850　　　　　　　　　　　　　　　　　　　　　　60
　　*Peter Voss*

6　Taking the Right Measures: The French Political and
　　Cultural Revolution and the Introduction of New Systems
　　of Measurement in Swiss Schools in the 19th Century　　73
　　*Lukas Boser*

7　Education Statistics, School Reform, and the Development
　　of Administrative Bodies: The Example of Zurich
　　Around 1900　　　　　　　　　　　　　　　　　　　　　　85
　　*Thomas Ruoss*

8　From Abstinence to Economic Promotion, or the International
　　Temperance Movement and the Swiss Schools　　　　　　98
　　*Michèle Hofmann*

## PART III
## The Internationalization of European Schooling in the Cold War　　111

9　The Implementation of Programmed Learning in Switzerland　113
　　*Rebekka Horlacher*

10　Global Comparison and National Application: Polls as a
　　Means for Improving Teacher Education and Stabilizing
　　the School System in Cold War Germany　　　　　　　　128
　　*Norbert Grube*

11　The National in the Global: Switzerland and the Council
　　of Europe's Policies on Schooling for Migrant Children
　　in the 1960s　　　　　　　　　　　　　　　　　　　　　　144
　　*Regula Bürgi and Philipp Eigenmann*

12　Language Structures in a Multilingual and Multidisciplinary
　　World: The Adaptations of Luxembourgian Language
　　Education Within a Cold War Culture　　　　　　　　　　157
　　*Catherina Schreiber*

13 Contesting Education: Media Debates and the Public Sphere in Luxembourg 174
*Thomas Lenz*

14 Globalization in Finnish and West German Educational Rhetoric, 1960–1970 183
*Matias Gardin*

**PART IV**
**Recent Developments** **197**

15 Calling for Sustainability: WWF's Global Agenda and Teaching Swedish Exceptionalism 199
*Malin Ideland and Daniel Tröhler*

16 From the Literate Citizen to the Qualified Science Worker: Neoliberal Rationality in Danish Science Education Reforms 213
*Jette Schmidt, Peer Daugbjerg, Martin Sillasen, and Paola Valero*

17 The European Educational Model and Its Paradoxical Impact at the National Level 227
*Lukas Graf*

18 Accelerated Westernization in Post-Soviet Russia: Coupling Higher Education and Research 241
*Viktoria Boretska*

19 Contesting Isomorphism and Divergence: Historicizing the Chinese Educational Encounter With the "West" 256
*Jinting Wu*

*Contributors* *269*
*Index* *275*

# PART I
# The Global and the Local in the History of Education

# 1

# BETWEEN THE NATIONAL AND THE GLOBAL

## Introduction

*Daniel Tröhler and Thomas Lenz*

Today's educational questions in both research and policy are discussed with regard to international or even global levels. While national educational policies are trying to adapt their educational systems to internationally accepted standards, research is trying to analyze these processes, to identify their historical roots, and to evaluate their desirability, impacts, and effects. However, although devoted to analyzing these developments, some of the research does more than analyze them—namely, it constructs them.

One of the most prominent attempts to construct rather than analyze these outlined developments is a model of institutional change developed at the Department of Sociology at Stanford University. The model has triggered an international research agenda called neo-institutionalism, which focuses on organizations in their cultural environment. In its first stage the model developed the notion of "loose coupling," describing the relationship between formal structures of organizations and their inner activities (Glassmann, 1973; Weick, 1976). The loose coupling model argues that the formal structures are not tightly linked to the inner practices within organizations and that the rules of the organizational game might be very different from the way the game is actually played. The inner activities are believed to have their own logic in terms of effectiveness and efficiency (Meyer & Rowan, 1977, pp. 341ff., p. 361; see also Meyer & Rowan, 1978, pp. 79ff.). Historical case studies in education endorse the idea that the phenomenon of loose coupling is not only *not* a disturbing factor but, quite on the contrary, a constitutive factor for an educational organization. Indeed, attempts to tightly connect formal structures and inner activities can lead to an annulment of the organization (Bosche, 2008). External expectations are mirrored in the adaptions of organizational structures and the definition of procedures of organizations (such as schools), whereas the inner activities (such as teaching) are hardly affected by organizational strategies—much to the chagrin of educational reformers. Whereas the outer shell of an organization and its rules and regulations can be revised rather quickly, its inner activities (the way the organization really does things) might not be very susceptible to change even in the long run.

The "world polity" thesis of neo-institutionalism assumes that there is something like a world society that leads to a global trend in the adaption of formal structures, which tend to be more or less the same in every (developed) nation-state (see, for instance, Meyer & Ramirez, 2000). According to this world polity thesis, (allegedly) successful models of organizing schooling are being globally disseminated. This dissemination works either through large international meetings and reports, such as the UNESCO Education for All conferences or the UNESCO Education for All *Global Monitoring Report*, or through the guidelines and conditions of the World Bank. Through these channels, the world polity thesis argues, specific models of organizing schooling become globally implemented, leading to a global isomorphism of schooling. UNESCO or the World Bank may be seen as contributing to the formal isomorphism of the educational systems throughout the world, and the Organization for Economic Co-operation and Development (OECD) may be identified as a player in harmonization on a more European scale.

The world polity thesis (at least on the naive reading) suggests that schools all over the world are in fact more or less the same. Accordingly, it is suggested that owing to specific "world forces," that is, some "cultural principles exogenous to any specific nation-state and its historical legacy" (Meyer & Ramirez, 2000, p. 115), the developments of schooling and curricula in the different nation-states "show surprising degrees of homogeneity around the world" (Meyer, 1992, pp. 2f.) and "variance across national societies is less noticeable than most arguments would have had it," so that we may speak of a "world curriculum" in the "global village," indicating the "relative unimportance of the national, so far as mass curricular outlines go" (pp. 6f.).

It is probably no coincidence that the idea of a "world society" steered by a regime called "world polity" has been suggested by sociologists (see also Luhmann, 1975; Beck, 1998; Castells, 2003). Sociology depends in its fundaments on the perception of a society, and society has been, from its very outset, a national construction, eventually becoming the epitome of the emerging nation-states, restricted to the respective nation-states and distinct from the "societies" of other nation-states. Against this background, it is understandable that in post-national times sociologists, realizing the slow eclipse of their object—society—would move to the next clustered "social" entity in a post-national era, the global "world society." What has been "true" in the nation-states—national society, education, policy, and politics—now applies to the world as a whole—world society, world curriculum, and world polity.

Notwithstanding the indisputable merits of the early neo-institutionalism, this book challenges the idea of transferring developments observed within the nation-states to a world-state. The book does not aim to challenge the fact that on an abstract level there are many formal similarities between different school systems that can be detected, but it does challenge the proposition that these similarities are still really similar on a less abstract level, on a level where different cultural systems of meaning "make" something else of something "similar." Rather than contributing to an intellectual globalizing of globalization (Tröhler, 2009), the book asks analytically how global or transnational pressures are translated into regional or national idiosyncrasies—or it asks how the model of "loose coupling" works on a regional or national level when it comes to global pressures.

The question of how a specific school organization (as an institutional heritage of an idiosyncratic culture) performs within the tensions between global agendas and national culture is hardly addressed by the dominant models and theories analyzing educational questions at an international level. It is here that this book sets in. It acknowledges that today's educational questions tend to be discussed more and more at international and global levels and that different national school systems are in fact more or less simultaneously adjusting to each other in more formal settings: It seems that the educational globe is harmonizing itself on both levels, the rhetorical and the organizational. Yet the attraction of this global formal affinity has led to a neglect of questions on how this harmonization process came about in different nation-states, how it interacted with national and/or cultural idiosyncrasies of national school systems, and to what extent rhetorical and formal organizational harmony actually erased national and/or cultural systems of reasoning and creating meaning (Tröhler, 2010).

The attractiveness of the perception of a harmonization of the educational globe might lie in its surprising stances, for modern mass schooling was undoubtedly established to help young states integrate their inhabitants into their respective nations. This integration has had two somewhat different aspects. One was to explain to inhabitants of different regions that they are now, and even foremost, citizens of a much bigger entity than the region and that they had to identify themselves with this whole, the state. The other aspect indicated the need to convince people who had been told they were free by nature to identify themselves with the new nation-state: Although it had been comparatively easy to unite people against a regime that was understood as unjust—the British and the French monarchies in the context of the American and French Revolutions—declaring all people free by nature (and that is by principle) made it of course much more difficult to make them into *loyal* or *good citizens* of the new constitutional state. It had been intellectuals who proclaimed people as being free by nature based on theories of natural rights, and it was again intellectuals who somehow reunited the people as citizens in the imagined community (Anderson, 1983) of the nation by uniting the ideas of the nation and the constitutional state, proclaiming the respective ideals of the social order and the visions of the good citizen, whereby these later served as a basis for the erection of the mass school system with its curricula through which these citizens actually had to be made (Tröhler, in press).

Whereas the transnationally shared belief was that citizens were not simply there but had to be "made," different nation-states developed distinct education systems and curricula through which this envisaged citizen was to be constructed (Tröhler, Popkewitz, & Labaree, 2011). Education policy and curricular developments were thus deeply shaped by traditional political entities and specific geographic and cultural path dependencies, even though transnational glances across the borders might have been much more common than the national(ist) rhetoric makes us believe.

The national framing of different educational systems is hardly questionable. However, as opposed to the political rhetoric largely stuck in national aspirations, there is little doubt that at least since the end of the Second World War, education policy and curricular developments have been determined fundamentally by international trends, supranational influences, and demands for global progress; the educational (or better: curricular) reform movement after Sputnik in 1957 is just a particularly striking example of the global harmonization of education. Within this framework, enabled by organizations like the Organization for European Economic Co-operation (OEEC)/OECD, the UNESCO International Institute for Educational Planning, the World Bank, and others, an international network of experts emerged—especially in the 1960s—that started to exert strong pressure on national and regional organizations (Tröhler, 2014). Domestic developments in education became more subject to influences from abroad. For instance, in 1972 UNESCO published a new report on education that argued enthusiastically that nations should tie their education policies closer to their entire state structures, social policy in particular. At a European level, the effort was to increase cooperation and mutual understanding and, thereby, mutual adaptation. Increased cross-national comparisons of very different education systems became popular in the press, too (UNESCO, 1972).

This dynamic internationalization of education should not be underestimated. At a formal level there were increasing dialogues between many European countries, such as the famous Royaumont seminar, held from November 23 to December 4, 1959, setting the agenda for New Mathematics in Europe. It was organized by the OEEC at the request of the United States (OECD, 1961; Bjarnadóttir, 2008; Rohstock, 2014). Organizations became active at supranational levels. Tight personal networks were created, linking the national and international and vice versa. Institutional channels were established for the transfer of ideas, policies, and curricula. These mutual adaptations between the systems led to a trend towards isomorphism, suggesting a teleology towards a unified and standardized (world) education system and curriculum. The result was an obvious gap between the political rhetoric in favor of this unified and standardized teleological process, on the one hand, and public discourses resulting from the distinct national agendas of education policy, on the other. It is this very gap that lies at the center of this book.

The general theoretical hypothesis linking the different chapters of this book is that when educational policy successfully transfers models from one system to another—that is, when one specific national policy or an amalgam of policies becomes global in its aspirations and is supported by supranational organizations—it will exert pressure on other national systems. This pressure will first lead to tension within local or national cultures that are expressed in the respective formal structures, the systems of governance, and the curricula. What exactly happens through this tension is culturally different, and what may look isomorphic at first glance (today's globalized harmonization) will turn out to be a culturally idiosyncratic blend of the global and the national upon closer inspection.

Therefore, the book starts out from the assumption that the linear progress "from national to global" emphasized in recent times is somewhat problematic. The motive for this linear interpretation is understandable yet often misleading, as William Pinar has observed: To escape (often unintended and unconscious) nationalism, researchers have recommended referring more to globalization as a phenomenon and introducing by that an epistemology that is likely to neglect the less intrusive notion of "international": "It is a question contextualized in our national cultures, in the political present, in cultural questions institutionalized in academic disciplines and educational institutions. It is a question that calls upon us to critique our own national cultures" (Pinar, 2003, p. 3).

When one observes the difference between curriculum policy and curriculum research, it is easy to underline Pinar's epistemological argument in favor of "international" over "global," and history shows why. This book will collect case studies underlining this analysis. It aims at understanding the development of the school and, with it, the curricula as idiosyncratic processes that result from complex negotiations between the global and the national.

This idea was also the general basis of a large 3-year research project funded by the National Research Fund in Luxembourg, the results of which suggest a better and more sophisticated understanding of the school (and its curriculum) as a culturally and historically grown system. The results of this research project were presented at an international conference at the University of Luxembourg and contrasted to findings of similar research conducted in other parts of the world, foremost Switzerland. Later, scholars with similar research agendas in other countries were invited to contribute to this overall topic. After thorough discussions and revisions, the examples drawn from the selected nation-states analyze differences and tensions within practices of policy, governance, and curriculum. By doing so, they offer new and improved ways of understanding the curriculum as a materialization of educational ideals that emerge out of adjustment to global trends and resistance against these trends. In the contexts of nationalism, cultural crises, and globalization, the comparative focus will help us to comprehend curricula as institutionalizations of the negotiation processes that emerge out of the tensions between national and global convictions and aspirations—processes in which the actual curricula are constructed, reformed, and adapted in idiosyncratic ways.

The book is divided into four parts. Part One, including this introduction and a chapter written jointly by Thomas S. Popkewitz, Yanmei Wu, and Catarina Silva

Martins, deals with the theoretical background and the question of what it means to reconstruct the cultural idiosyncrasy of national school systems against the background of transnational or global developments and pressures. Part Two, "Fabricating the Nation: National and International Impacts on Schooling in the Long 19th Century," will feature in-depth case studies from the long 19th century. Part Three, "The Internationalization of European Schooling in the Cold War," will focus especially on the Cold War era, as many international institutions important for the area of education got their specific shape during that period; it includes case studies from Switzerland, Germany, Luxembourg, and Finland. Part Four will focus on more recent developments, with case studies from Sweden, Denmark, Austria, Germany, Russia, and China.

We wish to thank, first of all, the National Research Fund in Luxembourg, which supported both the research project for 3 years and the international conference at the end of the 3 years. The project allowed us to engage in detailed studies without losing sight of the overall context. We also wish to thank the University of Luxembourg for providing excellent research conditions during this time period and through that for allowing us to help set the new university in the heart of Europe—founded in 2003—on a global agenda. And, finally, we wish to thank all those people engaged in the research project, be it as active researchers (Peter Voss, Anne Rohstock, Catherina Schreiber, Ragnhild Barbu, Geert Thyssen), external experts (Fritz Osterwalder, Bernd Zymek, Norbert Grube), organizers of the conference (Solange Wirtz, Andrea Hake, Marianne Graffé), authorities opening the conference (Mady Delvaux-Stehres, minister of national education and vocational training, Luxembourg, and Michel Margue, dean of the University of Luxembourg Faculty of Language and Literature, Humanities, Arts and Education up to 2013), discussants at the conference (Gert Biesta, Martin Lawn, Frank Ragutt, Bernd Zymek, Anne Rohstock, David F. Labaree, Julia Resnick, Eckhardt Fuchs, Fritz Osterwalder), or authors of this book.

Last but not least our thanks go once more to Ellen Russon, who edited the chapters written by people with very different linguistic backgrounds, making the book into a linguistically and formally coherent whole, and to Naomi Silverman, publisher at Routledge, for encouragement and assistance, and in particular to William F. Pinar, who generously accepted this book to be part of the Routledge Studies in Curriculum Theory series. We feel privileged to be able to present our research findings in this superb, internationally acknowledged book series.

## References

Anderson, B. (1983). *Imagined communities: Reflections on the origin and spread of nationalism*. London, UK: Verso.
Beck, U. (1998). *Perspektiven der Weltgesellschaft*. Frankfurt, Germany: Suhrkamp.
Bjarnadóttir, K. (2008). Fundamental reasons for mathematics education in Iceland. In B. Sriraman (Ed.), *International perspectives on social justice in mathematics education* (pp. 191–208). Missoula: University of Montana Press.

Bosche, A. (2008). *Schulsteuerung im 18. Jahrhundert: Eine historische Analyse der institutionellen Einbettung von Schulorganisation.* Saarbrücken, Germany: VDM Verlag.

Castells, M. (2003). *Das Informationszeitalter: Vol. 1. Der Aufstieg der Netzwerkgesellschaft.* Opladen, Germany: Leske+Budrich.

Glassmann, R. B. (1973). Persistence and loose coupling in living systems. *Behavioral Science, 18*, 83–98. doi:10.1002/bs.3830180202

Luhmann, N. (1975). Die Weltgesellschaft. In N. Luhmann, *Soziologische Aufklärung* (pp. 1–35). Wiesbaden, Germany: VS Verlag für Sozialwissenschaften.

Meyer, J. (1992). Introduction. In J. W. Meyer, D. H. Kamens, & A. Benavot (Eds.), *School knowledge for the masses: World models and national primary curricular categories in the twentieth century* (pp. 1–16). Washington, DC: Falmer Press.

Meyer, J. W., & Ramirez, F. O. (2000). The world institutionalization of education. In J. Schriewer (Ed.), *Discourse formation in comparative education* (pp. 111–132). Frankfurt, Germany: Peter Lang.

Meyer, J. W., & Rowan, B. (1977). Institutionalized organizations: Formal structure as myth and ceremony. *American Journal of Sociology, 83*, 340–363. doi:10.1086/226550

Meyer, J. W., & Rowan, B. (1978). The structure of educational organizations. In M. W. Meyer & Associates (Eds.), *Environments and organizations* (pp. 78–109). San Francisco, CA: Jossey-Bass.

Organization for Economic Co-operation and Development (OECD) (Ed.). (1961). *New thinking in school mathematics.* Paris, France: OECD.

Pinar, W. F. (2003). *The internationalization of curriculum studies.* Retrieved from http://www.riic.unam.mx/01/02_Biblio/doc/Internationalizaton_Curriculum_W_PINAR_(MEXICO).pdf

Rohstock, A. (2014). Verwissenschaftlichung und Programmierung des Klassenzimmers im Kalten Krieg. In P. Bernhard & H. Nehring (Eds.), *Den Kalten Krieg denken: Beiträge zur sozialen Ideengeschichte seit 1945* (pp. 257–282). Essen, Germany: Klartext.

Tröhler, D. (2009). Globalizing globalization: The neo-institutional concept of a world culture. In T. S. Popkewitz & F. Rizvi (Eds.), Globalization and the study of education [special issue]. *Yearbook of the National Society for the Study of Education, 108*(2), 29–48.

Tröhler, D. (2010). Harmonizing the educational globe: World polity, cultural features, and the challenges to educational research. *Studies in Philosophy and Education, 29*, 7–29. doi:10.1007/s11217-009-9155-1

Tröhler, D. (2014). Change management in the governance of schooling: The rise of experts, planners, and statistics in the early OECD. *Teachers College Record, 116*(9), 1–26.

Tröhler, D. (in press). Curriculum history. In J. Rury & E. Tamura (Eds.), *Handbook on history of education.* Oxford, UK: Oxford University Press.

Tröhler, D., Popkewitz, T. S., & Labaree, D. F. (Eds.). (2011). *Schooling and the making of citizens in the long nineteenth century: Comparative visions.* New York, NY: Routledge.

UNESCO (Ed.). (1972). *Learning to be: The world of education today and tomorrow.* Paris, France: UNESCO.

Weick, K. E. (1976). Educational organizations as loosely coupled systems. *Administrative Science Quarterly, 21*(1), 1–19. doi:10.2307/2391875

# 2

# PRACTICAL KNOWLEDGE AND SCHOOL REFORM

## The Impracticality of Local Knowledge in Strategies of Change

*Thomas S. Popkewitz, Yanmei Wu, and Catarina Silva Martins*

Our interest is to think about the relation of the global and the local as a history of the present. It approaches the distinctions through a path that leads us to think about the "reason" in teacher education research about teachers' practices as simultaneously about the global and local. The global is what is distant and abstract yet circulates as what is local and "practical" for changing teachers and teacher education reforms.

Practice is the modern-day version of alchemy. The medieval alchemist sought to find the elixir of life through transforming metals into gold. Practice is seen as the way to achieve contemporary perfection and heavenly bliss through valuing *and* changing the local everyday experiences and knowledge of teachers. The study of practice has multiple agendas: to achieve the enlightened citizen, to rectify social wrongs, and to create innovative and knowledge societies for "the global world" and inclusion for *all*. The study of practice in school change is expressed as enacting the commitments of democracy by taking seriously local knowledge and the people at the bottom of institutional life in school change.

Our intent is to ask about the historical conditions that make practice an object of reflection and action. Practice is a global discourse that is taken, ironically, as a way to promote local, indigenous reforms based on teachers' experiences and activities. Practice is the origin of change to develop professional expert teachers for improving children's learning of school subjects and for creating education systems that serve all children equally. U.S. teacher education reforms focus on "practice" to identify what novice teachers need to know to transform the school and revive its social commitments. Similarly, European teacher educators are seen as those "who teach (student) teachers how to link theory with practice and how to reflect on and evaluate their own practice in order to enhance their learning" (European Commission, 2013, p. 7). Academic arguments talk about the need for teachers to be reflective and to construct their own knowledge based on their practices and not on what the universities say are their practices (Schön, 1983). The word "practice" travels in current Chinese research on teacher "practice" to help teachers bring moral and emotional elements into a harmonious whole that promotes better teachers (Wang, 2009).

Our approach is to think about the systems of reason that order and classify "practice" as a strategy of educational change. Most of the discussion will consider U.S. research, with some attention to European and Chinese scholarship to recognize differences as well as similarities. When examined as a historical phenomenon, there is no such thing as "practical knowledge"—that is, direct knowledge of what people do that is not mediated through theories, narratives, and images. To foreshadow the discussion, the sciences of "practice" are theories about desired futures that are made into "facts" that are to initiate the envisioned future. Like theories of change, we argue that practice is paradoxical: It conserves its contemporaneous framework and excludes and abjects in its impulses to include. As a theory about reform and change, practice embodies styles of reasoning that conserve and stabilize. In terms of the social and cultural commitments to change teacher practices, the research strategy is impractical.

The history of the present is a method that asks about the knowledge of schooling as a problem of social epistemology (Popkewitz, 1991, 2008). The notion of the historical is not one of historicism—that is, the tracing of events and ideas of people from the past to the present. It is to look at the "reasoning" about the global and local in the notion of practice as a particular historical inscription in locating one's self in the world rather than in descriptions of geography, distance, and place. To study the historical is to understand the conditions that make it possible to "see" practice as an object of reflection and action. *Epistemology* directs attention to the rules and standards that order and classify what is seen and acted on as "practice." The *social* is to place the distinctions, categories, and classification assembled and connected as teacher "practice" within a grid of historical events that make possible what is seen and acted. The interest in social epistemology, then, is to take the commonsense and given objects of schooling and to make visible the historical principles that make possible what is talked about, "seen," acted on, and desired.

## Research on Teacher Practices: Theories and Desires of What Should Be

In American and European research, "practice" has a dual quality as an object of research. It is taken as something natural and seemingly self-evident about what teachers do. Research, it is asserted, is necessary in teacher education reform as it "must help novices learn how to *do* instruction, not just hear and talk about it" (Ball, Sleep, Boerst, & Bass, 2009, p. 459). There is research to identify the "core practices" that should guide teacher education, for example. The narrative of school change is critical of theories not directed towards practice. They are seen as having little worth or, at worst, as the work of the ivory tower, which has no relevance to what people "really do" or what really works to change schools.

A recent European report, *Supporting Teacher Educators for Better Learning Outcomes*, stresses the need for practice-oriented forms of research "which might better fit the context of teacher education" (European Commission, 2013, p. 24). The teachers' communities of practice are also seen as "safe spaces" that can enhance and promote reflection that could guide the future actions of novice teachers. The influential U.S. National Council for Research has even begun to think about changing practices as the criterion of relevance and rigor in education (Gutiérrez & Penuel, 2014). Chinese research expresses the concern that teachers have focused too much on acquiring a lot of theoretical knowledge that has been of little practical help in their teaching. The teacher's practical knowledge is to provide more constructive tools for teachers' professional development. The word "practice" travels in current Chinese research on teachers' practice to help teachers bring moral and emotional elements into a harmonious whole that promotes the education of students to be good citizens (Wang, 2009).

But to talk about practice is, ironically, not to get rid of theory but to look for a certain kind of theory. For some, practice "is the birthplace of new theories" (Shimoni, 2013, p. 46). Often theories are found in these same texts that discount theory. These theories give direction to what counts as the useful knowledge that teachers are to use to create change. In the research on teacher practices, for example, learning theories are "in," seen as providing useful knowledge for changing teacher practices. Other types of theories, such as critical ones, are seen as not serving practice and thus as not useful and impractical! Little does the discussion recognize that the opposition of "theory" and "practice" is constituted by self-referential/self-authorizing systems by which practice is made into an object of reflection and action!

Practice, then, has dual but overlapping qualities in research. It is intended to describe what teachers do, but the descriptions are bound to theories about what is to be noticed and described as practices. Particular organization, communication, and psychological theories order and classify what are seen as teacher practices but also the indicators of change.

### Practices as Making Kinds of People: The Teacher and the Trilogy of Children, Family, and Community

Reform-oriented research on teacher practice is about changing teachers into different kinds of people. The desired teacher in the United States is one who produces high scores on academic achievement tests. The abstractions considered as fulfilling this desire have different names: the expert, effective, authentic, and/or professional teacher. The names are not teachers who exist but fabrications that research calculates and measures to actualize the desired model of the teacher. The research is, to use the language of the research cited, to *transform* the attitudes, dispositions, and sensitivities of teachers to make them into "reflective practitioners."[1]

To be reflective in one's own practice is to be self-regulated. The research on practice aims to create a system of processes and procedures for teachers to engage in reflection and conscious deliberation that embodies the given models of instruction. But the norms and values of deliberation are not only about the solitary individual. The teacher is the kind of person who collaborates and participates in "communities," such as professional or learning communities. Community instantiates a space of collective belonging and home that speaks to both immediate affiliations *and* abstract norms and values that link individuality to the nation.[2] The gospel of teacher educators is that novices go to schools and learn the daily practices of the "real" teachers in the field, learning from the practices of those in the professional community and from "the community"; the latter typically refers to populations that the school has not been about to successfully accommodate—the poor and racially and ethnically different populations that are different from the unspoken "normal."

Practice is based on norms and values of stability. It takes what is given about schools as its reality and elides its historical and theoretical construction. "Reflective practitioners" is a common phrase about a type of people who change themselves through thinking about practices. The reflection on practice, however, embodies a theory of the mind (reflection) about the relation of individuality with the social. The reflective teacher is one who masters reflective skills. A distinction is made between expert and non-expert teachers. The expert engages with domain-related activities. Veteran teachers, for instance, can become experts "if they are well supported in the theorization of their practice" (Tsui, 2009, p. 437).

## *Making Kinds of People: The Expert Teacher*

The focus on practice is a system of classifying and ordering who teachers are as kinds of people. U.S. research on teacher practices has a particular historical assembly and connection of principles for actualizing the abstraction of the good teacher. One is the transmogrification of principles related to the North American enlightenment about progress into an instrumental grid that speaks of the mission of teacher education as "human improvement" (see Cohen, 1995; Grossman et al., 2009). Although the notion of human improvement is not explored as a precept, it is assumed that practice-based approaches to professional education will transform the dispositions, values, and attitudes of the teacher to achieve that improvement and reach system goals.

This is expressed in research's (re)visioning of the turn-of-the-century Social Question about the moral disorder of urban populations. The earlier Social Question focused on changing the immigrant and on the trilogy of the child, family, and community of urban poverty. Today's urban teacher education is also to change the trilogy through the "tailoring" of teachers "to possess specific sets of dispositions to fulfill ideal constructions of teacher quality and meet the instructional needs of each district" (Boggess, 2010, p. 65).

The mission of the teacher is given as that of the professional who produces social improvement. Grossman et al. (2009) assert that by identifying core practices, the teacher is a professional who can bring about social improvement. The commitment of the profession to social change is constituted through a theory about the desired teacher identity produced through interventions in practices. Research creates distinctions and classifications that order what should be and warrant interventions in teacher education. The abstraction of the teacher is a particular kind of person who organizes teaching through the three related activities of (1) taking the representations about knowledge given in the teaching of school subjects as what should be assessed to define successful teachers, (2) decomposing or analytically separating the elements in the processes of teaching to assess how that teaching is accomplished, and (3) defining the most efficient ways to engage in the previous two activities. The three activities comprise what it means to have the expertise of a professional. Teacher education aims to have the novice teacher approximate the activities that constitute the "core practices" of the professional.

The elements of the profession are not only what is done (practices) but also norms and values about the collective identity to be inscribed in each novice. The collective identity is spoken about as making the professional teacher. This kind of person is defined not only by the skills and knowledge that the teacher should have but also by the transformations of the habits of mind and meanings that the teacher has. Whereas the syntax of the theory is realist and about the "real setting of practice with actual clients" (Grossman & McDonald, 2008; Grossman et al., 2009), what is studied as practice is ordered and classified through theoretical principles to construct professional education as planning the nature of who people are as teachers.

This reflective practitioner is the kind of person constructed at the intersection of the positive notion of progress (social improvement), organizational theories of classroom management, and psychological knowledge on personal development. For example, an alternative teacher education certification program of Teach for America (TFA; 2013a, 2013b) has practice (called "actions") as the centerpiece of its rubric for training the teachers. Historically, a rubric was a heading on a document, or a direction in a liturgical book on how to conduct a church service. Today, a rubric is a "diagnostic" scheme to standardize ratings to support self-reflection about progress towards particular objectives. Categories are placed in an organizational grid in which a continuum of teacher proficiency levels is linked to observable acts. The explicit statement of standards in the rubric aims to minimize misinterpretation about what a teacher must do to be an Excellent Teacher. This entails providing rules and directives for classifying standardized criteria linked to learning objectives and assessment practices.

The rubric is the technology of becoming and self-purification. The link of salvation and science is expressed as desired actions classified as degrees of performance proficiency. Teachers' performance is divided into five levels ranging from Pre-Novice to Exemplary. The reflective teacher described in the rubric is a map to monitor teachers' moral development, which has little to do with particular skills. It is organized around six "commandments" that provide rules and standards to order reflection. The teachers are to "set big goals," "invest in students," "plan purposefully," "execute effectively," "continuously increase effectiveness," and "work relentlessly" (TFA, 2013b, p. 1).

The commandments form the constellation of the Excellent Teacher. The conflation of effectiveness and excellence in the rubric becomes the "reason" that guides correct forms of reflection in teacher education. The process of self-actualization is realized through the teacher's exhibiting of certain inner qualities that serve as indicators of excellent teaching and the effective teacher (TFA, 2013c, p. 1). The qualities are moral values that are related to particular Protestant (Calvinist) notions of how salvation is achieved (see Tröhler, 2011; see also Popkewitz, 2008). The above quote considers teacher excellence as the psychological qualities of "investing," working hard, and being purposeful, and these qualities produce a mode of living in which the teacher is impelled to "continuously increase effectiveness" (TFA, 2013c, p. 1).

The "transformation" is not only about who the teacher is and should be. The transformation of the teacher is connected to the trilogy of changing the child, the family, and the community, which is homologous with the Social Question at the turn of the 20th century. The Social Question was directed towards transforming the urban conditions that produced poverty, delinquency, family breakups, and sexual misbehavior. To change social conditions was to also change the child, the family, and the community in urban settings. The new Social Question is articulated in contemporary teacher education research on practice. The identified teacher practices or actions are not only about making the teacher as a particular kind of person. The attention to practice is to structure the development of low-achieving children in U.S. urban and rural areas.

The research on practice has a double task. It is intended to create the desired teacher, whose responsibilities are then to shape the urban trilogy of the child, family, and community. Urban children are positioned in research and policies as different from the unspoken values and norms, which tend to focus on characteristics that are often related to racially, ethnically, and economically poor populations (see Popkewitz, 1998). The strategy of urban reform is the "tailoring" of teachers through governing the dispositions and habits of the mind that are assumed as "intrinsic" to the individual, arguing that "dispositions are a more useful concept than beliefs because beliefs cannot be changed; however, dispositions can be taught as well as changed and assessed" (Boggess, 2010, p. 73).

In the teacher reform literature, a distinction is often made between the teacher's "actions" (in TFA's wording) and the foci of the research on core practices.

Whereas core practices are viewed as central processes and activities in making the professional teacher, TFA defines a developmental sequence that leads from being a novice to being an expert professional. Yet when viewed through the rules and standards of the reason that orders the different programs, the making of the teacher inscribed in the TFA rubric is homologous with the core practices. Each is concerned with the making of habits of the mind and inner psychological dispositions governing the patterns of social communication and interaction. Rather than the close monitoring of psychological states embodied in the developmental stages of TFA, the assessments of core practices take place through the development of "real-time" "in-the-moment" evaluation techniques with regard to how teachers implement the desired practices (Ball et al., 2009, p. 468). The assessment tools are formative and used in real time by teachers and teacher educators to produce particular habits and mentalities.

This concern with the interior of the teacher is found in the common reform of introducing teacher portfolios. Teachers document their continual development for purposes of assessment and self-assessment through bottom-up reasoning on practical experiences. Portfolios are thought of as a way of achieving "more conceptual ways of thinking" for the novice teachers to "reveal . . . their thinking" (Toom, Husu, & Patrikainen, 2014, p. 16). The assessment instruments are to govern the student teacher through the ethos of teachers' continuous obligation of self-formation. The focus is on governing the interior of the teacher.

If we compare Chinese research on practices that make the teacher professional, there seems to be an initial similarity. The research talks about collaboration, the development of skills, and teachers who are becoming more effective (articulating ideas better). But the similarities are a deception. "Practical" knowledge is not merely the replication of Western notions of rationality and expert knowledge. The notion of the profession is assembled with cultural nuances that are translated into English as the teacher's passion, love of students, collaboration, and serving as a model for students. However, the translations do not capture the semiotics of the Chinese characters through which they are expressed and their connection to Confucianism. We can only point to the need for further exploration, but Chinese philosophers speak of learning as the "unity of knowledge and practice" in developing moral education that is not necessarily built on Western notions of representation and identity (Wang, 2009, p. 113).

## Schools and Change as Systems

European and American research on teacher practices sees them as having a revolutionary potential to improve schools. The theory on change is ironically to conserve the existing framework of the reason that orders the objects of reflection and action. The categories constituting practice embody domains rendered as stable, representable forms that can be calculated, deliberated on, and acted on. This stabilizing is embodied in what is given as "the real" that is represented as teachers' practices. The realism of practice as the origin of change paradoxically gives a certainty to the very objects of schooling. The concern for change turns into producing variations of what is. To identify "high leverage practices," for example, is to learn what to do, which can apply "in any setting, regardless of variations" in curricula or teaching styles (Ball et al., 2009, p. 461). The assumption is one of certainty; that is, certain teacher actions and student learning are already known, and the problem is to provide greater efficiency to the processes of classrooms.

The certainty and conservatism in the research on teacher practices are not intended but are inscribed in the principles that are given as transforming practice. These principles embody teaching and the teacher as performing in a system. The ordering and classifying of the structuring and functioning of teaching relate to the system's performance outcomes—school achievement scores. The notion of system is to think about what holds "things" together in schooling as it relates to outcomes. But it also assumes the need for harmony and consensus in its elements or functional parts and for methods that enable the possibility of social interventions in different elements of the system to increase efficiency and harmony. The problem of research becomes to identify those parts that functioned well and those practices that disrupted the harmony of the desired models.

The language of systems and practice is made plausible through capturing the imaginary of the enlightenment. That imaginary privileges human reason and science in the service of progress and human agency. That imperative is (re)visioned as a symbolic model of an "instructional" system. That system "acts" as an organism. Agency has two qualities. One is through the interventions of research that identifies the core practices that increase the development, growth, and efficiency of the system. Research is to identity the specific units or elements (practices) of the system that can be redesigned to maximize utility. It is in this space of action that agency occurs. The second element of agency is providing clear distinctions for the ordering, assessment, and self-assessment of the decision-making processes of the teacher.

In research on teachers and teacher education, the system becomes the model in an experimentalist view of the individuals and society as an organism that grows and develops (see Easton, 1953; Simon, 1981). Systems analysis is the problem-solving tool. Analysis is to identify practices that could be codified and standardized to bring maximum efficiency in the evolution of the system. Teacher education reforms, for example, speak about capacity building across all levels of the school system, which is linked to ongoing professional development. The logic of research is to design the unity between "the pedagogical expertise and organizational conditions posited" (Matsumura & Wang, 2014, p. 5). Concepts of collaboration and community building are used as ways of increasing the effectiveness of research practices such as writing lesson plans (Pareja Roblin, Ormel, McKenney, Voogt, & Pieters, 2014, p. 184). Research should identify and then design interventions to change system elements that disturb its equilibrium (what is called the "achievement gap"). The change process embodied in practice research is, at least theoretically (and ironically), to maximize the ongoing system's efficiency.

The task of reflection and calculation inscribed in the symbolic system assumes, first, a consensus about what comprises the model and its parts, their relations, and the goals. Second, the calculation and administration of the system aim to bring it into a state of harmony and give it the stability needed to function effectively. The notion of utility and the "useful" serves as the value that gives the system consensus and harmony. It is assumed, for example, that the professional and expert teacher is a teacher who has a common language and common curriculum. Teacher education should enable the novice to internalize the core practices that give the system its effectiveness and efficiency. The consensus and harmony of the system that form the boundaries of what is possible are assumed in the following: "Approximations of practice . . . enable teacher education to address the gap between the practices we advocate in teacher education and those that novices are likely to see in the typical school setting" (Grossman & McDonald, 2008, p. 190).

Change is to achieve maximum utility in the sum of the given system's parts. Research gives functionality through ordering and creating finer and finer distinctions that find more points for intervention and administration. Successful learning is the sum of the different elements of the system's model of processes that are functional for achieving what are assumed as its goals and outcomes. Research is "to expose and analyze a set of core problems involved in building a useful and usable knowledge based in teacher education and to propose features of such a knowledge base crucial for addressing those problems of teacher education" (Ball et al., 2009, p. 459).

Practice is, paradoxically, a theory of change to actualize the desired principles about who the teacher should be and yet, at the same time, is bound to the given norms and values of the abstraction of the system's model. The core practices are analytic procedures to identify classifications of what already exists as representations of school subjects. The core practices to maximize the system performance are given, among other things, as the teacher posing problems to children, eliciting thinking, identifying criteria for calling on children in classroom lessons, and selecting representations (the curriculum) that organize instruction. Teaching is defined through making finer distinctions drawn from existing patterns in ordering the administration of the classroom. Core practice research, for example, focuses on the procedures that will give greater efficiency to the teacher's tasks while taking for granted the existing organization of classroom teachers. The old sense of writing a lesson plan for judging what is taught is now redesigned through an analytic that maintains the same ordering procedures but with a more discrete set of concepts in which the teachers "decompose" (analyze) and "recompose" teaching lessons with the intent to achieve what is assumed to be the defined outcomes.

The models of curriculum in the research assume there is consensus and harmony in what is taught as school subjects and in the measures of performance outcomes. The central research problem is to calculate, measure, and administrate teaching practices that, at least in U.S. schools, are intended to raise achievement scores and, more internationally, to promote a higher ranking in the Programme for International Student Assessment (PISA).

In the assumption of consensus and harmony is the alchemy of school subjects. The alchemy takes place through the tools and models that translate disciplinary knowledge into the curriculum (Popkewitz, 2004, 2013). The research on the expert and effective teacher treats existing curriculum models as transcendental models from which to identify the qualities and characteristics of the teacher and achievement. Yet, historically, the models of the curriculum are not designed for understanding the processes of producing disciplinary knowledge. Rather, the models of the curriculum are derived from psychologies and sociologies aiming to design the child, family, and community (the trilogy of the social sciences), which have nothing to do with the relation of the social, cultural, and epistemological processes that give form to the disciplinary fields that ostensibly form school subjects. What is defined as the practical knowledge of teaching is the ordering of conduct and the making of particular kinds of people (in science education, see McEneaney, 2003).

## Comparative Styles of Reason: The Paradox of Exclusion in Inclusion

In the previous sections, we explored practice in teacher education research as the complex process of theorizing and actualizing abstractions in the making of particular kinds of people, such as the Excellent Teacher. Principles related to systems, consensus, development, and stability ordered and classified what counted as practice and, ironically, change. This section explores a different but related set of limits of practice as a strategy of change. The limits stem from the comparative system of reasoning that paradoxically simultaneously excludes, abjects, and includes.

The comparative style of reasoning is embodied in the function/structure relation. Differences are instantiated in a continuum of values that distinguishes and divides what are given as the consensual norms. The consensus is articulated in the language of equality that expresses the desire for "all children" to learn. The "all" assumes a unity and consensus from which to "see" differences (see Popkewitz, 2008). This comparative style of reasoning organized the community sociology and psychologies of childhood as they formed at the turn of the 20th century in Europe and North America. The self was placed in a sequence of time that "projected degeneracy on the lower categories of the taxonomies of humankind rather than, as previously held, on doctrinal opponents in sectarian disputes" (Boon, 1985, p. 23).

In contemporary teacher research, this comparativeness is not given expression only in the norms of development and the stages in the making of the effective/expert teacher. It is also embodied in the rules and standards of "reason" that classify the trilogy of the child, family, and community that are recognized for inclusion through their recognition as different. The notion of diversity separates them from unspoken norms about the child who is not named as diverse; the distinctions of the at-risk or disadvantaged child assume principles about who is not at risk. Moving silently in the discourses of having "all children" learn are the characteristics and capabilities of the child who succeeds but whom "everyone knows," and who thus does not need to be represented. The processes of remediation to help a child achieve assumes the "other" child who succeeds and is placed at one end of the continuum of value embodied in the achievement gap.

Ironically, teacher research to correct social wrongs starts with the assumption of inequality even when the goal is equality. Rancière (1983/2004) argued that to begin with inequality to achieve equality actually (re)visions equality as inequality. The comparative inscriptions of difference to address fundamental wrongs produce the precondition of difference. The research on teacher practice reinscribes divisions that are to be erased at every step with science as the shepherd. Rancière argued that this epistemological position embodies a fear of democracy itself.

## Impracticalities?

In writing this chapter, we have thought about the divisions of global and local as distinctions that embody particular social epistemologies. What the local and the global mean is not a matter of micro or macro scales, in the specificities or the abstractions of daily life. Rather, our exploration considered the global and local as an inscription in a way of reasoning that partitions what is sensible in making kinds of people. Research on teacher practices, we argued, travels as simultaneously what is given as "real," local, and contextual, while at the same time embodying principles that perform as theories about what to "see," talk about, act, and hope for. Practice is an inscription of modes of thinking and acting about the world and the self. The locality of practice is a knowledge that is presented as a global and universal knowledge through the assumptions of systems. The abstractions about the kinds of teachers and the trilogy of the child, family, and community in the research serve as global, universalized knowledge about the interiorized habits of mind of the teacher. The useful and practical knowledge is a theoretical fabrication inscribed within a local space determined by the global possibilities of our times. A provocative question could be: Where were practices and local knowledge as objects of reflection and action before the theoretical ideas about them arose?

Our major focus was U.S. research with reference to European discourses and to differences in the "reading" of practice in current Chinese reform efforts. In the United States and Europe, practice is taken as something that can be recouped through good research on classrooms that gives value to the daily work of teachers. Practice as local knowledge is presented to counter the alienating and distancing qualities of globalization that seem to make teachers merely a cog in the statistical machines that compare school performances across nations and reduce education to equivalences given in numbers. The research on practice is seen as the exercise of democratic impulses to look after people in everyday life and to respect their daily experiences and "knowledge."

The local that practice epitomizes, however, is simultaneously theories about a desired world and desired people. The sciences of education "solve" the problem of studying the particulars that are observed, so as to standardize in a manner that could be projected as the resemblance of what would be the future. The philosophical operations of abstracting and generalizing about practice in the research inscribe the hope that the knowledge of research would actualize the future *already imagined in the notion of practice.*

## Notes

1. This phrase is drawn from organizational theory about productive members of organizations (Schön, 1983) that has taken a life of its own in multiple literatures, including education. A Google Scholar search yielded over 22,000 citations.
2. This reconfiguring of the boundaries of the citizen's belonging to the state is a continual historical process, as the French historian Renan recognized in the late 19th century. Today these relations and shifting boundaries are expressed through oppositions such as global and local and the need for contextual studies. What is important in this discussion is the inscription of "community" as a social concept for designing teacher relations with themselves (as professionals) and with children and families. In China and the United States, the relation of self, nation, and distant "things" is subject to particular universalizing discourses, of which practice is one example. In the European Union, the coordinates of belonging and home involve the creation of the European as a universalizing discourse from which to see the nation and citizens. This can be seen in the European journals on teaching and teacher education that continually juxtapose the nation with its "European" heritage (Popkewitz & Martins, 2013).

## References

Ball, D. L., Sleep, L., Boerst, T., & Bass, H. (2009). Combining the development of practice and the practice of development in teacher education. *The Elementary School Journal, 109*(5), 458–474. doi:10.1086/596996

Boggess, L. (2010). Tailoring new urban teachers for character and activism. *American Educational Research Journal, 49*(1), 65–95. doi:10.3102/0002831209358116

Boon, J. A. (1985). History and degeneration. In J. E. Chamberlin & S. L. Gilman (Eds.), *Degeneration: The dark side of progress* (pp. 1–23). New York, NY: Columbia University Press.

Cohen, D. (1995). Professions of human improvement: Predicaments of teaching. In M. Nisan & O. Schremer (Eds.), *Educational deliberations* (pp. 278–294). Jerusalem, Israel: Keter.

Easton, D. (1953). *The political system: Inquiry into the state of political science.* New York, NY: Alfred A. Knopf.

European Commission. (2013). *Supporting teacher educators for better learning outcomes.* Retrieved from http://ec.europa.eu/education/policy/school/doc/support-teacher-educators_en.pdf

Grossman, P., Compton, C., Igra, D., Ronfeldt, M., Shahan, E., & Williamson, P. (2009). Teaching practice: A cross-professional perspective. *Teachers College Record, 111*(9), 2055–2100.

Grossman, P., & McDonald, M. (2008). Back to the future: Directions for research in teaching and teacher education. *American Educational Research Journal, 45*(1), 184–205. doi:10.3102/0002831207312906

Gutiérrez, K., & Penuel, W. (2014). Relevance to practice as a criterion for rigor. *Educational Researcher, 43*(1), 19–23. doi:10.3102/0013189x13520289

Matsumura, L. C., & Wang, E. (2014). Principals' sensemaking of coaching for ambitious reading instruction in a high-stakes accountability policy environment. *Education Policy Analysis Archives, 22*(51), 1–37. doi:10.14507/epaa.v22n51.2014

McEneaney, E. (2003). Elements of a contemporary primary school science. In G. S. Drori, J. W. Meyer, F. O. Ramirez, & E. Schofer (Eds.), *Science in the modern world polity: Institutionalization and globalization* (pp. 136–154). Stanford, CA: Stanford University Press.

Pareja Roblin, N. N., Ormel, B. J. B., McKenney, S. E., Voogt, J. M., & Pieters, J. M. (2014). Linking research and practice through teacher communities: A place where formal and practical knowledge meet? *European Journal of Teacher Education, 37*(2), 183–203. doi:10.1080/02619768.2014.882312

Popkewitz, T. S. (1991). *A political sociology of educational reform: Power/knowledge in teaching, teacher education and research.* New York, NY: Teachers College Press.

Popkewitz, T. S. (1998). *Struggling for the soul: The politics of education and the construction of the teacher.* New York, NY: Teachers College Press.

Popkewitz, T. S. (2004). The alchemy of the mathematics curriculum: Inscriptions and the fabrication of the child. *American Educational Research Journal, 41*(4), 3–34. doi:10.3102/00028312041001003

Popkewitz, T. S. (2008). *Cosmopolitanism and the age of school reform: Science, education, and making society by making the child.* New York, NY: Routledge.

Popkewitz, T. S. (2013). The empirical and political "fact" of theory in the social and education sciences. In G. Biesta, J. Allan, & R. G. Edwards (Eds.), *Making a difference in theory: The theory question in education and the education question in theory* (pp. 13–29). London, UK: Routledge.

Popkewitz, T. S., & Martins, C. (2013). "Now we are European!" How did it get that way? *Sisyphus, 1*(1), 37–66. Available at http://revistas.rcaap.pt/sisyphus/article/view/2829

Rancière, J. (1983/2004). *The philosopher and his poor* (A. Parker, Ed. and Introduction) (J. Drury, C. Oster, & A. Parker, Trans.). Durham, NC: Duke University Press.

Schön, D. (1983). *The reflective practitioner: How professionals think in action.* New York, NY: Basic Books.

Shimoni, S. (2013). Teacher educators' discourses and languages. In M. Ben-Peretz with S. Kleeman, R. Reichenberg, & S. Shimoni (Eds.), *Teacher educators as members of an evolving profession* (pp. 43–60). Lanham, MD: MOFET Institute and Rowman & Littlefield Education.

Simon, H. (1981). *The science of the artificial.* Cambridge, MA: MIT Press.

Teach for America. (2013a). *Teaching as leadership comprehensive rubric.* Retrieved from http://www.teachingasleadership.org/sites/default/files/TAL.Comprehensive.Rubric.FINAL.pdf

Teach for America. (2013b). *Teaching as leadership framework.* Retrieved from http://www.teachforamerica.org/why-teach-for-america/training-and-support/teaching-as-leadership

Teach for America. (2013c). *Teaching as leadership framework*. Retrieved from http://www.teachingasleadership.org/sites/default/files/Teaching%20As%20Leadership%20Framework%20(One%20Pager).pdf

Toom, A., Husu, J., & Patrikainen, S. (2014). Student teachers' patterns of reflection in the context of teaching practice. *European Journal of Teacher Education, 37*, 1–21. doi:10.1080/02619768.2014.943731

Tröhler, D. (2011). *Languages of education: Protestant legacies in educationalization of the world, national identities, and global aspirations*. New York, NY: Routledge.

Tsui, A. (2009). Distinctive qualities of expert teachers. *Teachers and Teaching: Theory and Practice, 15*(4), 421–439. doi:10.1080/13540600903057179

Wang, C. (2009). The argument of teachers' practice: From comparative philosophy perspective. *Journal of Capital Normal University, Social Sciences Edition, 6*, 112–114.

# PART II
# Fabricating the Nation

National and International Impacts on Schooling in the Long 19th Century

# 3

# PEOPLE, CITIZENS, NATIONS

## Organizing Modern Schooling in Western Europe in the 19th Century: The Cases of Luxembourg and Zurich[1]

*Daniel Tröhler*

The development of the modern school system is closely linked to the emergence of nation-states after 1800. To legitimize national territories as political unities, the nation-states drafted constitutions determining the sovereignty of the territory and the inhabitants as national citizens. The territory was supposed to be defended by the army, and the newly defined national citizens—most of them having been subjects in the Ancien Régime—had to be "made" by the national school system and its curricula. The school came to be understood as the cradle of the nation, as we can read in 1828 in Luxembourg: "The primary schools are the cradle of the citizen. Therefore, the youth has to be trained in the practice of all the civic, moral, and religious virtues to which a true citizen has to become accustomed" (as cited in Witry, 1900, p. 34, freely translated here). Curricula reflect—as do constitutions—fundamental, taken-for-granted "cultural-cognitive" (Scott, 2001, p. 57f.) assumptions about the "good life" and the just social order made up by the ideal citizens, the "product" of the curriculum (Tröhler, in press).

Europe's first modern national school systems arose in Western and Northern Europe—that is, after some experiments in France and in the Napoleonic vassal states, in the Netherlands and Denmark in 1814, Norway in 1827, Switzerland from 1831 on, France in 1833, Belgium and Sweden in 1842, and Luxembourg in 1843. In the last quarter of the 19th century we find them in every nation-state. In the eyes of many contemporaries, this spread of national school systems was a symptom of progress, linear progress even, as can be seen on a map published on the occasion of the Paris World's Fair in 1878: "All of today's European governments emphasize the greatest importance of public education, its development and progress, understanding it as the most solid basis of the wealth, well-being, and morality of the nations" (L'instruction populaire en Europe, 1878, freely translated here). That sentence introduced a large European map assessing the progress of the national school systems.

**28** Daniel Tröhler

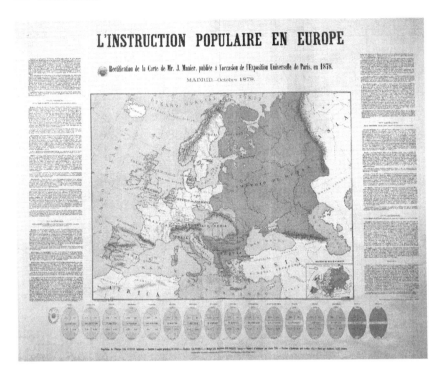

**FIGURE 3.1**

Figure 3.1 shows Europe's nation-states clustered in four categories of progress and shaded accordingly from light (most advanced) to dark (least advanced). The most advanced nation-states (*Pays très avancés*) include Sweden, Denmark, Germany, France, and Switzerland. The second best category (*Pays assez avancés*) includes Belgium, Norway, the Netherlands, Spain, and Great Britain—and it seems, Luxembourg, too, although it is not mentioned explicitly. The next category (*Pays arriérés*) is clearly rated much lower and includes Austria-Hungary, Italy, Greece, and Portugal. The very bad countries (*Pays très arriérés*) are limited to two countries only, Russia and Turkey.

As is the case in international country comparisons today, the message behind the comparison is clear: The best are not only the best but at the same time serve as models for worse countries, expressing the ideal for them to follow in their development. After all, you need to keep an eye on the neighbors; as an Organization for Economic Co-operation and Development (OECD) activist said in 1966 to the national delegates: "From the standpoint of practical politics, the consideration that really influences policy-makers, and even the people as well, is comparison with other countries. In this respect, nations resemble individuals—they want to keep up with the Joneses" (Harbison, 1966, p. 54).[2]

With the rise of crude nationalism towards the end of the 19th century, this *interpretation* of a linear-progressive expansion of the modern school systems was forgotten for nearly a century, until the Cold War, when global agendas in educational policy began to arise and be disseminated via transnational organizations such as UNESCO or the OECD (Tröhler, 2010b). Instead of emphasizing commonalities, singularities were sought and emphasized. It is in this nationalist context towards the end of the 19th century that the educational sciences became accepted and established as an academic discipline, and it seems that even today they still suffer from this nationalist birth defect. However, recent research—most of all in what is called neo-institutional sociology—rediscovered the parallels that were emphasized in the 19th century and interpreted them as expressions of an "exogenous" cultural phenomenon that was not the result of particular national idiosyncrasies but of "standard modern goals and standard strategies to attain these" (Meyer & Ramirez, 2000, p. 115). In other words, according to neo-institutional sociology, the modern school systems did indeed arise within the individual nation-states after 1800, but they followed a "universal and universalistic" agenda.

On an abstract macro-level this neo-institutional approach is fairly plausible and serves to relativize overly narrow nationalist views of the development of the school systems. However, as soon as we start to apply this view to both educational policy and educational research, we face serious problems. Of course, all the modern schools became a state affair sometime after 1800: Serious and ongoing fights with the church had to be borne, all of the nation-states drafted school laws that integrated all inhabitants in a uniform and consecutively organized school structure, and all of the countries established syllabi that were much more indebted to the modern sciences than previously in the Ancien Régime. And another fact seems evident, too, and supports the neo-sociological grand theory—namely, the fact that the people in charge of designing school laws often copied and pasted from other school laws. The Dutch school law of 1806, for instance, served as a model for a number of school laws to follow in other countries, and the Dutch school law itself had been influenced by the revolutionary school laws in France (Thyssen, 2013).

The problem we face when applying this sort of theory in policy and research lies first in the fact that the transnational travels of laws or syllabi are to be understood less as "copy and paste" and more as translations into what might be called the "genius loci." This cultural idiosyncrasy may not be as easily recognizable in the school laws and syllabi defining the school reality, but it is very obvious when it comes to the concrete organization of the school. This organizational aspect is a part of schooling that too often seems to be neglected in research. Even the protagonists of the neo-institutional narrative admit that the "evidence for the diffusion of standard models of educational funding and governance and the resultant world homogeneity is weak," but they expect, following their global-historical narrative, considerable standardization in this area of schooling, too (Meyer & Ramirez, 2000, p. 125). This faith expresses the intellectual agenda of globalizing globalization (Tröhler, 2010a) and misses an opportunity of understanding the history of schooling in a better way.

Whereas school laws and syllabi are designed to normatively define the ideal of the *future* citizen, the actual organization of the school shows precisely what it means to be a *current* citizen of a particular nation-state. My thesis is that within the actual organizations of the school systems we find organizational rules and practices that represent traditions (understood as handed-down cultural models of order or cultural systems of reasoning) that are older than new school laws and syllabi. And when the latter are "imported," they are always translated into these systems of reasoning. These handed-down systems of reasoning and organizing ensured cultural continuities, allowing the new school systems to be established in the context of nation-building. These cultural continuities, expressed most prominently in the organizational structures of the school, allowed the new school laws or the syllabi to be successfully implemented in the first place.

I would like to demonstrate this thesis in five steps, whereby I will focus comparatively on two territories, Luxembourg and Zurich, in full knowledge that Zurich was not an independent nation-state in the exact sense but was completely autonomous in terms of schooling. I focus first on the relation between central and local governance (section 1) and then address the question of communicative practices within the school system (section 2). I then analyze the manner in which the central authorities treated school teachers with regard to their professional and moral behavior (section 3) and detect how the teachers reacted and organized themselves (section 4). In a last step, I address cultural sustainability in the school systems and its relevance for research and policy (section 5).

## Central Versus Local Governance

The Canton of Zurich (the cantons are the states of the Swiss Confederation) is an impressive example of how the organization of the school and the school law are two distinct aspects of the school system. A year before the modern Zurich school law was passed in 1832, the new authorities of the regenerated canton—itself an immediate response to the July Revolution in France in 1830—passed two laws in which the organization of the public school was assigned to the greatest possible extent to the communes (the smallest political units) and the districts (Gesetz betreffend die Organisation der Gemeinds-Schulpflegen vom 19. November 1831). The people obtained an extended right to elect the members of the local school authorities, the school boards, and had a little less say in the election of the district school boards. These district school boards had the duty to support the lay members of the communal school boards, served as an appeal committee in case of disagreements in the communes, and were to be the professional tutors of the commune teachers. According to this principle of the local and regional organization of the school, the central administration of the Zurich school system was—at least until the end of the Second World War—extremely small. For all school levels from primary school up to university, it comprised only two ministers elected by the people of the canton and three further persons: the administrator of the upper high schools or grammar schools, the director of the cantonal publishing house for teaching materials, and a secretary (*Amtliches Schulblatt*, 1886, p. 3). This five-person agency was supported by a voluntary and unsalaried cantonal school board, elected by the members of parliament, and this board was in charge of "supervising all the schools in the canton" (Staatsverfassung für den Eidgenössischen Stand Zürich, 1831, § 70, paragraph 1).

In contrast, the administration in Luxembourg was—at least for the primary level—much more centralized and accordingly larger. The school law of 1842 defined the primary school as subordinate to the royal grand-ducal committee for instruction, composed of important officials and the inspectors nominated by the Grand Duke (Gesetz vom 26. Juli 1843, Nr 1709, über den Primär-Unterricht, Art. 59). These 18 persons were responsible for the approximately 120 communes—approximately two thirds of the number of communes in the Canton of Zurich—and for the development of Luxembourg's primary schools in the 19th century.

Given these organizational structures, it is not surprising that Luxembourg's authorities functioned largely top-down and obtained knowledge about the local schools by means of impressive statistics. The school law of 1843 had obligated every commune to deliver detailed data on their schools, including up to 62 individual items concerning the teachers, their level of education, school subjects, poor children (not able to pay school fees) and their fathers' occupations, money spent on renovation of school buildings, and heating costs (see Figure 3.2).

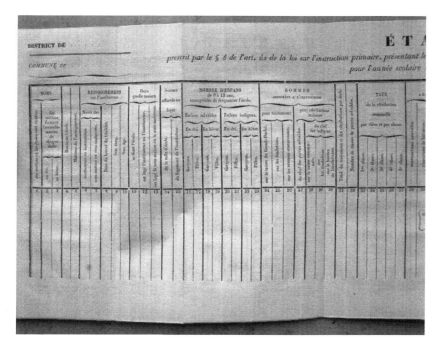

FIGURE 3.2

Year after year, every one of the approximately 120 communes delivered these detailed data to the central committee for instruction. The data, complemented by detailed reports by national inspectors, served as a basis for central decision-making on educational policy. These decisions made by the central committee for instruction had to be communicated and implemented.

## Practices of Communication

In contrast to Zurich, where knowledge was generated locally and decisions were often exchanged face-to-face, Luxembourg's central authorities needed an official gazette to serve as a communication tool to inform and instruct the school actors in the whole country. Simultaneously with the new school law in 1843, the central authorities therefore published the *Luxemburger Schulbote* [Luxembourg School Herald] to disseminate information and directives for teachers. It is not a coincidence that a comparable institution in Switzerland appeared much later, even though the Swiss modern school laws had mostly been passed before the Luxembourg school law. The Canton of Lucerne issued the first school paper in 1884, Zurich followed in 1886, and Bern in 1887, some 40 to 60 years after having passed the school laws.

This obvious time lag between Luxembourg and Switzerland in general and Zurich in particular points to the different motives and necessities originating in the fundamental decision about the relation of the local and the central. In its very first issue, the *Luxembourg School Herald* made clear: "*Luxembourg School Herald*. Under this headline, the royal grand-ducal committee for instruction publishes for the first time a periodical designed to inform the teachers of the Grand Duchy every time of all ordinances and decrees relevant for the school" (*Luxemburger Schulbote*, 1844, p. 1, freely translated here). Compared to this way of introducing the official gazette, the Swiss introductions were—owing to the local structures—much more moderate. Here is the very first, from the Canton of Lucerne: "The *Lucerne School Herald* enters today, somewhat hesitantly, the public sphere, in order to contribute together with all the other measures for the sake of public instruction, as much as it is possible, given its weak forces" (*Luzernisches Schul-Blatt*, 1884, p. 1).

Disseminating information was but one of the purposes of the *Luxembourg School Herald*. Among other functions, it also served as an interpretation model of its own progress. The data collected by the annual questionnaires were published in brief in the *Luxembourg School Herald* the following year, which conveyed to the public the state of the art of the school. But already in its 10th year of publication, the authorities drew up a balance sheet on the schools and interpreted the results, presented quantitatively and qualitatively, as a success story within the development of the new nation (see Figure 3.3).

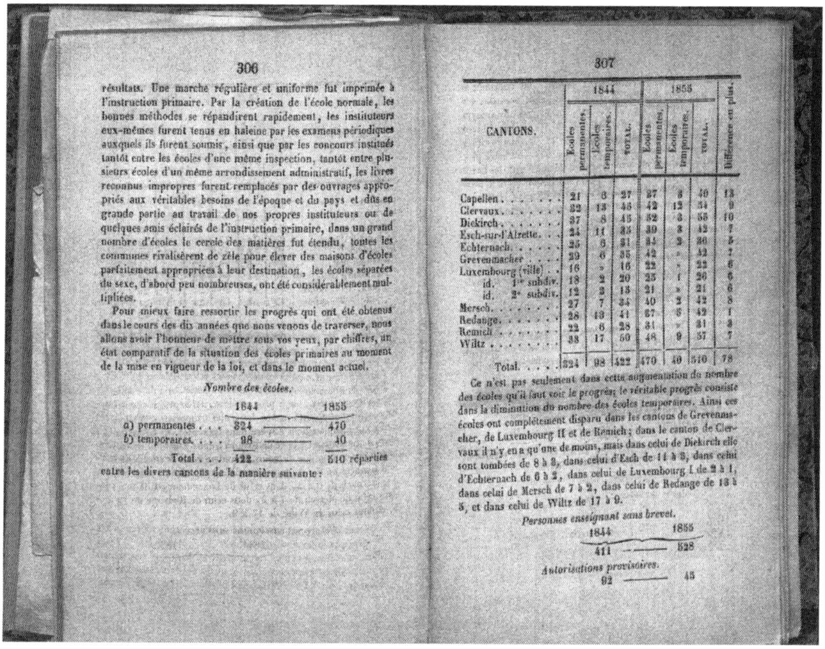

306

résultats. Une marche régulière et uniforme fut imprimée à l'instruction primaire. Par la création de l'école normale, les bonnes méthodes se répandirent rapidement, les instituteurs eux-mêmes furent tenus en haleine par les examens périodiques auxquels ils furent soumis, ainsi que par les concours institués tantôt entre les écoles d'une même inspection, tantôt entre plusieurs écoles d'un même arrondissement administratif, les livres reconnus impropres furent remplacés par des ouvrages appropriés aux véritables besoins de l'époque et du pays et dûs en grande partie au travail de nos propres instituteurs ou de quelques amis éclairés de l'instruction primaire, dans un grand nombre d'écoles le cercle des matières fut étendu, toutes les communes rivalisèrent de zèle pour élever des maisons d'écoles parfaitement appropriées à leur destination, les écoles séparées du sexe, d'abord peu nombreuses, ont été considérablement multipliées.

Pour mieux faire ressortir les progrès qui ont été obtenus dans le cours des dix années que nous venons de traverser, nous allons avoir l'honneur de mettre sous vos yeux, par chiffres, un état comparatif de la situation des écoles primaires au moment de la mise en vigueur de la loi, et dans le moment actuel.

*Nombre des écoles.*

| | 1844 | | 1855 |
|---|---|---|---|
| a) permanentes . . . | 324 | ——— | 470 |
| b) temporaires . . . | 98 | ——— | 40 |
| Total . . . | 422 | ——— | 510 réparties |

entre les divers cantons de la manière suivante:

307

| CANTONS. | 1844 Écoles permanentes. | 1844 Écoles temporaires. | 1844 TOTAL. | 1855 Écoles permanentes. | 1855 Écoles temporaires. | 1855 TOTAL. | Différence en plus. |
|---|---|---|---|---|---|---|---|
| Capellen . . . . . . . | 21 | 6 | 27 | 27 | 13 | 40 | 13 |
| Clervaux . . . . . . . | 32 | 13 | 45 | 42 | 12 | 54 | 9 |
| Diekirch . . . . . . . | 37 | 8 | 45 | 52 | 3 | 55 | 10 |
| Esch-sur-l'Alzette . . | 24 | 11 | 35 | 39 | 3 | 42 | 7 |
| Echternach . . . . . | 25 | 6 | 31 | 34 | 2 | 36 | 5 |
| Grevenmacher . . . . | 29 | 6 | 35 | 42 | » | 42 | 7 |
| Luxembourg (ville) . . | 16 | » | 16 | 22 | » | 22 | 6 |
| id. 1re subdiv. | 18 | 2 | 20 | 25 | 1 | 26 | 6 |
| id. 2e subdiv. | 12 | 3 | 15 | 21 | » | 21 | 6 |
| Mersch . . . . . . . | 27 | 7 | 34 | 40 | 2 | 42 | 8 |
| Redange . . . . . . . | 28 | 13 | 41 | 37 | 5 | 42 | 1 |
| Remich . . . . . . . | 22 | 6 | 28 | 31 | » | 31 | 3 |
| Wiltz . . . . . . . . | 33 | 17 | 50 | 48 | 9 | 57 | 7 |
| Total . . . . | 324 | 98 | 422 | 470 | 40 | 510 | 78 |

Ce n'est pas seulement dans cette augmentation du nombre des écoles qu'il faut voir le progrès; le véritable progrès consiste dans la diminution du nombre des écoles temporaires. Ainsi ces écoles ont complètement disparu dans les cantons de Grevenmacher, de Luxembourg II et de Remich; dans le canton de Clervaux il n'y en a qu'une de moins, mais dans celui de Diekirch elle sont tombées de 8 à 3, dans celui d'Esch de 11 à 3, dans celui d'Echternach de 6 à 2, dans celui de Luxembourg I de 2 à 1, dans celui de Mersch de 7 à 2, dans celui de Redange de 13 à 5, et dans celui de Wiltz de 17 à 9.

*Personnes enseignant sans brevet.*

| 1844 | | 1855 |
|---|---|---|
| 411 | ——— | 328 |

*Autorisations provisoires.*

| | | |
|---|---|---|
| 92 | ——— | 45 |

FIGURE 3.3

In particular, success was demonstrated by the quantitative growth of the individual schools from 422 to 520 units between 1844 and 1855. These pleasing numbers by themselves, the comment stated, demonstrated the true progress, which was expressed in the continuous elimination of the temporary schools that did not meet the regulations: "The true progress consists in the reduction of the number of temporary schools" (*Luxemburger Schulbote*, 1855, p. 307): Progress was not only quantitative growth but standardization of central guidelines.

In contrast, the statistical data collected in Zurich were very moderate in amount and hardly ever interpreted. In 1887, on the occasion of the 50th anniversary of the secondary schools, the central administration published a list of the students enrolled in the last 50 years, but they did this without any introduction or comment. The title was rather dry: "Overview of the enrollment of Zurich's secondary schools in the last 50 years," and page by page it included numbers that could easily have been (but were not) interpreted as a success story (see Figure 3.4a–b and Figure 3.5). In contrast to Luxembourg, the central authorities in Zurich waived this opportunity. Even in the case of the secondary schools, progress in Zurich never meant the progress in the central cantonal development. Schools were organized and largely controlled locally, and their success (or failure) was local.

Abonnementspreis.
Für das ganze Jahr Fr. 70 Cts.
inkl. Bestellgebühr und Porto.
Das Amtliche Schulblatt erscheint
je auf den 1. des Monats.

Einrückungsgebühr.
Die gedruckte Zeile 15 Cts.
Einsendungen und Gelder franco
an den
kantonalen Lehrmittelverlag.

# Amtliches Schulblatt

### des Kantons Zürich.

**II. Jahrgang.**      **Nr. 8.**      **1. August 1887.**

Inhalt: Besuch der zürch. Sekundarschulen in den letzten 50 Jahren, nebst Angabe der Eröffnungsjahre der einzelnen Sekundarschulen. — Beschluss des Erz.-Rates betr. das Lebet'sche Bilderwerk über nützliche Vögel. — Kleinere Mitteilungen. — Inserate.

Inhalt der Beilage: Gesetze und Verordnungen betr. das Unterrichtswesen. Neue Folge: Lehrplan des Technikums des Kantons Zürich in Winterthur, Studienplan der Tierarzneischule, Verträge.

## I. Übersicht des Besuchs der zürcherischen Sekundarschulen in den letzten 50 Jahren.

### A. Knaben und Mädchen.

| | 1836/37 | | 1846/47 | | 1856/57 | | 1866/67 | | 1876/77 | | 1886/87 | |
|---|---|---|---|---|---|---|---|---|---|---|---|---|
| | K. | M. | K. | M. | K. | M. | K. | M. | K. | M. | K. | M. |
| **Zürich** | | | | | | | | | | | | |
| Altstetten | | | *)17 | 2 | *)17 | 4 | 10 | 4 | 30 | 7 | 31 | 10 |
| Aussersihl | | | | | | | | | 107 | 57 | 127 | 80 |
| Birmensdorf | | | 12 | 2 | 13 | — | 13 | — | 14 | 3 | 21 | 4 |
| Dietikon | | | | | | | | | 25 | 4 | 30 | 8 |
| Enge | | | 26 | — | 50 | — | 53 | 27 | 35 | 29 | 64 | 54 |
| Fluntern | | | | | | | | | 30 | 12 | 28 | 27 |
| Höngg | | | **)15 | 5 | **)22 | 3 | **)22 | 8 | 21 | 18 | 24 | 6 |
| Hottingen | | | | | | | | | | | 66 | 49 |
| Neumünster | | | 24 | — | 54 | — | 105 | 60 | 105 | 119 | 137 | 99 |

\*) Schlieren.    \*\*) Oberengstringen.

**Bemerkung.** Die Unterscheidung von Knaben und Mädchen für das Jahr 1836/37 ist in den Akten nicht enthalten.

|  | 1836/37 | 1846/47 | 1856/57 | 1866/67 | 1876/77 | 1886/87 |
|---|---|---|---|---|---|---|
| Übertrag |  | 645 | 897 | 1356 | 2131 | 2462 |
| Andelfingen |  | 72 | 81 | 156 | 206 | 153 |
| Bülach |  | 87 | 99 | 160 | 237 | 186 |
| Dielsdorf |  | 58 | 90 | 112 | 165 | 136 |
|  |  | 862 | 1167 | 1784 | 2739 | 2937 |

*Mädchen.*

|  | 1836/37 | 1846/47 | 1856/57 | 1866/67 | 1876/77 | 1886/87 |
|---|---|---|---|---|---|---|
| Zürich |  | 11 | 157 | 360 | 626 | 770 |
| Affoltern |  | 15 | 18 | 15 | 53 | 43 |
| Horgen |  | 48 | 45 | 69 | 124 | 119 |
| Meilen |  | 37 | 48 | 52 | 85 | 82 |
| Hinweil |  | 28 | 32 | 51 | 114 | 89 |
| Uster |  | 7 | 9 | 27 | 51 | 61 |
| Pfäffikon |  | 17 | 13 | 21 | 34 | 23 |
| Winterthur |  | 10 | 15 | 42 | 273 | 311 |
| Andelfingen |  | 15 | 19 | 33 | 57 | 43 |
| Bülach |  | 32 | 23 | 32 | 71 | 56 |
| Dielsdorf |  | 4 | 17 | 28 | 31 | 44 |
|  |  | 224 | 396 | 730 | 1519 | 1641 |

*Total.*

|  | 1836/37 | 1846/47 | 1856/57 | 1866/67 | 1876/77 | 1886/87 |
|---|---|---|---|---|---|---|
| Zürich | 116 | 124 | 339 | 795 | 1309 | 1742 |
| Affoltern | 32 | 70 | 80 | 93 | 170 | 135 |
| Horgen | 116 | 137 | 203 | 249 | 369 | 385 |
| Meilen | 126 | 116 | 131 | 183 | 284 | 227 |
| Hinweil | 89 | 117 | 152 | 188 | 314 | 330 |
| Uster | 23 | 55 | 66 | 135 | 191 | 196 |
| Pfäffikon | 61 | 93 | 83 | 113 | 160 | 142 |
| Winterthur | 105 | 106 | 180 | 237 | 694 | 803 |
| Andelfingen | 70 | 87 | 100 | 189 | 263 | 196 |
| Bülach | 72 | 119 | 122 | 192 | 308 | 242 |
| Dielsdorf | 71 | 62 | 107 | 140 | 196 | 180 |
|  | 881 | 1086 | 1563 | 2514 | 4258 | 4578 |

FIGURE 3.4b

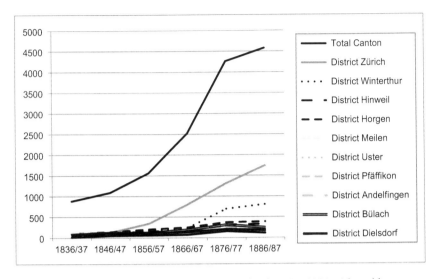

**FIGURE 3.5** Enrollments in Zurich's secondary school, 1836–1886, girls and boys
*Source: Amtliches Schulblatt des Kantons Zürich*, 1887, p. 97.

## Controlling the Professional and Social-Moral Behavior of the Teachers

In all of Europe's nation-states the conviction was shared that teachers were decisive in the failure or success of the school. Teachers as teacher-citizens were expected to educate students not only via their lessons but also by being good role models. It is not a coincidence that in Luxembourg, for instance, explicit civic instruction was introduced in the teacher education curriculum in 1848, decades before it became a subject in the primary school in 1912 (*Luxemburger Schulbote*, 1847, pp. 276f.; Schreiber, 2014, p. 84).

To organize schools meant therefore most of all to align the teachers to the authorities' expectations, and that is the reason the school laws always regulated teacher education and the system of certificates right from the start. However, the initial training was to be but one element, a *conditio sine qua non*, in aligning teachers to the overall national system of values; the teachers were also controlled in their professional and social-moral behavior after they were hired and had teaching positions. The practice of controlling depicts the way in which the national citizen was *actually* defined. It is here that the great differences between the individual nation-states become evident.

In Zurich, the fit between the expectations of the local authorities (mostly elected laymen) and the social-moral and professional quality of the teachers was largely secured in advance, because the school boards were responsible for electing the teachers. Intolerable conduct by teachers was often discussed in the realm of the communal school board, and in case of continuing disagreement the matter was handed over to the district school boards, whose primary function, however, was to advise and support the teachers in their quality. A comprehensive inspection of teacher quality in the whole canton was performed only once, in 1861/1862, when the minister of education, Hans Ulrich Zehnder, decided to conduct an extraordinary inspection, which he was legally entitled to do. However, the inspection results were sobering and showed worse results across the board than the visitation reports conducted by district school boards. These differences led to great unrest in the cantonal parliament, with the result that the central authorities never again dared to conduct a cantonal inspection (Kreis, 1933, pp. 427f.). Indeed, the central inspection of 1861/1862 was the only one in Zurich's entire school history, and anyone desiring to understand the practices of controlling the teachers has to consult the minutes of the local school boards, which requires a great deal of effort.

The situation in Luxembourg was totally different. The teachers were visited and evaluated by the inspectors twice a year regarding punctuality, neatness, moral-religious conduct, expertise in the school subjects, and didactic skills. Based on these elements the inspectors had to rate the teachers on a scale from "bad and nulls" to "distinguished." If we follow a statistical analysis of these evaluations across the 19th century, then the teachers improved considerably, for the two lowest categories had disappeared by 1912 (see Figure 3.6).

The data collected by the inspectors were used by the central authorities to organize the ongoing teacher education, which was organized along a formal ranking scale. As a rule, newly certified teachers started out at the lowest rank or level, and the central authorities decided which wage-relevant rank they were supposed to achieve in time intervals of two years. The *Luxembourg School Herald* published the names of all the teachers who had to take a further training course, including the precise level of the training course (*Luxemburger Schulbote*, 1858, pp. 20f.).

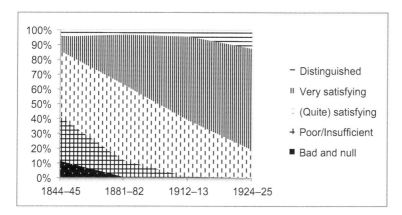

**FIGURE 3.6** Practical skills of the primary teachers according to the inspectors' reports
*Source*: Simmer, 1926, p. 79.

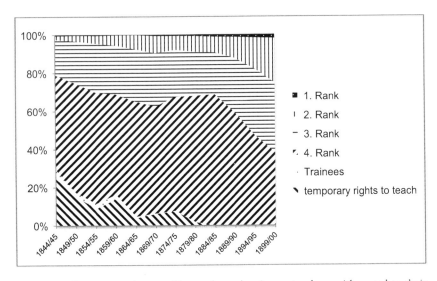

**FIGURE 3.7** Percentage change of Luxembourg's primary teachers with regard to their educational level, 1844–1900

*Source*: Simmer, 1926, p. 80.

This strategy was not followed solely to plan and ensure the careers of individual teachers; the aim was to develop the collective body of all teachers. If we follow the story told by the central authorities, their strategy was successful; the category "unqualified" and the lowest level, 4, disappeared by the turn of the century, whereas the upper three categories increased from 20% to 60% (see Figure 3.7).

Luxembourg's authorities were rather serious about their strategy to coerce the teachers to participate in continuing education. This is shown by the fact that teachers who did not follow the directive were immediately banned from employment temporarily and were denounced publicly in the *Luxembourg School Herald*—bilingually, of course:

> Removal of three school teachers. By decision of the royal grand-ducal committee for instruction, on 21 August and in accordance with article 92 of the school law on primary education, the teachers Zenner, Theodore, of Tandel, Manderscheid, Johann, of Kalborn, and Lulling, Niklas, of Merkholz were removed, because they did not attend the summer classes in the normal school.
> (Luxemburger Schulbote, *1846, p. 285*)

The public sanctioning of misbehaving school teachers was not limited to issues with their expertise in school subjects or didactic skills but included any kind of misbehavior. In every single issue of the *Herald*, published quarterly, fallible teachers were criticized severely and humiliated publicly, especially those "removed" teachers described as being "wicked with the most despicable vice incompatible with the dignity of a teacher, the vice of drunkenness" (*Luxemburger Schulbote*, 1845, p. 57). These fallible teachers were named and warned semi-anonymously, such as "the school teacher of L. . . ., whose debauchery while drinking led the school inspectors of the Canton L. . . ." to remove him from his job, and

> The teacher H. . . . of B. . . . in the Canton of Diekirch, has been rebuked by the royal grand-ducal committee for instruction because of his irregular behavior, his negligence in the implementation of his duties, and because of his unwise, reprehensible conduct on the occasion of the last community elections.
>
> (Luxemburger Schulbote, *1846, p. 285*)

These public humiliations could easily lead to the end of a career, as the following example shows: According to the complete directory of all teachers published in the same issue of the *Luxembourg School Herald*, the only possible person who could be "teacher H. . . . of B. . . . " was Mathias Hartz of Brandenbourg, Canton Diekirch, and a year later this Mathias Hartz had disappeared from the directory. The public humiliation by the central authorities had meant the end of his teaching career.

## The Teachers and the Question of Participation in Educational Policy

In the course of the 19th century, public humiliations of teachers disappeared in the same way that the bad teacher ratings and the low ranks of the teachers had disappeared. These handed-down data tell the story of Luxembourg's success in establishing a modern school system, not least because it seems that the central authorities were able to align the teachers to given and predefined professional and religious-moral norms. However, it is a story based on statistical data created by the central authorities, while the teachers appear to be comparatively passive. What were they doing?

Indeed, Luxembourg's teachers seem to have organized themselves only after several decades. In 1863—that is, 20 years after the school law was passed—the first teacher's journal was published, the *Luxemburger Schulblatt* [Luxembourg School Magazine]. However, it survived for only two years, and the next teacher's journal, the *Luxembourger Schulfreund* [Luxembourg School Friend] was published in 1872, some 30 years after the school law was passed. This delay was not limited to written communication: Regular general teacher assemblies were held only after 1871 (*Luxemburger Schulbote*, 1871, pp. 223–225).

In this respect, the contrast to Zurich could not be any greater. Although the Swiss cantons were rather reserved in terms of official gazettes published by the central authorities, the teachers themselves were very active. Between 1830 and 1844 three new teacher's journals were published in Zurich alone, each expressing very different views on organizing teachers and developing the school.[3] The teachers of Zurich were obviously much more politicized than their Luxembourger colleagues, which goes back not least to the specific institution that existed almost exclusively in Zurich—the school synod.

The Zurich school synod had been erected in the new constitution in 1831 and in the school law of 1832, and it was assigned high power even vis-à-vis the central administration (Tröhler, 2007). The synod was unique because it assembled all actors in the field—teachers and members of the cantonal and district school boards in Zurich—and gave them extensive rights to self-government (Gesetz über die Einrichtung der Schulsynode, 1831, §1); the members were able to elect their president from their midst (§4). Already starting in 1834, the *Verhandlungen der Schulsynode* [Proceedings of the School Synod] was published annually, containing professional or educational policy issues, didactic discussions, and educational-moral deliberations (*Bericht über die Verhandlungen der Zürcherischen Schulsynode*, 1834–1992).

In some respects, *Proceedings of the School Synod* was the equivalent of the *Luxembourg School Herald*, with the important difference that the *Herald* was top-down communication by the central authorities and the *Proceedings* were bottom-up communication by the actors in the field. Against this background, it is not surprising that beyond the constitutionally defined synod, teachers in Switzerland organized themselves in teacher's associations rather late: Bern was first, in 1892 (Graf, 1929), and Zurich followed in 1893 (Ziegler, 1993), shortly after the central authorities had decided to publish an official gazette. It is all the more striking that the Luxembourg teachers remained without any communication organs for such a long time and that they organized themselves only comparatively late, in 1884, and for 20 years solely as a benefit society for needy teachers. A teacher's union that fought for more rights for teachers was founded in Luxembourg only in 1905.

## Continuities

The differences between Luxembourg and Zurich regarding the ideas or shared convictions about how to organize schools, aimed at making the national citizen, go back to different systems of reasoning that originated long before the nation-states were founded. The Canton of Zurich had the institution of the school synod, assigning the teacher assembly comprehensive participatory rights in educational policy. This school synod was a copy of the church synod implemented in Zwingli's times in the 16th century; it was organized in a local and participatory way, as the entire school was defined in 1832. It is interesting to see that the school, emancipated from the supervision of the church, was designed to function in the same way that the church had functioned for 300 years, whereby the state cooperated for a considerable amount of time with the ministers in the communes. Two of the first five directors of the normal schools were clergymen, and, for decades,

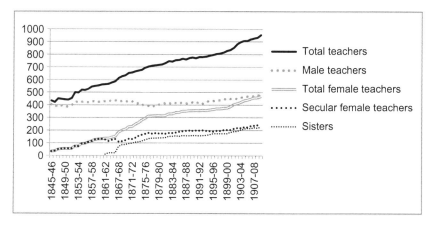

**FIGURE 3.8** Luxembourg's primary teachers, 1845–1910

*Note*: Including the nursery schools and upper primary schools
*Source*: Schooling as Institutional Heritage in Cultural Settings (SIHICS) teacher database.

the communal pastors were presidents of the local school boards; furthermore, for years, teachers had to serve as church sextons and cantors (Gesetz betreffend Aufhebung . . ., 1838). Similarly, the first directors of the Luxembourgish normal schools were priests, from the very beginning up to 1920, and teachers, once hired, were supervised by the local priests regarding their religious and moral conduct (Gesetz vom 26. Juli 1843, Nr 1709, Art. 57). The proportion of ecclesiastic or at least religiously trained actors had even grown throughout the 19th century: The extension of the primary schools in the 19th century happened largely through female teachers; whereas in 1900 approximately 50% of all the teachers were women, half of them were nuns and the other half had been trained in the boarding normal school run by the Soeurs de la Doctrine Chrétienne, the Sisters of the Christian Doctrine (see Figure 3.8).

In Luxembourg there was no regular institution similar to the Zurich school synod. We find semiannual conferences offered to the teachers that dealt with specific curricular and didactical questions, conferences that were precisely scheduled and communicated ahead of time via the *Luxembourg School Herald*. They were organized by the royal grand-ducal committee for instruction by publishing central questions related to schooling in the *Herald* and asking teachers to respond. The authors of the responses deemed to be the best were invited to the conference, where they further discussed their ideas, and their responses were published in the *Herald*.

We can see a correspondence between the school synod and the culturally institutionalized Reformed Church in Zurich, but we can also detect an analogy between the Luxembourgish school system and the institutionalized Catholic clerical and monarchical systems of order that were implemented in the school law of 1843: The organization was centralized and top-down,[4] which was executed not least to demonstrate in public the young state's ability to survive and organize itself. The first Grand Duke of Luxembourg was much praised for his tough top-down organization of primary schooling, whereas the previous liberal school regulation of the new Belgian government (to which Luxembourg had belonged from 1830 to 1839) was perceived as chaotic. In all educational historiography since, this top-down organization was worked into the national identity construction to demonstrate national progress and competitiveness: At the beginning stands the unloved *Schoulmeeschter* with his winter school, and at the end a modern, professional school system (Lenz & Rohstock, 2011, p. 64). Of course, we find local school administrations in the Grand Duchy as well, organizing the schools locally, but they did not have the same democratic legitimation or the same range of freedom to act that their colleagues in Zurich had. Integrated in the overall and top-down program of nation-building as an independent nation distinct from Belgium, the local stakeholders were meant to implement decisions made by the national stakeholders rather than to implement ideas that were deliberated in the local communities.

To be sure, the continuities that are so evident in both Zurich and Luxembourg are not ecclesiastic or even theological but tightly connected to cultural patterns or systems of reasoning in which the idea of the ideal citizen was interwoven, too, and this ideal was much less participatory in Luxembourg than in Zurich.[5] The practices of organizing the schools went along the lines of the handed-down value systems and cultural ideals of the respective nation-state and its citizens and helped to ensure the success and sustainability of the new school systems as defined by law and by the syllabi. More detailed studies show to what extent the normative parts of the school system (laws and syllabi) harmonized with the organizational practices, and what happened if they did not harmonize. The history of schooling then becomes a research model detecting the dynamic interaction of constitution and legislation, administration, the body of teachers, and the syllabi in their respective cultural contexts and milieus, the reconstruction of which has to include popular educational and pedagogical theories, debates on education policies, and historical statistics to detect the value systems of the educationalized nations after 1800 and their actual developments, which prove to be grounded in long cultural traditions. The results will be far from suggesting a "universal and universalistic" agenda, as it is advocated by the proponents of an alleged world culture or world polity (see Meyer & Ramirez, 2000, p. 115).

This cultural sustainability—allowing variations and innovation, of course—is not limited to enhancing academic knowledge on school systems but also serves as expertise for educational policy. In the same way that historical statistics belong to the methodological repertoire of research that aims to understand the development of school systems, modern quantitative investigations would profit from knowledge of the cultural path dependencies in the development of the school systems they are examining. For example, when in 1999 a large study on citizenship education explored the question, "How are political attitudes similar and different among samples of adolescents in the five countries?" (Hahn, 1998, p. 1), it did not take into account the different institutionalized values of citizenship but focused solely on classroom activities. After the principal investigator, Carole Hahn, did not succeed in explaining the inconsistencies in the given variables, she declared: "Whether they are rooted in culture, history, or some aspects of schooling is not evident"; rather, the result seemed to be a "combination of all those factors" (1999, p. 247). According to Hahn, the problem was that "political cultures" reflected various "distinct sets of values," and successful strategies in one place do not so readily apply in other cultures that have "differing traditions, values and meanings" (p. 231). This defines the frame of educational research, combining history, sociology, and education in cultural study aiming to build educational theories, and this is relevant for both future educational research designs and educational policy.

## Notes

1. I thank Peter Voss, Catherina Schreiber, and Nadine Geisler for helping me collect the sources.
2. This means that they strive to match their neighbors in spending and social standing. This is an American term of the 20th century. It originated with Arthur (Pop) Momand's comic strip in the *New York Globe* called "Keeping Up with the Joneses." Jones was a very common name, and "the Joneses" was merely a generic name for "neighbors" (retrieved August 19, 2011, from http://www.phrases.org.uk/meanings/216400.html).
3. *Zürcherische Schulzeitung* [Zurich School Journal] (1839–1845), *Zürcherischer Schulfreund* [Zurich School Friend] (1842–1843), and *Liberaler Schulbote* [The Liberal School Herald] (1844–1848).
4. Accordingly, the formal erection of an educational ministry did not take place until 1901 (Schreiber, 2014, p. 73): The culturally embedded top-down culture obviously did not even need, in the first 60 years, a distinct formal governmental organization and administration for schooling.
5. See also Ragnhild Barbu's chapter in this book.

## References

*Amtliches Schulblatt des Kantons Zürich* (1868–1969). Zurich, Switzerland: Verlag der Erziehungsdirektion.
*Bericht über die Verhandlungen der Zürcherischen Schulsynode* (1834–1992). Zurich.
Gesetz betreffend Aufhebung der Verpflichtung der Schullehrer zur Übernahme der Vorsingerstelle vom 27. September 1838. Zurich.
Gesetz betreffend die Organisation der Gemeinds-Schulpflegen vom 19. November 1831. Zurich.
Gesetz über die Einrichtung der Schulsynode vom 26. November 1831. Zurich.

Gesetz vom 26. Juli 1843, Nr 1709, über den Primär-Unterricht. Luxembourg.
Graf, O. (1929). *Der Bernische Lehrerverein: seine Geschichte, seine Arbeit und seine Ziele: ein Wort an die in das Amt tretenden Lehrer und Lehrerinnen—im Auftrage des Kantonalvorstandes des Bernischen Lehrervereins*. Bern, Switzerland: Bolliger & Eicher.
Hahn, C. L. (1998). *Becoming political: Comparative perspectives on citizenship education*. Albany, NY: SUNY Press.
Hahn, C. L. (1999). Citizenship education. An empirical study of policy, practices, and outcomes. *Oxford Review of Education, 25*(1–2), 231–250.
Harbison, F. H. 1966. Strategies for human resources development (1). In Organization for Economic Co-operation and Development (Ed.), *Human resources development. Training course. Lectures and methodological essays on educational planning. Bergneustadt, 6–24 July 1964* (pp. 39–54). Paris, France: Organization for Economic Co-operation and Development.
L'instruction populaire en Europe. Rectification de la Carte de Mr. J. Manier, publiée à l'occasion de l'Exposition Universelle de Paris, en 1878. Madrid, October 1878.
Kreis, H. (1933). Die zürcherische Volksschule von 1845–1872. In Erziehungsrat des Kantons Zürich (Ed.), *Volksschule und Lehrerbildung* (pp. 345–551). Zurich, Switzerland: Verlag der Erziehungsdirektion.
Lenz, T., & Rohstock, A. (2011). The making of the Luxembourger: Histories of schooling and national identity in the Grand Duchy. *Encounters on Education, 12*, 61–76.
*Luxemburger Schulblatt herausgegeben von mehreren Schullehrern des Grossherzogthums* (1863–1865). Luxembourg.
*Luxemburger Schulbote: Eine Zeitschrift, zunächst für die Schullehrer des Grossherzogthums Luxemburg bestimmt* (1844–1942). Luxembourg.
*Luzernisches Schul-Blatt: Amtliches Publikationsmittel des Erziehungsrathes des Kantons Luzern* (1884–). Lucerne.
Meyer, J. W., & Ramirez, F. O. (2000). The world institutionalization of education. In J. Schriewer (Ed.), *Discourse formation in comparative education* (pp. 111–132). Frankfurt, Germany: Peter Lang.
Schreiber, C. (2014). *Curricula and the making of the citizens: Trajectories from 19th and 20th century Luxembourg* (Unpublished doctoral dissertation). University of Luxembourg, Luxembourg.
Scott, W. R. (2001). *Institutions and organizations, 2nd ed.* Thousand Oaks, CA: Sage.
Simmer, L. (1926). *Etude sur la formation du personnel de notre enseignement primaire depuis 1815*. Luxembourg, Luxembourg: Joseph Beffort.
Staatsverfassung für den Eidgenössischen Stand Zürich. 1831. Zurich.
Thyssen, G. (2013). The stranger within: Luxembourg's early school system as a European prototype of nationally legitimized international blends (ca. 1794–1844). *Paedagogica Historica, 49*(5), 625–644.
Tröhler, D. (2007). Die Zürcher Schulsynode: Ein demokratisches Kuckucksei in der liberalen Ära Zürichs im 19. Jahrhundert. In C. Crotti, P. Gonon, & W. Herzog (Eds.), *Pädagogik und Politik. Historische und aktuelle Perspektiven. Festschrift für Fritz Osterwalder* (pp. 53–68). Bern, Switzerland: Haupt.
Tröhler, D. (2010a). Globalizing globalization: The neo-institutional concept of a world culture. In T. S. Popkewitz & F. Rizvi (Eds.), *Globalization and the study of education. 2009 Yearbook of the National Society for Studies in Education, Volume 108* (pp. 29–48). New York, NY: Wiley.
Tröhler, D. (2010b). Harmonizing the educational globe: World polity, cultural features, and the challenges to educational research. *Studies in Philosophy and Education, 29*(1), 7–29.

Tröhler, D. (in press). Curriculum history. In J. L. Rury & E. Tamura (Eds.), *Handbook on history of education*. Oxford, UK: Oxford University Press.

Witry, T. (1900). *Statistique historique du Grand-Duché de Luxembourg: La situation de l'enseignement primaire dans le Grand-Duché de Luxembourg pendant la période de 1815 à 1900*. Luxembourg, Luxembourg: V. Buck.

Ziegler, P. (1993). *Zürcher Kantonaler Lehrerverein, 1893 bis 1993*. Zurich, Switzerland: Zürcher Kantonaler Lehrerverein.

# 4

# EDUCATING THE CATHOLIC CITIZEN

## The Institutionalization of Primary Education in Luxembourg in the 19th Century and Beyond[1]

*Ragnhild Barbu*

The development of the modern public school in Europe in the 19th century is often equated with the secularization process in modern Europe. The narrative of the secularization paradigm describes the institutionalized separation between the secular and the religious, leading to the transition from a traditional to a modern society devoted to secular values and norms. In this process, nationalism becomes the new religion, a "worldly religion" that gradually replaces the church (Anderson, 1983). Further, the institutionalization of primary education becomes an important factor for ensuring nation-building. However, the secularization process is conducted *first* on an institutional level, as ecclesiastical sovereignty and church property, respectively, are transferred into the secular hands of the nation-state. Whether this transition from church to state also causes a "loss of religiosity" in society or schools is not easily confirmed.

Terms such as "post-secularism," the "post-secular turn," and "post-modernism" are currently used to highlight and discuss the "unexpected" persistence or resurgence of religion in society (Boeve, 2012; Bowie, 2012; Radford, 2012). However, according to Carr (2012), such "postal perspectives" overlook the pre-conditions of modernity; the discussion about what type of religious education should be offered in school is a distracting religious narrative that "may be considered of universal moral and spiritual significance" (p. 166). Moreover, the postal perspectives seem to omit the foundation of common beliefs and traditions on which national identities have been constructed, confusing the modern education system with a neutral and value-free institution.

The "invention" of the education system in Europe would not have been possible without Christianity (Fend, 2006), but the extent to which Christian traditions were pursued in public schooling varied across Europe[2] (Hahn, Bergmann,

& Luckmann, 1993). The "grammar of schooling" (Cuban, 1993; Tyack & Cuban, 1995)[3] concept requires school reforms to comply with the inner logic of the school to become successfully incorporated into institutionalized forms of schooling. This chapter engages with this concept, seeking to determine whether a grammar of Catholic schooling can be observed in the Catholic educational curriculum that emerged from the tension between a transnational church and local Catholic communities.

Luxembourg provides an interesting case study through which to analyze the relationship between religiosity and modernity, because Luxembourgish nationalism emerged as a Catholic nationalism. Specifically, the legal context of education facilitates the investigation of the importance of religion during the modernization process of the school system in Luxembourg. The central thesis guiding this chapter is that although the church lost its strong influence over public schooling as the nation-state emerged, Christian traditions and religious education continued to shape everyday educational practices far into the 20th century (and perhaps beyond), and educational philosophies remained strongly bound to religious content and ideologies.

In the first section below, I analyze and compare legal documents to investigate how, in the course of the modernization process, the influence of the church was gradually reduced by the various school acts instituted between 1843 and 1912 and how the primary school became increasingly *formally* secularized. Next, I outline how school regulations, textbooks, and curricular discourses existed in parallel with religious practice in daily educational practices and how teaching remained sacralized. I also compare Luxembourg with the Protestant Republic of Zurich to examine whether similar developments can be found in other European settings and/or to what extent such developments differ. In the final section, I discuss the assumed persistence of religion as an omnipresent principle in the context of schooling within the secularization paradigm.

## The Secularization Process of the Luxembourgish Primary School Law

Luxembourg's modern education system was developed between the mid-19th century and the beginning of the 20th century. The Luxembourgish government's implementation of its first school law in 1843 was the result of successful negotiations between the state and the vicar apostolic,[4] Jean-Théodore Laurent, that culminated in a compromise that favored the church. In subsequent years, several disputes on the school law (in 1881, 1898, and 1912) gradually reduced the influential position of the Catholic Church, which reached its lowest point with the school law of 1912. This law was established by the liberal-socialist government, which provoked a major conflict with the bishop. This school law remained in place until a new school reform was implemented in 2009, almost 100 years later.

## Religious Education and Instruction: The First School Law of 1843

The first Luxembourgish primary school law, in 1843, was inspired by the school laws of neighboring countries, especially Belgium, France, and Germany, but its treatment of the Catholic Church was unique (Voss, 2012; Thyssen, 2013). The 1843 school law has been called a "school concordat" (Goedert, 1957, p. 472), a (forced) compromise between the government and the clergy backed by the king and Grand Duke Wilhelm II in favor of Vicar Apostolic Laurent (Majerus, 1926, p. 239; see also Linster, 1968). The vicar apostolic was a strong personality and was intensely engaged in promoting the interests of the Catholic Church (Schmitt & Hellinghausen, 1990; Maas, 2000). In a letter to the king, Laurent expressed his dissatisfaction with the development of the school law and emphasized that national education or education in general can never prosper when it is not founded on religion (Vuillermoz, 1990). When the school law was finally passed in 1843, religion was given an important role in education and was to provide the foundation for teaching. According to the first article of the school law, religious and moral instruction was the most important task of the school.[5] Furthermore, the law guaranteed the Catholic Church control over educational matters and organization:

- In the hierarchy of school subjects, religion was considered the most important among the mandatory subjects (see note 5).
- The clergy taught religion and was allowed to pass this duty on to teachers. In that case, the teacher was supervised by the local priest.
- In addition to their certificate of qualification, aspiring teachers were required to hold certificates issued by the local priest and others confirming their moral suitability.
- The priest was a member of the local school commission and was always allowed to visit the school at any time.
- One third of the members of the national teaching committee, which oversaw daily school matters, textbooks, and teachers, were clergymen (Gesetz vom 26. Juli 1843).[6]

When this school law was passed in 1843, the Catholic Church secured an influential position within three major areas of education: teaching, textbooks, and the supervision of teaching staff (Majerus, 1926; Vuillermoz, 1990; also Schmitt & Hellinghausen, 1990). With the draft constitution of 1848, the discussion on the importance of the clergy and religious education as the central aim of schooling had gained new impetus. Notably, article 28, which assigned the state overall responsibility to provide education for all children in Luxembourg, was interpreted as an insult by the daily newspaper *Luxemburger Wort*, which asserted that the state alone could provide only instruction but not education ("Randglossen," 1848), which was considered more valuable than any practical knowledge.

## Compulsory Schooling and the Separation Between Secular and Religious Instruction: The School Law of 1881

In 1881 Director-General[7] Henri Kirpach submitted a new law to the parliament. The first draft proposed six years of compulsory schooling and the separation of secular and religious education. It also suggested that educational supervision should be performed by the state only. Although this document was the first to question the role of religious education, it was diplomatic enough to maintain a good relationship between church and state. Despite the resistance of the church, the 1881 school act was adopted, and six-year compulsory schooling was introduced. Religious and moral instruction had the highest priority among school subjects,[8] but the supervisory functions of the clergy were limited, although not abolished. The clergy alone remained responsible for the teaching of religious lessons and were restrained from delegating this duty to the teachers. The supervisory responsibility of the clergy was reduced to delivering religious lessons. In addition, the number of clerical representatives on the teaching commission was reduced to one: the bishop or his substitute. The moral certificates attesting to the religious convictions of aspiring teachers were still required (Gesetz vom 20. April 1881).[9]

The school act of 1881 was not acceptable to the Catholic Church. The supervisory role of the church and cooperative relationship between the state and the church were seen as violated, and critics mentioned that the "tendency of the law to treat the clergy as the necessary evil" ("Ein Räthsel," 1881, p. 1) appeared obvious.

As a consequence of the manifold and long-lasting opposition of the clergy to the school law of 1881, the parliamentary debates on the amendment of the school law of 1898 reintroduced priests' prerogative to delegate religious instruction to teachers and to call teachers to provide catechism training for approximately 15 minutes four times per week (Gesetz vom 6. Juni 1898, art. 20, p. 249). With this amendment, although the separation of secular and religious teaching was maintained, it was loosened, restoring friendly relations with the Catholic Church (Vuillermoz, 1990, p. 76).

## The Organizational Suppression of the Clergy and the Introduction of the Principle of Neutrality

With the institution of a bloc government in 1908—a coalition of the Liberal League and the Socialists—the separation of church and state was further promoted, especially through education legislation. Importantly, compulsory schooling was increased to seven years. The new thematic arrangement of the legal text rejected the prominent position of religion, placing compulsory schooling in the position of highest importance.[10] Despite the government's efforts to introduce a neutral and non-Christian education system and to abolish religious education, Luxembourgish education remained to some extent a Catholic institution designed to instill Christian virtues, and religious instruction maintained its primacy in the hierarchy of school subjects. The bishop or his representative retained a seat on the teaching committee.[11]

The role of the teacher, however, was extremely contested, because the teacher presented was a neutral teacher, which was seen to jeopardize the faith of the children. Citing education in the United States, a journalist at the newspaper *Luxemburger Wort* expressed concerns about the consequences of the mandated neutrality in school, asserting that it would lead to juvenile delinquency and to the brutalization of society, a trend that had become evident overseas ("Stimmen," 1912).

The new law also released the teacher from legal supervision by the clergy and from the duty to teach religious lessons or biblical history; the new law contained no reference to moral certificates or to school visits by the priest or clergy. The inspectorate became an organ of the state only. The debates in the press before and after the passage of the new school act testify to the deep division between the Catholic conservatives, who feared the de-Christianization of teachers and the public schools, and the liberals, who promoted the state monopoly of schools and freedom of instruction. Finally, the new school law introduced, for the first time, a legal option to decline to participate in the obligatory religious instruction (Gesetz vom 10. August 1912, art. 26, p. 770).

The Catholic and national reactions to the primary school law and particularly the developments in the school law after 1912 tend to suggest a story of loss, placing the Catholic Church in a marginalized position, but it might be more appropriate to describe it as a parallel position. Because the school question remained focused on the formal relationship between the state and the church and particularly on the wording of the law, the nationalization of education was persistently presented as a loss of religion, which does not reflect the actual situation: Religion remained central to public education, and it is unclear whether the formal separation between state and church had a natural impact on educational practices and habits.

## The Sacralization of Teaching and the Persistence of Catholic Heritage and Ideologies

Because the education system is shaped by forces beyond the legal, a large variety of influential factors must be identified and understood to reconstruct the meaning of education over time. In Luxembourg, public debate and the meaning-making process governing how education and instruction should be conducted and structured depended to a large degree on the teachers themselves (Rohstock & Lenz, 2012; Schreiber, 2014). Academic expertise and institutionalized organizations were not available in the 19th and early 20th centuries (Schreiber, 2014). Therefore, it is reasonable to assume that public assertions about how the education system should work represent how school was actually conducted.

## The Primacy of Catholic School Regulation (1845–Present) and Religious Themes in Textbooks

When the first school law was passed in 1843, Vicar Apostolic Laurent felt an urgency to familiarize children with Catholic rituals, practices, and prayers and to teach them to live Christian lives. He therefore introduced school regulations (Wagener, 1930). The purpose was to develop in children a habit of church attendance and to teach them Christian virtues whenever possible (Seiler, 1980). The pupils were also required to participate in processions during the six preparation days before communion and in diverse celebratory masses and processions. Evidence of student participation in the Octave de Notre Dame ceremony can be found in the reader, *Our Country: A Heimatbuch for Adults and Children*, which was regularly used in German classes. A passage reads, "Today is the day of the welcoming of the comforter (Virgin Mary). Now, She will begin her triumphal procession. Dull rings the Bourdon bell as the children of the city open the procession. And now follow in a colorful sequence the "Normal School," the *Kolleg*, societies, musicians, flags, angels, first communicants, men and women" (Hary, 1916, p. 95). The scene described suggests that in addition to primary school children, student teachers and secondary education students also participated. Even though this is only an indication of such praxis, it still reflects the ideal situation.

In addition to Bishop Johannes Josef Koppes's advice to use Catholic books in reading classes,[12] school readers included, to varying degrees, religious texts and prayers that could comprise up to one third or even half of the book. Significantly, almost all of the textbooks used in the 19th century and early 20th century were edited by teachers and began with a prayer or a description of one's relationship with God.[13]

Singing, introduced as a school subject in 1881, became an important method for inculcating nationalist and religious ideals in students. In an April 1895 edition of the Catholic teacher journal *Luxemburger Schulfreund*, an editorial offered teachers "the tools . . . to educate the mind of his/her pupils during singing lessons as scheduled" ("Und welche Mittel," 1895, p. 85). The advantages of singing were considered to lie principally in the simplicity of the texts: "These songs [themselves] will teach the children how to feel with their heart what the text is expressing and how to transfer these feelings into the singing" (p. 86). In particular, the rhymes were seen as good practice for memory, providing an important basis for further specialization. The songbooks dealt with nature themes, love for the homeland, and, most importantly, religious topics, which were considered essential to the true development of the children's minds.

Readers and songbooks are among the many examples that illustrate the permeation of textbooks by religiously inspired topics and customs. Religious messages were also included in history, geography, *Heimatkunde*, and school plays.

## *The Religious Foundation of Teacher Education and Employment*

Another area of Catholic influence can be identified in teacher education. The teacher education program was steeped in Catholic tradition (Institut Supérieur d'Études et de Recherches Pédagogiques [ISERP], 2000), and for a long time professors and school directors were primarily clergymen. Although the school law of 1912 made teacher education exclusively a state matter, teacher education remained embedded in Catholic tradition until the second half of the 20th century, primarily because the professors and school directors of the Normal School were mostly clergymen. For the separate female teacher class of the Normal School, this tradition lasted the longest and ended only when the Pedagogical Institute replaced the Normal School in 1961.

The first official teacher education school, the *École Normale*, or Normal School, was founded in 1845.[14] Studies focused on "catechism, the study of the Bible, reading and the study of German and French texts and the respective grammars, and arithmétiques" (ISERP, 2000, p. 12). The class for female teachers was officially opened 10 years later. Before this, female teachers had received instruction in provisional settings that were either led by congregations or conducted through cooperation between the director of the Normal School and several congregations (Simmer, 1926).

Moreover, school regulations were implemented in the Normal School, providing the guiding principles for the school's daily practices. The majority of the articles addressed in the regulations were dedicated to the religious duties of a teacher and the necessity of cultivating religious practices at school, mandating daily attendance of mass, participating in communion at least six times per year, and participating in the two major processions in Luxembourg: the Octave de Notre Dame and "Te Deum" singing (Wagener, 1930).

The regulations were further enhanced by customs, such as the strong domination of Catholic leadership in the Normal School. After more than 50 years of Catholic leaders in the management of the Normal School, the first lay director was appointed in 1916.[15] Moreover, the bishop traditionally nominated the professors of teacher education, which led to a significant representation of clergymen in the Normal School in general.[16] However, not only were the teachers and directors of the teacher school religious, but also the recruitment practices for primary school teachers show clear preferences for ecclesiastical teachers. The members of the various Luxembourgish congregations enjoyed good reputations (Simmer, 1926) and were voluntarily recruited as teachers for both private and public schools[17] (Müller, 2000).

However, despite the major changes instituted by the school law, the sacralization of teaching and teacher education occurred on many levels. Teacher education especially was dominated by a religious heritage that first began to diminish in the second half of the 20th century, when its organizational structure was changed and the Pedagogical Institute was installed.

## The Ideal of the Christian Citizen in Concepts of Modern Schooling in Luxembourg and the Republic of Zurich

Similar to the famous dancing procession at Echternach,[18] the separation of religious and secular education recognized by the school law followed the rhythm of three steps forward and two steps back. The school question was mainly addressed through diplomatic compromises between state and church that preserved their friendly partnership (Pauly, 1982) by delegating moral education to the Catholic Church. A "neutral" proposition establishing how and by whom moral education should be defined after the emergence of the nation-state was never made. On the contrary, within the Luxembourgish construction of the citizen, religion became an element that overlapped and was combined with educational philosophies, making a distinction between religious and secular impossible.

The illustration on the cover page of the first edition of the monthly journal *Haus und Schule* (1922) (see Figure 4.1) portrays precisely the cultural interrelations affecting schooling in Luxembourg. There are four buildings in the picture; on the left side is the family house, where the mother stands in the door holding a baby and small children play in front of the house. In the middle of the picture is the church, and one can see children leaving it to go to elementary school. On the right side of the picture there are two school buildings. In the back is the high school, where two male adolescents are standing in front of the entrance, and at the front is the elementary school, to which far more children go than to the high school. In the center of the picture we see the father, the priest, and the teacher engaged in conversation, with the priest in the middle as the binding element. The state is not made visible, but it appears as the cultural product of the overall scene.

The case of Luxembourg is not the exception that proves the rule. Modern schooling in the Republic of Zurich, Switzerland, from 1770 to 1870 shows indications of similar developments, but they apparently occurred much earlier (Tröhler, 2011). The initiation of the modernization process of the *Volksschule* of the Republic of Zurich was grounded in the religious-political heritage of Switzerland, which is built on the central principles of Zwinglianism,[19] i.e., republican ideas of self-government. Although the church was officially separate from the school, such was not the case in practice. Similar to Luxembourg, it was self-evident that ecclesiastical authorities controlled to a great degree the organization and supervision of the public education system: "Particularly at the lower school levels, a great part of the school culture remained church culture, or religious culture, for decades after 1831" (Tröhler, 2011, p. 159). By 1870, the *Volksschule* had finally become a secular school under public control, ensuring a fair balance between the political and the religious.

This balance finds further support in an examination of the textbooks or teaching materials used at the time. For the central subjects, e.g., reading, writing, and singing, religious content was preferred, and there was extensive use of catechisms

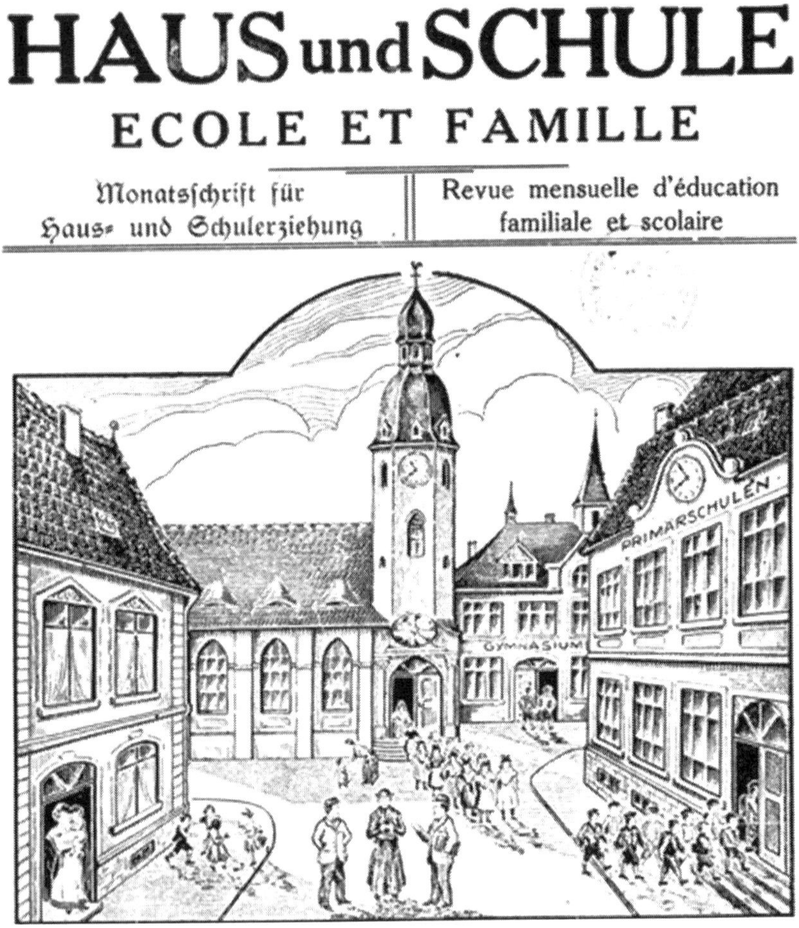
HAUS und SCHULE
ECOLE ET FAMILLE
Monatsschrift für
Haus- und Schulerziehung
Revue mensuelle d'éducation
familiale et scolaire
PRIMARSCHULEN
GYMNASIUM

FIGURE 4.1 Cover illustration of *Haus und Schule*, 1922

(De Vincenti & Grube, 2011). As in Luxembourg, regular prayers before the lesson were a common practice in rural schools across the Republic of Zurich (p. 284). In contrast to the dominant authority of the priest in the communes of Luxembourg, the priests in the communes of the Republic of Zurich encountered obstacles in performing their duties, such as the election of schoolmasters.

The school regulations assigned the priest to supervise the school. However, as an inquiry confirmed, the priests were typically excluded from electing schoolmasters (p. 285). Interestingly, the same inquiry revealed that most of the priests in rural areas did not even know that such regulations existed, and the communes were not interested in altering this fact; they self-confidently "insist[ed] on exercising their rights and reject[ed] any interference from the outside" (p. 287).

The practices associated with the election of schoolmasters in rural areas in the Republic of Zurich represent the importance of both the republican idea of self-regulation promoted by the distinctiveness of civic groups, e.g., the Examiners Committee, and the right not to be ruled by others. In contrast to these (Protestant) republican ideals, Luxemburg, which encouraged Catholic, civic, and monarchical virtues, was clearly dominated by religious and clerical authority that was relatively resistant to change. In contrast to the growing independence of the communes in the Republic of Zurich, the communes in Luxembourg remained closely associated with the church.[20]

## Considerations

It is evident that the modernization of the public education system led to the formation of a secular school, separating state and church on institutional and normative levels. However, several indicators mark the persistence of religion and informal religious modes of thought within a "Catholic grammar of schooling" in ways that trouble the concept of a secular school.

The Luxembourgish school was imagined as a Catholic school and was established as such through the permeation of Catholic thought and practices in daily school life, and this is reflected in the schools' teaching, textbooks, and teacher education. Luxembourg is uncontestably embedded in a Catholic tradition, and nationalism did not replace religion. Instead, a Catholic nationalism was shaped; Christian virtues still define the Luxembourgish vision of a good Catholic citizen. For example, the Virgin Mary, patron of Luxembourg, is an important symbol of this Catholic nationalism and represents the religious-national unification of the people (Schmitt & Hellinghausen, 1990). Religious expression and the national longing for Christian values and symbols—reflected, for instance, in the appreciation of the Holy Sacraments as important life events—were inculcated at school and supported the construction of the Catholic citizen. These values are also reflected in the distinct need for rituals and symbols in Luxembourgish society, which is particularly visible in the common "consumption of sacraments" (Fehlen, 1998).

The relationship between modernity and religion is being questioned, and the assumption that the contradiction between scientific theory and religion would result in a new moral order of society and in the marginalization of religion has not materialized. Today, the secularization paradigm has been contested in recent scientific discussions (Stark, 1999; Casanova, 2008; Gorski & Altinordu, 2008; Gabriel, Gärtner, & Pollack, 2012), and new paradigms focus mainly on the changes in individual relationships. For example, the "rational-choice" or "invisible religion" paradigms focus on aspects of de-institutionalization (Hellemans, 2005) but remain weak on justifications regarding the social system. The unexpected persistence or resurgence of religion should be carefully examined, not as a "postal" development but as a cultural practice that accommodates religious narratives and practices even in contexts claiming to be scientific and value-free.

## Notes

1. A draft version of this chapter was presented at the conference "Between the National and the Global: Developments of Modern School Systems," February 14–16, 2013, University of Luxembourg. Advice given by Catherina Schreiber, Anne Rohstock, and Frederik Herman was very helpful during the development of this chapter. I would also like to thank Peter Liwowski for the image processing.
2. The implementation of public schooling, i.e., compulsory education offered by the state, provoked several "school conflicts" across Western Europe. For example, conflicts arose during the Bataafsen Republiek (the Netherlands) between 1793 and 1806, and the first school conflict in Belgium occurred between 1879 and 1914.
3. The main thesis of the concept of the "grammar of schooling," a concept developed in the United States in the last decade of the 20th century, is that attempts to exercise influence on schooling need to be pursued within the inner logic of schooling to be successfully implemented. The "cultural construction of schooling" functions in a selective way and might even allow adaptation of the reform to specific needs.
4. According to Roman Catholic law, an apostolic vicariate is a diocese on probation. The vicar apostolic inherits the jurisdiction for the territory of the apostolic vicariate; his position is similar to that of bishop but differs in its relationship to the pope.
5. "Primary education considers necessary: religious and moral teaching, German and French reading, writing, original elements of both languages, and arithmetic" (Gesetz vom 26. Juli 1843, art. 1, p. 561; freely translated here). It was further added that the teaching of French could be dismissed for several reasons.
6. See the following articles of the Gesetz vom 26. Juli 1843: art. 51, p. 577; art. 75, p. 584; art. 57, p. 579; art. 59, p. 580; and art. 73, p. 583.
7. The position of director-general was the highest position in the government and was supported by three additional director-generals. Henri Kirpach held the position of director-general for domestic policy, including education.
8. "The obligatory subjects of primary education are, 1st, religion; 2nd, German language; 3rd, French language; 4th, arithmetic, and the system of weights and measures; 5th, original elements of geography; 6th, original elements of the history of the country; 7th, singing and also, for the girl's schools, handiworks" (Gesetz vom 20. April 1881, Tit. 1, art. 1, p. 369; freely translated here).
9. See the following articles of the Gesetz vom 20. April 1881: art. 72, p. 389; arts. 20 and 22, pp. 374; art. 26, p. 375; art. 73, p. 389; and art. 52, p. 383.
10. "Each child that has passed the age of 6 years on the first of November must attend the instruction in the subjects listed in article 23 of the actual law for seven consecutive years" (Gesetz vom 10. August 1912, chap. 1, art. 1, p. 761; freely translated here).
11. See the following articles of the Gesetz vom 10. August 1912: art. 22, p. 769; art. 23, p. 769; art. 68, p. 783; and art. 74, p. 785f.
12. School readers "should not only foster the spirit [of the child] but should also have a stimulating and purifying effect upon [the child's] mind, will, memory and all his soul powers. Bible history and the handbook for religious instruction, the catechism, should therefore be his favorite books" ("Fasten-Hirtenbrief," 1897; freely translated here).
13. See, for example, the *Lesebuch für die obersten Klassen der Primärschulen des Großherzogthums Luxemburg* (Stehres, 1851); *Der Kinderfreund, Ein Büchlein für die Schuljugend des Luxemburger Landes* (Mersch, 1883); *Luxemburger Kinderfreund, neues Lesebuch für die Mittelstufe der Primärschulen* (Goedert & Reynald, 1912); and *Vaterländisches Lesebuch für die Luxemburger Volksschule: Oberstufe* (1916).

14. It offered a three- to four-year training program to students who had finished either the *ecole primaire superieur* or three years of *lycée*.
15. Up to 1916, the directors of the Normal School included Jean Majerus (1844–1852), a former priest, followed by Michel Müller, the vicar of Remich (1853–1880), and Jean Majerus (1852–1875), a priest in Hemstal, and later Jacques Meyers (1881–1916), a professor of religious instruction at the Normal School.
16. The described employment praxis became a major point of discussion during the parliamentary debate in 1958 (Projet de loi portant modification de la loi du 10 août 1912). This nomination practice clearly contradicted the constitutional rights and duties of the state and was interpreted as the exception to the rule. In this example, it is obvious that traditions and habits existed even after being discontinued by the school law.
17. New teachers that were recruited, especially between 1845 and 1875, were typically female teachers (Institut national de la statistique et des études économiques du Grand-Duché du Luxembourg [STATEC], 1990) who had been trained under the supervision of sisters of various congregations or by nuns.
18. Echternach is the oldest city in Luxembourg and a commune where a religious dancing procession occurs every year on Whit Tuesday.
19. Huldrych Zwingli (1484–1531) was a Zurich reformer who stressed the importance of close collaboration between the state and the church. Zwingli's ideal republic was both republican and Christian.
20. See also Daniel Tröhler's chapter in this book.

## References

Anderson, B. (1983). *Imagined communities: Reflections on the origin and spread of nationalism.* London, UK: Verso.

Boeve, L. (2012). Religious education in a post-secular and post-Christian context. *Journal of Beliefs and Values, 33*(2), 143–156. doi:10.1080/13617672.2012.694058

Bowie, R. (2012). Human rights education and the post secular turn. *Journal of Beliefs and Values, 33*(2), 195–205. doi:10.1080/13617672.2012.694062

Carr, D. (2012). Post-secularism, religious knowledge and religious education. *Journal of Beliefs and Values, 33*(2), 157–181. doi:10.1080/13617672.2012.694059

Casanova, J. (2008). Public religions revisited. In H. de Vries (Ed.), *Religion: Beyond the concept* (pp. 101–119). New York, NY: Fordham University Press.

Cuban, L. (1993). *How teachers taught: Constancy and change in American classrooms 1890–1990.* New York, NY: Teachers College Press.

De Vincenti, A., & Grube, N. (2011). The masters of republicanism? Teachers and schools in rural and urban Zurich in the 18th and 19th centuries. In D. Tröhler, T. S. Popkewitz, & D. Labaree (Eds.), *Schooling and the making of citizens in the long nineteenth century: Comparative visions* (pp. 282–302). New York, NY: Routledge.

Fasten-Hirtenbrief für das Jahr 1897. (1897, March 8). *Luxemburger Wort, 50*(67), 8.

Fehlen, F. (1998). Weide meine Lämmer, zähle meine Schafe. *Forum für Politik, Gesellschaft und Kultur, 173*(2), 6–12.

Fend, H. (2006). *Geschichte des Bildungswesen: Der Sonderweg im europäischen Kulturraum.* Wiesbaden, Germany: VS Verlag.

Gabriel, K., Gärtner, C., & Pollack, D. (Eds.). (2012). *Umstrittene Säkularisierung: Soziologische und historische Analysen zur Differenzierung von Religion und Politik.* Berlin, Germany: Berlin University Press.

Gesetz vom 26. Juli 1843 über den Primär-Unterricht/Loi sur l'instruction primaire. In *Verordnungs- und Verwaltungsblatt des Großherzogthums Luxemburg/Mémorial legislative et administrative du Grand-Duché de Luxembourg, 39,* 1843, 561–592.

Gesetz vom 20. April 1881 über den Primär-Unterricht/Loi sur l'instruction primaire. In *Verordnungs- und Verwaltungsblatt des Großherzogthums Luxemburg/Mémorial legislative et administrative du Grand-Duché de Luxembourg, 32,* 1881, 369–408.

Gesetz vom 6. Juni 1898, wodurch das Gesez vom 20. April 1881 über die Organisation des Primärunterrichtes abgeändert, und dasjenige vom 6 Juli 1876 über die Lehrergehälter revidiert wird, *Memorial des Großherzogthums Luxemburg,* Montag, 6. Juni 1898, 249–260.

Gesetz vom 10. August 1912 über den Primär-Unterricht/Loi sur l'instruction primaire. In Verordnungs- und Verwaltungsblatt des Großherzogthums Luxemburg/Mémorial legislative et administrative du Grand-Duché de Luxembourg, 61, 761–798.

Goedert, J. (1957). *Jean-Théodore Laurent, 1804–1884.* Luxembourg, Luxembourg: Impr. V. Buck.

Goedert, N., & Reynald, R. (Eds.). (1912). *Luxemburger Kinderfreund, neues Lesebuch für die Mittelstufe der Primärschulen.* Luxemburg, Luxembourg: Joseph Beffort.

Gorski, P. S., & Altınordu, A. (2008). After secularization? *Annual Review of Sociology, 34,* 55–85. doi:10.1146/annurev.soc.34.040507.134740

Hahn, A., Bergmann, J., & Luckmann, T. (1993). Die Kulturdeutung der Religion in der Gegenwart der westlichen Gesellschaften. *Kölner Zeitschrift für Soziologie und Sozialpsychologie, 33,* 7–15. doi:10.1007/978-3-322-94248-7_1

Hary, A. (1916). *Unser Land: Ein Heimatbuch für große und kleine Leute.* Luxemburg, Luxembourg: G. Soupert.

*Haus und Schule: Monatszeitschrift für Haus- und Schulerziehung.* (1922). Cover page, vol. 1, 1922.

Hellemans, S. (2005). Die Transformation der Religion und der Großkirchen in der zweiten Moderne aus Sicht des religiösen Modernisierungsparadigmas. *Schweizerische Zeitschrift für Religions- und Kulturgeschichte, 99,* 11–35.

Institut national de la statistique et des études économiques du Grand-Duché du Luxembourg (STATEC). (1990). *Statistiques historiques 1839–1989, Luxembourg.* Luxembourg, Luxembourg: éditpress.

Institut Supérieur d'Études et de Recherches Pédagogiques (ISERP). (2000). *La formation de l'instituteur au Luxembourg.* Luxembourg, Luxembourg: ISERP.

Linster, G. (1968). La question scolaire: ses racines dans notre histoire politique. In *Almanach culturel 1968.* Esch-sur-Alzette, Luxembourg: Impr. Coopérative Luxembourgeoise.

Maas, J. (2000). La question scolaire au Grand-Duché de Luxembourg. In A. Neuberg (Ed.), *Le choc des libertés: L'Eglise en Luxembourg de Pie VII à Léon XIII (1800–1880)* (pp. 103–106). Bastogne, Belgium: Musée en Piconrue.

Majerus, N. (1926). *La situation légale de l'église catholique au Grand-Duché de Luxembourg.* Luxembourg, Luxembourg: Impr. St. Paul.

Mersch, K. (1883). *Der Kinderfreund, Ein Büchlein für die Schuljugend des Luxemburger Landes. Mit vielen Originalzeichnungen von Prof. D. Pletsch.* Luxemburg, Luxembourg: D. Bück.

Müller, G. (Ed.). (2000). *Theologische Realenzyklopädie: De Gruyter Studienausgabe Teil II.* Berlin, Germany: De Gruyter.

Pauly, M. (1982). Von der staatlichen Kontrolle zur Partnerschaft: Kurzer Überblick über die Beziehungen zwischen Kirche und Staat in Luxemburg. *Landeskundliche Vierteljahresblätter, 28*(1), 14–27.

Projet de loi portant modification de la loi du 10 août 1912 concernant l'organisation de l'enseignement primaire et création d'un institute pédagogique, No. 479, continuation de la discussion générale—Lecture et vote des articles—vote sur l'ensemble par appel nominal, avec dispense du second vote constitutionnel. In 38me séance de Chambre de Deputés, Mercredi, 18.6.1958, document C-1957-O-038-0004, 1825–1856.

Radford, M. (2012). Faith and reason in a post secular age. *Journal of Beliefs and Values, 33*(2), 229–248. doi:10.1080/13617672.2012.694065

Randglossen zu dem Entwurfe der neuen Verfassungsurkunde. (1848, May 28). *Luxemburger Wort*, no. 20, p. 1.

Ein Räthsel. (1881, September 3). *Luxemburger Wort, 34*(205), 1.

Rohstock, A., & Lenz, T. (2012). A national path to internationalization: Educational reforms in Luxembourg, 1945–70. In C. Aubry & J. Westberg (Eds.), *History of schooling: Politics and local practice* (pp. 108–126). Bern, Switzerland: Peter Lang.

Schmitt, M., & Hellinghausen, G. (1990). *Kirche im Werden und Wachsen eines Volkes: Vol. 2*. Strasbourg, France: Editions du Signe.

Schreiber, C. (2014). *Curricula and the making of the citizens: Trajectories from 19th and 20th century Luxembourg*. Dissertation. Luxembourg 2014.

Seiler, E. (1980). *Der Religionsunterricht in den staatlichen Sekundarschulen: zur heutigen Situation*. Luxembourg, Luxembourg: Impr. Saint-Paul.

Simmer, L. (1926). *Étude sur la formation du personnel de notre enseignement primaire depuis 1815. Programme publié à la clôture de l'année scolaire 1925–1926*. Luxembourg, Luxembourg: Editions Joseph Bedford.

Stark, R. (1999). Secularization, R.I.P. *Sociology of Religion, 60*(3), 249–273.

Stehres, P. (1851). *Lesebuch für die obersten Klassen der Primärschulen des Großherzogthums Luxemburg*. Luxemburg, Luxembourg: D. Bück.

Stimmen aus der Neuen Welt über den neutralen Unterricht. (1912, February 10 and 11). *Luxemburger Wort, 65*(41–42), 2.

Thyssen, G. (2013). The stranger within: Luxembourg's early school system as a European prototype of nationally legitimized international blends (ca. 1794–1844). *Paedagogica Historica, 49*(5), 625–644. doi:10.1080/00309230.2013.786105

Tröhler, D. (2011). Classical republicanism, local democracy, and education: The emergence of the public school of the republic of Zurich, 1770–1870. In D. Tröhler, T.S. Popkewitz, & D. Labaree (Eds.), *Schooling and the making of citizens in the long nineteenth century: Comparative visions* (pp. 153–176). New York, NY: Routledge.

Tyack, D., & Cuban, L. (1995). *Tinkering toward utopia a century of public school reform*. Cambridge, MA: Harvard University Press.

Und welche Mittel stehen dem Lehrer zu Gebote, um die Gemüthsbildung seiner Schüler durch den Gesangsunterricht planmäßig zu pflegen? (1895, April 15). *Luxemburger Schulfreund, 14*(8), 85–87.

*Vaterländisches Lesebuch für die Luxemburger Volksschule: Oberstufe* (10th ed.). (1916). Luxemburg, Luxembourg: V. Bück.

Voss, P. (2012). Der bürokratische Wendepunkt von 1843: Die Primärschule im Prozess der Luxemburger Nationalstaatsbildung des 19. Jahrhunderts. In M. Geiss & A. De Vincenti (Eds.), *Verwaltete Schule: Geschichte und Gegenwart* (pp. 53–70). Wiesbaden, Germany: Springer VS.

Vuillermoz, G. (1990). *Das Luxemburgische Primarschulgesetz: eine rechtsgeschichtliche und kirchengeschichtliche Untersuchung*. Luxemburg, Luxembourg: Impr. Saint Paul.

Wagener, J. (1930). *Enseignement primaire*. Luxembourg, Luxembourg: Impr. J. Beffort.

# 5

# EARLY SCHOOL EVALUATION AND COMPETENCY CONFLICTS BETWEEN PRIMARY AND SECONDARY SCHOOLS IN LUXEMBOURG AROUND 1850

*Peter Voss*

After gaining independence in 1839, the government of the Grand Duchy of Luxembourg made the establishment of an operational school system one of its top priorities. The circumstances for such an undertaking, however, were far from ideal (Calmes, 1983; Diederich, 1989; Pauly, 2011; Voss, 2012). This becomes evident in a letter to Johann Heinrich Pestalozzi in 1818 by Heinrich Stammer, a professor at Luxembourg's Athenäum. In the letter Stammer described the Grand Duchy as a "tiny country in the dark depths of a forest." He considered the capital city, like all other towns and villages, to be poor and referred to Luxembourg as a "purely Catholic country," a fact that he felt was patently obvious to any observer. In fact, Stammer felt that the backwardness of the school system in the Grand Duchy was due in no small part to what he described as Luxembourg's unenlightened Catholicism (Horlacher & Tröhler, 2013, pp. 462–467). For the most part Stammer's description of the situation in Luxembourg still held true a good quarter of a century later. Practically all of the tentative progress that had been made in laying the foundations of a school system during the period of Dutch rule from 1815 to 1830 had been reversed by the events of the Belgian revolution from 1830 to 1839. Around 1840, only two thirds of Luxembourg parishes had a primary school, and roughly half of those operated only in winter (Calmes, 1983, p. 266).

These were the circumstances that faced the new administration when it took on the task of reorganizing the school system at the beginning of the 1840s. The primary school act of 1843 made the establishment of a primary school in every parish of Luxembourg a legal requirement.

The reorganization of the secondary school system had begun even earlier. Originating as a Jesuit college, the Athenäum was Luxembourg's only complete secondary school. It was a grammar school approximately equivalent to a German

*Gymnasium* or a French *Lycée* and was dedicated to the delivery of a traditional classical education, which was naturally of benefit only to young boys rather than young girls. In 1841 the Athenäum incorporated an *école industrielle*. At the same time the two existing town colleges (*collèges municipaux*) in Diekirch and Echternach were placed under state supervision and converted into pre-grammar schools (*Progymnasien*). As such, these two schools offered the same courses available during the first four years at the Athenäum, including Latin and Greek. Students graduating from the *Progymnasien* in Diekirch or Echternach could then transfer to the prestigious institute in the capital to complete their studies. In 1848 the school in Echternach was renamed as a secondary vocational college (*Mittel- und Gewerbeschule/Ecole moyenne et industrielle*) (Müllendorf, 1894; Müller, 1856; Schmit, 1989, 1999; Stehres, 1880; Thill, 1897).

As a result of this historical background, schools in Luxembourg at the beginning of the 19th century were characterized by strong Habsburg, French, Dutch, and Belgian influences. The main inspiration in the rebuilding phase in the mid-19th century was taken from Luxembourg's two largest neighbors, France and Prussia, and the school systems of the Grand Duchy of Baden and the Kingdom of Württemberg, for instance, also exerted an influence. At the same time, however, Luxembourg also aspired, like any other independent nation, to set up its own unique state school system.

A particular idiosyncrasy was the premise that, with the exception of the university, a comprehensive, differentiated school system covering all fields of education could be established within the parameters of Luxembourg's nation building process and in such a small country. Indeed the expectation was to create a school system that was on a par with the systems in other countries, for example, France or Prussia. This policy was clearly being pursued from a "position d'isolement," in which Luxembourg found itself since independence, a point emphasized by the minister Norbert Metz in a speech in 1853 (Thill, 1897, p. 27). In a small, extremely poor country with a population of just 200,000, however, this project was almost immediately hampered by financial, institutional, and personnel limitations. Aside from the need to bring about a significant shift in the mentality of the population toward education, a problem also faced in other countries during that period, Luxembourg lacked the requisite resources—in terms of money, know-how, trained teachers, and even, as will be discussed later, pupils—to build the kind of school infrastructure required to fulfill the modern institutional ideal.

In light of this particular idiosyncrasy we can assume that although the primary and secondary schools in the Grand Duchy of Luxembourg in the mid-19th century were intended to form part of a continuous, complementary educational pathway, the severe transitional problems suffered over a period of decades brought the entire school system to the brink of collapse. If the implementation of the primary school system is viewed as a bottom-up process and that of the secondary, in contrast, as a top-down process, the transition problems between the two levels of schooling in Luxembourg can be attributed to the fact that the secondary school system was tied to a classical "German" educational ideal.[1] The dominant clerical influence on secondary education led to the setting of standards that the primary schools of Luxembourg in the 19th century could not sufficiently prepare their pupils to meet. Furthermore, the strict adherence to a theologically legitimate and humanistic educational ideal stood in open contradiction to the prerequisites for the creation of a mercantile, educationally emancipated society. In end effect, a significant proportion of the population was excluded from participation in the education system beyond the primary school level. As such, this system can also be interpreted as a strategy by the ruling elite of the Grand Duchy, made up of public servants and clerics, to perpetuate their hold on power.

## Case Study of Echternach, 1851–1852

A conflict that occurred between the primary and secondary schools in Echternach from 1851 to 1852 will serve to illustrate this thesis.

### *Prelude*

On October 29, 1851, the teachers' conference of the secondary vocational college in Echternach filed a complaint at the highest level concerning the "deplorable conditions" at the primary school in Echternach.[2] The complaint stated that in order to operate successfully, the secondary vocational college was reliant on the town primary school to provide suitable recruits. However, despite 300 pupils attending the state primary school, it had "yet to produce a single candidate" who was "even halfway prepared." The pupils usually possessed absolutely no "positive knowledge" whatsoever. Their spirits had been robbed of "all flexibility, all elasticity and all productivity." As a result, the pupils were unable with all the will in the world to "rouse themselves from their own stupor." "Will power and a thirst for knowledge," which the primary school was surely responsible for awakening and strengthening, had instead been all but "completely destroyed." "A sense of morality" was "nowhere to be seen in most cases." In 1849 only three pupils from Echternach enrolled at the secondary vocational college, but in 1850 there were 18 candidates—all of whom, however, were described as absolutely "dissolute." The results of the entrance exams of 1851 showed no signs of improvement. Not only had the secondary school suffered since its establishment from the "state of desolation at the local primary school," but its whole existence was in the meantime in serious danger. The teacher conference therefore urgently requested a "complete reorganization of the local primary school" so that the secondary vocational college could look forward to receiving "at least reasonably well prepared pupils" in the future. Only in this way would the school be in a position to compete successfully with other secondary schools in the country.

## The Course of Proceedings

These allegations, leveled in 1851 against the primary school in Echternach and, in particular, against the teacher, Mathias Georg Zacharias Werner, were nothing new. The archives contained three similar letters from previous years. However, this particular complaint, filed in October, set off a series of correspondence between the relevant authorities and resulted in a drawn-out inquiry.

At the end of August 1852, nearly a year into the proceedings, a commission undertook a thorough inspection of the primary school, which confirmed the allegations. The commission attested to a remarkably high level of performance in the girls' classes but also criticized the poor performance of the boys. The commission recommended structural alterations and, in particular, strict separation of boys and girls. The female teachers were, with a single exception, afforded praise and encouragement, whereas the male teachers were severely reprimanded. A younger junior colleague was installed to assist the leading teacher, Werner, with the delivery of his lessons, in particular in his "problem subjects" of French and mathematics. That was considered the end of the matter, and the file was closed. It would appear that Werner was not willing to accept these recommendations, however, as his name no longer appeared in the records as a primary school teacher in the Duchy of Luxembourg from the beginning of the 1852–1853 school year, presumably because he had quit his post ("Allgemeines Verzeichnis der Personen," 1853).[3]

The important point as far as the inquiry commission was concerned would seem to be that in Werner they had succeeded in identifying the main guilty party and had sanctioned him accordingly. A new teacher was installed in his position at the Echternach primary school. Order had been restored. Thanks to the reorganization of the primary school, the secondary school in Echternach could now also look forward to a brighter future: *Quod erat demonstrandum.*

## The Allegations Against the Primary School in Echternach

The allegations leveled at the primary school by the teachers' conference at the secondary vocational college—but also from all sides during the course of the inquiry—can be summarized as follows:

- The primary school delivered too few pupils, and those who did enroll at the secondary vocational college were poorly prepared for further studies. This in turn endangered the existence of the higher school. The boys graduating from the primary school were apparently not even able to successfully complete the simplified preparatory course that had been introduced to the syllabus to ease their transition to the next level of schooling.
- Teaching at the primary school in such a populous town as Echternach was in a sorry state overall. Graduates from schools in neighboring villages were

- better equipped than Echternach pupils to succeed at the secondary vocational college.
- The girls' classes in the primary school in Echternach, especially the higher-level classes, were achieving better results than the boys' classes.
- As the teacher of the higher classes in the boys' section of the primary school, Werner was primarily responsible for the poor results achieved by the pupils and for their subsequent failure to achieve the necessary standards at the secondary vocational college.
- Werner's teaching methodology in general and in particular his approach to teaching French were not up to "a level that met current standards." Werner was described as too old, incompetent, and "a spent force in his subjects areas." (ANLux, G-0291) He was no longer considered fit to fulfill his duties and could only do harm to his pupils.

In a 12-page "rebuttal," Werner rejected the "unjustified" allegations leveled against him.[4] According to Werner, the main reason for the "unsatisfactory state of affairs" at the primary school was "overcrowding" in the lower classes. The hopelessly overfilled classes were resulting in extremely limited progress. By the time pupils reached the higher-level classes, they were so far behind that it was practically impossible for them to catch up. Werner also pointed out that the primary school also suffered from very irregular attendance in the lower classes. Pupils would sometimes remain in the first-year class until the age of 12 without mastering basic reading and writing skills. Such overly long periods in the first-year class led to a stagnation in pupils' motivation and enjoyment of learning. On top of this, many students chose to leave school after celebrating their First Communion, cutting short their school careers.

Werner also noted that pupils were being lured away from primary school before they had completed their regular school lives. In Werner's own words, pupils were leaving just at a point where "they could have formed the core of a good class."

## *Discussion of the Allegations*

It is clear that the causes of the problems at the secondary vocational college were being sought exclusively at the primary school, focusing on the operating conditions and on the incompetence of individual teachers. If the secondary vocational college was unable to fulfill its mandate, this could only be the result of the poorly run primary school. In contrast, the running of the secondary school and the competency of its teachers were never up for discussion. It was therefore logical to conclude, from this perspective, that correcting the problems at the primary school would automatically ensure the future success of the secondary vocational college in Echternach.

Werner actually defended himself using exactly the same line of argumentation that his critics had used against him. He lamented the fact that pupils entering his class did not have the necessary knowledge to succeed at that level and therefore could not be adequately prepared for entry to the secondary vocational college in the time available to him. In this way the buck was being passed down: from the secondary vocational college to the graduating class at the primary school and from there on to the lower level classes.

## The Reality in the Echternach Primary School

Werner's point about "overcrowding" is doubtless an important factor in the alleged falling performance levels at the primary school in Echternach. When the school was inspected in August 1852, a total of 571 pupils were being taught by just seven teachers.[5] The lower levels in particular were hopelessly overcrowded. The teacher of the *Classe préparatoire*, which had been introduced in 1851 to relieve pressure on the upper classes, was supervising 155 pupils, 80 girls and 75 boys. The burden in the upper classes was somewhat lighter: Werner had 66 boys in his class, and his female colleague was teaching 48 girls. Nearly two thirds of the pupils attending the school on the day of inspection were exempt from tuition fees on the grounds of poverty.

The problem of overcrowding was further exacerbated by the limited space available. The school was spread over several buildings. For example, the 48 second-year girls had to walk through the first-year classroom to get to their lessons, causing continual disruptions and disturbances. The inquiry described even the new schoolhouse as "relatively unsuitable" for teaching purposes. The sporadic attendance, also noted by Werner, was a further problem facing the primary schools of Luxembourg in the 19th century. In the school year of 1851–1852, a total of 2,020 children within the compulsory school age range of 6–12 years resided in the Canton of Echternach. An inspection during the winter months found only approximately four fifths of the children (1,650) at school, and in the summer that figure fell even further to less than two thirds (1,240) ("Rapport général sur l'état de l'instruction primaire," 1852). Under such circumstances, it is hardly surprising that teachers had to go to great lengths just to keep their lessons effective or that the school careers of many pupils took longer than expected.

## Pedagogical Suitability and Didactics

Werner was accused by his critics of no longer fulfilling the conditions required for the performance of his duties due to a combination of his advancing years and his antiquated teaching methods, which were described as out of touch with the findings of the latest pedagogical research. This critique was directed at a 56-year-old, who in 1851 could look back on a 32-year career in the service of the school system, the last 18 years of which had been spent in Echternach. Werner had also run an evening school in the town for many years. However, it was not only for his service history that Werner was well known in the Luxembourg primary school system. He was in fact one of a total of only 13 teachers in the Grand Duchy to hold an official teaching qualification (*brevet*) at level 2, placing him among a select elite of teachers ("Allgemeines Verzeichnis der Personen," 1852). During his years of service in the parish of Mersch, he was described by the *Commissaire de district* as "one of the best teachers in the country."[6] As well as being a teacher, Werner was also a renowned writer of patriotic songs, which were published in several magazines (Wilhelm, 1996). The allegation leveled by the primary school inspector, Michel, that Werner was particularly poorly qualified to teach French seems especially unusual, considering that Werner had published not only a German but also a French language teaching book (Werner 1838a, 1838b). In fact, his *Kleine französische Sprachlehre* had been reprinted many times, with a new edition appearing in 1852. Michel also accused Werner of only being concerned with superficial matters when mentoring his pupils ("façonner ses élèves") rather than being truly concerned to provide them with a complete, robust education ("leur donner une instruction qui soit durable").[7] According to Michel, although Werner spoke of the love he felt for his pupils, he had a fundamental problem with discipline in class, allowing his pupils too much freedom and failing to impart to them the necessary respect and fear of the authority of a teacher. In Werner's classes it seemed to Michel more likely that the pupils would strike their teacher than the other way around.

Although the majority of the comments were negative, some parties did attempt to offer a more balanced view. The commission that inspected Werner's teaching in 1852, for example, admitted to having expected far worse than they actually found in reality.[8] However, even the more well-meaning observers were of the opinion that Werner could have solved several of the problems identified with a little more effort on his part. His less experienced female colleagues, some of whom were as young as 20 years old, were considered more competent and dynamic in this respect, in particular in the subjects of mathematics and French, in which his performance had been adjudged to be substandard. At least in the eyes of the school administration, it was they who represented the future of education in Luxembourg, whereas schoolmaster Werner, nearing the end of his career, embodied the *Ancien Régime* of the school system of the pre-1843 era.

The fact that the blind spot in the argumentation of the one side and the uncomfortable truth in the argumentation of the other were not discussed speaks volumes about the conflict between the two schools in Echternach. This is epitomized by the fact that an important point raised by Werner in his defense was not taken up in subsequent discussions: the role of the secondary school in the conflict.

## Echternach as a School Location

According to Werner, the conversion and elevation of the status of the *Collège municipal* to a *Progymnasium* in 1841 represented an overambitious project: "Had Echternach been at the center of a more extensive country with a very significant inflow of candidates from surrounding areas," then "this school would surely have been in a position to guarantee the successful development of a significant area of the Grand Duchy." However, because Echternach was located "in the far northeastern border region" and was in direct competition with both the Athenäum and the pre-grammar school in Diekirch, the school was forced to rely "almost exclusively on the youth of the town of Echternach itself."[9]

The powers had been aware that Echternach was not necessarily the ideal location for a pre-grammar school since 1843 at the latest.[10] Although it had only 4,400 residents, it was the second most populous town in the Grand Duchy after Luxembourg (population 21,000). Having been established around a once important Benedictine monastery disbanded during the French Revolution, there was little apart from the monastic educational tradition and the existing *Collège municipal* in favor of developing the town into a center of education *avant la lettre*. The peripheral location on "l'extrême frontière" of the Grand Duchy had already been noted to be a handicap by Missy, the rector of the pre-grammar school in Echternach. Approximately 40 kilometers west of the capital, Luxembourg, and directly on the border with Prussia, it had very little by way of a surrounding catchment area. Despite the enrollment of two foreign students at the Echternach pre-grammar school in 1845, there was little hope of a significant inflow of pupils from Prussia. Therefore, the student body had to be recruited almost exclusively from the town itself, which ultimately proved to be an inadequate source of pupils. According to Missy's annual report of 1843, the few wealthy families in Echternach clearly did not have many boys of the appropriate age to attend the pre-grammar school, and the families with plenty of children could not afford to allow their young boys to study at that level. The surrounding villages were even poorer than the town and were also only sparsely populated.

In addition, as Werner went on to state in his rebuttal, Echternach was an "agricultural town" inhabited mainly by "carters and day laborers." Irrespective of their difficult material circumstances, "the population at large was yet to appreciate the benefits of higher education" and therefore "did not feel the need to send their children to the secondary vocational college." Werner interpreted the high levels of absenteeism at the primary school and the tendency for pupils to stop attending school completely after receipt of their First Communion as indicators of the lack of desire to obtain a school education.

## Classical Versus Vocational Education

In 1841 the *Collège municipal* was converted into a pre-grammar school with compulsory lessons in Latin and Greek, despite the fact that prominent local inhabitants would have preferred to see the establishment of a secondary vocational college.[11]

In 1842 the local council was already pushing for modern languages to be given more emphasis in the syllabus (Thill, 1897, pp. 8, 12). The council also called for young people to be offered an education that would provide them with the skills necessary to pursue a career in industry or commerce should they choose to do so. The Echternach council raised these concerns repeatedly in the years to come, but they always fell on deaf ears in Luxembourg. Any plan to make it easier for young people who "only (*uniquement*)" aspired to the occupations mentioned above to obtain an adequate education for this purpose was deemed "unacceptable (*inadmissible*)." It was considered to be the function of the final-year class of the primary school to fulfill that goal. Ultimately, the pre-grammar school was considered "a full-fledged branch of the Athenäum." In 1844 the deputy head teacher of the pre-grammar school was forced to dispel rumors that it was to be converted into a secondary comprehensive school (*Realschule*) according to the Prussian ideal or even that the school was facing closure.

The repeated complaints of the local council did, however, finally bear fruit in 1848. On July 23 of that year, a new law reclassified the pre-grammar school as a secondary vocational school. The syllabus remained practically unchanged, however. Although the original intention was to exclude Latin and Greek, both subjects were reinstated in response to government pressure. Although participation in Greek and Latin lessons was officially "optional (*facultative*)," in reality all pupils were de facto students of the languages of Plato and Cicero. Both of these languages had a strong link to religious studies, which was without question the most important part of the curriculum. The Catholic cleric, Missy, remained in the office of rector even though the local council considered him unsuitable to direct a secondary vocational college.[12] Missy did not relinquish his position until six years later, in 1854, when he entered an order of Trappist monks, living out the rest of his days in the Oelenberg Abbey in Alsace.

The renaming of the school therefore did not actually lead to any significant practical changes. In fact, its labeling as a secondary vocational college could even be considered misleading, because it continued to operate as a feeder for the Athenäum and, as such, also continued to prepare its pupils to attend the higher classes at that institution. It is hardly surprising, then, that the Echternach school was reinstated as a pre-grammar school 20 years later, in 1869.

In the year of the 1848 reform, Missy felt obliged to strongly convey the importance of the "old classical languages" and to reaffirm the high regard with which this area of study was held at his school. According to Missy, Latin and Greek were the "main cornerstones of a real ... and truly humane education" and protected against "superficiality and shallowness." Without the classical languages, he saw the specter of a "superficial education, empty hearts, hollow heads, great darkness, and vain arrogance" appearing on the horizon (Thill, 1897, p. 21).

The hopes of the school commission of Echternach, expressed just weeks before the school conversion in 1848, to create an "appropriately equipped vocational secondary school that better met the requirements and aspirations of its pupils," had therefore not been realized. This lack of real change also denied the "families of the town, who, for the most part due to mid or low income levels, could not afford to send their children to study at institutes elsewhere, the opportunity to see their children receive an education that was becoming more and more necessary with the ever increasing demands being placed upon them." As a result of pressure from the government, the church, and the faculty, the school adhered to a classical curriculum that failed to reflect the needs of the community. In effect, it was this adherence that resulted in Echternach failing to fulfill the expectation that the school would draw a "significant pool of pupils from within and from outside the town." School planning in Echternach had thus continued in spite of, rather than in response to, the needs of the local community, the "consumers," leaving boys who would perhaps have attended a secondary vocational school with no alternative but to prematurely end their school careers after primary school.[13]

This situation is also reflected clearly in the school enrollment statistics. In the 1840s there were already only around 50 pupils attending the Echternach pre-grammar school. That number rose briefly to a peak of 88 pupils in 1848, when the school was converted to a secondary vocational college, only to dip back to 50 in the early 1850s, which is perhaps a good indication of the false hope that had been placed in the reclassification (Thill, 1897, p. 67). Two thirds of the pupils were exempt from tuition fees on the grounds of poverty or made only a partial contribution. It is also important to note in this context that one third of pupils enrolling in school would leave the institution again during the course of the school year to return to farming ("retournés à la charrue") or to take up another occupation, or because they were unable to afford to continue their schooling as a result of "acute poverty."

It was not until the second half of the 1850s that the number of pupils attending the secondary vocational college rose above 90. Unfortunately, it is impossible to tell from the information available today whether this development was attributable to improvements at primary school level, to the change in rectors, or indeed to a combination of such factors.

Although Latin and Greek had been described by the director-general himself in 1849 as only "minor secondary branches" of the syllabus, the rector, Missy, had been attracting criticism since the reclassification in 1848 for his refusal to accept the diminishing importance of the classical languages at the secondary vocational college.[14] It would appear, in fact, that other circumstances at the school at that time were also not ideal. In 1850 the curators expressed concern regarding the rector's frequent absences and regarding the apparent inability to fill two vacant teaching posts at the school.[15] In addition, the clerical teaching staff was accused of placing too much emphasis on religious studies in day-to-day lessons, which was causing considerable "disharmony" between them and their secular colleagues.

In light of these difficulties, it therefore seems fair to assume that the allegations raised against the primary school and Werner a year later may have also been partly motivated by a desire to divert attention away from what was happening at the secondary vocational college itself.

All things considered, it is therefore hardly surprising that the secondary school in Echternach—whether in the guise of a pre-grammar school or a secondary vocational college—was fighting for survival from its very inception in 1841 right up to 1868. Numerous applications were filed with the Chambre des Députés to convert the school into an upper primary school (*école primaire supérieure*) or an agricultural college or even to close it down completely. This goes to show that the fate of the school in Echternach was a very controversial topic at the highest levels of politics in the Grand Duchy. Demands made by representatives of the emerging mercantile middle classes in Luxembourg, led by Norbert Metz, for the introduction of an "instruction intermédiaire" between the traditional "instruction supérieure" and "instruction primaire" were initially unsuccessful, however (Thill, 1897, p. 27).

## Conclusion

The case study of Echternach charts the conflict-ridden creation of a school system as part of a nation building process in an emerging pre-industrial market society. Although the primary and secondary schools were at least theoretically intended to be consecutive and complementary and to represent a smooth educational pathway, the reality was far less harmonious. This was certainly due in part to the fact that the Luxembourg primary school system was failing to cope adequately from 1839 on owing to the sharp increases in school enrollments and the under-qualified teaching staff. Even more pivotal, however, was the pronounced asymmetry between the primary and secondary schools. The secondary school was setting the standards and requirements, but the primary school was simply unable to comply. Another interesting point to come out of this conflict is the intractability of the originally "German," clerical humanistic educational ideal in the face of such strong opposition from the increasingly influential urban community, especially considering that the municipal council was responsible for supporting the school financially. As evidenced by the case of Werner, the ultimate cause of the crisis in the school system was the conflicting views of those responsible with regard to the role of the school system.

The losers in the conflict described here were undoubtedly the pupils. The young boys in the impoverished country town of Echternach were denied the opportunity to continue their education at a vocational school. The young girls were even less fortunate. Although they clearly outperformed the boys at the Echternach primary school, their choices were even more limited than boys'. The only two options available to the young girls were to enter the boarding school for *höhere Töchter* (young ladies) or to take up a handicraft like needlework. In mid-19th century Luxembourg, the idea of opening up further education to girls as well as boys or even of allowing girls to take the place of boys at the secondary vocational college remained, for the time being, out of the question.

## Notes

1. On the "German" educational ideal, see Tröhler (2012).
2. ANLux, G-0291: "Schreiben der Lehrer-Konferenz der Mittel- und Gewerbeschule Echternach an den Regierungs-Präsidenten und Generalverwalter des öffentlichen Unterrichts in Luxemburg," October 29, 1851. Sources beginning with "ANLux, G-0291" are documents from the folder G-0291: Réclamations contre l'organisation des écoles (1842–1855). No. 185/51: Améliorations à introduire dans les écoles primaires d'Echternach.
3. Werner died in 1862 in Mersch, Luxembourg; see Wilhelm (1996, p. 124).
4. ANLux, G-0291: "Erwiderung auf die, von der städtischen Schulkommission und der Professoren-Konferenz der Mittelschule in Echternach gegen den Lehrer Werner erhobenen Klagepunkte, in Betreff auf seine amtliche Pflichterfüllung," November 28, 1851.
5. ANLux, G-0291: "Etats statistiques," August 1852.
6. ANLux, G-0291: No. 350–51, Commissaire du district de Grevenmacher, Réponse à la dépêche du 16 août 1851, September 6, 1851.
7. ANLux, G-0291: L'inspecteur d'écoles du canton d'Echternach au secrétaire de la Commission royale-grand-ducale d'Instruction, January 15, 1852.
8. ANLux, G-0291: Procès-verbal, Commission pour l'examen des écoles de la ville d'Echternach, August 23, 1852.
9. See note 4.
10. ANLux, H-0656: Missy: "Rapport sur le progymnase d'Echternach rendu à la fin de l'année scolaire 1842–1843," September 15, 1843.
11. See note 10.
12. ANLux, G-0304: Le collège des bourgmestre et échevins de la ville d'Echternach à l'Administrateur général, September 9, 1848.
13. ANLux, G-0291: 24. Sitzung der Schulkommission, Echternach, September 15, 1848.
14. ANLux, G-0304: Willmar à Missy, February 22, 1849.
15. ANLux, G-0304: "Extrait du registre aux délibérations du collège des curateurs de l'école moyenne et industrielle de la ville d'Echternach," October 26, 1850.

## Archival Sources

Archives Nationales du Luxembourg (ANLux): Fonds modernes (1795–1880), Régime constitutionnel (1842–1856):

Instruction Primaire:

- G-0291: Réclamations contre l'organisation des écoles (1842–1855). No. 185/51: Améliorations à introduire dans les écoles primaires d'Echternach
  Enseignement Supérieur et Moyen:
- G-0304: Personnel des Progymnases (1848–1852)
- H-0656: Inspection périodique des établissements—Rapports sur la situation des études (1843–1855).

## References

Allgemeines Verzeichnis der Personen, welche im Großherzogthum Luxemburg das Schullehreramt ausüben. Schuljahr 1851–1852. (1852). *Luxemburger Schulbote, 9*, 3–16.

Allgemeines Verzeichnis der Personen, welche im Großherzogthum Luxemburg das Schullehrer-Amt gesetzlich ausüben. Schuljahr 1852–1853. (1853). *Luxemburger Schulbote, 10*, 3–18.

Calmes, A. (1983). *Histoire contemporaine du Grand-Duché de Luxembourg, Vol. 5: La création d'un Etat 1841–1847*, 2nd edition. Luxembourg, Luxembourg: Saint-Paul.

Diederich, V. (1989). Notre enseignement primaire—essai historique. In *Mémorial 1989. La société luxembourgeoise de 1839 à 1989* (pp. 337–368). Luxembourg, Luxembourg: Editions Mosellanes.

Horlacher, R., & Tröhler, D. (Eds.). (2013). *Sämtliche Briefe an Johann Heinrich Pestalozzi. Kritische Ausgabe, Vol. 5: August 1817–1820*. Zurich, Switzerland: Verlag Neue Zürcher Zeitung.

*Der Luxemburger Schulbote / Le Courrier des Ecoles. Eine Zeitschrift zunächst für die Schullehrer des Großherzogthums Luxemburg bestimmt* (1844–1942), Vols. 1–99. Luxembourg, Luxembourg: V. Bück.

Müllendorf, A. (1894). Le Gymnase de Diekirch de 1830 à 1894. In *Gymnase Grand-Ducal de Diekirch. Programme publié à la clôture de l'année scolaire 1893–1894* (pp. 1–87). Diekirch, Luxembourg: Schroell.

Müller, F. (1856). *Königlich-Großherzogliche Mittel- und Gewerbschule zu Echternach. Programm herausgegeben am Schlusse des Schuljahres 1855–1856 mit einer Abhandlung über das Unterrichtswesen früherer Zeiten in der Stadt Echternach*. Luxembourg, Luxembourg: V. Brück.

Pauly, M. (2011). *Geschichte Luxemburgs*. Munich, Germany: Beck.

Rapport général sur l'état de l'instruction primaire dans le Grand-Duché de Luxembourg pendant l'année scolaire 1850 à 1851. (1852). *Luxemburger Schulbote, 9*, 49.

Schmit, M. (1989). Aperçu d'un siècle et demi d'enseignement supérieur et moyen. In *Mémorial 1989: La société luxembourgeoise de 1839 à 1989* (pp. 395–407). Luxembourg, Luxembourg: Les Editions mosellanes.

Schmit, M. (1999). *Regards et propos sur l'enseignement supérieur et moyen au Luxembourg: essai documentaire*. Luxembourg, Luxembourg: Beffort.

Stehres, P. (1880). *Die Diekircher Mittelschule von ihrer Gründung bis zu ihrer Erhebung zu einem Staatsprogymnasium*. Diekirch, Luxembourg: Schroell.

Thill, J. (1897). Le Collège d'Echternach comme établissement de l'Etat depuis sa création jusqu'en 1897. In *Progymnase Grand-Ducal d'Echternach. Programme publié à la clôture de l'année scolaire 1896–1897* (pp. 1–68). Luxembourg, Luxembourg: V. Bück.

Tröhler, D. (2012). The German idea of *Bildung* and the anti-Western ideology. In P. Siljander, A. Kivelä, & A. Sutinen (Eds.), *Theories of Bildung and growth: Connections and controversies between continental educational thinking and American pragmatism* (pp. 149–164). Rotterdam, the Netherlands: Sense Publishers.

Voss, P. (2012). Der bürokratische Wendepunkt von 1843: Die Primärschule im Prozess der Luxemburger Nationalstaatsbildung des 19. Jahrhunderts. In M. Geiss & A. De Vincenti (Eds.), *Verwaltete Schule: Geschichte und Gegenwart* (pp. 53–70). Wiesbaden, Germany: Springer.

Werner, M.G.Z. (1838a). *Kleine deutsche Sprachlehre für Anfänger*. Luxemburg, Luxembourg: Schmit-Brück; Echternach, Luxembourg: J. Joerg. (Republished in 1841)

Werner, M.G.Z. (1838b). *Kleine französische Sprachlehre für Anfänger*. Luxemburg, Luxembourg: Schmit-Brück. (Republished in 1841 and 1852)

Wilhelm, F. (1996). M. G. Z. Werner, instituteur et poète, et la naissance du sentiment national luxembourgeois. *Récré, 1*, 107–126.

# 6

# TAKING THE RIGHT MEASURES

The French Political and Cultural Revolution and the Introduction of New Systems of Measurement in Swiss Schools in the 19th Century

*Lukas Boser*

This chapter tells a story about a balancing act that is located between global and national requirements. It is the story of the introduction of new measures and weights and, in particular, the metric system in Switzerland over the course of the 19th century. School is also an aspect of this story, because it was an institution that was assigned the task of preparing young people in the best possible way for their future lives amid local, national, and global challenges. In the course of this chapter, many different actors emerge who, each with different interests and intentions, were involved in introducing (or opposing) new systems of measurement in Switzerland: politicians, scientists, and administrative staff but also teachers and, notably, schoolbook authors. Although by the end of the 19th century the metric system had been successfully established in Switzerland, this is not a resounding success story. Rather, the story that is told here is one of diverging expectations for the future, political deliberations, contradictions and obstructions, local dictates and international pressure to adapt, *neophilia* and *neophobia*—and, finally, it is a story that is sometimes also characterized by the irony of history.

## Measures and Weights

Units of measurement and weight are among the oldest objects that humans use to bring order into their world and to organize social exchange. One can hardly imagine the exchange of goods and information without common units of measurement and weight, and it is thus not surprising that every culture, regardless of time and place, defined, used, and left traces of such units (Crease, 2011). In this process measures and weights have always been caught up in the balancing act that is the subject of this conference volume. As the times changed, so did the extent to which measures and weights were required to meet local, regional, national, and international demands. Their purpose was to organize local exchanges among people; to structure geographic areas, such as nations; and to establish order across space and time (Witthöft, 1988; Boser, 2010). And beyond their practical function as a means of measuring and weighing, units of measurement and weight also had an additional important property: They represented structures of power, ownership, and belonging (Linklater, 2003). In many cultures and periods of history measures and weights referred to a higher, i.e., usually divine, world order. The Bible, for example, states in no uncertain terms what order applies in the world and who established it: "You shall do no wrong in judgment, in measures of length or weight or quantity. You shall have just balances, just weights, a just ephah, and a just hin: I am the Lord your God, who brought you out of the land of Egypt" (Leviticus 19.35–36; see Crease, 2011). The potency of the symbolism of measures and weights was such that throughout the centuries, many secular and religious masters also appropriated them. Many old measures and weights were initially anthropomorphic (i.e., they referred to parts of the human body, such as the foot, the ell, or the thumb) or were taken from nature (for example, the carat or grain weight). Most of the units of measurement were easily understandable and adapted to everyday life. The French king's foot, which was widely used, is a good example for this. On the one hand, it symbolized the king's sphere of power, and on the other, it also referred to the fact that the king guarantees the legality of this unit of measurement. It was unambiguous what the king's foot referred to—the length of the foot and the king's authority.

## Standardization of Measurements and the Beginnings of the Metric System

With the exception of a few rare units of measurement that were widely used, the measurements and weights in Europe in the early modern period were characterized mainly by their variety and their regional confinement (Zupko, 1990). Every dominion, every market town, and practically every valley had its own units of measurement and weight. Units of measurement such as the ell or the foot could be found with varying lengths in numerous regional variations (Tuor, 1976). Nevertheless, they were "ni défectueuses, ni inférieures" (Marec, 1990, p. 135). The variety was the result of the properties of the old units of measurement described above; it was not random and served a purpose.

However, in the course of the 18th century, two groups became increasingly displeased with the heterogeneity of measures in use, natural scientists and statesmen/civil servants. In line with the general trend in the natural sciences towards the standardization of the systems of classification and denomination—see especially the works of Linnaeus (1707–1778) and Lavoisier (1743–1794)—natural scientists recognized the urgent need to standardize measures and weights (Boser, 2010). Statesmen and civil servants were spending more and more time dealing with the rationalization of governance and the related statistics (Porter, 1986; Scott,

1998). For these enlightened men, the diversity of measures and weights was a source of great irritation that needed to be remedied in the shortest possible time.

In the course of the 18th century, the standardization of metrology was discussed across Europe. Time and again, scientists and statesmen suggested the introduction of new standardized systems, none of which, however, were able to establish themselves. Nevertheless, scientists in particular were not to be discouraged, and the members of the French Academy of Sciences in Paris tried once again to create a standardized system of measurement (Bigourdan, 1901; Alder, 2002). Although the scientists involved in the development of the new units of measurement suffered greatly from the effects of the Revolution—the chemist Lavoisier and the mathematician Condorcet (1743–1794) even lost their lives—the circumstances at the time were favorable for metrology reform. This was due to the scientists finding new, powerful allies in politics. The young republic was in search of new symbols to set it apart from royalism and to symbolize its enlightened ideals. The new measures and weights came at just the right time. Scientists including Condorcet, Laplace (1749–1827), Borda (1733–1799), Méchain (1744–1804), and Delambre (1749–1822) joined forces with politicians such as Talleyrand (1754–1838) and Prieur de la Côte d'Or (1763–1832) to achieve metrology reforms. The scientists and politicians also recognized a new means to implement this reform. Whereas their predecessors had put their hopes largely in the power of laws and decrees, Talleyrand, Prieur, Laplace, and their fellow campaigners now counted on the opportunities that public education provided. Prieur (1790) wanted a catechism to be written that would familiarize children with the new measures, and Laplace (1795/1912) held lectures on the issue at the *École Normale*, the newly founded teacher training college in Paris. However, these efforts were hardly successful, as will be shown below.

The French natural scientists who wished to find universal laws and universal order in nature, or, in other words, to "perceive whatever holds the world together in its inmost folds" (Goethe, 1808, Faust I, verse 382), also laid claim to universal validity for the new system of measurement. The new measurements were to be recognized equally throughout the world. At the end of the 18th century the members of the Republic of Letters regarded the national specificities in the field of metrology as hindering the advancement of science. For politicians it was particularly important that the new units of measurement could be presented as a French achievement. In the course of the genesis of the metric system these national considerations became increasingly important, which ultimately led to universality becoming replaced by national symbolism (Boser, 2010). To ensure that the new system would at least find the required international acceptance in the sciences, French scientists organized an international conference on the metric system in 1798–1799, held in Paris. Men of learning from all over Europe were invited to jointly review the French calculations and measurements and to decide on the final definition of the metric system. Among the conference participants was a delegate from the Helvetic Republic, Johann Georg Tralles (1763–1822), who in the spring of 1799 was even awarded the privilege of writing the official conference report. Shortly thereafter, Tralles returned to Switzerland—with a meter and a kilogram in his luggage.

## Between Central State, Confederation, and Federal State

But when Tralles returned home, Switzerland was going through turbulent times. In 1799 Switzerland was only in its second year as a unified nation. Up to 1798 it had been a confederation, a union of 13 sovereign states that had come into existence through a mesh of alliances. In 1798 the French first militarily defeated and then replaced the confederation with a unitary state. If this new state, or rather its institutions, were to become fully functional, the most important aspects of organizing a nation-state, such as finances, taxation, a customs system, and so on, had to be standardized as soon as possible. For this reason, the government also set itself the task of standardizing the system of weights and measures. This turned out to be difficult. Promoting an existing system of measurement to the status of the national standard appeared to be impossible, since the individual Swiss cantons (states) would have begrudged another canton's units of measurement being treated preferentially. Thus, the creation of new measures that did not carry a historical burden and were free of neighborly hostility was called for. With Tralles, the Helvetic Republic now had a recognized expert in this field, and he was assigned the task of developing a standardized system of measurement for Switzerland (Tralles, 1801a, 1801b). Tralles was a staunch advocate of introducing the metric system in the whole of Europe. But he also realized that certain political considerations spoke against this, and he therefore developed a specifically Swiss version of the system that did justice to the Helvetic Republic's national independence. It is interesting to note that in the introduction of the new system, Tralles did not make provisions for the educational measures that his French colleagues had planned. In his eyes, introducing the new units of measurement was a purely administrative process, and there was also nobody within the government of the Helvetic Republic that associated the introduction of the new system of measurement with national education. In any case, there was little time for them to introduce a new system, because already in 1803 the Swiss unitary state once again disappeared from the map of Europe. Under the guidance of Napoleon, the Helvetic Republic was replaced by a confederation of cantons, which had regained their sovereignty.

These political upheavals further exacerbated the problem of the heterogeneous units of measurement, because now the cantons were eager to establish their own units of measurement. In many cantons, the necessity of standardizing units of measurement had long been the subject of debate, but it was clear that the meter and the kilogram—the former occupying power's units of measurement—could not be used at the cantonal level. Hence, within a short time there was a return to the old measures and weights. Notable exceptions were the cantons that owed their existence to the French occupation in the first place. For example, the canton of Vaud was a new Helvetic creation, which in 1803 faced the challenge of determining a new system of measurement to establish an effective state administration. In Vaud, which borders on France, there were strong tendencies towards adopting the metric system. However, in the *Grande Nation* itself, despite all of the administrative and educational efforts, the metric system was hardly able to establish itself and was even intermittently replaced by the *système usuel*, which was strongly influenced by the old weights and measures. With this *système usuel* the Napoleonic administration attempted to achieve the national standardization of measures and weights that they so urgently required (Alder, 2002). In the end, in 1822, the government of Vaud decided to introduce a cantonal system of measurement that was based on the French *système usuel* (Develey, 1823). This decision was not accepted by everyone; one of the most influential critics was Emmanuel Develey (1764–1839), a mathematician and schoolbook author. As early as 1802 Develey had published an arithmetic book for primary schools, in which he explained the metric system in detail and praised it as the system of measurement of the future (Develey, 1802). Develey also dedicated a relatively large portion of his book to the old measures and weights, probably for pragmatics reasons. In 1802 it was not yet clear whether the new system would be able to establish itself. As a teacher, Develey saw it as his duty to prepare his pupils not only for a desired future but also for a future that did justice to the historically evolved local conditions and requirements. For the rest of his life, Develey remained a staunch supporter of the introduction of the metric system. Although he aired his grievances over the variety of national measures and weights, his argument in favor of the metric system was its intrinsic logic, which he praised with the words, "quelle simplicité! quelle uniformité! quelle beauté" (Develey, 1802, p. 306).

Although in the first 30 years of the 19th century the Swiss cantons preferred cantonal metrology solutions, the goal of national standardization was never given up entirely. However, it was clear that the metric system could serve as a reference but not as a national system of measurement. It was too much a symbol of France to be able to symbolize an independent Swiss nation. In 1835, following several years of negotiation that were characterized by failures and setbacks owing to the cantons' incompatible political interests, 12 cantons were finally able to agree on a standardized system of measures and weights, which was scheduled to become valid in 1838 (Furrer, 1889; Dubler, 2011). Politicians and scientists played an equal part in developing the new system, which in shape and title was a thoroughly Swiss system, even though the individual units were defined in reference to the meter and the kilogram. This reference to the metric units of measurement had nothing to do with France but rather with science. Modern systems of measurement were characterized by being determined through the methods of natural science, and in this context the metric system was the method of choice for the scientists in Switzerland. Some of these scientists had witnessed the development of the meter in France and Tralles' project in the Helvetic Republic as attentive observers and now drew on their experiences from this period (Boser, 2010). In 1835 and 1838 the introduction of the new system of measurement was again considered to be a purely administrative act. The cantonal education laws, regulations, or curricula did not require the new measures to be turned into a school subject to be taught at primary school. This is fairly astonishing, because already in 1828 an expert from the canton of Vaud had reported that the acceptance of the new system in his canton was directly related to the population's level of education. According to this expert's statements, it was primarily uneducated citizens who refused to accept the new system (Boser, 2010).

In reality, in the years following 1838, some schoolbook authors in cities such as Bern and Zurich still used the old cantonal measures. This meant that the arithmetic problems in schoolbooks certainly largely corresponded to the everyday life of the population, who continued to use these old units of measurement. In general, the population was very reluctant and slow to adopt metrology changes (see Weber, 1976). Opposition to new measures and weights had a long tradition, particularly among the rural population. The peasants feared that when new measures were introduced, their tax burden would increase (Blickle, 2012). However, a large part of the schoolbook authors welcomed the national standardization of metrology and tried to support it through their books (Heer, 1841; Lehner, 1842). Their arithmetic problems no longer referenced people's everyday life and now looked to the future, a future in which they foresaw the prevalence of the national units of measurement. This approach by the schoolbook authors led to a kind of self-fulfilling prophecy. By preparing pupils for a certain future, the authors contributed to bringing about precisely this future. The 12 cantons' new system of measurement was an important step towards national integration, which had not been achieved politically but was already in progress on an economic level. Through their association, the 12 cantons took an important step towards creating a homogeneous national economic area.

The situation in the canton of Vaud, which had not participated in this standardization of measures, was slightly different. As mentioned above, the canton of Vaud had just put much effort into the introduction of a new system. The decision to not participate in the national standardization was probably made because yet another change would have resulted in (even more) reluctance and resistance on the part of the population. Accordingly, pupils in Vaud continued to learn that canton's own units of measurement and weight (Lochmann, 1835; Hermann, 1842). Develey's book, in which both the old and the metric units of measurement had a prominent place, remained the exception (Develey, 1839).

In 1848 the Swiss cantons united to form a federal state. To establish an administration at the level of the nation-state, the system of weights and measures that had been negotiated in 1835 was constitutionally declared mandatory for the entire nation. The cantons that still had their own systems of measurement were given until 1856 to introduce the new system. On this occasion, again, no educational measures to support the transition were prescribed. The explanation for this is simple: The newly formed federation had no authority over the schools. The responsibility for organizing the school system remained entirely with the cantons. But now teachers and schoolbook authors took the initiative themselves, because they saw it as their duty to contribute to the implementation of the national system of measurement. Schoolbook author Johann Caspar Hug (1821–1884) wrote, for example: "When a system of this magnitude is to be introduced, the schools in particular must contribute to its actual introduction among the people" (1854, p. 106). It is interesting to note that arguments like this, which were based on the people, the state, and the nation, were made primarily by schoolbook authors whose cantons were not required to introduce a new system because they had already done so in 1838. In places where no great changes had to be introduced, it was evidently easier to point out the role of the schools in the process of nationalization. In the cantons where the formation of the federal state actually did entail changing the metrology system, the situation was altogether different. In the canton of Vaud, arithmetic books largely ignored the new Swiss units of measurement. Although the canton of Vaud belonged to the federal state, schoolbook authors appear to have found the cantonal customs and requirements more important than the national legislation (Faucherres, 1854; Blanc, 1858). As was the case in 1838, it appears as though the authors of arithmetic books did not wish to cause even more confusion and opposition. An example from an arithmetic book of 1858 illustrates the complicated situation that confronted some sections of the population of the canton of Vaud:

> One day, a winegrower from Lavaux receives three letters: An innkeeper from Romont offers him 0.55 centimes for a federal jug of wine, a hotel keeper from Langenthal offers him 60 centimes but specifies how much he wishes to acquire in the customary units of measurement of Bern, and a coffeehouse owner in Lausanne will pay 52½ centimes for a cantonal jug of wine (Canton of Vaud measure). For three days the poor winegrower has been racking his brain over which offer is the best.
>
> *(Blanc, 1858, p. 62)*

## National Integration and International Innovations

In the years following 1848, arithmetic book authors in Bern, Zurich, and the canton of Vaud varied in their choice of measures and weights for their arithmetic examples. Some of them oriented themselves towards the nation and the legally prescribed weights and measures, regardless of whether they were used by the population or not. Others based their arithmetic examples on the local or cantonal customs and conditions and used cantonal units of measurement, which were still highly popular. In doing so, however, all of them overlooked (or ignored) a development that some of their colleagues had already anticipated at the beginning of the 19th century: Also in Switzerland, the metric system had started to establish itself as the standard.

This can be well illustrated by means of some examples. In the 1830s the Swiss military leadership initiated a large-scale cartography project under the responsibility of Guillaume-Henry Dufour (1787–1875). To compile the necessary data, Dufour and his colleagues looked to already existing maps. In cases where maps were missing or too inaccurate, new land surveys and calculations were carried out. To allow this data to be compared, the meter was taken as a basis. Dufour had learned how to use the French units of measurement, which had been new at the time, as a student at the *école polytechnique* and the *école du génie* in Paris. Using the meter as the measure of comparison when drawing the map of Switzerland corresponded to his practical experience. Among the scientifically educated geodesists and cartographers of the time, the use of metric units of measurement appears to have already been common practice. For example, contracts with the cartographer Johann Jakob Sulzberger established payments based on square centimeters of map drawn (Gugerli & Speich, 2002).

However, what makes the cartography project particularly noteworthy regarding the units of measurement used is that Dufour chose the meter and not the legally prescribed Swiss measure not only as the unit of measurement for the land surveys and calculations but also for all publications. Evidently, nobody appeared to be bothered by this: The first draft of the map in 1837 contained the preliminary results of the land surveys in meters, and this did not result in Dufour being forced to change this representation, even after a new national system of measurement was introduced in Switzerland. From that time on, the official overview of Switzerland, which was visualized for the first time by Dufour's map, always used meters. Dufour had created a standard for Swiss cartography (Dufour, 1865).

However, the meter was becoming established not only in the field of science and technology but also in the domestic area. In the second half of the 19th century fashion-conscious ladies looked to Paris. The latest fashion trends were designed there, and the trends spread from Paris throughout the world by means of fashion magazines. To enable women who could not buy their clothes from the couturiers in Paris to dress *à la mode*, measurements were attached to the magazine pictures so that the clothes could be copied. The specifications were frequently given in meters and centimeters. Thus, these units of measurement gained increasing acceptance in the field of textiles. The 1860 book *Das fleissige Hausmütterchen* (The industrious little housemother), by Susanna Müller (1829–1905), used metric measures in the instructions on sewing and knitting.

Last, international affiliations were also important for the dissemination of metric measures. In 1853, for example, statisticians from various countries including Switzerland met for the Congrès général de Statistique (Statistical Conference). At the congress it was decided that, in future, national statistics should be published in standardized units to allow international comparison. For weights and measures, the metric units were set as the standard (Cox, 1958). This decision had an impact far beyond the still relatively small of group of statisticians. In the modern state administrations, statistics were increasingly used as the basis for governing. And now that statistics were recorded using a certain unit of measurement, it did not take long for the public administrations to begin using it as well.

During the second half of the 19th century this and other developments resulted in the meter being increasingly seen as the unit of progress (Boser, 2012). As a result, more and more people in Switzerland demanded that the metric system be publicly recognized, so that Switzerland would not lose touch with progress. It is not without a certain irony that the authors of schoolbooks in the 1850s and 1860s—who had repeatedly stated that they saw it as their most important task to teach their pupils useful knowledge—largely missed this decisive change in metrology. Although the metric units of measurement turned up in teaching material in Zurich and Bern sporadically, usually in connection with the railway or postage system or Dufour's land survey data, nothing in these schoolbooks indicated that the metric system had long since become widespread and was also already being taught at the polytechnic school in Zurich, for instance, or at the teacher training institute in Bern (Pasche, 1865; Boser, 2012). Only in the canton of Vaud did a teacher see the urgent need for a schoolbook with the new units of measurement, if the arithmetic classes were actually to continue to live up to the claim of being useful (Pasche, 1865). In the canton of Vaud—in addition to Develey's resilient book, which was still in use—the following years saw the development of several arithmetic books in which the metric measures featured prominently.

## Between the National and the Global

The Swiss Federal Council was not fundamentally opposed to the introduction of the meter in Switzerland. However, it became apparent that replacing the Swiss system with the metric system required a constitutional amendment, which could be accomplished only with the population's and the cantons' approval. Constitutional amendments were exposed to the interplay of political forces and were therefore frequently difficult to accomplish. In the end, the Federal Council's solution was a typically Swiss compromise. As of 1868 the metric system was officially tolerated in Switzerland. Thereby, the government legalized the practice of using metric units, which had long since become established in the field of science and technology, in public administration, in trade, and in many other areas of everyday life. Some schoolbook authors interpreted this as a sign that the time had come to provide teaching materials for the metric system. However, this did not mean that from then on all authors of arithmetic books incorporated the new measures into their books. For the time being, a few of them kept to the old Swiss units of measurement or took their time revising their books (Rüegg, 1869; Zähringer, 1869). This situation once again reflected how difficult it was for schoolbook authors to assess what knowledge would become important to their pupils in the future. If the process of international standardization were to continue, then it would certainly be appropriate to teach the metric measures at school. But what would have happened if the local customs had prevailed? And if the population had resisted the introduction of the new system after all, would it then not have been better to have taught the old units of measurement at school? Between 1868 and 1878 there were various alternatives to deal with this situation. There were schoolbooks that were based exclusively on the metric system and others that used only the Swiss units of measurement. Some authors again sought a compromise and incorporated both systems into their books.

But using two systems was not satisfactory either. It made metrology needlessly complicated and contradicted the increasing international trend towards the meter asserting itself as the sole applicable standard. In 1868 Prussia introduced the metric system (Koller, 1869), and in June 1870 an article in the renowned science journal *Nature* proclaimed: "The battle of the Standards is over, and we may say the Meter has gained the victory" ("The Unit of Length," 1870). Hence, the anonymous author of the article desired the introduction of this unit in Great Britain as soon as possible. He was not in favor of granting concurrent validity to multiple measures, as had been done in Switzerland. He based his opinion on his view of education. In particular, he believed that the teachers would not be able teach their pupils two systems of measurement, because they simply lacked the time: "With all the desire of the teachers to introduce it [the meter] in the schools, they find that they cannot teach the old and new tables. They cannot afford the time."

In 1874 the population approved a constitutional amendment that enabled the introduction of the metric system as the definite and sole system in Switzerland. In corresponding draft legislation from 1874, the schools were subsequently given the task of teaching the units of measurement "in order for the people of Switzerland to familiarize themselves with the new measures and weights and over time to grow fond of them" (Federal Council, 1874, p. 716). In 1875 it was determined by law that as of 1 January 1877, the metric units of measurement and weight would become Switzerland's official measures. Although the law no longer mentioned the schools, schoolbook authors immediately published new books (Gaillard-Pousaz, 1875; Zähringer, 1877). The official introduction of the metric system created the expectation that metrology in Switzerland would now actually be standardized. When the Swiss Military Department started testing whether young recruits actually understood the metric system in 1876, this signified the definite breakthrough for the new system. No canton wished to achieve worse scores on these tests than the others. As a result, by 1883 the metric units of measurement were included in all the cantonal primary school curricula and in almost all arithmetic textbooks (Ernst, 1884). Thus, the originally French meter, which had turned into an international standard, became the first truly national unit of measurement in Switzerland.

## References

Alder, K. (2002). *The measure of all things: The seven-year odyssey and hidden error that transformed the world.* New York, NY: Free Press.

Bigourdan, G. (1901). *Le Système Métrique des Poids et Mesures. Son établissement et sa propagation graduelle, avec l'histoire des opérations qui ont servi à déterminer le mètre et le kilogramme.* Paris, France: Gauthiers-Villars.

Blanc, S. (1858). *Recueil de problèmes de calcul de tête et d'arithmétique.* Lausanne, Switzerland: S. Blanc.

Blickle, P. (2012). *Unruhen in der ständischen Gesellschaft 1300–1800.* Munich, Germany: R. Oldenbourg.

Boser, L. (2010). *Natur—Nation—Sicherheit.* Nordhausen, Germany: Traugott Bautz.

Boser, L. (2012). *Modernisierung, Schule und das Mass der Dinge* (Doctoral dissertation). University of Bern, Bern, Switzerland.

Cox, E. F. (1958). The metric system: A quarter-century of acceptance (1851–1876). *Osiris, 13*(15), 358–379.

Crease, R. P. (2011). *World in the balance: The historic quest for an absolute system of measurement.* New York, NY: W.W. Norton.

Develey, E. (1802). *Arithmétique d'Émile.* Paris, France: (s.n.).

Develey, E. (1823). *Précis du nouveau système des poids et mesures du Canton de Vaud en Suisse.* Lausanne, Switzerland: Hignou Ainé.

Develey, E. (1839). *Arithmétique d'Émile.* Lausanne, Switzerland: Marc Ducloux.

Dubler, A.-M. (2011). Masse und Gewichte. In *Historisches Lexikon der Schweiz* (HLS). Retrieved from http://www.hls-dhs-dss.ch/textes/d/D13751.php

Dufour, G.-H. (1865). Schlussbericht des Herrn General Dufour über die topographische Karte der Schweiz. *Bundesblatt, 17/1*(10), 203–216.

Ernst, H. (1884). Die mathematischen Fächer. In H. Wettstein (Ed.), *Schweizerische Landesausstellung, Zurich 1883: Bericht über die Gruppe 30: Unterrichtswesen* (pp. 181–217). Zurich, Switzerland: Orell Füssli.

Faucherres, H. (1854). *Problèmes d'arithmétique sur les questions ordinaires de la vie.* Lausanne, Switzerland: Georges Bridel.

Federal Council. (1874). Botschaft des Bundesrathes an die hohe Bundesversammlung, betreffend die obligatorische Einführung des neuen metrischen Mass- und Gewichtsystems. *Bundesblatt, 26/3*(10), 713–722.

Furrer, A. (1889). *Volkswirtschaftslexikon der Schweiz.* Bern, Switzerland: Schmid, Franke & Co.

Gaillard-Pousaz, F. (1875). *Le système métrique des poids et mesures et la transformation des mesures suisses en mesures métriques.* Lausanne, Switzerland: D. Lebet.

Goethe, J. W. von (1808). *Faust: Eine Tragödie.* Tübingen, Germany: Cotta.

Gugerli, D., & Speich, D. (2002). *Topographie der Nation: Politik, kartografische Ordnung und Landschaft im 19. Jahrhundert.* Zurich, Switzerland: Chronos.

Heer, J. (1841). *Methodisches Lehrbuch des Denkrechnens, sowohl im Kopfe als mit Ziffern, für Volksschulen. Dritter Theil: Das Exempelbuch enthaltend. Zweite Abtheilung.* Zurich, Switzerland: Friedrich Schulthess.

Hermann, F. (1842). *Éléments de calcul pour les écoles primaires.* Lausanne, Switzerland: Marc Ducloux.

Hug, J. C. (1854). *Die Mathematik der Volksschule: Ein methodisches Handbuch für einen dem Wesen der Volksschule entsprechenden und alle ihre Stufen umfassenden Unterricht.* Zurich, Switzerland: Friedrich Schulthess.

Koller, A. (1869). *Archiv des Norddeutschen Bundes und des Zollvereins.* Berlin, Germany: Fr. Kortkampf.

Laplace, P.-S. de (1912). Neuvième séance. Sur le nouveau système des poids et mesures. In P.-S. de Laplace, *Oeuvres complètes de Laplace* (pp. 133–145). Paris, France: Gaultier-Villars. (First published 1795)

Lehner, J. (1842). *Uebungsbuch im Kopf- und Zifferrechnen, bestehend in fünf Abtheilungen mit einem Schlüssel, zunächst für Berner Volksschulen*. Bern, Switzerland: (s.n.).

Linklater, A. (2003). *Measuring America: How the United States was shaped by the greatest land sale in history*. New York, NY: Plume.

Lochmann, J.-J. (1835). *L'aide des instituteurs, des pères et mères de famille. Recueil de problèmes sur la numération et les quatre premières règles le l'arithmétique etc.* Lausanne, Switzerland: Samuel Delisle.

Marec, Y. (1990). Autour des résistances au système métrique. In B. Garnier & J.-C. Hocquet (Eds.), *Genèse et diffusion du système métrique* (pp. 135–144). Caen, France: Ed.-Diffusion du Lys.

Müller, S. (1860). *Das fleissige Hausmütterchen: Mitgabe in das praktische Leben für erwachsene Töchter*. Herisau, Switzerland: C. J. Meisel.

Pasche, L. (1865). *Problèmes d'arithmétique des poids et mesures et ses rapports avec les poids et mesures suisses de 1851*. Lausanne, Switzerland: Pache.

Prieur de la Côte d'Or, C. A. (1790). *Mémoire sur la nécessité et les moyens de rendre uniformes, dans le royaume, toutes les mesures d'étendue et de pesanteur*. Dijon, France: (s.n.).

Porter, T. M. (1986). *The rise of statistical thinking, 1820–1900*. Princeton, NJ: Princeton University Press.

Rüegg, H.-R. (1869). *Das Rechnen in der Elementarschule: Ein Wegweiser für Lehrer und Lehrerinnen*. Bern, Switzerland: J. Dalp.

Scott, J. C. (1998). *Seeing like a state*. New Haven, CT: Yale University Press.

Tralles, J. G. (1801a). *Bericht der Festsetzung der Grundeinheiten des von der fränkischen Republik angenommenen Metrischen Systems von dem zu diesem Geschäfte Abgeordneten der helvetischen Republik*. Bern, Switzerland: National Druckerey.

Tralles, J. G. (1801b). *Vortrag über die Einführung von einerley Maaß und Gewicht in der helvetischen Republik*. Bern, Switzerland: National Druckerey.

Tuor, R. (1976). *Mass und Gewicht im alten Bern*. Bern, Switzerland: Haupt.

The unit of length. (1870). *Nature, 2*(33), 137.

Weber, E. (1976). *Peasants into Frenchmen*. Stanford, CA: Stanford University Press.

Witthöft, H. (1988). Metrologische Strukturen und die Entwicklung der alten Mass-Systeme: Handel und Transport—Landmass und Landwirtschaft—Territorium/Staat und die Politik der Massvereinheitlichung. In H. Witthöft, J.-C. Hocquet, & I. Kiss (Eds.), *Meterologische Strukturen und die Entwicklung der alten Mass-Systeme* (pp. 13–24). St. Katharinen, Germany: Scripta Mercaturae.

Zähringer, H. (1869). *Aufgaben zum Kopfrechnen für schweizerische Volksschulen*. Zurich and Glarus, Switzerland: (s.n.).

Zähringer, H. (1877). *Aufgaben zum Kopfrechnen für schweizerische Volksschulen*. Zurich, Switzerland: (s.n.).

Zupko, R. E. (1990). *Revolution in measurement: Western European weights and measures since the age of science*. Philadelphia, PA: The American Philosophical Society.

# 7

# EDUCATION STATISTICS, SCHOOL REFORM, AND THE DEVELOPMENT OF ADMINISTRATIVE BODIES

## The Example of Zurich Around 1900

*Thomas Ruoss*

Since the early 19th century, education statistics have served as planning criteria for the governmental administration of education (Voss, 2012). Moreover, they have also served the function of accountability to the government and of legitimization for the administrative bodies. The administrative bodies in particular needed legitimization during the period of their establishment, to "assert, to stabilize organizationally, and to introduce themselves as legitimate custodians of education issues" (Geiss, 2012, p. 72).[1] Beyond that, historians stress the normalizing function of statistics, in that they establish a standardized language (Tanner, 1995; Desrosières, 2005). To make national and international comparisons possible through a common language of numerical data, educational policy-makers began to address the challenge of homogenizing education statistics[2]—and especially so in federal Switzerland. To delineate this development and to exemplify the relationship between a political rhetoric of institutional homogenization and the advancement of school reforms, we need to examine regional needs and reservations related to statistical inquiries. I first describe the explicit aims related to the homogenization, diffusion, and institutionalization of education statistics at the turn of the 20th century as instances of political rhetoric and then look at statistical reports and school structures to investigate the implicit and empirically verifiable significance of education statistics for educational policy and administration in the case of Zurich.

The establishment of a specific kind of data-based knowledge within the administration of education led to an upgrading of statistics as an argument of education policy. This led to the strengthening of the position that the keepers of that knowledge had. In my opinion, though, the promotion of comparative cantonal observation led neither to homogenization of cantonal education statistics nor to homogenization of cantonal education systems in the short term. But those involved in the education administration in Zurich preferred to create pressure to advance domestic school reform through comparative observations. Nonetheless, the contents and the aims of this kind of statistical knowledge were not beyond dispute.

## Nationalizing Schooling Through Statistics: An Instance of Political Rhetoric

From the late 1860s, and with a first climax at the World Exhibition in Vienna in 1873, education statistics in Switzerland turned into a project with a national range. Internationalization was central to this development, first as an external impetus and then as an internal legitimization (Ruoss, 2013). After 1874, the Swiss Confederation's supervision of cantonal education systems answered to a constitutional mandate (Criblez & Huber, 2008), and the cantons were asked to surrender their statistical reports on education. The attempt by a national secretary of education within the Federal Statistical Office to institutionalize this federal supervisory function failed in a national referendum of 1882, with the consequence that the confederation semi-officially delegated the production of Swiss-level[3] education statistics to the cantonal education administration in Zurich. With a guarantee underwritten by the confederation, the cantonal secretary of education of Zurich published the *Yearbook of the Education System in Switzerland* (*Jahrbuch des Unterrichtswesen in der Schweiz*) between 1889 and 1912. The *Yearbook* presented the development of cantonal education systems with comparative structural data on an annual basis. These kinds of statistics were characterized by full-scale surveys of the schools based on standardized questionnaires, stocktaking of structural data (concerning pupils, teachers, infrastructure, and financing), and comparative presentation of the findings.

Emma Lucia Bähler,[4] advocate of the statistical comparison of education systems, declared in 1914 that the "Swiss public school [*schweizerische Volksschule*][5] as a national entity has been realized" (1914, p. 25), and she pointed to education statistics to support her claim: "Education statisticians have to be credited for creating a situation in which we can now speak of a Swiss public school" (p. 50).

As Hartmann (2011) points out, though, this statement requires some relativization, since statisticians in the pre-war period experienced strong legitimization pressures during the expansion of their field, and they therefore had a vested interest in discursively overemphasizing the political relevance of statistics. Bähler's statement therefore has to be understood primarily as having a normative aim.

Albert Huber[6] (1902) aimed to develop a Swiss public school through "a slow and organically implemented reconfiguration of conventions and customs, of laws and institutions." According to Huber, the failure to nationalize education statistics in the national referendum of 1882 was a blessing in disguise for the aim of homogenization, since only through working "quietly" could cantonal mistrust of comparative statistics be avoided (p. 52).[7]

As early as 1880, Johann Caspar Grob[7] demanded the implementation of "the idea of a Swiss public school" (1880, p. 1). In the preface to the first issue of the *Yearbook*, Grob (1889, p. iii) presented his program for the realization of this aim. He spoke of "the mutual observation of the conditions of schooling," which would offer "fundamental benefits to each canton as well as to the nation state," "uncovering shortcomings" so that "public opinion in the country will urge the overcoming of these shortcomings." This program can be summarized as being more extensive mutual observation on the basis of direct intercantonal comparisons, leading to knowledge of one's own canton's deficiencies and to increased public pressure within the cantons. The cantons had to adapt their own education systems and could now copy existing models. This means that the focus had to be on homogenization of the cantonal education systems. This political agenda can be found unchanged in the 1906 report by a commission of the Swiss Conference of Cantonal Ministers of Education (EDK) that recommended supporting the *Yearbook* (Bericht der Kommission vom 28. Juni 1906, p. 13, StALU A 1271 / 114) and in the 1914 obituary of Huber written by Bähler (1914, p. 37 f.).

In the following sections I will demonstrate why this unvaried proclamation of the same program nevertheless shows such a high level of persistence—and that this program of isomorphism *avant la lettre* does not document homogenization of either education statistics or education systems.

## Diffusion and Institutionalization of Education Statistics

The education administrators in Zurich were also active on a national Swiss level. As the first standing secretary of the EDK between 1898 and 1912, Huber was the conduit for the transactions of the EDK (Manz, 2008). In 1906 the minister of education of the Canton of Ticino demanded an increased level of homogeneity between the cantonal accountability reports and called for the EDK's participation in the *Yearbook*. The first commission report to address these issues was devised by Huber; this report showed in detail all the deficits found regarding how the cantons published education statistical data, and it outlined the implications for action (Bericht der Kommission vom 28. Juni 1906, StALU A 1271 / 114). On Huber's advice the commission did not impose an obligation on the cantons, as it had initially intended: "It would neither have been good nor wise, and we therefore have to refrain from the declaration of certain wishes or even rules. We can be content if we can configure the statistical reports more consistently" (Kreisschreiben vom 24. August 1907, p. 3, StALU A 1270 / 121). Finally, the commission even abstained from imposing a standardized exemplary statistics sheet. But the EDK at least decided in 1906 to support the *Yearbook*, and therefore education statistics on the Swiss level. Grob's program became the program of the EDK.

Education statistics became an intercantonal project with a national scope, with the aim to develop the production of statistics itself and lead to a (more) consistent Swiss public school not through regulation but through mutual observation. At the same time, this kind of education statistics also became a symbolic element of consolidation of the EDK, since only the statistical tables facilitated the concise and uniform representation of a supposedly homogenized system of schooling across the whole of Switzerland.

This program of education statistics initiated by the EDK did not proceed unproblematically, however, something that again throws light on configurations within the Canton of Zurich. A dispute in 1911 on the federal level concerning the preparation of national education statistics for the Swiss National Exhibition in Bern substantiates this. Under the supervision of Federal Councilor Schobinger, a dispute took place between Huber and his opponent, Friedrich Zollinger,[8] with Huber being able to assert that he "basically represent[ed] the opinion of the EDK" (Protokoll vom 10. August 1911, p. 5, BAR E80 Nr.600 Bd.79. 1911–1914). In particular, Huber argued against the claim that comparison of education statistics was a form of continuous evidence-based observation of cantonal school systems.[9]

Zollinger, for his part, asked for a stronger emphasis on thematic inquiries, particularly concerning youth welfare and the architecture of school buildings,[10] and he argued that many of the statistical details compiled would not be of current or permanent value for the education administration, nor for the general public: "What we do not need is dead data material. We need stimulating text in the first instance" (Protokoll vom 10. August 1911, p. 11, BAR E80 Nr.600 Bd.79. 1911–1914). The interest in education statistics, according to Zollinger, should be "not only on the arrangement of instruction and its interior and exterior preconditions" (1901, p. 204).

With the support of the EDK, Huber overcame Zollinger's objections. National education statistics were supported financially by the confederation, with a Bureau of Education Statistics being established in Zurich under the leadership of Bähler, which in the long term became a center of competence for Swiss-level education statistics. But in the cantonal administration in Zurich, the Huber–Zollinger dispute had further implications. Starting in 1914, the Cantonal Statistical Office in Zurich published annually a survey concerning the school leavers' vocational choices (Statistisches Bureau des Kantons Zürich, 1914).[11] In 1919 the cantonal education administration was extended.[12] A youth welfare office was founded in Zurich as part of the education administration; Zurich was the first cantonal administration to add such an office (Desiderato, Lengwiler, & Rothenbühler, 2008). Zollinger drafted the appropriate decree. Even if the youth welfare office was not established as a consequence of or with the aim of engaging in statistical investigation,[13] the appreciation of and requirement for data-based knowledge stood in distinct contrast to Zollinger's antecedents in the education administration. The argument concerning the extension of the education administration was also a dispute about the prerogative of interpretation concerning the aims and methods of education statistics.

## Reviewing the Aim of Homogenization

### Homogenization of Education Statistics

The homogenization of education statistics contained in cantonal accountability reports had been a continuous demand since the 1880s—first by the *Yearbook* editors and then by the EDK. The accountability reports of Bern and Zurich were already described as role models during that time (Chatelanat, 1879; Grob, 1891, p. x).[14] To assess the rhetoric of homogenization used at the time, I will compare the reports of the postulated statistical models of Bern and Zurich with those of St. Gallen, Schaffhausen, Neuchâtel, Basel-Stadt, and Appenzell Ausser-Rhoden between 1880 and 1915.[15] I will concentrate on primary education, as, according to the statistical commission of the EDK, it was the most homogenized level of schooling at the time (Bericht der Kommission vom 28. Juni 1906, StALU A 1271 / 114).

The data on primary schools that were periodically published in the *Yearbook* tell us which basic data could be continuously compiled by and compared between the cantons. This concerns the following categories: gender of pupils, gender of teachers, absentees, and sites of schools.

First, I will deal with the published *contents* according to these categories. The reports of Bern and Zurich contained almost matching data for the whole period. Basel-Stadt had also collected these data for the whole period. Schaffhausen, Appenzell Ausser-Rhoden, and St. Gallen had continuously adapted their education statistics before 1915. However, before 1905, and in some areas for even longer, Appenzell Ausser-Rhoden did not differentiate between genders for either pupils or teachers. Neuchâtel, for its part, published all these data in its report of 1905. The publication of data then decreased considerably over the following years to the point where only data concerning school divisions were published. Homogenization of even the most fundamental categories of data was therefore not achieved in the cantons under study, and some of them even show the opposite development.

All data published in addition to these categories differ in each canton, which means that we can identify extensive diachronic changes within the Cantons of Bern and Zurich themselves. A homogenization is not verifiable in this regard. What can be found is a high level of alteration of the published categories in the ostensibly model reports of the Cantons of Bern and Zurich and at the same time a tendency to stability in the categories of the other five cantons.

The *presentation* of statistical data by the majority of the cantons under study always took place in the form of charts. Only Neuchâtel and Basel-Stadt were exceptions. In the Neuchâtel report, we can see multifaceted charts that differ according to attributes and political granularity. These incoherent charts do not even allow a comparison between types of schooling within the canton. After the turn of the century, these data were simply no longer published. In Basel-Stadt, before the turn of the century, many of the data cannot be found in charts but instead were given in the running text. After that, however, we can see a clear use of charts. A certain homogenization thus had occurred with regard to the presentation of data. Before 1915 the statistical data of Basel-Stadt in particular, and (with limitations) also those of Neuchâtel, increasingly resemble the data of the other cantons. Admittedly, all five of the other cantons displayed a high consistency in their presentation, which did not differ substantially from that used by Bern and Zurich.

Thus, processes of adaptation can indeed be found in cantonal education statistics for some parts of their presentation and contents. But these did not keep up with the demands of the contemporary actors under study. The samples analyzed were too incoherent and in part contradictory. This has to be understood against a background in which processes of adaptation should have been most probable in the cantons and at the levels of schooling under study.

Nevertheless, the demand for an "increase in discipline concerning education statistics" (Bähler, 1914, p. 52) was not without effect. As just described, the willingness of cantonal ministers of education to initiate a corporate statistical agenda increased after the turn of the century. The institutionalization of comparisons between education statistics within the EDK confirms this development.

## *Homogenization of Education Structures*

The hypothesis that "frequent statistical investigations led to an institutional homogenization of . . . education systems" (Voss, 2012, p. 67) cannot be confirmed with such linearity in the case of Switzerland. The education systems under study vary considerably on the structural level. With the school law of 1899 the Canton of Zurich extended its education system to a compulsory eight-year primary school.[16] In the Canton of Bern, a nine- to ten-year primary school had already existed since the early 19th century. Far into the 20th century, quite different types of schooling co-existed in St. Gallen (at least six types during the period under study), depending on the geographical location. In the Canton of Neuchâtel, nursery school (*école infantine*) was part of compulsory schooling. The Canton of Basel-Stadt was unusual, owing to its education system and its introduction of four years of primary and four years of lower-secondary schooling. In contrast, Appenzell Ausser-Rhoden had had a system of seven years of *Alltagsschule* and two years of *Übungsschule* since a decree of 1878.

An example will show how the rhetorical postulate of the model function of the Zurich school system was questioned by contemporary politicians. As early as 1879, the Canton of Schaffhausen passed a school law introducing compulsory education for eight years. Schaffhausen then criticized the failure of the neighboring Canton of Zurich to extend compulsory education: "The 'Schwabengängerei' [migration to Germany] is dwindling! But in contrast an alarming 'Zürichgängerei' [migration to Zurich] has prevailed in some places . . . This education [in Zurich] can obviously not be adequate according to our law" (Grob, 1890, p. 69 f.). Pupils in the Canton of Schaffhausen were thus behaving subversively and avoiding compulsory education by going to schools in the Canton of Zurich. It is therefore apparent that Zurich could not have served as a structural model for the considerably smaller Schaffhausen. On the contrary, I will demonstrate how the education statisticians in Zurich took advantage of the comparison with other cantons to advance domestic school reforms.

## Advancement of Domestic School Reforms

The warnings from Schaffhausen concerning the inadequate education system in Zurich echoed warnings that had been made before: During the second half of the 19th century, there had already been a number of demands to reform the education system in Zurich. In 1872 and again in 1888, two drafts of a law had been rejected in referendums. Further revised drafts failed even earlier in the parliamentary process (Gassmann, 1933). Not before 1899 did a new school law find a majority in support, with a reorganization of the lower-secondary level and therefore an extension of compulsory education being the central aims.

Zurich education statisticians were involved in the drafting of this school law as legislative and executive authorities as well as education administrators. Statistics became a significant tool in the argument for the domestic need for reform. Huber was at one point both secretary of education and actuary for the cantonal board of education. The board of education took five years to prepare the draft. Huber was also a member of the parliamentary commission for this school law. Since his election to the cantonal parliament, Grob had been anxious to advance school reform. The parliament elected him president of the parliamentary commission for the school law. And as head of the communal city school in the city government, he submitted a written response to a draft law consultation to the cantonal board of education. Grob was able to draw on his statistical knowledge to clarify the need for reform:

> If we compare the number of pupils per class with the number in other cantons, the Canton of Zurich occupies one of the last positions. Education statistics for the school year 1893/94 reveal that the number of pupils per class is only higher in the Cantons of Appenzell A.-Rh. und Appenzell I.-Rh.
> *(Vernehmlassungsantwort des Vorstandes des Schulwesens der Stadt Zürich an die Sachkommission zum Gesetz betreffend der Volksschule, STaZH M 35.114)*

After the public consultation, the need for school reform was discussed using statistical comparison in various volumes of the *Amtliches Schulblatt*, the official journal of the education administration of the Canton of Zurich, which was under Huber's editorship:

> For the appraisal of the draft of this law, as well as for the conditions of our public school [*Volksschulverhältnisse*] in general, it should be interesting to discover how some other cantons organize their public schools [*Schulwesen*] . . . Through several issues of our journal, . . . the explanation necessary will be provided with statistical brevity.
>
> *(Huber, 1897, p. 1)*

Through statistical comparison, deficiencies in the education system in Zurich were illustrated in tables: substandard compulsory education, an inadequate number of *Fortbildungskurse* (secondary schools after compulsory education), and an above-average number of pupils per primary school class: "To implement the new school law, policymakers referred to relevant comparisons, again to Schaffhausen and Thurgau, but also internationally to Baden, Württemberg and Sachsen" (Locher, 1900, p. 3).

Without describing in more detail the emergence and implementation of the reform process for public schooling in Zurich, this example shows the embeddedness of Zurich education statisticians in these processes in terms of form and content. Statistics were used by statisticians to compare their own education system to other education systems, so as to illustrate the need for reform in general and to legitimize the contents and processes of ongoing reforms. The administration used statistics as a means to influence the processes of school reform in a formative manner[17]—a function that management science describes as "Vorbereitungsherrschaft" (Franz, 2013, p. 29 f.). Steiner-Khamsi (2003, p. 377 f.) calls this kind of transfer

> a means of decontextualization and deterritorialization of controversial school reforms . . . Read this way, externalization as the reference to models which exist beyond one's own education systems is a strategy of legitimization to enforce controversial reforms in one's own country or context.

Statistical comparison had already been used in Zurich in the 1890s to point to inadequate conditions in public schooling as part of a successful strategy of promoting school reform.

## Conclusion

We should not overestimate the potential of comparative education statistics to homogenize education structures in the short term. At the same time, the example of Zurich illustrates the significance of statistics for the development of the cantonal education administration: The Zurich school reform of 1899 showed how the administration was able to interact in a political process by means of statistical comparisons and to push statistical activities at different political levels.

Education statisticians in Zurich managed to institutionalize education statistics at different political levels. Promoting a national institutionalization of statistical comparisons strengthened their position within the Canton of Zurich with a twofold effect: the formation of school reforms and the stabilization of the administrative body. But there was no general consensus regarding the understanding and implementation of education statistics. This was part of a dispute over the prerogative of interpretation concerning relevant methods and data.

The function of statistics can therefore be located on a time scale. Accountability and legitimization through the production of visibility, comparability, and mutual observation—in short, as a passive means of governmental representation—gradually lost their value and legitimacy after the turn of the century. Since the early 20th century education statistics have been a tool on the cantonal level for dealing with specific questions and challenges and for generating projections and evidence-based planning.

## Notes

1. All quotations cited in this chapter have been translated.
2. In the following, I orientate myself to a neo-institutional terminology in line with DiMaggio and Powell (1983).
3. In current policy analysis concerning Switzerland, it has become common to differentiate between the national level (the responsibility of the confederation) and the Swiss level ("gesamtschweizerisch": the responsibility of intercantonal actors) (Lehmann, 2013).
4. In 1912 Bähler (1885–1970) became the head of the Bureau of Education Statistics and was thereby appointed by Albert Huber to carry out research for the Swiss National Exhibition in Bern in 1914. She would dominate the work in education statistics on the Swiss level for the next four decades.
5. Including primary and lower-secondary education under local public control, which was compulsory and free of charge.
6. Huber (1863–1913) started his career as an education administrator in 1882 when J. C. Grob appointed him to the position of assistant for national education statistics for the Swiss National Exhibition in Zurich (Grob, 1883) and then as assistant in the cantonal administrative body. Huber succeeded Grob in 1892 as cantonal secretary of education. He was named head of national education statistics for the Swiss National Exhibition in Geneva (Huber, 1896/1897) in 1896, and he initiated the fourth round of national education statistics for the Swiss National Exhibition in Bern in 1914 (Huber, 1915). Huber was, at times together with Grob, a representative of the centralist Democratic Party (Demokratische Partei) in the cantonal parliament.
7. Grob (1841–1901) was a long-time secretary of education in the Canton of Zurich (1875–1892) as well as a member of the communal parliament (1886–1892), the city government (1892–1901), and the cantonal parliament (1872–1874 and 1893–1901). Grob organized the national education statistics for the Swiss National Exhibition in Zurich in 1883 (Grob, 1883).
8. Zollinger (1858–1931) was Huber's successor as cantonal secretary of education (1900–1930) and head of the Swiss Society for School Hygiene (Schweizerische Gesellschaft für

Schulgesundheitspflege). Zollinger had already been the secretary of education of the city of Zurich (1892–1900) under Grob's leadership.
9. What has not been discussed is the fact that the demand for the previous level of comprehensive national education statistics at the Swiss National Exhibition in Geneva in 1896 was far lower than expected: According to a circular issued by the Central Library, "a mass of books amounting to more than 8000 volumes" (Korrespondenz vom 7. Mai 1904, BAR E80 Nr.599 Bd. 79. 1904) of this edition had to be discarded despite being available for free.
10. Such thematic inquiries had been conducted even more frequently since the late 19th century, also as a consequence of the Swiss Society for School Hygiene's initiative and in an international comparative manner (Hofmann, 2013).
11. The city education administration also carried out periodic surveys concerning lower-secondary students' spare-time activities and work, starting in 1915.
12. At the time of Grob's inauguration in 1892, the office of the cantonal director of education and, with it, the hub of the governmental education administration consisted solely of three full-time civil servants. By 1914 the body of the education administration in Zurich had grown to six positions, increasing the differentiation of duties and hierarchization of functions (PHZH FBib: ZH HB I 1 ff.). In the meantime, the number of pupils in public schools had also grown, albeit not in the same proportions. Besides that, there was an administration of cantonal upper-secondary schools, an administration of teaching materials, and a supervisory agency for *Fortbildungsschulen* (secondary schools after compulsory education) and *Arbeitsschulen* (handicraft lessons). There are various references to adjuncts in the governmental budgets. Reorganization and a comprehensive extension of the cantonal education administration in Zurich were not undertaken until the 1940s (Illi, 2008). Administrative duties had been performed mainly by the elected local lay supervision (Tröhler, 2008).
13. The establishment of the youth welfare office in the Canton of Zurich took place in the context of class struggle and unemployment but also older debates about social welfare, youth protection, and the establishment of criminal law and a penal system relating to young offenders (*Jugendstrafrecht und Jugendmassnahmenvollzug*) (Criblez, 1997).
14. The publication of periodic accountability reports (which for a long time did not appear annually in each canton) including statistical data can also be understood as a result of homogenization.
15. Huber (1905, p. v) explicitly applauded these five cantons for adapting their reports to those published by Bern and Zurich. This series of reports is accessible in the Swiss National Library.
16. It had previously had a six-year *Alltagsschule* (all-day school) and a subsequent three-year *Ergänzungsschule* (two mornings per week). Under the law of 1899, pupils had to attend primary school every day for a period of eight years.
17. It needs to be noted that an expanded contextualization of this school reform would modify the significance of statistics in relation to other relevant themes. Statistical arguments did not assert themselves in every aspect.

## Archival Sources

### *Research Library Pestalozzianum*

PHZH FBib: ZH HB I 1 ff.: Regierungsetat des Kantons Zürich (1885–1915).

## State Archives Lucerne / Archive of the Swiss Conference of Cantonal Ministers of Education (EDK)

StALU A 1270 / 121: Kreisschreiben (1897–1907).
StALU A 1271 / 109–114: Protokolle der Konferenzen (1897–1906).

## State Archives Zurich

STaZH M 35.114: Sachkommission zum Gesetz betreffend der Volksschule (1898).

## Swiss Federal Archives

BAR E80 Nr.599 Bd.79. 1904: Schweizerische Schulstatistik (1904–1906).
BAR E80 Nr.600 Bd.79. 1911–1914: Schweizerische Schulstatistik (1911–1914).

## References

Bähler, E. L. (1914). Dr. jur. Albert Huber: 1863–1913: Ein Lebensbild. *Jahrbuch des Unterrichtswesens in der Schweiz, 26,* 1–57.
Chatelanat, A. (1879). Statistische Nachrichten über das Unterrichtswesen der Schweizer Kantone im Jahr 1877. *Zeitschrift für schweizerische Statistik, 1–2,* 54–81.
Criblez, L. (1997). Die Pädagogisierung der Strafe: Zur Geschichte von Jugendstrafrecht und Jugendmassnahmenvollzug in der Schweiz. In H. Badertscher & H.-U. Grunder (Eds.), *Geschichte der Erziehung und Schule in der Schweiz im 19. und 20. Jahrhundert* (pp. 319–356). Bern, Switzerland: Haupt.
Criblez, L., & Huber, C. (2008). Der Bildungsartikel der Bundesverfassung von 1874 und die Diskussion über den eidgenössischen "Schulvogt." In L. Criblez (Ed.), *Bildungsraum Schweiz* (pp. 87–129). Bern, Switzerland: Haupt.
Desiderato, S., Lengwiler, U., & Rothenbühler, V. (2008). *Jugendhilfe Kanton Zürich 1918–2008: Zwischen Professionalität und politischem Kräftemessen.* Zurich, Switzerland: Lehrmittelverlag des Kantons Zürich.
Desrosières, A. (2005). *Die Politik der Grossen Zahlen: Eine Geschichte der statistischen Denkweise.* Berlin, Germany: Springer.
DiMaggio, P. J., & Powell, W. W. (1983). The iron cage revisited: Institutional isomorphism and collective rationality in organizational fields. *American Sociological Review, 48,* 147–160.
Franz, T. (2013). *Einführung in die Verwaltungswissenschaft.* Wiesbaden, Germany: Springer.
Gassmann, E. (1933). Die zürcherische Volksschule von 1872 bis 1932. In G. Guggenbühl, A. Mantel, H. Gubler, H. Kreis, & E. Gassmann (Eds.), *Volksschule und Lehrerbildung. 1832–1932. Festschrift zur Jahrhundertfeier* (pp. 557–689). Zurich, Switzerland: Erziehungsrat des Kantons Zürich.
Geiss, M. (2012). Opportunismus der Kommunikation: Die Einheit der Bildungsverwaltung als methodisches Problem. In M. Geiss & A. De Vincenti (Eds.), *Verwaltete Schule: Geschichte und Gegenwart* (pp. 71–82). Wiesbaden, Germany: VS Springer.
Grob, J. C. (1880). *Berichterstattung über das schweizerische Unterrichtswesen auf Grundlage der im Jahr 1878 erschienenen offiziellen Jahresberichte. Vom schweiz. Departement des Innern angeordneter Separatabdruck aus der Zeitschrift für schweizerische Statistik.* Bern, Switzerland: K. J. Wyss.

Grob, J. C. (Ed.). (1883). *Statistik über das Unterrichtswesen in der Schweiz im Jahr 1881.* Im Auftrag des schweizerischen Departements des Innern auf den Zeitpunkt der schweizerischen Landesausstellung in Zürich 1883. Zurich, Switzerland: J. Schabelitz.

Grob, J. C. (1889). Vorwort. *Jahrbuch des Unterrichtswesens in der Schweiz, 1887, 1,* iii–iv.

Grob, J. C. (1890). Allgemeiner Jahresbericht des Unterrichtswesens in der Schweiz im Jahr 1888. *Jahrbuch des Unterrichtswesens in der Schweiz, 1888, 2,* 9–128.

Grob, J. C. (1891). Vorwort. *Jahrbuch des Unterrichtswesens in der Schweiz, 1889, 3,* ix–xiv.

Hartmann, H. (2011). *Der Volkskörper bei der Musterung Militärstatistik und Demographie in Europa vor dem Ersten Weltkrieg.* Göttingen, Germany: Wallstein Verlag.

Hofmann, M. (2013). Kongresse, Komitees und Koryphäen. Internationalität als Legitimation für die schweizerischen Vertreter der Schulhygienebewegung in der ersten Hälfte des 20. Jahrhunderts. *Bildungsgeschichte. International Journal for the Historiography of Education (IJHE), 3*(1), 36–45.

Huber, A. (Ed.). (1896/1897). *Schweizerische Schulstatistik 1894/95.* Bearbeitet im Auftrage des schweizerischen Departements des Innern in Bern für die Landesausstellung in Genf 1896. Zurich, Switzerland: Buchdruckerei des Schweizerischen Grütlivereins.

Huber, A. (Ed.). (1897). *Amtliches Schulblatt des Kantons Zürich, 12*(1), 1 January, 1–3.

Huber, A. (1902). Stadtrat Johann Kaspar Grob 1841–1901: Eine biographische Skizze. *Jahrbuch des Unterrichtswesens in der Schweiz, 1900,* 14.

Huber, A. (1905). Vorwort. *Jahrbuch des Unterrichtswesens in der Schweiz, 1903, 17,* iii–v.

Huber, A. (1915). *Schweizerische Schulstatistik.* Bern, Switzerland: Kommissionsverlag A. Francke.

Illi, M. (2008). *Von der Kameralistik zum New Public Management: Geschichte der Zürcher Kantonsverwaltung von 1803 bis 1998.* Zurich, Switzerland: Chronos.

Lehmann, L. (2013). *Zwang zur freiwilligen Zusammenarbeit: Steuerungsinstrumente und interkantonale Governance in der schweizerischen Lehrerinnen- und Lehrerbildung.* Bern, Switzerland: hep Verlag.

Locher, A. (1900). *Die innere Einrichtung der Achtklassenschule: Bericht der XIer-Kommission.* Zurich, Switzerland: G.B.Z.

Manz, K. (2008). Die Bundessubventionen für die Primarschule: Analyse einer bildungspolitischen Debatte um 1900. In L. Criblez (Ed.), *Bildungsraum Schweiz* (pp. 155–181). Bern, Switzerland: Haupt.

Ruoss, T. (2013). Historical change in the production and legitimisation of education statistics in Switzerland. *European Educational Research Journal, 12*(1), 95–107. doi:10.2304/eerj.2013.12.1.95

Statistisches Bureau des Kantons Zürich (Ed.). (1914). *Die Berufswahl der im Frühjahr 1913 aus der Volksschule ausgetretenen Schüler.* Zurich, Switzerland: Buchdruckerei Geschwister Ziegler.

Steiner-Khamsi, G. (2003). Vergleich und Subtraktion: Das Residuum im Spannungsfeld zwischen Globalem und Lokalem. In H. Kaelble & J. Schriewer (Eds.), *Vergleich und Transfer: Komparatistik in den Sozial-, Geschichts- und Kulturwissenschaften* (pp. 369–397). Frankfurt, Germany: Campus.

Tanner, J. (1995). Der Tatsachenblick auf die "reale Wirklichkeit": Zur Entwicklung der Sozial- und Konsumstatistik in der Schweiz. *Schweizerische Zeitschrift für Geschichte, 45,* 94–108.

Tröhler, D. (2008). Verwaltung und Aufsicht der Zürcher Volksschule. In D. Tröhler & U. Hardegger (Eds.), *Zukunft bilden: Die Geschichte der modernen Zürcher Volksschule* (pp. 55–68). Zurich, Switzerland: NZZ Libro.

Voss, P. (2012). Der bürokratische Wendepunkt von 1843: Die Primärschule im Prozess der Luxemburger Nationalstaatsbildung des 19. Jahrhunderts. In M. Geiss & A. De Vincenti (Eds.), *Verwaltete Schule: Geschichte und Gegenwart* (pp. 53–70). Wiesbaden, Germany: VS Springer.

Zollinger, F. (1901). *Weltausstellung in Paris 1900: Bestrebungen auf dem Gebiete der Schulgesundheitspflege und des Kinderschutzes*. Bericht an den hohen Bundesrat der schweiz. Eidgenossenschaft. Zurich, Switzerland: Artistisches Institut Orell Füssli.

# 8

# FROM ABSTINENCE TO ECONOMIC PROMOTION, OR THE INTERNATIONAL TEMPERANCE MOVEMENT AND THE SWISS SCHOOLS

*Michèle Hofmann*

In the 19th century alcoholism became a major social problem. With the onset of the Industrial Revolution, the consumption of (hard) alcoholic beverages increased. The 1830s are known in the literature as the period of the "first liquor wave" (Tanner, 1994, p. 52). The breakthrough of mechanized factory production and wage employment resulted in a decrease of self-sufficiency within families and thereby in a dietary degradation among large parts of the population. Alcohol served the purpose of "quenching thirst, appeasing hunger and forgetting woes in one go" and became "a foodstuff for the lower classes, which was equally as important as it was miserable" (pp. 50–51).

In response to this development the first "temperance" societies were formed. These societies required their members to be completely abstinent from distilled beverages and to exercise the greatest possible restraint with regard to other alcoholic beverages. Some societies expressly addressed children. In Preston in England (1834) and in Dumfries in Scotland (1837), for example, temperance societies for children were founded (Zollinger, 1902, p. 193). Among other things, the temperance societies attempted to combat alcoholism by publishing treatises, educational pamphlets, and folk tales. In Switzerland, well-known writings of this kind are Jeremias Gotthelf's (1797–1854) short stories in *How Five Girls Perish Pitifully From Liquor* (1838) and *Dursli the Liquor Drunkard* (1839). Gotthelf combated the "liquor plague" not only in his function as an author but also as a school inspector. Albert Bitzius (Gotthelf's legal name) was the school inspector of several villages in the Canton of Bern. School children visiting pubs and the alcohol problems of teachers were the theme of various letters Bitzius addressed to the local school commissions and Bern's department of education in the 1830s (Derron, 2009, pp. 24–25). This shows that alcoholism did not even stop at the school's doors.

After the commotion about alcohol consumption had ebbed somewhat periodically, a second "liquor wave" started to arouse emotions and, particularly in the United States, Great Britain, and Continental Europe, led to the founding of new societies and organizations that advocated sensible moderation in the consumption of alcohol or even complete abstinence (Schwelle, 2013, pp. 95–96). In 1877 the Blue Cross, the first organization in Switzerland that not only required complete abstinence of its members but also looked after alcohol-addicted persons, was formed. The founder of the Blue Cross was Louis-Lucien Rochat (1849–1917), a pastor from the Canton of Vaud. He had gotten to know the abstinence movement in England, which had convinced him that abstinence was the only therapy for dipsomania and that those who wished to help alcoholics must be abstinent themselves (Hölzer, 1988, pp. 24, 29; Zürcher, 1997, p. 12).

In Switzerland, the abstinence or temperance movement became an important social movement at the end of the 19th century. At this time, teachers also started to become involved. In 1899 the Swiss Association of Abstinent Teachers was founded and took up the fight against alcohol in schools. Its members modeled their association on international endeavors in this field and were networked beyond the national borders.[1] This chapter illustrates how abstinent teachers in Switzerland campaigned for prevention of alcoholism. Initially, their concerns met with little interest or even opposition, as is shown in the first section. In the 1920s they finally met with approval; now the focus was on topics such as milk and fruit. These two agricultural products lent themselves to being advertised as typically Swiss. Hence, the abstinent teachers' efforts were now supported by the strong Swiss agricultural lobby. This cooperation proved to be very productive: Countless lesson planning ideas on the topic of milk and fruit were published (section 2); in addition, posters and protective booklet sleeves were designed, and school campaigns were initiated (section 3).

## Demand for Total Abstinence by Teachers

The abstinent teachers considered alcoholism to be the "greatest social ill" and pointed out its "manifold perils" (Staub, 1900, p. 706). In their view, alcohol threatened "the young being . . . even before it sees the light of day—because the great majority of descendants of drinkers are already born with a hereditary burden of abnormal tendencies, mental defectiveness, epilepsy, sickliness, nervousness" (Waser, 1900/1901, p. 14). Hence, the schools were to educate young people "in the spirit of abstinence and sobriety" ("Bekämpfung des Alkoholismus," 1903). The best measure to achieve this—and on this the abstinent teachers after the turn of the century agreed, and they never tired of repeating it—was "the good example set by the teacher" (Buchmann, 1903).

Since the early 19th century, the international anti-alcohol movement had been split into two factions: the "moderate" and the "abstinent" (Hölzer, 1988, p. 35). The moderate faction regarded the consumption of small quantities of spirituous beverages as unproblematic; the abstinents advocated complete abstinence from alcohol (pp. 35–36). With its demand for complete abstinence for teachers, the members of the Swiss Association of Abstinent Teachers belonged to the second faction. This radical demand was one of the reasons that at the beginning of the 20th century, they were only modestly successful at drawing attention to their concerns. In the years following the founding of the association, they also found little acceptance and even opposition from their colleagues. In 1902 the association's president, Heinrich Volkart (1852–1905), stated in the *Swiss Teachers' Journal* that the association was "often and readily accused by fellow teachers" of being fanatical (1902, p. 262). Not least, the abstinent teachers were "accused of portraying only the negative side of the alcohol issue" (W. W., 1907, p. 406). This criticism referred in particular to the book *Graphical Tables With Accompanying Text on the Alcohol Issue*, published in 1907 by Jakob Stump (1864–1926) and Robert Willenegger (see Stump & Willenegger, 1907). The extensive tables showed alcohol in relation to other factors, including crime, illness, mortality, and degeneration. It was one of the first textbooks for anti-alcohol education in Switzerland. In their introduction, Stump and Willenegger emphasized the "successes" that abstinent teachers had achieved in the fight against alcohol in other countries. "Numerous edicts by the highest school authorities, decrees and laws" in Prussia, Austria, France, Belgium, England, Scandinavia, Canada, and the United States were given as proof (pp. ix–x).

An additional demand that the abstinent teachers frequently made at the beginning of the 20th century was for alcohol-free school trips and celebrations. This can be found in a petition that the Association of Abstinent Teachers addressed to the federal and cantonal authorities in 1903. This suggests that at the time it was customary for school children to drink alcohol, at least occasionally. In addition, abstinent teachers carried out various investigations between 1912 and 1915 at schools in Zurich, Basel, and Bern, interviewing children from 6 to 14 years of age. Heinrich Steiger (1889–1977), a secondary school teacher in Zurich, summarized the results in a presentation he gave in 1915: "24% of school children aged between 6 and 14 live abstinently. Frequent or even regular, daily consumption of spirituous beverages can be found with 19.1% of the school children" (1915, pp. 111–112). For Steiger, only children who had never drunk a drop of alcohol in their lives counted as abstinent. In 1912 he himself had carried out a survey on alcohol consumption among his pupils. He had been motivated to do this by reading a report about the Tenth International Anti-Alcohol Congress, held in 1905 in Budapest. Steiger's interest in the international abstinence movement is also reflected in the fact that he compared the results of his survey to results in other countries. He reached the conclusion that although more children lived abstinently in Switzerland than elsewhere, "these figures nevertheless represent food for thought" (p. 112). In particular, Steiger advocated educational measures in the fight against alcohol consumption among school children. Both the children themselves and their parents and teachers were to be educated about the "alcohol issue" (pp. 120–121).

Already shortly after 1900, anti-alcohol education had been included in the abstinent teachers' demands, but at the time it did not have top priority. In addition, the demands at that time were rather unspecific with regard to teaching materials. Only in exceptional cases were descriptive suggestions made as to how the issue might be implemented in the classroom: "[S]uitable sections about alcohol and alcoholism" (Frey, 1903/1904, p. 103), "appropriate reading passages" ("Alkoholfrage," 1904), and chapters in schoolbooks "which are designed to contribute to the fight against alcoholism" ("Bekämpfung des Alkoholismus," 1903) were demanded, without specifying what exactly this meant or giving concrete examples.

Barely any schoolbooks for anti-alcohol education existed in the years following 1900. The exceptions were Stump and Willenegger's *Graphical Tables*, mentioned above, and a storybook, *From a Fresh Spring* (*Aus frischem Quell*, 1908). After the storybook was published by the Association of Abstinent Teachers in 1908, the association founded its own publishing house. In 1910 it published the first booklet in the teaching material series *Fountain of Youth*; additional volumes followed in the 1920s and 1930s. Two additional series were published after 1930, *Check for Yourself!* and *Healthy Youth*. By the 1950s more than 50 titles had been published that achieved a broad circulation and were republished in part by the Swiss youth literature institution in later years. After 1920, in parallel to the publication of an abundance of teaching materials, anti-alcohol education shifted to become the focus of the abstinent teachers.

## Lesson Outlines and Schoolbooks About Fruit and Milk

The international abstinence movement reached its historical zenith with Prohibition in the United States. This nationwide Constitutional complete ban on alcohol was adopted in 1919 and remained in place until 1933. The United States was not the only country to attempt to bring alcohol abuse under control through strict prohibitions. Prohibition was implemented in Canada from 1917 to 1927 and also in Ireland (1915–1922), Finland (1919–1933), and Russia (from 1914 into the 1920s) (Schwelle, 2013, p. 105). At the same time as the "international endeavors for the good" ("Bernischer Verein," 1925/1926, p. 401), as the Swiss abstinent teachers called Prohibition, they too succeeded in gaining attention for alcoholism prevention. This success was owed to two topics (fruit and milk) for economic reasons.

In the second half of the 19th century, Switzerland developed into Europe's most fruit tree–rich country in relation to its population size. Large quantities of fruit could be exported. The expansion of fruit growing resulted not only from good sales prospects but also from the decline of viticulture, which was afflicted by parasites and disease, and of grain growing, which was exposed to competition from imports. Towards the end of the 19th century, the canning industry and cider mills boosted the demand for fruit. Subsequently, thanks to private and state measures, fruit growing was systematically promoted, and the fruit trade was coordinated. However, after a record harvest in 1922, the fruit market collapsed, and owing to the worldwide economic crisis, the exports suffered a severe decline (Schumacher, 2010, pp. 349–350). At the same time, the dairy industry, which since the end of the 19th century had developed into a main branch of the Swiss agricultural sector, was struggling with sales problems. In the spring of 1920, after the lifting of nearly all the wartime economic measures, the reduction of crop cultivation—which had needed to be extended because of the First World War—and the high volume of dairy product imports resulted in an ongoing sales crisis that caused a massive collapse of the milk price. The price erosion was further aggravated by the worldwide economic crisis (Stadler, 2009, p. 578).

In the course of the worldwide economic crisis, the opponents of alcohol found partners in the milk and fruit producers, who were willing to support their cause. The two topics of milk and fruit not only could be advertised as typically Swiss but also proved to be excellently suited for anti-alcohol education. By the end of the 1920s at the latest, they had turned into *the* central topics of the debate. School children were to learn that fruit and milk were healthy and natural foodstuffs, and simultaneously their attention was to be directed to the harmfulness of alcohol. The abstinent teachers' efforts to take up fruit and milk as teaching topics benefited the producers and were actively supported by them. As a result of this collaboration, countless lesson planning ideas, examples, and lesson outlines on these topics were developed, published, and made available to Swiss teachers—in some cases free of charge.

In contrast to earlier demands regarding anti-alcohol education, the abstinent teachers now illustrated in a manner that was descriptive and customized to specific levels of schooling how the topics of milk and fruit should be treated in the classroom. The authors were in agreement that a specific school subject need not be created for anti-alcohol education but that instruction on milk and fruit should flow into the existing school subjects at all levels. The teachers' own abstinence, which had been demanded forcefully in the years following 1900, scarcely played a role anymore, because any teacher could and should give classes on milk and fruit. Naturally, it was also possible for non-abstinent teachers to dedicate classes to the topics of milk and fruit without reference to alcohol avoidance.

Most of the lesson planning ideas were for the school subjects of mathematics and nature studies. For example, a secondary school teacher from Wattenwil, Fritz Schuler, explained exercises for the topic of fruit in arithmetic classes in the *Journal for Healthcare* in 1927 (see Schuler, 1927). Schuler was a member of the Association of Abstinent Teachers. He started his article with what he viewed as two poor examples, which "by means of frequent repetition present alcohol to the child as a necessity of life" (p. 276). The first arithmetic exercise was as follows: "From an $18¾$ hl barrel of wine, a landlord fills three smaller barrels of $4⅗$ hl, $3⁷⁄_{10}$ hl, and $5¼$ hl. How much wine will remain in the large barrel?" (p. 276). And the second exercise: "A family buys a small barrel of wine for 49.95 francs at 55 centimes per liter.

How many liters does the small barrel contain?" (p. 276). Exercises of this nature had been widespread in arithmetic books since the 19th century. Schuler wanted to replace them with exercises that opposed alcohol, and he provided over 60 sample arithmetic exercises in the article: For example, the school children calculated the Swiss fruit crop yield, the "wealth of our country," and subsequently determined the sugar content of the harvest (pp. 277–279). They calculated the expenditures for alcoholic beverages, put these in relation to the federal debts, and determined how many family houses could have been built with this money (pp. 281–282). Or, based on statistical data from Holland, Sweden, Scotland, England, Denmark, and Switzerland from 1880 to 1922, they calculated "the reduction of tuberculosis mortality as a percentage" in relation to the "annual per capita consumption of pure alcohol" (p. 286). Exercises like this, in which crop yields, expenditures, or national debts were calculated, were typical for the arithmetic books of this time. Schuler took the existing exercises as a basis and supplied them with new content that would serve in the fight against alcohol at school.

In the opinion of Adolf Hartmann (1882–1959), a teacher at the cantonal school of Aarau, there was "hardly another scientific topic that [offered] as much stimulation for biological, physical, and chemical observations . . . as the topic of fruit" (1933, p. 711). The experiments on the topic of fruit can be illustrated using the "18 chemical experiments for school and national education" that Hartmann (1933) presented in an article in the *Journal for Hygiene*. Hartmann, who held a degree in chemistry from the University of Zurich, played a pioneering role in researching and promoting alcohol-free fruit processing. He addressed the latter, or to be more specific the production of apple juice, in the introduction to the article: Thanks to "unexpectedly great progress with regard to commercial and family farming production of apple juice," the "large part of the difficulties in processing fruit[2] may now be considered as largely overcome" (p. 699). He added that apple juice was "the great practical fruit preserve, which maintains all the healthy fruit ingredients and can be preserved for as long as required" (p. 699). He lamented, "Regrettably, the concept of improved appreciation of fruit and apple juice is still far from having permeated all the municipalities and families" (p. 700). Hartmann wanted to change this, namely, using educational measures: "It is necessary to treat the benefits of the new possibilities of processing fruit at schools and in national education courses, not only in words and writing but also by means of illustration and experiments" (p. 700). Hartmann explained what this instruction might be like using experiments he had developed himself. The experiments were on the process of fermentation and "the superiority of sugar from our fruit over refined sugar" (p. 701). For instance, the school children determined the nutritional value of unfermented and fermented fruit drinks, learning that in the process of fermenting fruit and grape juices, a large part of the fruit elements are destroyed: "Thus, fermentation is in large part the destruction of most valuable human foodstuffs" (p. 709). In the same vein as Schuler's arithmetic examples, the school children were to be taught by means of chemistry experiments on the same topic areas (fruit, sugar, fermentation, and alcohol) that consuming fruit in its unfermented form is the better alternative. Ironically, such experiments at school also taught the children a great deal about producing alcohol.

Many arithmetic exercises and experiments for nature study classes were also proposed on the subject of milk. The school children were to calculate, for example, a family's daily, weekly, monthly, and annual expenditure for milk (see Fröhlich, 1934, p. 241). An example from the field of nature study is an experiment presented in 1934 by a former teacher and head of the Swiss Central Office for the Fight Against Alcoholism in Lausanne, Max Oettli (1879–1965), in the *Swiss Teachers' Journal* (Oettli, 1934). In Oettli's (1934) experiment, the children were to find out which elements milk contained by heating a drop of milk on a razor blade:

> In general, milk smells extremely foul at the beginning of the heating process. . . . The first elements to evaporate are the fatty acids, such as the foul-smelling butyric acid and the like, which are formed by the bacterial decomposition of the cream. And subsequently, when the milk starts to burn it smells wonderful: of burnt sugar. Milk contains *sugar*. . . . As soon as the flame extinguishes, a small thread of smoke arises. It stinks of burnt protein. Milk contains *protein*! We continue the heating process. A sort of oil flows over the blade. We heat it. It smells like when mother is making omelets. . . . And finally we also make use of our eyes. Black carbonaceous residues remain on the blade. If we heat the blade to red heat under an air flow, which is achieved by holding the blade at an angle to the flame, the black color turns white. The coal incinerates. Milk contains *ash*.
>
> (p. 230)

Here, the reference to abstinence from alcohol is not self-evident, so it was the teacher's task to establish the link after the experiment. In Oettli's opinion, the objective was to "enlighten the boys and girls about the *value* of sugar, fat, protein, ash, so that they marvel at the miracle of milk, and they no longer regard it as merely baby food but resolve to drink it also during military service and to order milk instead of beer when playing cards at the pub!" (p. 230). The schoolbook *Milk* by Schuler (1931) also contained various experiments on milk. The publication was made available to the teachers free of charge by the propaganda office of the Swiss milk commission.

In addition to mathematics and nature studies, suggestions for planning anti-alcohol lessons based on milk and fruit were also made for other school subjects: language lessons (German), home economics, drawing, life science, singing, handicrafts and needlework, history, geography, and gymnastics. In language classes, for example, pupils wrote down a "milk experience" or learned adjectives: "The pear is sweet, soft. The apple is rosy, ripe. The plum is juicy, sugar-sweet. Inversion: The rosy, ripe apple" (Eberli, 1936, p. 139; Huggler, 1940, p. 690). In home economics classes, the school children were to learn to prepare "a truly tasty dairy dish"

(Tschiffely, 1936, p. 125). Drawing assignments included, for example: "Paint (directly with the paintbrush) native fruits from memory" (Eberli, 1930, p. 165). For singing lessons, the abstinent teachers recommended "a cheerful shepherds' song" (Eberli, 1936, p. 140). In handicraft classes, the children were to build a "two-wheeled milk cart from a matchbox, with sticks as an axle and cork discs as wheels" (Fröhlich, 1934, p. 241). In history classes, one could "carry out historical examinations about the long history of fruit in our country" (Hartmann, 1933, p. 711). And, finally, the abstinent teachers presented teaching units that were structured according to topics and were not associated with any particular school subjects. These lesson outlines were intended primarily for teaching in the lower classes. They had titles such as "Milk, the Ideal Drink," "Ripe Apples," and "Milk in a Bottle."

## Visual Material, Protective Exercise Book Covers, and School Campaigns

Articles published by abstinent teachers also repeatedly suggested employing large-format educational illustrations, posters, and protective book covers on the topics of fruit and milk. With regard to visual material, "small-format" illustrations were recommended in particular for the promotion of public health. These were published by the Swiss Central Office for the Fight Against Alcoholism and "provided free of charge to all teachers who committed themselves in writing to put them to their intended use" (Keller, 1936b, p. 123). In 1936 Anna Keller (1879–1962), a teacher from Basel, showed in the *Swiss Teachers' Journal* how to use the small-format illustration entitled "Ruthli" in the lower grades (Keller, 1936a). The illustration shows a small girl who is drinking a glass of milk, and the caption reads: "Ev'ry drop so good and sound / and makes those cheeks so red and round" (p. 84). Keller told a story revolving around "young Ruthli," who "had become so pale and so whiny after a bout of whooping cough" (pp. 84–85). "The doctor said: 'The child must drink milk'. 'She does not like it', the mother replies. 'Take her out to the countryside, into the sun and the fresh air!' That is why Ruthli is now in the countryside and has been living in a splendid farmhouse with her mother for some weeks now" (p. 85). Here, after having seen a calf drinking, Ruthli wanted milk too: "Pleased, the mother fetched a glass, filled it to the brim, and Ruthli drank and thought about the calf and closed her eyes. Then she said to her mother: 'Ah! Good!'" (p. 85). School children were to learn that milk is good not only for calves but also for children, as the end of the story reveals: "Soon Ruthli has to return to the town. Her father will be pleased to see a healthy, lively child! She will have to continue drinking milk when she returns to the town. Oh, but she wants to! For it so good, so sweet and so healthy" (p. 85).

In addition to schoolbooks, the Association of Abstinent Teachers also published themed protective covers for exercise books. Several themes associated with fruit and milk were available, including "Fruit and Apple Juice," "Grapes and

Grape Juice," "Pro Milk," and "Cowherd's Song." In 1930 a competition was held to find suitable themes—a competition entry had to be "an artistically designed protective cover, which can be used for exercise books and possibly also for textbooks and which is graphically designed both to meet the stated purpose and to bring about an alcohol-critical attitude in the pupils" ("Wettbewerb," 1930). The published protective covers were available in batches of 100, 500, 1,000, or even 10,000 and were made of "strong paper, which can be colored in with watercolors or crayons" (Swiss National Library, n.d.). The abstinent teachers praised them as a "beautiful gift to the Swiss young people" and a useful tool for milk and fruit classes (Nagel, 1934, p. 308).

To supplement anti-alcohol education, various school campaigns were initiated. In this area, too, the abstinent teachers collaborated with the milk and fruit producers. At the beginning of the 1930s, the school milk program was introduced: Pasteurized milk in glass bottles was handed out to school children as a refreshment during the morning break (Moser & Brodbeck, 2007, p. 206). The Association of Abstinent Teachers participated in the school milk program from the beginning. In 1938, on the occasion of the association's 40th anniversary, its president, Moritz Javet (1883–1960), stressed the commitment to school milk: With the support of the abstinent teachers, "modern day bottled milk [has been] introduced as a refreshment in over 200 villages and towns with many schoolhouses and classes. 60,000 school children have become acquainted practically with bottled milk" (Javet, 1938). An additional school initiative was the Pro Juventute fruit donation. The abstinent teachers supported this initiative as well. Since 1927 Pro Juvente, a Swiss foundation dedicated to supporting children and youth, collected fruit every year for schools in communes (the smallest political units in Switzerland) in mountainous regions and pursued an educational purpose: "The children are to get to know and appreciate the value of the apple, grow accustomed to it and when they grow up, to not want to do without fruit" (Michel, 1941, p. 1). The Schweizerwoche [Swiss week] also carried out school campaigns. This association was committed to domestic production and organized an annual essay competition, in which between 20,000 and 30,000 school children participated every year. In 1929 the topic of the competition was milk. The task was as follows: What do I know about Swiss milk, and how it is used? In 1929 the association decided to "place *Swiss fruit and its appreciation* in the focus of the school campaign" ("Schweizerobst," 1937, p. 828).

Against the backdrop of the crises in the fruit and dairy markets, these two competition topics illustrate that the children were to be educated to consume Swiss products. The abstinent teachers and the producers agreed that it was the duty of public schools to convey the "value of fruit that has been grown in one's own country" (Schmid, 1927, p. 327). Resources to achieve this objective included a large-format educational illustration entitled "Swiss Fruit" and a lesson outline entitled "On the Value of Our Fruit." In this period tropical fruits were viewed increasingly as competition to domestic production. This was reflected by negative press coverage of fruit from abroad. The competing products were portrayed as being almost as unhealthy as alcohol. In 1927 a member of the Swiss fruit and winegrowers' association's fruit-growing commission warned in the *Swiss Teachers' Journal* about the "increasing addiction to foreign fruit" to which young people were particularly prone (Schmid, 1927, p. 327); the author considered foreign fruit to be as harmful as sweets:

> Nowadays our youth has many more opportunities to buy tropical fruits and sweets than they used to. Kiosks, pastry shops, banana booths, we can find in abundance in the towns, and soon also in every village. Frequently, the child is not able to resist the longing for the delicious goods that are offered for sale here. The healthy and natural longing for fresh fruits is quenched with tropical fruits or, what is even less desirable, spoilt with sweets.
>
> (p. 327)

With regard to milk, the abstinent teachers and the producers argued that the Swiss population had become alienated from this typically Swiss product and that the youth needed to be trained to "better appreciate and to consume more milk" (Nagel, 1932/1933, p. 178). In connection with the topic of milk, the simple and healthy eating and living habits of the ancestors were invoked, and rural (alpine) life was idealized. For instance, in the lesson outline "Milk, the Ideal Drink," published in 1934 in the journal *Swiss School*, Josef Hauser, a teacher from Neuallschwil, recommended visiting a farm: A "tour through the stable, barn, cellar, through the meadows and orchards opens the child's eyes to many a thing that up to now it has passed by heedlessly" (1934, p. 1139). The visit to the farm "can now easily be followed up by a new weekly target, precisely, 'Milk, the ideal drink'" (p. 1139). And by addressing this topic in the classroom "the children's respect for the cow is strengthened, . . . and in their eyes, the farmer takes the place he deserves" (p. 1139). Crucial here are the farmer's activities on an alp (pp. 1139–1141). Thus, the Swiss farmer was portrayed as a shepherd. This image of farmers, which can also be found in other articles on the topic of milk, must be seen in light of the mythologization and idealization of the Swiss Alpine and herdsman's life that began in the 18th century and that was not least influenced by outside forces (see, e.g., Boerlin-Brodbeck, 1998).

## Conclusion

In Switzerland, the international anti-alcohol movement found its expression last but not least in the abstinent teachers' association. Initially, association members were committed to complete abstinence from alcohol. With this demand they found little acceptance on the part of their fellow teachers. They were also criticized of portraying the "alcohol issue" only in negative contexts (crime, illness, mortality). Later, in the 1920s, the abstinent teachers successfully gained media attention by focusing on milk and fruit and advocating the teaching of these topics in the schools. Here, the international anti-alcohol endeavors found a specifically Swiss manifestation. With the support of the strong farm lobby, countless lesson planning ideas were developed, many of which were also published in pedagogical journals. Education on milk and fruit was to be carried out at all school levels, and lesson ideas specific to each school level were developed. Prevention of alcohol consumption was oriented particularly towards younger school children. This is illustrated by lesson outlines that were intended for cross-curricular education in the lower grades and that bear titles such as "Ripe Apples" and "Milk in the Bottle" and also by school experiments that were commended as suitable for children. The protective book covers also addressed the younger school children, as we can see in the fact that they were designed to be colored in with watercolors and crayons. By means of the topics of milk and fruit, a minimization or trivialization of the alcohol issue took place, which stands in sharp contrast to the initial portrayal of alcohol in the context of criminality, illness, and mortality, as can be found in the *Graphical Tables* published by Stump and Willenegger (1907). The strict abstinence that had been forcefully demanded in the years following 1900 no longer played a role. What had started out as a great international social reform movement eventually turned into a national measure for promoting the economy.

## Notes

1. The abstinent teachers in Switzerland cultivated relations with associations in other countries that pursued the same goals and also organized mutual visits. There was also a society with the name International Teachers' Association Against Alcoholism. Overall, the abstinence movement was highly international (see Schrad, 2010).
2. The "difficulties in processing fruit" referred to problems associated with preserving fruit: "Until a few years ago, it was not possible to prevent fruit from undergoing rapid self-decay. Rot and fermentation quickly destroy many fruits" (Hartmann, 1933, p. 699). What Hartmann omitted: Producing liquors also represented a mode of preserving fruits and thus of conserving resources.

## References

Alkoholfrage. (1904). *Schweizerische Blätter für Schulgesundheitspflege, 2*, 65.
*Aus frischem Quell*. (1908). Bern, Switzerland: Gustav Grunau.
Bekämpfung des Alkoholismus. (1903). *Schweizerische Lehrerzeitung, 48*, 127.
Bernischer Verein abstinenter Lehrer und Lehrerinnen. (1925/1926). *Berner Schulblatt, 58*, 401–403.
Boerlin-Brodbeck, Y. (1998). Das Bild der Alpen. In *Die Erfindung der Schweiz 1848–1948* (pp. 76–87). Zurich, Switzerland: Schweizerisches Landesmuseum.
Buchmann, F. X. (1903). Mit was für Mitteln kann die Lehrerschaft den Schäden des Alkoholismus entgegenwirken? *Pädagogische Blätter, 10*, 297.
Derron, M. (2009). Kinder und Lehrer im Wirtshaus: Ein Fallbeispiel aus der Arbeit eines Schulkommissärs. In B. Mahlmann-Bauer (Ed.), *Jeremias Gotthelf und die Schule* (pp. 24–29). Bern, Switzerland: Basisdruck.

Eberli, A. (1930). Obst—Gärung—Alkohol. *Schweizerische Lehrerzeitung, 75*, 164–166.
Eberli, A. (1936). Eine Milch-Woche in der Oberklasse. *Schweizer Schule, 22*, 135–141.
Frey, M. (1903/1904). Die unverheiratete Frau im Dienste der Abstinenzbewegung. *Schweizerische Lehrerinnenzeitung, 8*, 101–107.
Fröhlich, O. (1934). Von der Milch: Lektionsskizze für die 2. und 3. Klasse unter Berücksichtigung des Gesamtunterrichts. *Schweizerische Lehrerzeitung, 79*, 239–241.
Hartmann, A. (1933). Das Obst als Nahrungsmittel: 18 chemische Versuche für Schule und Volksbildung. *Schweizerische Zeitschrift für Hygiene und Archiv für Wohlfahrtspflege, 13*, 699–716.
Hauser, J. (1934). Die Milch, das ideale Getränk: Eine Lektionsskizze für das 4. od. 5. Schuljahr. *Schweizer Schule, 20*, 1138–1141.
Hölzer, C. (1988). *Die Antialkoholbewegung in den deutschsprachigen Ländern (1860–1930)*. Frankfurt, Germany: Peter Lang.
Huggler, M. (1940). Unser Obst: Gesamtunterricht für die Unterstufe. *Schweizerische Lehrerzeitung, 85*, 689–691.
Javet, M. (1938). Nüchternheitsarbeit in den Schweizer Schulen. *Schweizerische Lehrerzeitung, 83*, 641.
Keller, A. (1936a). Kleinwandbild Nr. 88. *Schweizerische Lehrerzeitung, 81*, 84–85.
Keller, A. (1936b). Ein Spiel vom Kindlein, das die Milch nicht mag. *Schweizer Schule, 22*, 123–125.
Michel, D. (1941). Pro Juventute Obstspende 1940. *Pro Juventute, 22*, 1–5.
Moser, P., & Brodbeck, B. (2007). *Milch für alle: Bilder, Dokumente und Analysen zur Milchwirtschaft und Milchpolitik in der Schweiz im 20. Jahrhundert*. Baden, Switzerland: hier + jetzt.
Nagel, K. (1932/1933). Aus dem Tätigkeitsbericht des Schweiz. Vereins abstinenter Lehrer und Lehrerinnen. *Schweizerische Lehrerinnenzeitung, 37*, 177–178.
Nagel, K. (1934). Schweizerischer Verein abstinenter Lehrer und Lehrerinnen. *Schweizerische Lehrerzeitung, 79*, 308–309.
Oettli, M. (1934). Kindertümliche Schulversuche mit Milch. *Schweizerische Lehrerzeitung, 79*, 229–230.
Schmid, G. (1927). Mehr Schweizerobst und weniger Südfrüchte. *Schweizerische Lehrerzeitung, 72*, 327–328.
Schrad, M. L. (2010). *The political power of bad ideas: Networks, institutions, and the global prohibition wave*. Oxford, UK: Oxford University Press.
Schuler, F. (1927). Ein volksgesundheitliches Rechenbuch. *Schweizerische Zeitschrift für Gesundheitspflege, 7*, 276–287.
Schuler, F. (1931). *Die Milch: Versuche und Betrachtungen*. Bern, Switzerland: A. Francke.
Schumacher, R. (2010). Obstbau. In *Historisches Lexikon der Schweiz* (Vol. 9, pp. 348–351). Basel, Switzerland: Schwabe.
Schweizerobst—Reichtum der Heimat—Quell der Gesundheit: Aufsatzwettbewerb der Schweizerwoche in den Schulen des Landes. (1937). *Schweizerische Lehrerzeitung, 82*, 827–828.
Schwelle, W. P. (2013). *Alkohol: Die mächtigste Droge der Welt: Vol. 1*. Solothurn, Switzerland: Nachtschatten Verlag.
Stadler, H. (2009). Milchwirtschaft. In *Historisches Lexikon der Schweiz* (Vol. 8, pp. 576–579). Basel, Switzerland: Schwabe.
Staub, F. (1900). Hat die Schule die Pflicht, gegen das grösste soziale Übel, den Alkoholismus, zu kämpfen und mit welchen Mitteln? *Pädagogische Blätter, 7*, 706–710, 737–742.

Steiger, H. (1915). Über Genuss geistiger Getränke bei Schulkindern. *Jahrbuch der Schweizerischen Gesellschaft für Schulgesundheitspflege, 16*, 92–121.

Stump, J., & Willenegger, R. (1907). *Graphische Tabellen mit Begleittext zur Alkoholfrage.* Zurich, Switzerland: Rob. Willenegger.

Swiss National Library (SNL). (n.d.). V Schweiz 14 [Miscellaneous/propaganda].

Tanner, J. (1994). Drogen und Drogenprohibition—historische und zeitgenössische Erfahrungen. In R. Renggli & J. Tanner (Eds.), *Das Drogenproblem: Geschichte, Erfahrungen und Therapiekonzepte* (pp. 21–122). Berlin, Germany: Springer.

Tschiffely, D. (1936). Die Milch im hauswirtschaftlichen Unterricht. *Schweizer Schule, 22*, 125–127.

Volkart, H. (1902). Der schweiz. Verein abstinenter Lehrerinnen und Lehrer. *Schweizerische Lehrerzeitung, 47*, 262–263.

Waser, H. (1900/1901). Abstinenten-Ecke: Die Schule gegen den Alkohol. *Schweizerische Lehrerinnenzeitung, 5*, 13–16.

Wettbewerb für alkoholgegnerische Heftumschläge. (1930). *Schweizer Schule, 16*, 375.

W. W. (1907). Zur Alkoholfrage. *Schweizerische Lehrerzeitung, 52*, 406–407.

Zollinger, F. (1902). *Bestrebungen auf dem Gebiete der Schulgesundheitspflege und des Kinderschutzes: Bericht an den hohen Bundesrat der schweiz. Eidgenossenschaft über die [an der] Weltausstellung in Paris 1900 gemachten Beobachtungen.* Zurich, Switzerland: Orell Füssli.

Zürcher, R. (1997). *Von Apfelsaft bis Zollifilm: Frauen für die Volksgesundheit.* Hünibach, Switzerland: Schweiz. Bund abstinenter Frauen.

# PART III
# The Internationalization of European Schooling in the Cold War

# 9

# THE IMPLEMENTATION OF PROGRAMMED LEARNING IN SWITZERLAND

*Rebekka Horlacher*

Continuously throughout their history, schooling and teaching have shown a certain methodological and technological inclination. At the beginning of the 19th century it was the Pestalozzi Method that promised to be the most efficient and cost-effective means of educating a growing student population in reading and arithmetic. After only a few years, methods then called the Monitorial System, advanced by Andrew Bell, a Scottish cleric, and Joseph Lancaster, an English Quaker, assumed a similarly promising role. The start of the 20th century saw great educational hopes invested in film and radio; today those hopes reside in newer computer technologies and in E-learning in particular. But the expectations placed in programmed learning and teaching machines were comparatively great—and perhaps even greater—nearly 50 years ago (Cuban, 1986, p. 3; Cuban, 2001, p. 16; Miller, 2004; Jacottet Isenegger, 2008; Bosche & Geiss, 2010).

In July 1963 Carl-Heinz Evers, a German policymaker, Social Democratic Party member, and public school official in Berlin, summarized these expectations in the foreword to a publication released following the First International Conference on Programmed Learning and Teaching Machines. It was no accident that the conference was held in Berlin, as Evers stated in no uncertain terms, for the city endeavored "through cosmopolitan sensibility and an openness to new things to render compellingly visible the virtues of a democratic way of life" (1964, p. vii). Furthermore, Evers asserted, Berlin was firmly convinced that "the great challenge of our time—to provide the ever growing population with an ever improving education—can only be met if the latest scientific and technical knowledge is set in service to the educational process" (p. vii). James B. Conant, a chemist, scientific policymaker, and diplomat, and the honorary chairman of the conference, reached the same conclusion in the published conference proceedings. Conant (1964) compared programmed learning to the invention of the automobile, arguing that the automobile represented far more than a new means of transportation, as the American car industry had given birth to an entirely new urban infrastructure, thereby transforming society as a whole.

These rather euphoric expectations and promises also met with vociferous skepticism, of course. Skeptics feared that the implementation of teaching machines in the classroom would have a fundamentally negative effect on teaching, that the art of instruction would suffer or disappear (Hilgard, 1964, p. xii), and that the "living teacher" would somehow be replaced (Corell, 1969, p. 1). However, at least at this initial stage, objections of this kind were unable to dampen the enthusiasm for emergent technologies and the promise they held for revolutionizing schooling and teaching.

In the post-war era, programmed learning[1] became one of the dominant themes of pedagogy and school development on both sides of the Iron Curtain (Tröhler, 2013). Systems on either side of that divide shared the conviction that "ever mounting and shifting demands," as the highly developed industrial nations viewed them, could be met only by the "adaptation of educational standards and establishments to the changing needs and circumstances of the present and particularly of the future" (Vogt, 1965, p. 9). The challenges identified included the necessity of streamlining a system that was experiencing a sharp increase in the number of students and a concomitant lack of qualified teachers; the fact that there existed a greater amount of relevant educational content relative to earlier eras that needed to be imparted; classroom deficiencies that could be traced back to insufficient knowledge of teacher performance and teaching methodologies; the classroom focus on the teacher rather than the student; the dominance of oral teaching methods; and, finally, the fact that too little weight was given to independent student work (p. 10ff).[2] According to Soviet psychologist Alexei Nikolajewitsch Leontjew and Soviet pedagogue Pjotr Jakowlewitsch Galperin, these challenges could be met not only by "broadened and improved *research related to classroom instruction*" but also "by growth in the scope of application of *mathematical and cybernetic methods*," which is to say through "*programmed learning* and *teaching machines*" (Vogt, 1965, p. 12; see also Leontjew & Galperin, 1969).

If not the "founder" of the concept of programmed learning, American psychologist B. F. (Burrhus Frederic) Skinner is nevertheless one of the critical forefathers of the concepts of behaviorism and cybernetics that underpin it. In a lecture entitled "The Science of Learning and the Art of Teaching," delivered in March 1954 at the conference Current Trends in Psychology and the Behavioral Sciences at the University of Pittsburgh, Skinner articulated what might be considered a "foundational text" of the programmed learning movement. Skinner stated at the outset that the past few years had seen great progress in the field of behavioral research, noting that this had led to "much more effective control of behavior" (1954/1962, p. 18). According to Skinner, this progress was primarily attributable to new experiments that were able to isolate with a greater degree of precision the individual stimuli that brought about a change in behavior. By identifying these stimuli, it would then be possible to subdivide the teaching process into practical component parts, so that each could be better understood, controlled, and imparted to students. Skinner asserted that this approach opened the door to a new understanding of the relationship between psychology and pedagogy and altered the belief that had been predominant since William James' (1899) *Talks to Teachers on Psychology*. James had maintained that no "definite programs and schemes and methods of instruction for immediate schoolroom use" (p. 7) could be derived from psychology as science, governed as it was by the apparently ungovernable law of consciousness. But according to Skinner (1965), experimental behavioral analysis had "produced if not an art at least a technology of teaching from which one can indeed deduce programs and schemes and methods of instruction" (p. 427). Critical to the success of this application of psychological principles to the classroom context would be the articulation of clear objectives, each of which was to be attained in a discrete instructional sequence: "Programming undertakes to reach one goal at a time" (p. 440). More importantly, Skinner stated that classroom instruction should be oriented to "certain other kinds of behavior" and not just the so-called "facts and principles" (p. 441). Moreover, he believed that this ambitious and aspiring young science would have ripple effects that would be felt in "economics, government, law, and even religion" (p. 442).

Thus, experimental psychology not only promised a better basic understanding of learning and teaching processes but also—when paired with appropriate pedagogical programming and teaching methods—offered the possibility of more fully satisfying the ever-growing demands of modern society. Enhanced knowledge of learning and teaching processes would make classroom instruction more efficient in general, thereby also solving the problem posed by a student population that was outgrowing the number of qualified teachers.

This international debate on programmed learning was also taken up in Switzerland. But how, and what were the arguments in the Swiss debate? Who actively took part in the dissemination of the program, how, and to what end? And, lastly, how was programmed learning received among the actual target audience, the teachers? I will explore these questions through specific examination of the Department of Programmed Learning at the Pestalozzianum[3] in Zurich, Switzerland. In the first part of this chapter, I shed light on who first implemented the programmed learning model in Switzerland, specifically in the Canton of Zurich (Switzerland is divided into states, or cantons), as well as the arguments they gave to support it. I then trace the history of the Department of Programmed Learning and what it accomplished up through 1988, when, in collaboration with the Pestalozzianum's continuing education program for teachers, the Department of Computer Science was established. As we will see, this change in name from Programmed Learning to Computer Science reflects a significant change in perspective related to content. It shows how the initial enthusiasm gave way to a particular disillusionment, and how the concept of programmed learning was transformed into a media education project. In the final section, I examine the extent to which we might consider this specific experience with programmed learning typical of efforts to reform Swiss schools or comparable to experiences in other countries.

## The Implementation of Programmed Learning in the Canton of Zurich

In January 1964, only six months after the international conference in Berlin mentioned above, the Pestalozzianum organized a lecture series in collaboration with the Zurich teachers' association (Pestalozzianum, n.d.).[4] Six months later, on July 14, 1964, the Zurich Education Council[5] asked the Pestalozzianum to inquire into the use of technical teaching aids in the classroom (Erziehungsrat, 1964). The council also commissioned the Pestalozzianum to draw up programs specifically tailored to the current material circumstances of the Zurich school system and to test these out in practice. Reports were to be made on the outcomes of these attempts, and a language laboratory was established.[6]

Shortly thereafter, in 1965, the Pestalozzianum offered its first introductory course in programmed learning (Pestalozzianum, 1965; see Schweizerischer Pädagogischer Verband, 1956), which generated a great deal of interest. Educators were now able to learn about and utilize the technology on their own, without relying on outside assistance, foreign or otherwise. That same year, the question of programmed learning was also raised in political debates.[7] Two years after the first major international conference on programmed learning was held in Europe, the matter was regarded as so important that not only were state and local departments established and continuing education courses offered for it, but steering and oversight committees were also formed to monitor the reforms; even at the parliamentary level this educational issue was debated heatedly. The overall judgment acknowledged certain difficulties, which by then were rather well known, such as the time-consuming nature of the work of developing these programs and the considerably limited choices.[8] However, especially the educational administration was convinced that all the experience up to this point demonstrated the programs' efficacy, particularly in certain fields. Industry, or occupational training, seemed the most promising, because there, in contrast to the academic classroom, "the emphasis is not placed on the student's personal development" (Stadtrat Zürich, 1965). In this way, a distinction was drawn between public schooling and vocational training according to the varying requirements each had to fulfill. Whereas upbringing and personal development were given priority in the public schools, vocational training was primarily concerned with imparting and acquiring knowledge, making it ideal for programmed learning applications.

In 1967 the Pestalozzianum offered a continuing education seminar in programming,[9] in collaboration with Brown, Boveri, and Cie, which sent a consultant and an assistant to Zurich. Course participants could actually take a device—called a "promentaboy"—home with them. Detailed minutes of a programming course offered in April 1968 provide concrete information on the content.[10] The four-day course, led by educational psychologist Franz Kollerics of Mannheim, featured a short presentation on the evolution of programmed learning, referring as far back as Comenius and Plato. After defining particular terms, many of them essentially deriving from behaviorist theory, the presentation moved on to discuss possible contemporary applications and to clear up any potential misunderstandings regarding the technology, the purpose of this being to make clear not only the scope of applications but also the enormous potential the method had to offer. Programmed learning was not meant to be used merely as test preparation but was intended to be understood as *education*, or *Bildung, itself* (Horlacher, in press). The method had even produced positive results in "alleviating neurotic disturbances" and had demonstrated some success in so-called problem children and children with brain injuries; "mongoloid children" had even apparently learned to read "with the help of these programs" and were therefore now "mature for schooling" (Hauser, 1968, p. 7). Teaching machines were further presented as a tool properly suited to the modern, industrialized, and engineered world that could be perfectly utilized to prepare students for the changed world that awaited them. In this, the most ardent hopes of the era are clearly expressed, hinged as they are to applied technologies. The technologies were in no way perceived as threatening but rather as liberating, as a release from repetitive, boring, and strenuous work (even within the home); now that machines could perform these tasks neatly, conveniently, and efficiently, more time would be available for leisure (Hauser, 1968, p. 8).

In 1967 Alois Stadlin, prorector of a business school, commented in an annual report on "initial attempts and experiences at our own school" (p. 1). Stadlin, too, mentions programmed learning's origins in behavioral research and both animal and educational psychology, but he also emphasizes that programmed learning might be explained "through the praxis and psychology of the classroom" (p. 1) as well, with reference to its four central tenets: namely, the categorization of educational content, student empowerment, immediate feedback, and personalization of the learning process. A focus on classroom instruction would of course be preserved throughout the process. Programmed learning, beyond offering an alternative to the previously dominant model of teacher-centered instruction, was to supplement rather than replace the personal student–teacher relationship,[11] and it became clear that students, too, needed to get acquainted with the new methods to effectively utilize all that they had to offer (pp. 4–5).

These varied experiences led Stadlin to conclude that programmed learning could be a meaningful method. However, he allowed that one still needed to determine exactly what sort of content might be best imparted in this way; of course, one needed to consider that the students were more quickly fatigued by the concentrated nature of the work, which meant that lessons needed to be kept under 30 or 45 minutes. Nevertheless, Stadlin thought the introduction of programmed learning might free up time and space in the classroom for "educationally effective conversation" (1967, p. 7). The efficiency with which programmed learning conveyed information was its greatest asset, for, according to Stadlin, more time could thus be devoted to "the pedagogical."

## The Department of Programmed Learning Is Established

In 1968, nearly five years after the conference in Berlin, the Zurich Ministry of Education held a press conference on "modern technical teaching aids" (Pestalozzianum, 1968). This was the government's reaction to a series of articles published in the Zurich daily newspaper, the *Tages-Anzeiger*, criticizing the canton's lack of a proper educational research center; this was connected with the fear that the Zurich school would lag behind in teaching improvements. The aim of the press conference was not just to brief the community on programmed learning. A presentation on audio-visual learning processes was also offered, reports were made on experiments currently underway in the schools, interested parties were invited to tour a language laboratory, and the press was given the opportunity to take part in a programmed learning course.

Before the conference, a meeting took place between the editor of the newspaper, Rolf Lerf; the Pestalozzianum's director, Hans Wymann; and Max Gubler, a member of the Zurich Education Council and later director of the Zurich Teachers' Training College. On the agenda were options for implementing programmed learning in the city's schools, with particular reference to the difference between developments happening around the globe and their realization on a national level. In an interview, Gubler noted the rapid dissemination of programmed learning throughout the United States, which at least in part compensated for the country's egregious teacher shortage. One negative consequence of this aspect of programmed learning's success, however, was that it reinforced the popular bias that it would replace teachers altogether. According to Gubler, the question now arose as to how and under what conditions the American model might be imported and adapted to conditions pertinent to Swiss schools (cited in Lerf, 1968, p. 3). The series of newspaper articles mentioned above provoked criticism from readers, mainly teachers, who feared a decline in focus on educating the "whole person" and a deterioration of learning and teaching to the mere provision and acquisition of information (p. 8). With this, the debate on programmed learning broadened into a debate on "correct" concepts of schools and curricula.

Stadlin was one of many voices addressing the fears expressed in the newspapers. In an article printed in the magazine of the association of commercial employees, *Schweizerisches Kaufmännisches Zentralblatt*, Stadlin (1968) pointed out that programmed learning could not replace teachers and that in recent years the concept had developed from a small, isolated idea, reminiscent of behavioral psychology and conditioning, into what he termed "learning through insight." This evolution, he wrote, was due in large part to the influence of Gestalt psychology, which delineates "greater, more challenging steps in the learning process," as opposed to "merely verbal or blind-associative learning." In support of his argument, he cited the paragon of Swiss education, Johann Heinrich Pestalozzi, and Pestalozzi's concept of "elementarizing." Now, as then, the concern was to craft a "more stable" and therefore more successful teaching method; in doing so, instruction would necessarily be bound to eternal laws, as Pestalozzi would have it, or to science, as was the case when Stadlin was making his argument. In both cases, however, what remained unresolved was the problem of selecting the appropriate materials. The issue could be addressed only from a "methodological" and, more crucially, a "pedagogical point of view." Here Stadlin made it abundantly clear that fears concerning "mechanized" teaching were wholly unfounded. Programmed learning did not make mindless machines of students and teachers: The primacy of pedagogy in the curricula and the schools remained intact, and technology functioned to serve pedagogy rather than overrule it.

This defense of programmed learning did not go uncontested. Wolfgang von Wartburg (1968), a historian and *Gymnasium* teacher, issued an adamant critique of programmed learning, charging that, despite all modifications or reforms it may have undergone since its inception, the concept was still causally linked to and confined by the idea of conditioning, that it was little more than propaganda, and that, because it styled itself as "better" and "more efficient," it was exerting a debilitating effect on the deeply valued methodological freedom of the classroom. The separation between knowledge acquisition and educational upbringing that programmed learning proposed was utterly ill conceived, as, according to Wartburg, "the first principle of every humanistic education is that the two must constitute an inseparable whole." This principle of his was grounded not in educational content or organization but rather in moral conviction and expressed skepticism with respect to learning that was not uncharacteristic of debate on the issue in the German-speaking world: "Real and effective *education* does not take place until the teacher personally shapes and brings the *material knowledge* to life; and *knowledge* likewise can be imparted if and only if it is transformed—personalized and brought to life—into an agent of *education*, which is to say, of character building."

This dispute makes clear the battle lines separating the critics and the proponents of the new method. While one side waved the flag of modernity, progress, science, and the future, the other side stood in defense of personality, affinity, and holism. The debate thus not only came back around to the question posed by William James, as to whether useful teaching methods might be derived from psychology or whether teaching was an art of its own, but also vividly demonstrated the divergent conceptions of engineering and technology. Whereas the one side conceived of technology as an educational support, the other saw it as little more than an educational threat.

Despite the ideological debate and the divergent views on engineering and technology, more and more teachers were getting trained in programming, a number of Zurich communities were looking into establishing language laboratories, and teaching materials were being developed for programmed learning. Be that as it may, a persistent topic in the wider discussion on programmed learning remained the lack of appropriate teaching materials. Moreover, the number of initiatives, experiments, and individually undertaken activities was increasing, making some kind of general coordination all the more desirable. To this end, at the start of the 1970s the Department of Programmed Learning decided to publish a bulletin (Pestalozzianum Zürich & Pädagogische Arbeitsstelle, 1970) that would enable "reciprocal knowledge exchange" and that would be "oriented to addressing individual issues in connection with the development, testing, and implementation of learning programs" (*PU-Bulletin* No. 1, p. 1). Further bulletins appeared at irregular intervals thereafter, reporting on the latest trends, educational conferences (*PU-Bulletin* No. 2), and activities within the department. And so we can see that the initial euphoria about the new method had given way to a more realistic estimation of the possibilities programmed learning had to offer, that useful programs were in short supply, and that the concept of programmed learning, however widely known, was still rarely practiced (*PU-Bulletin* No. 3). And increasingly the talk was turning away from programmed learning and towards computer-supported teaching (*PU-Bulletin* No. 4).

## From Programmed Learning to Media Education

In February 1972 the Society for Teaching and Learning Methods was established. Its mission was to address issues pertinent to programmed and computer-assisted learning as well as to other media in use in the classroom (Gesellschaft für Lehr- und Lernmethoden, 1972). Participants at the founding meeting consisted not only of faculty and school administrators: Scientists and scholars were also delegated to represent private industry, and several members of the military took part. The projects that this new society would initiate represented a clear shift away from the classical model of programmed learning and towards an educational model supported by a variety of technical aids such as computers and television.[12] An article in the *PU-Bulletin* (No. 7, p. 1) reflected the trend:

> The time is now past for any further debate on programmed learning replacing teachers or on the complete automatization of the classroom . . . No one believes in the absolute authority of programmed learning anymore. We've long since realized that this is merely one of many possible methods in the repertoire available to our schools.[13]

Programmed learning was being redefined, as the Society for Programmed Instruction confirmed at its annual conference in Wiesbaden, Germany, in 1974. At the conference, titled Media as a Partner, it was made evident that henceforth discussion would have to center on how media in general might be most sensibly utilized in the classroom. In this way, past mistakes made in the implementation of programmed learning might be avoided, such as the inordinate faith that had been invested in programmed learning, which of course had only led to extreme disappointment and complete renunciation of the concept (*PU-Bulletin* No. 8, p. 7). In Switzerland, this new, broader term "media" encompassed computer-assisted learning, even as it had before the conference (*PU-Bulletin* No. 3, p. 2). By the mid-1970s computer-assisted learning had already established itself as one possibility among a variety of instructional methods; of these, none were deified or demonized in and of themselves but were in fact being pragmatically applied to particular classroom circumstances.[14]

In 1980 one of the biggest, most well-known German textbook publishing houses announced that they would cease publishing programming-related teaching materials, at which point the Department of Programmed Learning was forced to consider, more or less seriously, whether its own work would soon be hopelessly outdated (*PU-Bulletin* No. 21, p. 1). Nonetheless, Christian Rohrbach, author of the article and head of the department, pointed out a key difference between Germany and Switzerland in how each dealt with programmed learning, as notably less discussion was devoted to programmed learning in Switzerland compared to Germany. According to Rohrbach, Germany remained mired in ideological debate, whereas the Swiss were taking a more pragmatic approach to reform. The difference in approaches may offer an explanation as to why programmed learning was in fact able to assert itself in Switzerland as a pedagogically feasible option. The Swiss expected less of the method, Rohrbach continued, so their disappointment with it was proportionally less acute. He went on to distinguish between the pedagogical and the educational—the pedagogical being understood as restricted to the practical structuring of concrete classroom scenarios, whereas the educational remained linked in the imagination to fantasies of rescue and salvation—arguing thus that programmed learning in Switzerland had only ever been regarded from a pedagogical point of view.

For whatever reason, the Department of Programmed Learning continued to grow in popularity among teachers in the Canton of Zurich and—as it was the only department of its kind in the country—among teachers throughout German-speaking Switzerland (Schweizerische Koordinationsstelle für Bildungsforschung, 1980, p. 3). The department continued to publish programmed teaching materials, and then, in 1983, it even offered a *demonstration program on programmed learning*. The following year the personal computer and its use in the classroom became a topic in the ongoing discussion on programmed learning (*PU-Bulletin* No. 27, p. 3), and just one year after that, in 1985, the first programmed teaching aid appeared specifically concerning the computer (*Wie ein Computer funktioniert* [How a computer works]). In the book the talk was now of "computer science," and the *PU-Bulletin* even changed its name to include a "c" in the acronym—*PcU-Bulletin*—further evidence that computers and computer science had become the new core concern of the former Department of Programmed Learning. The department consequently turned its attention to putting together handouts on LOGO, an educational programming language. Over the course of the next five years, a definitive transformation took place, turning the former Department of Programmed Learning into the Department of Computer Science and into a site concerned with deploying new media in the public schools.

This reorientation is reflected in later editions of the *PcU-Bulletin*, which continued to be published through 1993. It became more and more obvious that the many and varied applications of new media had superseded programmed learning (*PcU-Bulletin* No. 28, p. 2) and that the new role of the department would be one of mediator between teachers and the latest advances in computer science. The final *PcU-Bulletin* plainly states this reorientation, not only declaring the publication's own realignment but also informing its readership that the department would now carry on its earlier work in the field of media and communications (*PcU-Bulletin* No. 39, p. 1).

## A Typical Example of Educational Reform?

We cannot say conclusively whether or not the implementation of programmed learning in the Canton of Zurich might be considered characteristic of how schools in general deal with innovation and reform. More than a single case study would be required for that (see, e.g., Bosche, 2013). With a view to the question of the national and the international in schooling, however, we can say a number of things: first, that an international conference on programmed learning was the impetus behind the activities that began to take place in Zurich, yet quickly thereafter Swiss sovereignty and individuality—which is to say the sovereignty and individuality of the Swiss schools—came to the fore. Swiss schools certainly benefited from a global exchange of ideas in their practical application—and, above all, in the practical introduction of teaching materials and pedagogical practice—but there was a need to adapt them to local contexts for real student benefits. This fact is evident in the repeated complaints made concerning the high production costs of teaching materials, which is why so few were available, most of them "foreign."

I might also say a few words concerning how the arguments on programmed learning unfolded quite differently in Switzerland and Germany. The arguments in the bulletins issued by the Department of Programmed Learning reveal a fundamental difference between the Swiss and the German systems in their relationship to innovation and reform. The Germans tended more towards a discussion of concepts at the ideological or categorical level, and the Swiss focus was more pragmatic, inquiring as to whether method A or material B would be more or less functional in the classroom. If so, the method or material would be applied; if not, it would be rejected.

Nonetheless, ideological questions were not entirely absent from the more pragmatic Swiss debate. Whether the new method would prove to be a blessing or a curse for teaching, education, and schooling was also up for discussion—a discussion that accompanied each and every technological innovation that happened there. And just as every new method was understood by one side to be a comprehensive solution, for the other side it heralded calamity. This was true not only with regard to programmed learning. Indeed, the topic of new media in the classroom has triggered an equally fractious debate. However, these debates reveal less about any given method than they speak to the habitual tendency of pedagogy and education to put itself in the position of a cure-all for society's ills, thereby casting every new method as either a panacea or pest, take your pick.

## Notes

1. Programmed learning refers here to any pedagogical setting that is formulated based on clearly delineated stages of learning, offers immediate feedback to the student, and can be implemented largely without direct support from a teacher.
2. In the United States in particular there was staunch and ardent support for the inclusion of the natural sciences in the curriculum, and the reforms that were being fought over were aimed at remedying technological backwardness, which the successful Soviet Sputnik project had made drastically apparent to the American public and which in turn effected an increased awareness of the state of scientific instruction in U.S. schools.
3. The Pestalozzianum, a primarily state-funded foundation dedicated to continuing education for teachers, was for a long time mainly a library and resource center for teachers; since the 1950s, with the support of the Zurich Education Council, it has been entrusted with the development, implementation, and supervision of new teaching materials and methods (Horlacher, 2009). In doing so, the Pestalozzianum has played an academic supporting role for educational administrations in Switzerland, which in the 1950s and 1960s were still extremely small. The administrations handle in particular the financial aspects of the educational system and some organizational aspects, among them curriculum development (see Tröhler, 2008; Horlacher & De Vincenti, 2014, pp. 483–488).
4. Issue 24 (1964) of the *Schweizerische Lehrerzeitung* [Swiss teachers' journal] contained another article on the subject of programmed learning by Fred W. Schmid (1964), accompanied by a short piece by Hans Biäsch (1962/1964) and a piece on teaching machines by Hans Wenke (1963/1964). A report by M. Rychner on the Berlin conference in July 1963 also made its way into print (Rychner, 1964). We may assume that the content of these articles was similar to that discussed in the Pestalozzianum lecture series. Each article was conceived with the intention of easing any fears the teachers may have had regarding the idea of machines or technology in the classroom and furthermore of convincing them of the advantages offered by these new methods, without at the same time overindulging in blind enthusiasm or failing to recognize existing (or persisting) problems.
5. The founding of the Zurich Education Council dates back to a recommendation by Philipp Albert Stapfer, minister for science and art in the Helvetic Republic; Stapfer established it in 1798, following the French model. Council members were to be appointed by the government, but various interest groups also had the right to make recommendations. In many Swiss cantons, the education council is now one of the few institutions remaining from the period of the Helvetic Republic. Today the education councils are mainly responsible for curriculum and textbooks, regulations, and coordination of the schools.
6. That same October, the Schulwarte in the Canton of Bern—an institution comparable to the Pestalozzianum in Zurich for continuing teacher education—organized a national

conference with the aim to broaden awareness of programmed learning, debate its relative advantages and disadvantages, and develop strategies for the future. A further goal was to launch an educational organization to survey the field and advise on related issues in an independent manner, free from the influence of publishers or other interest groups. The initiative itself was in a sense an expression of a widespread unease, stirrings of which could already be felt at the conference in Berlin. The unease was related to the need for change, because programmed learning—or, more precisely, the teaching materials and teaching machines it required—was simply not going to manufacture itself. It quickly became clear that publishers and commercial business interests were going to play an important role in implementing and disseminating this new method, just as it also became evident that major American and German publishers might be the only ones in a position to do so. Swiss educational policymakers therefore feared "foreignization," or excessive foreign influence in schools, which would expose a critical distance between developments on a global level and the implementation of change at a local one.

7. In an interpellation dated September 23, 1965, the head of the Zurich faction of the Free Democratic Party (Freisinnig Demokratische Partei), Magnus Wolfensberger, asked the Zurich school council (*Schulvorstand*) what sort of "significance" he might attribute "to programmed learning and the future development of teaching methods" and inquired whether the council, "in light of a possible adaptation of these methods to the conditions of our classrooms," was prepared to "support and facilitate, where necessary, these attempts in the city of Zurich."

8. That certain obstacles stood in the way of implementing programmed learning in Zurich's public schools is also attested to in the correspondence that took place between Hans Wymann, director of the Pestalozzianum, and various publishing houses and other vendors of teaching machines and learning programs. However, here the discussion focused more on technical problems than on skepticism regarding the method as such. Wymann's exchange with the Heidelberg branch of Brown, Boveri & Cie (today the ABB Group)—the company responsible for the production, sales, and distribution of teaching machines in the German-speaking world—details the challenges that had to be overcome before these machines would be field-tested and sufficiently well engineered to be ready for mass production.

9. The Pestalozzianum not only sought to further educate teachers in programming but also planned to partner with local schools to execute and evaluate learning programs (see Pädagogische Arbeitsstelle, 1967). It was in contact, for instance, with trade schools that were likewise actively grappling with the issue and that had formed their own network with members from the Federal Office for Industry, Trade, and Labor (Bundesamt für Industrie, Gewerbe und Arbeit, as of 1998 the State Secretariat for Economics, Staatssekretariat für Wirtschaft) and the Swiss Federal Institute of Technology Zurich. These schools were likewise engaged in realizing teaching efforts of their own.

10. The demand for this course was also very high. Although two sessions were held, many teachers had to be put off until the course could be offered again at a later date. Interest in the new method was still quite considerable. Moreover, an analysis done following the session was positive, indicating that the participants felt they would profit quite a bit from it.

11. The mercantile union business school's forays into programmed learning were primarily motivated by earlier, particularly Swiss models; the Institute for Pedagogy at the Technical University of Aachen is the only institution outside of Switzerland that was mentioned by name.

12. The Society for Teaching and Learning Methods (Gesellschaft für Lehr- und Lernmethoden) also reached out to the Fribourg Task Force on Curriculum (Arbeitsgruppe für Curriculum), which was founded at around the same time and was committed to implementing the American curriculum studies in Switzerland (see Horlacher & De Vincenti, 2014, p. 483).
13. In the very same year (1972), the Commission of the European Communities entrusted the European Institute for Professional Training in Paris with an examination of the overall situation concerning programmed learning. The results of the inquiry were more or less the same as in Switzerland (Commission of the European Communities, 1972). The main advantages were seen as less study time needed for the same results, better individual performance, greater homogeneity of results, and the fact that programmed learning was a way to handle the shortage of trained teachers (p. 2). This last point was not a great problem (or the subject of great discussion) in Switzerland.
14. This moderate approach is evinced by assorted bulletins in which can be found frequent and various references to and reviews of new programs; further evidence can be found in the relatively high number of requests made to the Pestalozzianum for textbooks available from their library.

## References

Biäsch, H. (1964). Vom Anlernen zum programmierten Lernen. *Schweizerische Lehrerzeitung*, *109*(24), 736–737. (First published 1962)

Bosche, A. (2013). *Schulreformen steuern: Die Einführung neuer Lehrmittel und Schulfächer an der Volksschule (Kanton Zürich, 1960er- bis 1980er-Jahre)*. Bern, Switzerland: hep.

Bosche, A., & Geiss, M. (2010). Das Sprachlabor—Steuerung und Sabotage eines Unterrichtsmittels im Kanton Zürich, 1963–1976. In Sektion Historische Bildungsforschung der Deutsche Gesellschaft für Erziehungwissenschaft (DGfE) (Ed.), *Jahrbuch für Historische Bildungsforschung* (Vol. 16, pp. 119–139). Bad Heilbrunn, Germany: Klinkhardt.

Commission of the European Communities. (1972, March). *Programmed teaching in the European Community*. Information [Social Policy] 10/72. [EU Commission—brochure]. Brussels, Belgium: European Communities. Retrieved from http://aei.pitt.edu/id/eprint/7637/

Conant, J. B. (1964). Address of welcome. In Pädagogische Arbeitsstelle/Sekretariat Pädagogisches Zentrum (Eds.), *Bericht Internationale Konferenz Programmierter Unterricht und Lehrmaschinen, 9.–15. Juli 1963* (pp. ix–x). Berlin, Germany: Franz Cornelsen.

Corell, W. (1969). Einleitung. In W. Corell (Ed.), *Zur Theorie und Praxis des programmierten Lernen* (pp. 1–13). Darmstadt, Germany: Wissenschaftliche Buchgesellschaft.

Cuban, L. (1986). *Teachers and machines: The classroom use of technology since 1920*. New York, NY: Teachers College.

Cuban, L. (2001). *Oversold and underused: Computers in the classroom*. Cambridge, MA: Harvard University Press.

Erziehungsrat des Kantons Zürich. (1964, July 14). *Technische Hilfen im Unterricht, Beschluss*. Nachlass Wymann (Fachstelle Programmierter Unterricht, 2). Forschungsbibliothek Pestalozzianum Zürich, Zurich, Switzerland.

Evers, C.-H. (1964). Vorwort—Preface. In Pädagogische Arbeitsstelle/Sekretariat Pädagogisches Zentrum (Eds.), *Bericht Internationale Konferenz Programmierter Unterricht und Lehrmaschinen, 9.–15. Juli 1963* (pp. vii–viii). Berlin, Germany: Franz Cornelsen.

Gesellschaft für Lehr- und Lernmethoden. (1972, February 5). *Programm der konstituierenden Generalversammlung*. Nachlass Wymann (Fachstelle Programmierter Unterricht, 53). Forschungsbibliothek Pestalozzianum Zürich, Zurich, Switzerland.
Hauser, M. (1968). *Programmierkurs, Protokoll*. Nachlass Wymann (Fachstelle Programmierter Unterricht, 19). Forschungsbibliothek Pestalozzianum Zürich, Zurich, Switzerland.
Hilgard, E. R. (1964). Introduction. In Pädagogische Arbeitsstelle/Sekretariat Pädagogisches Zentrum (Eds.), *Bericht Internationale Konferenz Programmierter Unterricht und Lehrmaschinen, 9.–15. Juli 1963* (pp. xi–xvi). Berlin, Germany: Franz Cornelsen.
Horlacher, R. (2009). Von der Geschichte der Pädagogik zur Historischen Bildungsforschung: Das Pestalozzianum zwischen Universität und Lehrerseminar. In M. Caruso, H. Kemnitz, & J.-W. Link (Eds.), *Orte der Bildungsgeschichte* (pp. 221–236). Bad Heilbrunn, Germany: Klinkhardt.
Horlacher, R. (in press). Bildung *or the cultural conceptualizing of education: German origins and international misunderstandings*. New York, NY: Routledge.
Horlacher, R., & De Vincenti, A. (2014). From rationalist autonomy to scientific empiricism: A history of curriculum in Switzerland. In W. F. Pinar (Ed.), *International handbook of curriculum research* (pp. 476–492). New York, NY: Routledge.
Jacottet Isenegger, D. (2008). Unterrichtstechnologien und moderne Schule. In C. Crotti & F. Osterwalder (Eds.), *Das Jahrhundert der Schulreformen: Internationale und nationale Perspektiven, 1900–1950* (pp. 369–385). Bern, Switzerland: Haupt.
James, W. (1899). *Talks to teachers on psychology and to students on some of life's ideals*. New York, NY: Henry Holt.
Leontjew, A. N., & Galperin, P. J. (1969). Die Theorie des Kenntniserwerbs und der programmierte Unterricht. In W. Corell (Ed.), *Zur Theorie und Praxis des programmierten Lernen* (pp. 108–123). Darmstadt, Germany: Wissenschaftliche Buchgesellschaft.
Lerf, R. (1968). *Die Vorbereitungen sind in vollem Gange*. Nachlass Wymann (Fachstelle Programmierter Unterricht, 20.) Forschungsbibliothek Pestalozzianum Zürich, Zurich, Switzerland.
Miller, D. (2004). Die *Reusability* pädagogischer Aspirationen und ihre Potenzierung durch technologische Innovationen. *Zeitschrift für pädagogische Historiographie, 10*(1), 10–15.
Pädagogische Arbeitsstelle. (1967). *Antwort auf Interpellation Oehrli betr. technischer Unterrichtshilfen*. Nachlass Wymann (Fachstelle Programmierter Unterricht, 13). Forschungsbibliothek Pestalozzianum Zürich, Zurich, Switzerland.
Pestalozzianum. (1965, April 22). *Brief an die Teilnehmer des Einführungskurses in das Programmieren* [Letter]. Nachlass Wymann (Fachstelle Programmierter Unterricht, 5). Forschungsbibliothek Pestalozzianum Zürich, Zurich, Switzerland.
Pestalozzianum. (1968, March 27). *Einladung zur Pressekonferenz vom 16. April*. Nachlass Wymann (Fachstelle Programmierter Unterricht, 20). Forschungsbibliothek Pestalozzianum Zürich, Zurich, Switzerland.
Pestalozzianum. (n.d.). Einladungskarte [Invitation announcement]. Nachlass Wymann (Fachstelle Programmierter Unterricht, 1). Forschungsbibliothek Pestalozzianum Zürich, Zurich, Switzerland.
Pestalozzianum Zürich & Pädagogische Arbeitsstelle (Eds.). (1970–1993). *PU-Bulletin* [Periodical]. Zurich, Switzerland: Pestalozzianum Foundation.
Rychner, M. (1964). Berliner Konferenz für programmierten Unterricht und Lehrmaschinen Juli 1963. *Schweizerische Lehrerzeitung, 109*(24), 739–744.
Schmid, F. W. (1964). Der programmierte Unterricht zwischen Forschungslabor und Klassenzimmer. *Schweizerische Lehrerzeitung, 109*(24), 725–735.

Schweizerische Koordinationsstelle für Bildungsforschung. (1980). *Permanente Erhebung über Bildungsforschungsprojekte, Nr. 80:013*. Aarau, Switzerland: Schweizerische Koordinationsstelle für Bildungsforschung.

Schweizerischer Pädagogischer Verband (SPV). (1965). *Jahresbericht* [Annual report]. Schulgeschichte (SPV II,2). Forschungsbibliothek Pestalozzianum Zürich, Zurich, Switzerland.

Skinner, B. F. (1962). The science of learning and the art of teaching. In W. I. Smith & J. W. Moore (Eds.), *Programmed learning: Theory and research, an enduring problem in psychology* (18–33). Princeton, NJ: Van Nostrand. (First published 1954)

Skinner, B. F. (1965). The technology of teaching. *Proceedings of the Royal Society of London Series B, Biological Sciences, 162*(989), 427–443. doi:10.1098/rspb.1965.0048

Stadlin, A. (1967). *Der programmierte Unterricht: Erste Versuche und Erfahrungen an unserer Schule* [Draft of annual report]. Nachlass Wymann (Fachstelle Programmierter Unterricht, 17). Forschungsbibliothek Pestalozzianum Zürich, Zurich, Switzerland.

Stadlin, A. (1968, June 14). Missverständnisse um den programmierten Unterricht. *Schweizerisches Kaufmännisches Zentralblatt, 24*, 7.

Stadtrat Zürich. (1965). *Auszug aus dem Protokoll vom 29. Oktober 1965*. Nachlass Wymann (Fachstelle Programmierter Unterricht, 6). Forschungsbibliothek Pestalozzianum Zürich, Zurich, Switzerland.

Tröhler, D. (2008). Verwaltung und Aufsicht der Zürcher Volksschule. In D. Tröhler & U. Hardegger (Eds.), *Zukunft bilden: Die Geschichte der modernen Zürcher Volksschule* (pp. 54–68). Zurich, Switzerland: NZZ Libro.

Tröhler, D. (2013). The technocratic momentum after 1945, the development of teaching machines, and sobering results. *Journal of Educational Media, Memory, and Society, 5*(2), 1–19.

Vogt, H. (1965). *Programmierter Unterricht und Lehrmaschinen an Hoch- und Fachschulen der Sowjetunion*. Munich, Germany: Manz.

Wartburg, W. von (1968). Notwendige Bemerkungen zum Problem des Programmierten Unterrichts. *Schweizerisches Kaufmännisches Zentralblatt, 33*, 5.

Wenke, H. (1964). Lehrmaschinen. *Schweizerische Lehrerzeitung, 109*(24), 737–738. (First published 1963)

Wolfensberger, M. (1965, September 23). *Interpellation an den Schulvorstand der Stadt Zürich, 23. September 1965*. Nachlass Wymann (Fachstelle Programmierter Unterricht, 6). Forschungsbibliothek Pestalozzianum Zürich, Zurich, Switzerland.

# 10

## GLOBAL COMPARISON AND NATIONAL APPLICATION

Polls as a Means for Improving Teacher Education and Stabilizing the School System in Cold War Germany

*Norbert Grube*

In the 19th century, the rise of the nation state was greatly affected by the use of statistics (Osterhammel, 2009, p. 60). The surveying of an extended area was intended to help with and prepare for the development of the national territory, and statistics were used to describe and legitimate new frontiers. Furthermore, especially in the United States in the early 20th century, statistics developed into a new tool to gauge popular attitudes, media consumption, consumerism, and the acceptance of values and norms in a complex society. By defining these values as national values, poll statistics helped engineer the national average. This average enabled norms to be set about what is right or wrong, especially because the polls' audience used the average as a point of reference and comparison for its own attitudes. In this sense, the statistical average might have affected the self-orientation of the public and reinforced the adoption of the norms of what was perceived as the majority and the rejection of certain opinions of the assumed minority (Igo, 2007; Converse, 2009). Although the results of opinion polls were also published with the aim to hold a mirror up to the public, they were much more frequently used to predict voters' political preferences and interests and thereby to gain political power through targeted election campaigns. Foremost, polls were used to prepare preventive national social policy (Foucault, 2004, pp. 188, 191, 197–201). They were a means of improving the efficiency of governmental interventions and decisions in the context of the national welfare state. In the global competition between the nation states, governments, entrepreneurs, managers, and scientists legitimized their need for statistics on the population by asserting the necessity of efficient utilization of human resources and human capital. In particular, motivation, willingness, and ability to work have been the focus of social inquiries since the late 19th century (Oberschall, 1997). The relationship between nutrition, reproduction, family life, health, working conditions, and crime has stood at the center of sometimes implicitly racist social surveys. Around the beginning of the 20th century, it was eugenic beliefs and propaganda that encouraged the gauging of the people and the use of statistics to define the population as a racial corpus. A highly illustrative example of the early adaptation and application of statistical methods is the global temperance movement, which carried out surveys on drinking habits and used targeted abstinence propaganda that addressed individual target groups, such as teachers, workers, or criminals (Grube & De Vincenti, 2013). Frequently, the consequence of these surveys was the demand for increased and intensified education.

In this chapter, I analyze the connection between polls and educational policy. I focus on one of the oldest poll agencies in Germany: the Allensbach Institute of Public Opinion Research, which was founded in 1947 by Elisabeth Noelle-Neumann (1916–2010) (Viswanath, 1996). In the 1950s and 1960s the Allensbach Institute performed polls on behalf of the Baden-Württemberg ministry of education. In Germany, school policy is the responsibility of the state governments, and this case study of Baden-Württemberg provides the opportunity to reflect on national debates over educational reforms. In my analysis of the Allensbach polls, I concentrate on four aspects: first, the motivation behind the new West German government's use of polls as a new globally applied tool for surveying popular attitudes towards schools during the Cold War; second, polls' presentation of national coherence through the monitoring of popular support for educational policies; third, the legitimation of school reforms using polls; and, fourth, the role that polls played in combating the teacher shortage.

## Public Opinion Polls as a Means of Re-education, Governmental Spin-Doctoring, and Monitoring of Educational Policy in West Germany in the 1950s

In Germany, survey research was implemented in the context of post-war re-education. The Allied governments, especially the Office of Military Government, United States, used polls and quantitative methods to observe the process of democratization in West Germany (Weischer, 2004). The pollsters legitimized their methods with the promise of efficient planning and organization of the process of political re-education. "Make the world [or at least West Germany] safe for democracy"—this lofty global goal, which U.S. President Woodrow Wilson proclaimed in the aftermath of the First World War—served as a legitimization for the utilization of empirical social research in the Unites States but also particularly for opinion polls in post-war Western Europe after 1945 (Crespi, 1952). In the context of the post-war promises of peace, democracy, and welfare, polls became a tool of political planning in the Western world—and this in spite of a number of controversial debates concerning their legitimacy. Although most of the idealistic goals of democratic re-education failed, polls to survey the West German population became established (Kruke, 2007). Since the 1950s they have contributed towards construing the population of West Germany as a single political body. The goal of survey research was to support the process of democratization and reconstruction by gauging the population's knowledge of the political and economic system and of the government's policy and reputation. Generating knowledge about the public sphere was regarded as an important prerequisite for the establishment of national cohesion against the perceived powerful Bolshevist collective in the bipolar conflict of the Cold War.

Against this ideological and political backdrop, schools were assigned a central role in the endeavor to create a new generation of democratic citizens who would believe in capitalism, entrepreneurship, hard work, the social welfare state, and a national parliamentarian system. The social researchers were to find out whether the schools were fulfilling their mission of political education. An even more important expectation placed on social researchers was to undertake survey-based research into the relationship between parents and school education—on parents' expectations of the schools, their concerns, and their hopes for the future. Analogously to the Gallup Institute in the Unites States since the 1930s (Tyack & Cuban, 2001, pp. 13, 49), post-war polls in West Germany were intended to gauge the population's agreement and satisfaction with the schools (Noelle & Neumann, 1956, p. 223). However, such polls not only resulted from ambitions to monitor and optimize educational reforms but were also used, particularly in the context of elections, to cater to the opinion of the majority of the public. In 1953, a federal election year in West Germany, the Christian Democratic Party commissioned the Allensbach Institute to survey parents' attitudes towards schools. The poll report revealed widespread reservations about schools, or rather about educational bureaucracy (Institut für Demoskopie Allensbach [IfD]-Report 276, 1953, pp. 1–2). The respondents also rejected denominational schools and were in favor of nondenominational Christian schools. The pollsters advised the Christian Democrats to take these results into account to increase their reelection chances (IfD-Report 578, 1957, p. 13).

However, the surveys on the public acceptance of educational policies were not used only as a means to ensure what was known as triumphant election campaigns. Polls were also widely regarded as an important tool for the mobilization of human resources in the Cold War era, and in this context they represented a basis for preparing for improvements in the school education system. In the 1960s, in almost every Western European nation, ministries of education, entrepreneurs, managers, and trade associations demanded better exploitation of human capital and talents, particularly with regard to rural areas (Dahrendorf, 1965, p. 31; Posch, 1967; Friedeburg, 1992, p. 348). In Germany, managers of large corporations, such as the chemical company BASF and the industrial companies Mannesmann, Siemens, and Bosch, together with sociologists, such as Theodor W. Adorno (1903–1969) and Elisabeth Noelle-Neumann of the Allensbach Institute, and pedagogues, such as Georg Picht (1913–1982), initiated what was known as the *Ettlinger Kreis* (Ettlinger circle) (Sauer, 1999; Bergmann, 2002). This informal group called for science-based educational planning and for the efficient implementation of reforms. The reforms were seen as a means of achieving a technological and educational lead over the Eastern Bloc (Bergmann, 2002, p. 121; Conze, 2009, p. 244; Tröhler, 2010). Commissioned by the Ettlinger circle, the Allensbach Institute surveyed parents' support for school reforms in the late 1950s (IfD-Report 645, 1958), such as the proposed extension of the number of years of school education, improved English lessons, an increase in the number of secondary school pupils, and improvement of vocational education to meet the demands of the technological and chemical industries. In the report they submitted to the Ettlinger circle, the Allensbach pollsters pointed out that two fifths of the parents wished to send their children to university preparatory upper secondary school (*Gymnasium*), but only a quarter of the parents indicated that their children actually attended upper secondary school (IfD-Report 645, 1958, p. 22). The reason for this difference between educational ambitions and the reality in West Germany in the 1950s was seen as the cultural gap between teachers at upper secondary schools, who predominantly belonged to the upper middle class, and most working-class parents (pp. 30–32). The issue was that working-class parents were concerned about their children being disadvantaged because of their unfamiliarity with the habits and language of the upper middle-class teachers. Similar concerns had existed in the United States in the 1940s (Tyack & Cuban, 2001, p. 24). Although demands for equal educational opportunities were popular at the time, this perceived gap between teachers and parents increased the proletarian parents' distance from school education (IfD-Report 645, 1958, p. 63).

The pollsters' inquiry into how one could mobilize people and increase their commitment to educational progress (IfD-Report 645, 1958, p. 46) was picked up by German ministers of education, including Wilhelm Hahn (1909–1996) in Baden-Württemberg. A few years later, in the mid-1960s, Hahn implemented a development plan for the schools. Hahn, a former professor of Lutheran theology and president of the University of Heidelberg, was a supporter of modern and neo-liberal conservatism (Friedeburg, 1992, pp. 340, 352–354; Gass-Bolm, 2005, p. 241). Hahn and his assistant secretary of state, Paul Harro Piazolo (1926–2000), were the main supporters of the plans of the German Science Council. The two politicians founded numerous research groups, whose members included Georg Picht,[1] Elisabeth Noelle-Neumann, sociologist Ralph Dahrendorf, and pedagogue Andreas Flitner. To a certain extent, this was the same group of people who were involved in the Ettlinger circle.

Hahn believed in school education as a tool of preventive and future-oriented population policy (Foucault, 2004) by the welfare state, aimed at creating self-dependent, skilled, and responsible citizens as well as promoting popular involvement in common welfare and political participation. Simultaneously, Hahn's support of these neo-liberal premises was also aimed at gaining support and affirmation for the existing political system and government. In Hahn's opinion, education was a weapon in the Cold War. As is illustrated by a newspaper article published in the *Stuttgarter Zeitung* in November 1960, "Superior Teachers Won the War" (cited in Conze, 2009, p. 244), this was a popular point of view at the time. The article emphasized that with its 2.4 million teachers and 104,000 professors, the Soviet Union was much better prepared for the Cold War than was West Germany, where the universities had only 200,000 students and 9,000 lecturers. The article declared a state of alarm and asserted that a nation requires many academics "if it will be strong." Hahn (1968, p. xiii) picked up on such statements and reproduced the deep faith in education as an instrument of prosperity, social balance, and harmony, or even national cohesion. For Hahn, education was a key factor for improving efficiency and achieving success and optimal performance. He believed that it was the quality of education that decided whether or not "we win the competition between opposing social systems and what place we will attain among other cultural and economic nations" (cited in Stein, 1974, p. 565).

According to Hahn, the success of educational policy depended on national affirmation and cohesion between the government and the people. His firm conviction in the necessity of a single coherent political body motivated Hahn to monitor public opinion using polls and to guide the public using propaganda, publicity, and media agenda setting. This might be the reason why almost half of the members of the research group Hahn formed to combat the teacher shortage were journalists; the group was led by Karl Stanislaus Becker (1907–1986), who also officiated as the commissioner of media for the Catholic Deutsche Bischofskonferenz (German Bishops' Conference) (Gabel, 1999).

## Federal Competition and National Cohesion: How Polls Monitored the Support for Educational Policy in the 1960s

In 1968 Hahn commissioned the Allensbach Institute to carry out polls to measure popular support for his educational reforms. He wanted to find out what the consequences were of the public debate on educational policy (IfD-Report 1607, 1969, pp. 1, 4). In a dualistic manner of thought that was characteristic of the bipolar conflict of the Cold War, the pollsters explored popular expectations about the consequences of a scenario where one nation spent a lot on schools and universities while another nation did not.[2] The questionnaire presented eight responses from which the interviewees could choose. The responses reflected Hahn's beliefs about education as a field of international competition. Moreover, these multiple choice questions presented only positive effects of educational reform—a fact that may indicate that education had already been taken for granted as an efficient and favorable instrument of preventive policy during the Cold War. The predefined response choices were based on the assumption that education is an important factor for the advancement of the national economy and technology, the standard of living, social-psychological well-being, and the nation's international prestige:

> The entire field of technology will be better developed in those nations that spend more on education;

In a nation that spends a great amount on education, the economy will develop more favorably;

There, where a great deal is spent on education, the people will be happier;

In a nation that spends a great deal on education, the people's income will increase and the standard of living will be higher;

The culinary arts will be better developed in a nation that spends a lot on education;

A nation that spends more money on education will win more victories in soccer games;

A nation's worldwide reputation will be higher if a great deal is spent on education;

The more a nation spends on education, the less it will be involved in wars.

*(IfD-Report 1607, 1969, n.p.)*

While exploring popular convictions regarding the suggested advantages of education, these predefined responses reduced education to an instrument for the prosperity of the national welfare state, whereas statements about possible disadvantages of this type of utilitarian economic focus in education were missing.

Table 10.1 illustrates another questioning technique (Noelle-Neumann & Petersen, 2005, pp. 156–163) that was used to explore approval of educational policy. This technique simulates a dialogue between the minister and the population that in reality never took place. In fact, it is not a dialogue at all, because the questions touch only on governmental and political statements that the respondents could applaud. Only for well-informed respondents was it apparent which statements spoke in favor of the government.

The simulated dialogue in Table 10.1 referred to the public debate over two main possibilities for educational reforms: opening up higher education to the majority or following an elitist approach to education that would limit access to schools of higher education. The respondents' opinions concerning the simulated dialogue corresponded with Hahn's aims. As we will see below, in contrast to many Social Democrats of the time, Hahn did not want to change the school systems. As a believer in law and order he disapproved of the Social Democrats' reforms, such as the educational guidelines in Hessen or mixed-ability classes (Sauer, 1999, pp. 161–163; Gass-Bolm, 2005, pp. 394–396). Although he wanted to increase the number of students at the universities, he also pled for a select academic elite. He therefore voted in favor of improvements in vocational education, because this would fulfill the demands of industry and the economy without opening up the institutions of higher learning to the masses.

Hahn's endeavor to mobilize the public in favor of educational reforms while also appeasing those who criticized the insufficiency of schools was a difficult one. Whereas a majority of the respondents supported the governmental reform to close rural single-class schools in favor of larger school centers (see Table 10.2), 63% of the respondents negated the statement that teachers at large schools could

**TABLE 10.1** Higher Education or Vocational Education?

Question:
Recently much has been undertaken to get more children to attend upper secondary schools (*höhere Schule*). There are two opinions regarding this issue: Which of the two do you agree with?

|  | Baden-Württemberg | | |
| --- | --- | --- | --- |
|  | General population[a] (%) | University graduates[b] (%) | Parents of school children and students[c] (%) |
| The most pressing issue in the Federal Republic is to increase the number of young people who attain higher education and complete secondary school examinations (*Abitur*). To keep pace in the world of the future *we* [italics added] need many more people who have attended schools of higher education. | 34 | 41 | 39 |
| It is not the number of students that counts but their quality. The main thing *we* need in the world of the future is a scientific elite group. Therefore, only the gifted and not the mass population should attend upper secondary schools. | 55 | 48 | 53 |
| Indifferent | 11 | 11 | 8 |

Allensbach Archives IfD-Survey 285 (IfD-Report 1607, 1969, p. 17ff):
[a] Adults in Baden-Württemberg older than 16 years ($N = 614$). This poll was conducted on January 8–18, 1968.
[b] Graduates who had completed university ($N = 190$). This poll was conducted on February 14–25, 1968.
[c] Fathers and mothers of pupils and students younger than 21 years ($N = 199$). This poll was conducted on February 14–28, 1968.

**TABLE 10.2** Progress Through Neighborhood Schools?

Question:
Overall, do you or do you not have the impression that the neighborhood schools represent progress for *our* [italics added] school system?

|  | Baden-Württemberg, January/February 1968 | | |
| --- | --- | --- | --- |
|  | General population (%) | University graduates (%) | Parents of school children and students (%) |
| Yes, they represent progress | 55 | 83 | 62 |
| No, they do not represent progress | 9 | 5 | 11 |
| Undecided, no opinion | 9 | 8 | 9 |
| Never heard of neighborhood schools | 27 | 4 | 18 |

Allensbach Archives, IfD-Survey 285 (see Table 10.1 for details).

**TABLE 10.3** Attention to Each Child in Schools?

Question:
Overall, what is your impression of the lessons *at our schools* [italics added]? Can the teachers pay enough attention to each individual child, or is the attention paid not enough?

| | Baden-Württemberg, January/February 1968 | | |
|---|---|---|---|
| | General population (%) | University graduates (%) | Parents of school children and students (%) |
| Not enough | 63 | 71 | 64 |
| Enough | 12 | 9 | 14 |
| Undecided | 19 | 15 | 19 |
| No opinion | 6 | 5 | 3 |

Allensbach Archives, IfD-Survey 285 (see Table 10.1 for details).

adequately look after the needs of every child (see Table 10.3) (IfD-Report 1607, 1969, p. 12).

The choice of *Nachbarschaftsschulen* (neighborhood schools) as the name of the new school centers may have intended to suggest or even simulate a revitalized local community. But this term could not overcome popular concerns regarding the overly bureaucratic and confusing nature of large schools, which the public associated with the dehumanizing organization of large numbers of pupils.

As can be seen from the tables, the poll was carried out with three different target groups: the university graduates and the parents of school children emulate a dualistic and opposing pair, and these groups of course also belong to the population as a whole. But the tabular layout of the comparison implied a deviation of these distinct social groups from the general population. The data about the general population created an average with which the results of the two specific target groups, the university graduates and the parents, were compared. Therefore, the average was intended to be construed as a standard and a kind of norm (Igo, 2007). For the governmental reformers, the average served as a guide for the successful implementation of school reforms. School reformers had to convince the average German of their plans, allowing the average to be presented as the norm, against which opponents could be marked as dissenters. But there is also another—somewhat concealed—statistical narrative: The graduates' support for educational reforms was above average; those who had benefited from education could serve as a guide or avant-garde for those who would benefit from educational reform in the future. On the other hand, depending on what was in line with the government's strategies, the findings regarding the attitudes of the school children's parents could serve as a legitimization to preserve the established school system and teaching methods.

A closer look at the questionnaire and the characteristic style of the questions suggests that the Allensbach poll was intended to legitimize the educational policy in Baden-Württemberg. The questions contained many personal and possessive pronouns in the first person plural: *we* and *our*. As a kind of hidden agenda, this style indicates and promotes community and identification with the federal state of Baden-Württemberg. And this indirect appeal to state patriotism can be seen as a rhetorical attempt at exploring the support for schools and education in Baden-Württemberg.

This is particularly true with regard to the question that personifies the state of Baden-Württemberg as a political actor (see Table 10.4). This concealed the actual politicians who were responsible for educational policy, as the state became the personified subject of the comparison. Simultaneously, this poll promoted intra-national comparisons rather than global competition. It reinforced the nation as the reference framework: The data created the average for the state of Baden-Württemberg, and the "*we*-style" of the questionnaire was intended to simulate or even strengthen the identification with the state. At the same time, other federal states were not explicitly mentioned but were referred to implicitly, because "we" always implies the existence of "the others." Therefore, the questionnaire reflects the federal competition in the fields of education and schooling in West Germany and points to (intra-) national comparisons and agenda setting.

**TABLE 10.4** Better Schools in Baden-Württemberg?

Question:
If you compare Baden-Württemberg . . . with the other German states, do you believe that *Baden-Württemberg* is more or less committed to its schools and universities and all issues regarding education than the overall average?

| | Baden-Württemberg, January/February 1968 | | |
| --- | --- | --- | --- |
| | General population (%) | University graduates (%) | Parents of school children and students (%) |
| More | 27 | 47 | 27 |
| Equally committed | 49 | 36 | 49 |
| Less | 7 | 9 | 9 |
| Undecided, do not know | 17 | 8 | 15 |

Allensbach Archives, IfD-Survey 285 (see Table 10.1 for details).

## Gauging Popular Opinion in the 1960s: Legitimization for Equality of Educational Opportunities, or Scholarships for Outstanding Pupils?

As has been shown, increasing national prosperity was one of the main objectives behind Minister Hahn's decision to expand school education and to exploit human capital with a particular focus on rural areas. Improvements in vocational education were to correspond with the industrial and technological needs of entrepreneurs. For example, Hahn supported the founding of new universities such as the one in Constance and increased pupil access to upper secondary schools (Conze, 2009, p. 247). However, he also tried to limit the scope of his reform. He resolutely advocated the national German tripartite school system (consisting of the *Gymnasium*, *Realschule*, and *Hauptschule*) and opposed endeavors to change the system by establishing comprehensive schools. According to Hahn, equality of educational opportunity was the result of left-wing ideologies that would degrade cultural achievements and productive efficiency (Wissenschaftszentrum Bonn, 1978; Gass-Bolm, 2005, p. 387).

It was certainly on behalf of Hahn that in 1965 the Allensbach Institute attempted to trivialize the heated debate on equality of educational opportunity by claiming that the population had already agreed to this political demand (IfD-Report 1226/II, 1965, p. 2). The pollsters did concede that social background and one's father's profession could restrict educational opportunity: 70% of the children of entrepreneurs, managers, and civil servants but only 13% and 10% of the children of farmers and unskilled workers, respectively, attended upper secondary schools (*Gymnasien*) (p. 12). Thus, only a minority of lower-class and lower middle-class children attended these schools of higher education. But the pollsters found that family size was a stronger determinant than economic status for whether or not the children of farmers and unskilled workers attended upper secondary schools. Therefore, the Allensbach Institute investigated these parents' efforts to enable their children to attend secondary schools. The pollsters posed as advocates of the parents by pointing out the arduous efforts of many farmers and workers to send at least one of their children to upper secondary school (pp. 22, 25). The pollsters stated that the "quasi-natural selection" of only a few outstanding pupils from families with many children reduced the risk that these pupils would drop out of upper secondary school. Thus, it was found that successful educational achievement at secondary schools not only depended on social class but also on family size, family support, and, most of all, the individual student's assertiveness and skills. Accordingly, individual working-class children completed upper secondary school as successfully as pupils from wealthy families. However, the Allensbach pollsters warned that the problem of school dropouts could worsen if the number of working-class children who gained access to secondary schools without prior selection increased (p. 32).

The Allensbach researchers suggested that attendance at secondary schools depended only on the willingness of the parents: "Educational opportunities do not only depend on the size and generosity of our institutions of learning but also on whether the parents understand the value of secondary or higher education" (IfD-Report 1226/II, 1965, p. 4). The Allensbach pollsters therefore conducted a further survey on popular awareness regarding education. Again, a simulated dialogue was used in the questionnaire. It was to reveal whether the respondents believed that outstandingly gifted children should necessarily receive higher education, or whether basic education was believed to provide a sufficient basis for promising job opportunities. When the question was formulated in this way, two thirds of the respondents answered that higher education was favorable. But many of the lower-class and lower middle-class parents surveyed were uncertain as to whether higher education ensured a good job and whether, owing to their lack of cultural capital, their children would be able to keep up with middle-class children at upper secondary schools.[3] The conclusion of the report on these survey findings was not very original: It included demands for educational counseling; for effective, earmarked grants to enable talented children from the lower classes to attend upper secondary schools and complete higher education; for infrastructural improvement of children's walking and bicycling routes to school; and for construction of schoolhouses in rural areas (pp. 18, 20). With its focus on the size and the values of families as the decisive criteria for educational opportunities, the Allensbach Institute implied that family policy measures instead of educational reforms would improve the educational exploitation of human capital (p. 37; similarly, see Jürgens, 1964, pp. 94–95). This recommendation legitimized Hahn's preference for stabilizing the existing school system and contradicted the Social Democrats' attempts to reform the educational system.

Ten years later, in 1977, during the conflict over the founding of comprehensive schools in various German states, the Allensbach Institute supplied the government of Rhineland-Palatinate along with Prime Minister Helmut Kohl and the Christian Democrats in North Rhine-Westphalia with similar findings. The new Allensbach survey recommended not risking experiments in educational policy, because more than 50% of the parents surveyed agreed with the statement in the questionnaire that the existing teaching methods represented the best solution for the education of their children. The same questionnaire showed that 54% of the parents feared that school education could overburden the children (IfD-Report 2348, 1977, pp. 1, 7). A report concluded that campaigns against establishing comprehensive schools should take into account the population's fear that anonymity in huge schools would lead to a large number of the teachers neglecting the pupils' potential (IfD-Report 2349, 1977, pp. 52–54). By claiming to represent the voice of the parents, the reports attempted to portray left-wing reform plans as ideologically driven.

## The Ideal Teacher for the People: Teacher Images and Teacher Shortage From the 1960s

The success of school reforms depended on training teachers and preventing teacher shortages. The employment of a sufficient number of teachers was one of the central aspects of the government's attempt to stabilize the existing German tripartite school system and to develop human talents. However, West Germany was not alone in this predicament: Educational and sociological researchers demonstrated that in the 1960s almost every nation faced teacher shortages. In 1963 a joint study by UNESCO and the Swiss International Bureau of Education, founded in 1925 by Jean Piaget, identified teacher shortages as a serious global problem. Interviews with 83 national ministers of education throughout the world revealed a lack of teachers in 75% of the nations (Posch, 1967, p. 29).

Minister Wilhelm Hahn (1968, p. xiii) also took this global study into consideration, because the teacher shortage endangered his reforms to strengthen the German school system and make it more efficient. However, the international statistics from UNESCO and the International Bureau of Education did not only serve as a basis for the global adoption of the Western concept of schooling: Arguably, as the wealth of global research and international comparisons suggests, surveys and applied research studies also represented a means to harmonize the educational globe (Tröhler, 2010). Moreover, these studies had a stabilizing effect on how the national school systems were perceived. In fact, international tabulations and reporting dominated and strengthened the specific national perspective on educational policy. International data was studied through national lenses. For example, the Austrian researcher Peter Posch (1967, pp. 31, 37–40) analyzed data from several nations, including, for example, a German study on the teacher shortage that was carried out on behalf of the Ettlinger circle, mentioned above. The study, conducted in 1960 and published in 1962, predicted a shortage of more than 80,000 teachers in Germany for the year 1970.

Through his research group on combating the teacher shortage, Hahn commissioned another poll from the Allensbach Institute to measure the popular image and prestige of teachers and to identify adolescents' and parents' attitudes towards the teaching profession. Again, this social survey was to provide a basis for harmonization of the relationship between government policy and society. By exploring sociocultural attitudes, it was to prepare an effective combination of educational and family policy.

The results of the Allensbach poll were disillusioning: Teachers had an unalluring image among the 521 surveyed 18- and 19-year-old sixth-formers (*Primaner*) at university preparatory upper secondary schools (*Gymnasien*) in Baden-Württemberg in 1967. According to the Allensbach pollsters, the reasons for this negative image were the young people's Epicurean aims of life and the fusion of hedonistic and altruistic values with wishes to receive and accomplish important tasks (Noelle-Neumann & Schmidtchen, 1968, pp. 150–152). The sixth-formers who were efficient and successful at school aspired to find jobs in the fields of business, technology, and industry (pp. 154–156, 205). Talented students rejected at an early stage the prospect of becoming teachers, whereas mediocre and inefficient upper secondary school graduates had two strong motives to become upper secondary school teachers: In part, they admired the ostensibly pedagogical ideals of community and altruism, but mainly it was the promise of security and a good standard of living that influenced their choice in favor of teaching careers.

These results were disastrous for Minister of Education Hahn's attempts to mobilize educational resources without changing the existing school system. Therefore, he was forced to intensify his publicity campaign for his reform. However, Hahn did not manage to put an end to criticism by the media. In 1969 a report on the shortage of more than 3,000 teachers in Baden-Württemberg published in the German weekly magazine *Der Spiegel* forced him to establish an emergency reserve (*Alarmreserve*) of 100 (young) teachers ("Mikätzchen und Gastarbeiter," 1969). A few months later, another *Der Spiegel* story ("Unmasse Stoff," 1969) criticized the failure of educational planning. The articles stated that the 375-page book *Action Program to Combat the Teacher Shortage* (*Aktionsprogramm gegen den Lehrermangel*), which had been published by the Baden-Württemberg ministry of education, was little more than a dust collector and did not contribute towards alleviating the disastrous shortage of teachers in Baden-Württemberg. This criticism also applied to the polls because survey results were broadly included in this book (Noelle-Neumann & Schmidtchen, 1968). Furthermore, not only the press but also the audit division complained about expensive, laborious, and inefficient educational planning.

## Summary and Outlook

Even though educational planning appears to have failed, polls, ratings, and output measurements have become established as potent methods to stabilize and legitimize national educational reforms and policy throughout the world. Applied mainly in national contexts or merely to compare one's own country with others, social surveys construe and reproduce the national body by creating "the average," even if the population is divided into segregated social target groups.

Polls have been used to generate national cohesion and support for government policies. Depending on the government's strategy, polls provided a basis to legitimize the necessity of radical reforms of the school system or, as was the case with Wilhelm Hahn, to gain support for the existing system. Hahn was open-minded about preventive scientific educational planning. By using what was perceived as a modern tool (social surveys), he tried to stabilize the tripartite German school system (Hahn, 1968) and forge it into a weapon for the future-oriented international contest that was the Cold War. It was an attempt to simultaneously mobilize and harness human capital through educational reforms. The selection of pupils through the transfer to upper secondary schools was to be sustainable. One could say that reforms in family policy rather than educational reforms, such as the general guidelines for education by Ludwig von Friedeburg in Hessen, represented the preferred proactive instrument of Hahn and the Allensbach Institute.

Hahn's primary point of reference was the nation. In his view, the characterization of the nation as a strong and efficient "body" was the precondition for competing in the Cold War. Therefore, Hahn viewed the teacher shortage as "an issue concerning our national existence" and emphasized that "the current generation of pupils and students will influence the consciousness and the basis of our people's vitality [*Vitalgrundlage unseres Volkes*] in the next millennium" (Hahn, 1968, pp. xiv, xxi).

The national narrative can also be distinguished in a range of other social research studies that presented international data collections and comparisons concerning teacher shortages and school education, such as Posch's study on teacher shortage in 1967 (pp. 150–152). Some sociologists even reveal nationalist or racist tendencies in their research. For example, an Allensbach report rightly accused Hans-Wilhelm Jürgens (b. 1932), an anthropologist and, beginning in 1974, the first director of the Federal Institute for Population Research in West Germany, of supporting Social Darwinism (IfD-Report 1226/II, 1965, pp. 3, 30; Etzemüller, 2007, p. 119). Jürgens' (1964) study on the influence of family size on children's educational careers concluded that the most talented and strongest child in a family with many children would be successful and gain entry to upper secondary school. However, this statement and Jürgens' research approach bore similarities to the conclusions that the Allensbach pollsters themselves had drawn. This example demonstrates the strong national roots of internationally active sociologists and pollsters. In spite of the global application of polls and social research, and the wealth of international comparisons during the ideological conflict of the Cold War, the nation remained the primary point of reference in educational debates and politics in West Germany.

## Notes

1. Picht was head of a German private school, Birklehof, in the Black Forest from 1946 to 1955 and a member of the German commission for education. In 1965, one year after his famous article on the German *Bildungskatastrophe* (educational disaster) (see Bergmann, 2002), Picht became a professor of theological philosophy at the University of Heidelberg, of which Minister Hahn was a former president.
2. "Suppose in one country, a great deal of effort goes into schools and universities, whereas in another country, no particular effort is spent. What do you believe will be the consequences if one nation spends *a great deal* on schools and universities—can you determine the consequences with the help of this list?" (IfD-Report 1607, 1969, p. 3).
3. This reasoning brings to mind similar findings by Pierre Bourdieu (1987, pp. 515, 518), who stressed the uncertainty of the petty bourgeoisie in the face of education.

## Archival Sources

### Archives of the Allensbach Institute of Public Opinion Research/Institut für Demoskopie Allensbach (IfD) (unpublished poll reports)

IfD-Report 276. (1953). Eltern und Schule. Ergebnisse einer Eltern-Befragung im Bundesgebiet und in West-Berlin im Auftrag der Bundesgeschäftsstelle der CDU.

IfD-Report 578. (1957). Konfessionsschule und konfessionelle Lehrerausbildung. Die Meinung der Eltern schulpflichtiger Kinder in Baden-Württemberg, im Auftrag der Gewerkschaft Erziehung und Wissenschaft, Baden-Württemberg.
IfD-Report 645. (1958). Studien zur Schulfrage (I). Ergebnisse von Bevölkerungsumfragen im Auftrag des Ettlinger Kreises (Dr. Ing. e.h. Hans Freudenberg).
IfD-Report 1226/II. (1965). Familie und Bildungschancen. Repräsentativerhebungen über die Bildungswege der Nachkriegsgeneration im Auftrag des Bundesministeriums für Familie und Jugend.
IfD-Report 1607. (1969). Bildungspolitik in Baden-Württemberg. Umfragen in der Bevölkerung, bei Akademikern und Eltern von Schulkindern. Im Auftrag des Kultusministeriums von Baden-Württemberg.
IfD-Report 2348. (1977). Werden die Kinder von der Schule überfordert? Ein schulpolitischer Aspekt der demoskopischen Erhebung in Rheinland-Pfalz.
IfD-Report 2349. (1977). Das Volksbegehren gegen die kooperative Schule. Umfrage in Nordrhein-Westfalen.

## References

Bergmann, S. (2002). Die Diskussion um die Bildungsreform in der Nachkriegszeit (Georg Picht). In G. Brakelmann & T. Jähnichen (Eds.), *Gesellschaftspolitische Neuorientierungen des Protestantismus in der Nachkriegszeit* (pp. 101–126). Münster, Germany: Lit.
Bourdieu, P. (1987). *Die feinen Unterschiede: Kritik der gesellschaftlichen Urteilskraft*. Frankfurt/Main, Germany: Suhrkamp.
Converse, J. (2009). *Survey research in the United States: Roots and emergence 1890–1960*. New Brunswick, NJ: Transaction.
Conze, E. (2009). *Die Suche nach Sicherheit: Eine Geschichte der Bundesrepublik Deutschland von 1949 bis in die Gegenwart*. Munich, Germany: Siedler.
Crespi, L. (1952). America's interest in German survey research. In Institut zur Förderung öffentlicher Angelegenheiten (Ed.), *Empirische Sozialforschung. Meinungs- und Marktforschung. Methoden und Probleme* (pp. 215–217). Frankfurt/Main, Germany: Institut zur Förderung öffentlicher Angelegenheiten.
Dahrendorf, R. (1965). *Arbeiterkinder an deutschen Universitäten*. Tübingen, Germany: Mohr.
Etzemüller, T. (2007). *Ein ewigwährender Untergang: Der apokalyptische Bevölkerungsdiskurs im 20. Jahrhundert*. Bielefeld, Germany: Transcript.
Foucault, M. (2004). *Geschichte der Gouvernementalität:Vol. 2. Die Geburt der Biopolitik*. Frankfurt/Main, Germany: Suhrkamp.
Friedeburg, L. (1992). *Bildungsreform in Deutschland: Geschichte und gesellschaftlicher Widerspruch*. Frankfurt/Main, Germany: Suhrkamp.
Gabel, H. (1999). Becker, Karl Stanislaus. In B. Ottnad (Ed.), *Baden-Württembergische Biographien* (Vol. 2, pp. 30–33). Stuttgart, Germany: Kohlhammer.
Gass-Bolm, T. (2005). *Das Gymnasium 1945–1980: Bildungsreform und gesellschaftlicher Wandel in Westdeutschland*. Göttingen, Germany: Wallstein.
Grube, N., & De Vincenti, A. (2013). Die Abstinenzbewegungen gegen das alkoholisierte Volk: Zirkulation wissenschaftlichen Wissens in Schule und Öffentlichkeit in der Schweiz um 1900. *Bildungsgeschichte: International Journal for the Historiography of Education (IJHE), 3*(2), 209–225.
Hahn, W. (1968). Der Lehrer in der Schule und in der Gesellschaft von morgen. In Kultusministerium Baden-Württemberg (Ed.), *Aktionsprogramm gegen den Lehrermangel:*

*Analysen und Vorschläge für Baden-Württemberg vorgelegt vom Arbeitskreis Lehrermangel des Kultusministeriums Baden-Württemberg* (pp. xiii–xxii). Villingen, Germany: Neckar-Verlag.

Igo, S. E. (2007). *The averaged American: Surveys, citizens, and the making of a mass public.* Cambridge, MA: Harvard University Press.

Jürgens, H. W. (1964). *Familiengröße und Bildungsweg: Untersuchungen über den Bildungsweg von Kindern aus unterschiedlich großen Familien.* Stuttgart, Germany: Enke.

Kruke, A. (2007). *Demoskopie in der Bundesrepublik Deutschland: Meinungsforschung, Parteien und Medien 1949–1990.* Düsseldorf, Germany: Droste.

Mikätzchen und Gastarbeiter: Lehrermangel in Deutschland. (1969, August 25). *Der Spiegel, 35,* 110.

Noelle, E., & Neumann, E. P. (Eds.). (1956). *Jahrbuch der öffentlichen Meinung. Vol. 1: 1947–1955.* Allensbach, Germany: Verlag für Demoskopie.

Noelle-Neumann, E., & Petersen, T. (2005). *Alle, nicht jeder: Einführung in die Methoden der Demoskopie.* Berlin, Germany: Springer.

Noelle-Neumann, E., & Schmidtchen, G. (1968). Lehrer für das Gymnasium: Umfrage unter Primanern, Eltern und Studienräten. In Kultusministerium Baden-Württemberg (Ed.), *Aktionsprogramm gegen den Lehrermangel: Analysen und Vorschläge für Baden-Württemberg vorgelegt vom Arbeitskreis Lehrermangel des Kultusministeriums Baden-Württemberg* (pp. 135–375). Villingen, Germany: Neckar-Verlag.

Oberschall, A. (1997). *Empirische Sozialforschung in Deutschland 1848–1914.* Munich, Germany: Karl Alber.

Osterhammel, J. (2009). *Die Verwandlung der Welt: Eine Geschichte des 19. Jahrhunderts.* Munich, Germany: Beck.

Posch, P. (1967). *Der Lehrermangel: Ausmaß und Möglichkeiten der Behebung.* Weinheim, Germany: Julius Beltz.

Sauer, T. (1999). *Westorientierung im deutschen Protestantismus? Vorstellungen und Tätigkeit des Kronberger Kreises.* Munich, Germany: Oldenbourg.

Stein, E. (1974). Bildung im Dienste des Wohlstandsidols. In G. Leibholz, H.-J. Faller, P. Mikat, & H. Reis (Eds.), *Menschenwürde und freiheitliche Rechtsordnung. Festschrift für Willi Geiger zum 65. Geburtstag* (pp. 561–578). Tübingen, Germany: Mohr.

Tröhler, D. (2010). Harmonizing the educational globe: World polity, cultural features, and the challenges to educational research. *Studies in Philosophy and Education, 29,* 7–29.

Tyack, D., & Cuban, L. (2001). *Tinkering toward utopia: A century of public school reform.* Cambridge, MA: Harvard University Press.

Unmasse Stoff. (1969, November 10). *Der Spiegel, 46,* 104.

Viswanath, K. (1996). Elisabeth Noelle-Neumann (1916–). In N. Signorelli (Ed.), *Women in communication* (pp. 300–311). Westport, CT: Greenwood.

Weischer, C. (2004). *Das Unternehmen "Empirische Sozialforschung": Strukturen, Praktiken und Leitbilder der Sozialforschung in der Bundesrepublik Deutschland.* Munich, Germany: Oldenbourg.

Wissenschaftszentrum Bonn (Ed.). (1978). *Mut zur Erziehung: Beiträge zu einem Forum am 9./10. Januar 1978 im Wissenschaftszentrum Bonn-Bad Godesberg.* Stuttgart, Germany: Klett-Cotta.

# 11

## THE NATIONAL IN THE GLOBAL

Switzerland and the Council of Europe's Policies on Schooling for Migrant Children in the 1960s

*Regula Bürgi and Philipp Eigenmann*

The contribution made by international governmental organizations to modern educational policy is virtually ubiquitous; major players include UNESCO as well as organizations only tangentially concerned with education policy, such as the Council of Europe, the European Union, and the Organization for Economic Co-operation and Development (OECD). The dominant theoretical explanation for this phenomenon is the world culture theory of neo-institutionalism (Schriewer, 2012). This theory is based on the idea that nation-states are surrounded by a world culture that legitimizes their existence even while compelling them to organize themselves according to the dominant principles of the world culture, a pressure that is turning them increasingly isomorphic, at least on a formal level (Meyer, Boli, Thomas, & Ramirez, 2005). According to the theory's proponents, international organizations serve as "diffusion agents" in this process, operating as the vehicles by which "virtual" world culture is disseminated (Meyer & Ramirez, 2005, p. 216–233; Drori & Krücken, 2009, p. 17).

The advocates of world culture theory have, indeed, demonstrated a set of global convergences, but the theory is silent about the historical genesis of worldwide models (Carney, Rappleye, & Silova, 2012). In this chapter, we seek to generate insights for closing this gap by focusing on the policies developed by the Council of Europe during the 1960s regarding the education of migrant children.[1] With its first resolution on school education for the children of migrant workers, issued in 1970 (Resolution (70) 35, 1970), the Council of Europe laid the cornerstone for subsequent European policy on immigration and schooling.

By examining the historical genesis of Resolution 35, we will attempt to elucidate the process by which a key model for international education policy was developed. We also seek to show the sources that were evoked to support it. The Council of Europe did not unilaterally draft Resolution 35, for its ideas did not arise out of the blue. Rather, the policy was highly contingent on the experience and expertise of the individual nation-states that were the members of the Council of Europe. National expertise on education policy was a product of national processes of negotiation and debate and by no means a homogeneous unit. As the Council of Europe's resolution largely drew on expertise specific to individual nations, we would argue that its recommendations ultimately united discourses that had taken place at the national level and reflected their lines of conflict—yet these discourses were repackaged in a universalist language. Thus, even before an international model could achieve its isomorphic impact on individual nation-states, it owed its own genesis to a number of different previously existing national policies and discourses.

Our analysis employs a multilayered approach. It is focused on the Council of Europe and presents the processes and debates that took place inside this organization, but it also takes a specific look at one of the member states in an attempt to draw broadly applicable insights. Since the Council of Europe viewed Switzerland as a country with a sophisticated history of dealing with the education of immigrant children (RS/SEM 2, 28–30 Oct. 1968), and Switzerland was generally viewed as a model with respect to its policies toward migrant workers (Berlinghoff, 2013, p. 181), we have selected the rationales and discourses that took place in Switzerland to analyze in depth. In this connection, we will examine internal documents and minutes from Council of Europe meetings together with the references to Switzerland that they contain. This multilayered approach allows us to describe the specific argumentation and its discursive references. Our goal is to make transparent those elements that are virtually invisible in the official resolutions and studies, and thereby to unlock the "black box" that international organizations present to the outside world with respect to the genesis of their policies.

We will develop our argument in four stages: In the first section, we briefly introduce Resolution 35 of 1970 and its contents, as well as the Council of Europe. Next, we show the historical context underlying the new effort and the specific concerns to which it was responding. Third, we examine how the Council of Europe gathered information for developing Resolution 35, including what information was selected. In the fourth section, we show the outcome of the negotiations in the Council of Europe and the extent to which it reveals the lines of argumentation and discourses of individual nations and their governments, thereby resulting in a multilayered and ambiguous product. In the last section, we demonstrate the persistence of a nation-state–based understanding of schools in international models, leading us to the conclusion that to understand universalist notions of a common world culture, it is necessary to extract the "ingredients" specific to national contexts.

## The Council of Europe and Resolution 35, School Education for the Children of Migrant Workers

Most international organizations in Europe, such as the OECD and the European Economic Community (the predecessor of the European Union), did not include education for the children of immigrant workers on their agendas before 1970,[2] except for the Council of Europe, which became the very first organization to establish a committee on school education for children of migrant workers in 1968 and then adopted a resolution on this issue in 1970. The establishment of the Council of Europe was the product of two intersecting historical circumstances: the end of the Second World War and the beginning of the Cold War. It had been founded as an intergovernmental organization in 1949 by 10 Western European governments[3] with the main objectives "to achieve a greater unity between its members" and to facilitate "their economic and social progress" (Statute of the Council of Europe, 1949, Article 1).[4] This very broad mandate opened the door to numerous policy concerns, including economic, social, cultural, and scientific issues.[5] Within this frame, education (Holtz, 2000, p. 21) and migration became part of the agenda for the Council of Europe starting in the 1950s.[6] But these two strands of Western European policy cooperation—education and migration—were not combined until 1968, when the committee on school education for the children of migrant workers was set up, whose work culminated in Resolution 35 in 1970.

The legally non-binding Resolution 35 consisted of three pages, introduced by a statement of principles on the issue. In addition, it contained a broad set of policy recommendations that addressed both immigration and emigration countries. Emigration countries were asked to provide their citizens with information about the education system of the country of immigration, to announce the arrival of children, and to prepare "standard records providing information on their school career and health" (Resolution (70) 35, 1970, p. 85). The immigration countries were encouraged to establish "special classes" to guide the children toward "gradual integration into normal classes" (p. 85). These special classes were to focus especially on teaching the language of the receiving country, and the resolution emphasized that they should last only so long as absolutely necessary. In addition, it was stated that regular teachers should have knowledge about the educational system of the countries of emigration, and "specialist teachers" should be engaged to teach the children about "the civilisation and language of their country of origin" (p. 86). In sum, the recommendations in the legally non-binding resolution were mainly directed at issues concerning the organization of schooling; issues pertaining to curricula were scarcely mentioned, such as suggestions for educational techniques or textbooks.

### Demographic Change as an Impetus

The Council of Europe merged the policy areas of education and migration by creating a committee to deal with both issues in the 1960s, responding to a quantitative challenge facing most Western European immigration countries in the wake of the liberalization of family reunion policy for migrant workers.[7] This policy change was strongly supported by the Council of Europe through its Social Charter, ratified in 1961, which encouraged its members to support the reunion of migrant worker families. Consequently, a shift had occurred in the demographic structure of the immigrant population in the receiving countries.[8] The growth in the numbers of foreign children forced social policy makers to cope with this new challenge and to provide these children with an education, because many were not attending school at all.[9] Indeed, it was the Advisory Committee of the Special Representative for National Refugees and Over-Population that first proposed the idea in the mid-1960s.[10] In 1966 it submitted the following suggestion to the Committee of Ministers—the highest body of the Council of Europe:

> [A]ppropriate measures *should* be applied in immigration countries to facilitate *access* and *readmission* [italics added] by immigrant worker's children to schools and vocational training establishments in such countries.
>
> *(RS 17, 7 Dec. 1966)*

This suggestion was taken into account by the ministers' deputies in 1967 and resulted in the establishment of a committee on school education for children of migrant workers in 1968, which was responsible for the 1970 Resolution 35. The origins of the policy makers' concerns are evident in a summary presented at the very first meeting of the committee in 1968, when it declared that its purpose was "encouraging attendance by migrant workers' children at the schools" (RS/SEM 1, 17 Apr. 1968). The main focus, however, was on immigration and the demographic challenges it created, and not on education, so the work of the committee was subsumed under the organization's "social structure and welfare" mandate and not as part of its educational agenda (Europarat, 1967, p. 32).

## Calling for Expertise

Despite the classification of education for migrant children as part of the social policy function of the Council of Europe, the committee representatives were selected from the areas of educational policy or educational administration in member states. Two members were selected from the Council for Cultural Cooperation—the unit of the Council of Europe that had typically dealt with matters of education.[11] At the same time, the committee included national-state representatives in its deliberations, such as school inspectors and educational consultants from immigration and emigration countries. The members agreed from the very beginning to seek expert advice regarding educational issues:

> [T]he educational study [. . .] will require an analysis of scholastic systems and a knowledge of the ideas of teaching proper [. . .] and can be carried out only by an *expert* [italics added].
>
> *(RS/SEM 3, 17 Apr. 1968, p. 2)*

The task of gathering expertise was assigned to Pierre Malenfant, an official from the French Ministry of Education. Malenfant put together a questionnaire for surveying member states. The states' expertise proved to be important both for quantitative data on numbers of foreign children attending public schools and for qualitative information about the relevance of so-called special classes. Since the reports were submitted by individual member states, they did not provide a homogeneous or comprehensive picture. Accordingly, Resolution 35 was primarily informed by the arguments that had been made in the course of national debates and discourses rather than by consistent positions adopted by each individual state, which becomes rather obvious in the case of Switzerland.

## *Quantitative Information: Facts and Figures*

As noted above, the committee's first attempt to gather information was a questionnaire that it sent to the member countries. The questionnaire focused specifically on statistical data and legal issues, since these facts were relevant to the committee's main concern about children's school attendance. Its aim was to record and compare social conditions in the various member states through facts and figures—a form of knowledge creation and comparison that was enjoying a boom during the Cold War.[12]

This method of information gathering was problematic in several respects: First, the most populous members of the Council of Europe, including West Germany, France, and the United Kingdom, did not respond to the questionnaire at all.[13] Second, the statistical data lacked comparability,[14] as some countries maintained no records on the number of immigrant children and thus seemed to be quite unaware of "the problem" (RS/SEM 2, 20 June 1968; Chmielorz, 1985, pp. 90).

However, this was not the case for Switzerland. Switzerland proved to be a different challenge for the Council of Europe owing to its heterogeneous educational system, which varied considerably on the cantonal level.[15] Switzerland had no national ministry of education and thus lacked any established pathway of communication for gathering nationwide information.[16] The committee's main source of information on Switzerland was the Swiss Information Centre for Teaching and Education (CESDOC),[17] whose head, Eugen Egger, became part of the council's committee. At that time, the CESDOC, founded in 1962, was the main intercantonal[18] institution dealing with Swiss education policy.

The manifold systems for organizing education policy within Switzerland complicated the gathering of aggregate national data. Indeed, the figures reported to the committee of the Council of Europe were quite discrepant: The CESDOC reported that 53,330 foreign children were attending Swiss schools in 1969,[19] which differed from the number provided by the government of Italy with regard to Italians in Switzerland. Furthermore, it also conflicted with the figure of 14,000 foreign children attending Swiss schools that had been reported in a Council of Europe document a year earlier (RS/SEM 2, 17 May 1968, p. 3). In addition, this older report had assumed that there were many Italian children of school age in Switzerland who were not attending school at all (RS/SEM 2, 17 May 1968, p. 3), something that was not mentioned by Egger.[20]

These selective and somewhat contradictory figures as well as the absence of any quantitative information from the largest countries[21] completely stymied the committee's discussion of quantitative issues. Ultimately, the lack of reliable data sabotaged international exchange about quantitative social realities. As a result, the children who were not attending school were overlooked, even though their situation had been the initial motivation for setting up the committee.

## Qualitative Information: "Special Classes"

The committee undertook a far more detailed discussion of appropriate qualitative interventions for educating migrant children, especially about "special classes" and their funding. From these discussions, we can determine and classify the different approaches advocated by the delegates. For their part, the immigration countries made efforts to provide special classes for immigrant children to accelerate their integration into regular classes. On the other hand, emigration countries—assuming that these children would be returning home—wanted to see special classes set up to assure preservation of their native language and cultural heritage, and sometimes even to teach the syllabus of the country of origin. For example, the Italian representative emphasized the importance of "the teaching of the Italian language and certain subjects relating to the history, geography and civilization of their own country to the children" (RS/SEM 1 (final), Addendum II, 2 Oct. 1968, p. 1).

But the opinions of individual member states were also not at all homogeneous: For Switzerland as an immigration country, Eugen Egger, head of the CESDOC, who was the Swiss representative on the committee, pointed out that some cantons did, indeed, provide "special classes" for immigrant children in both the host language and the language of origin (RS 150, 12 Nov. 1969, p. 1)—and, in fact, this had been standard practice in Switzerland. However, in the committee of the Council of Europe, he did not give voice to the heated debate about immigrant education that was then taking place in Switzerland. In fact, at the time Switzerland was in the midst of a contentious debate not only about special classes as a means of integrating foreign children but about Italian schools with an Italian syllabus. This debate was characterized by recurrent references to the concept of "assimilation," and arguments centered around the political battle cry of Switzerland being "overrun by foreigners" (*Überfremdung*).[22]

The lines of conflict between the immigrants' home and adopted countries were also clearly manifest at the level of national politics. Egger represented the position of the receiving country, Switzerland, by promoting assimilation and adaptation. By contrast, a Swiss Catholic clergyman, Michael Jungo—another Swiss expert whose reports the committee used as a source—supported the position of the emigration country, Italy, by highlighting the importance of having immigrant children maintain the Italian language and cultural heritage while away from home.

Thus, the positions that the committee ultimately included as references were selective. It is not surprising that the data from Egger and his CESDOC were included, since—as mentioned above—the CESDOC was the official institution dealing with public education in Switzerland at the inter-cantonal level. More puzzling is the fact that the committee referred to the position of Jungo, a clergyman who did not officially represent Switzerland's opinion. Ultimately, the "Contact Point" for Italians in Zurich, an association representing and balancing the Italian and Swiss interests equally, was not invited to share its well-known expertise on immigration and education, although it had been given an opportunity to comment on an earlier Council of Europe resolution on immigration and social services in 1968 (SSA: Ar 48.20.1).

## The Multilayered Meanings of Resolution 35

Looking at the specific example of conflicts about "special classes" also illustrates how the committee's discussions ultimately coalesced into a resolution that was burdened by a number of conflicting approaches. Especially in the formulation of the justifications for the policy recommendations in the resolution, there were several different and at times contradictory frames of reference. In their final recommendation to the Committee of Ministers, the committee expressed support for special classes for "reception and integration teaching" and, moreover, favored "maintenance teaching"—meaning classes conducted in the language and culture of the country of origin—as a supplement to the regular curriculum. However, it emphasized the need for close liaison with the regular school to prevent "ghettoization" (Chmielorz, 1985, p. 109).

Although the committee was unambiguous in making these recommendations in its informal statement, these three points were somehow vitiated in the official version of Resolution 35 enacted by the Council of Europe. The first point—special introductory classes—was watered down with a "possibly" and an "if need be":

> *Possibly* to establish, *if need be* [italics added], in co-operation with the authorities of the countries concerned, in areas where a sufficient number of migrant workers' families live, special classes or courses designed to assist the gradual integration of the children into the normal classes of the country of immigration.
>
> *(Resolution (70) 35, 1970, p. 85)*

This sort of conditional wording provided receiving countries with legitimate backing for very different measures. At the same time, in a subsequent paragraph, Resolution 35 also addressed the second point—the official recommendation for schooling in the culture and language of origin. However, it did not explicitly recommend special classes for this purpose, and it kept the recommendation for schooling of this kind hidden between the lines.[23] Ambiguous formulations, or rather the avoidance of an explicit position, bear witness to the fact that the passage of this resolution was dependent on a majority vote by the members of the Council of Europe and was thus necessarily a compromise.

Nevertheless, the more diverse the interests and objectives of the involved actors were, the more the resolution failed to take a clear stance. The simultaneous activation of multiple levels of reference, which tended to stand in diametrical opposition to each other, led to overlapping attributions of meaning in the text of the resolution. In the resolution, the Council of Europe essentially asserted four different legitimating reasons for the schooling of migrant children (Resolution (70) 35, 1970, p. 84):

1. Education as an "inalienable right"
2. Maintaining the cultural heritage of the country of origin
3. Promoting adaptation or integration in the receiving country
4. And, in keeping with the Article 1 of the statute of the Council of Europe, the objective of a "greater unity between its members."

*(Statute of the Council of Europe, 1949, Article 1)*

These four points were prefixed to the recommendations made in the resolution and provided them with legitimacy. At first glance these points would seem unproblematic. Yet if we consider the ways they interconnect with claims and objectives emerging from particular conditions in specific nation-states, they become fraught with meaning, and the four points reveal profound lines of conflict.

The first argument—school education as a right—served as the overarching justification for the committee's recommendations. Formulated as a fundamental and, indeed, universal human right, this source of legitimacy could not be questioned. At the same time, the right to an education did not by itself prescribe specific goals or particular systems for organizing the schools to best implement this right. However, the linkage between the second and third forms of legitimation—maintaining cultural heritage and promoting adaption or integration—proved to be conflict-laden, because the former responded to a demand from the emigration nations and the latter reflected a concern of the immigration nations. This conflict, which was also intensely expressed within the national politics of each immigration nation, could be overcome only through compromise. Ultimately, it was this compromise that shaped the wording of Resolution 35, diluting the ideas and objectives that had originally been communicated by the Committee of Ministers so unambiguously.

It is clear that in its official policy the Council of Europe tried to do justice to both opposing approaches favored by its member states, so as to increase the resolution's legitimacy, and ended up justifying its policy recommendations with two opposite arguments. In this way, the Council of Europe supported its "European" program for educating migrant children based on national arguments, even though this stood in opposition to its mandate to create greater unity between its members. This contradiction was made possible by the document's ambiguous use of the term "integration," which could be understood in terms of each individual member state or in terms of European unity. With respect to "promoting adaptation" (the third rationale), "integration" could only be understood to mean adaptation to the nation-state—and in Switzerland this directly related to the national discussion on the fear of being "overrun by foreigners" (*Überfremdung*). However, the same term, "integration," is used in the fourth rationale in reference to European unity, which actually implied the weakening of the prerogatives of the nation-states. This framework of legitimization ultimately reflected the orientation and referential context of the Council of Europe, as established in its statute.

The success of the educational policy that emerged from this process is demonstrated by the fact that after 1970 a number of other international organizations began placing the education of children of migrant workers on their educational policy agendas and promoting special classes (Ogay, 1992). This opened the door for many different national education policies for educating immigrant children and served to stimulate the emergence of the now well-established sub-discipline of "intercultural education."

## Extracting the Ingredients of World Culture

The Council of Europe, created in the dual contexts of the aftermath of the Second World War and the onset of the Cold War, wished to fulfill its mandate of promoting "European unity" in all policy areas, including those related to migration and education. The council's 1970 policy recommendations for educating the children of migrant workers, as formulated in Resolution 35, could only be successful if the experiences and expectations of individual member states were integrated into the genesis of the resolution.

Thus, the work that took place inside the "black box" of the Council of Europe was marked by ambivalence between its overarching aims of strengthening European unity and its need to rely on national expertise. Using the example of the genesis of the Council of Europe's policy for the education of children of migrant workers, we have shown how a universalistic—or rather world-cultural—mission was substantially shaped by existing debates and discourses about educational policy within individual European nation-states and by their bilateral negotiations. As a consequence, the argumentation for the resolution can only be understood in the context of the various discourses taking place in individual states and the national views about public education. In contradistinction to an overarching policy aim "to achieve a greater unity between its members" (Statute of the Council of Europe, 1949, Article 1), the Council of Europe actually supported a European, universalistic, nation-state model of public schools. To this extent, European policy on education was still nothing more than the aggregate of the educational policies of Europe's nation-states—homogenized and repackaged into a European frame of reference.

The analysis carries the theoretical implication that models that circulate internationally do not arise "out of the blue" but rather from "cultural frames of meaning" (*kulturelle Bedeutungswelten*) (Schriewer, 2007) that are specifically coded at the level of the nation-state and are then transformed at the international level into what is then termed "world culture" and identified as "isomorphic." However, the supposedly universalistic culture is actually still imbued by principles native to specific nations, and depending on the perspective, it is laden with different meanings. Thus, the ingredients used to develop the international model of education policy discussed herein must be taken into account when analyzing the ways and extent to which this model was ultimately "reintegrated" into nation-state policies. Accordingly, to adequately understand transnational exchange, we must begin by determining precisely what was transferred. Only by elucidating the individual "ingredients" can we arrive at a deeper understanding of how an internationally generated program interacts and dovetails with systems of meaning specific to national contexts.

## Notes

1. The policy area of migration proves informative for the issue at hand, since migration, as a genuine international phenomenon, requires interdependent relationships between states (Glick Schiller, Basch, & Blanc-Szanton, 1992).
2. They did not follow suit until after the 1970s but then with a huge number of publications; the OECD joined as late as the 1980s. However, all of these organizations were engaged with educational as well as migration issues during the 1960s (Ogay, 1992, p. 14).
3. Founding members: Belgium, Denmark, France, Ireland, Italy, Luxembourg, the Netherlands, Norway, Sweden, and the United Kingdom. Further members: Austria, Cyprus, Greece, Iceland, Malta, Switzerland, Turkey, and West Germany. Switzerland joined in 1963 (Europarat, 1967).
4. The Council of Europe had an overall mandate that was not limited to the realm of economics, unlike the Organization for European Economic Co-operation (OEEC, the forerunner of the OECD) or the European Coal and Steel Community (ECSC, the forerunner of the European Union). Similar to UNESCO its statutes are primarily oriented to pacifism (Europarat, 1967, p. 14).
5. For recent literature on the Council of Europe, see Bond (2012) or Brummer (2008).
6. See Europarat (1959), Europarat (1967), or Europarat (1970).
7. For Switzerland, see Niederberger (2004) or Mahnig and Piguet (2003); for West Germany, see Mattes (2005).
8. For Switzerland, see Piguet (2006).
9. On the significant number of unregistered children of immigrant workers who were not attending any school, see Ricciardi (2010).
10. This committee, assembling high-ranking officials from every member state and representatives of other international organizations (such as the International Labour Organization, the European Economic Community, and the OECD), has been dealing with the challenges of migration since its foundation in the mid-1950s (Chmielorz, 1985, p. 9). The Consultative Assembly pushed in the mid-1960s as well for a committee on migrant workers, which was established in 1966 (Europarat, 1967, p. 40) and resulted in two resolutions on this issue, in 1968 and 1969 (Reid & Reich, 1992, p. 3).
11. The Council for Cultural Cooperation was founded in 1961 based on the intergovernmental treaty of the European Cultural Convention (1954). Its work was dedicated to

structural questions concerning educational equivalence between the members, textbook improvements, foreign language teaching, and teacher education (Europarat, 1970, p. 39; Wassenberg, 2012, p. 178).
12. See Grube in this volume.
13. The Council of Europe documents provide no explanation as to why these countries did not respond. Whereas the omission might be explained in the case of West Germany by its federal system of organization (see note 16), and in the case of United Kingdom by its very different immigrant situation from that in continental Europe (Steedman 1979), the omission of France is conspicuously puzzling, especially since it was the specific area of competency of the preparer of the report, Pierre Malenfant.
14. Every member state defined substantial criteria such as "migrant worker" differently (Chmielorz, 1985, p. 87).
15. The same applies, if to a lesser extent, to the Federal Republic of Germany and may be the reason that country did not respond to the Council of Europe questionnaire (see note 14).
16. According to the federal constitution, it is the federal government that is responsible for international relations, but at the same time the cantons enjoy broad sovereignty with regard to the educational system.
17. On the history of the CESDOC, see Gentinetta (1997).
18. The institution cannot be characterized as national but rather as inter-cantonal, since it was not led by a department of the national Swiss government but was founded to coordinate education policy between the different cantons.
19. The information within his report was collected throughout the cantons in the previous years (Hirt, 2009, p. 366).
20. On the contradictory reports on Italian children in Switzerland, see also Barcella (2012).
21. Since the Council of Europe was financed by means of a contributions system that was keyed to the size of the countries, West Germany, England, and France bore a major part of the cost.
22. On the genesis of the term *Überfremdung* at the beginning of the 20th century, compare Kury (2003); for the discourse of *Überfremdung* in the 1960s and 1970s in Switzerland, compare Buomberger (2004).
23. For example, in the recommendation for adequate teacher education in the country of origin: "to educate the children of migrant workers abroad, in the civilisation and language of their country of origin" (Resolution (70) 35, 1970, p. 86).

## Archival Sources

### Archive of the Council of Europe, Strasbourg, France

Statute of the Council of Europe, 1949.
Resolution (70) 35: School Education for the Children of Migrant Workers, 27 Nov. 1970.
RS and RS/SEM; School Education for the Children of Migrant Workers.

### Swiss Social Archives, Zurich, Switzerland (SSA)

Ar 48; Zürcher Kontaktstelle für Italiener und Schweizer [Zurich Contact Point for Italians and Swiss]

# References

Barcella, P. (2012). *"Venuti qui per cercare lavoro". Gli emigrati italiani nella Svizzera del secondo dopoguerra*. Bellinzona, Switzerland: Fondazione Pellegrini Canevascini.

Berlinghoff, M. (2013). *Das Ende der "Gastarbeit". Europäische Anwerbestopps 1970–1974*. Paderborn, Germany: Ferdinand Schöningh.

Bond, M. (2012). *The Council of Europe: Structure, history and issues in European politics*. London, UK: Routledge.

Brummer, K. (2008). *Der Europara: Eine Einführung*. Wiesbaden, Germany: VS Verlag für Sozialwissenschaften.

Buomberger, T. (2004). *Kampf gegen unerwünschte Fremde: Von James Schwarzenbach bis Christoph Blocher*. Zurich, Switzerland: Orell Füssli.

Carney, S., Rappleye, H., & Silova, I. (2012). Between faith and science: World culture theory and comparative education. *Comparative Education Review, 56*(3), 366–393. doi:10.1086/665708

Chmielorz, A. (1985). *Der Europarat und die Migration in Europa*. Frankfurt, Germany: Peter Lang.

Drori, G. S., & Krücken, G. (2009). World society: A theory and a research program in context. In G. Krücken & G. S. Drori (Eds.), *World society: The writings of John W. Meyer* (pp. 3–35). Oxford, UK: Oxford University Press.

Europarat. (1959). *Der Europarat 1949–1959*. Strasbourg, France: Presse- und Informationsabteilung des Europarats.

Europarat. (1967). *Der Europarat*. Strasbourg, France: Presse- und Informationsabteilung des Europarats.

Europarat. (1970). *Der Europarat: Presse- und Informationsabteilung des Europarates*. Nancy, France: Berger-Levrault.

Gentinetta, P. M. (1997). Schweizerische Dokumentationsstelle für Schul- und Bildungsfragen CESDOC. In H. Badertscher (Ed.), *Die Schweizerische Konferenz der kantonalen Erziehungsdirektoren 1897 bis 1997* (pp. 237–241). Bern, Switzerland: Paul Haupt.

Glick Schiller, N., Basch, L., & Blanc-Szanton, C. (1992). *Towards a transnational perspective on migration: Race, ethnicity, and nationalism reconsidered*. New York, NY: New York Academy of Sciences.

Hirt, M. (2009). *Die Schweizerische Bundesverwaltung im Umgang mit der Arbeitsmigration: Sozial-, kultur- und staatspolitische Aspekte. 1960 bis 1972*. Saarbrücken, Germany: Südwestdeutscher Verlag für Hochschulschriften.

Holtz, U. (2000). 50 Jahre Europarat: Eine Einführung. In U. Holtz (Ed.), *50 Jahre Europarat* (pp. 9–37). Baden-Baden, Germany: Nomos.

Kury, P. (2003). *Über Fremde reden: Überfremdungsdiskurs und Ausgrenzung in der Schweiz 1900–1945*. Zurich, Switzerland: Chronos.

Mahnig, H., & Piguet, E. (2003). Die Immigrationspolitik der Schweiz von 1948 bis 1998: Entwicklung und Auswirkungen. In H.-R. Wicker, R. Fibbi, & W. Haug (Eds.), *Migration und die Schweiz: Ergebnisse des Nationalen Forschungsprogramms "Migration und interkulturelle Beziehungen"* (pp. 65–108). Zurich, Switzerland: Seismo.

Mattes, M. (2005). *"Gastarbeiterinnen" in der Bundesrepublik. Anwerbepolitik, Migration und Geschlecht in den 50er bis 70er Jahren*. Frankfurt, Germany: Campus.

Meyer, J. W., Boli, J., Thomas, G. M., & Ramirez, F. O. (2005). Die Weltgesellschaft und der Nationalstaat. In G. Krücken (Ed.), *John W. Meyer. Weltkultur: Wie die westlichen Prinzipien die Welt durchdringen* (pp. 85–132). Frankfurt, Germany: Suhrkamp.

Meyer, J. W., & Ramirez, F. O. (2005). Die globale Institutionalisierung der Bildung. In G. Krücken (Ed.), *John W. Meyer. Weltkultur: Wie die westlichen Prinzipien die Welt durchdringen* (pp. 212–234). Frankfurt, Germany: Suhrkamp.

Niederberger, J. M. (2004). *Ausgrenzen, Assimilieren, Integrieren: Die Entwicklung einer schweizerischen Integrationspolitik*. Zurich, Switzerland: Seismo.

Ogay, T. (1992). *De l'éducation des enfants de migrants à l'éducation interculturelle. Les activités des organisations internationales: Conseil de l'Europe, Communauté européenne, OECD, UNESCO.* Bern, Switzerland: Office fédérale de l'éducation e de la science.

Piguet, E. (2006). *Einwanderungsland Schweiz*. Bern, Switzerland: Haupt.

Reid, E., & Reich, H. H. (1992). *Breaking the boundaries: Migrant workers' children in the EC*. Clevedon, UK: Multilingual Matters.

Ricciardi, T. (2010). I figli degli stagionali: bambini clandestini. *Studi Emigrazione, 47*(180), 872–886.

Schriewer, J. (2007). *Weltkultur und kulturelle Bedeutungswelten: Zur Globalisierung von Bildungsdiskursen*. Frankfurt, Germany: Campus.

Schriewer, J. (2012). Meaning constellations in the world society. *Comparative Education, 48*(4), 411–422. doi:10.1080/03050068.2012.737233

Steedman H. (1979). The education of migrant workers' children in EEC countries: From assimilation to cultural pluralism? *Comparative Education, 15*(3), 259–268. doi:10.1080/0305006790150304

Wassenberg, B. (2012). *Histoire du Conseil de l'Europe (1949–2009)*. Brussels, Belgium: Peter Lang.

# 12

# LANGUAGE STRUCTURES IN A MULTILINGUAL AND MULTIDISCIPLINARY WORLD

## The Adaptations of Luxembourgian Language Education Within a Cold War Culture

*Catherina Schreiber*

### "The Vodka Is Potent, but the Meat Is Rotten": What Cybernetics and Linguistic Confusion Have to Do With Structural Language

Popular jokes often mirror cultural concerns of the time of their first mention. A famous joke of the Cold War period went around about a computer that the CIA (Central Intelligence Agency) had built to translate from English to Russian and Russian to English. The director of the CIA was invited to test the machine and entered, "The spirit is willing but the flesh is weak." The machine cranked and groaned, and Cyrillic letters appeared on the screen. When the CIA translated the result back into English, trying to check the correctness of the translation, the result was "The vodka is potent, but the meat is rotten." A similar "apocryphal tale" that went around in the early 1960s claimed that the computer translation of "out of sight, out of mind" yielded the phrase "invisible insanity" (Budiansky, 1998, p. 80).

Stories like these problematize the idea that any kind of problem can be solved by an automatized process, whose algorithms provide it with a certain idea of structure as the main parameter. Concretely, the tales referred to hurdles of communication that turned the Iron Curtain into a linguistic one as well. In fact, at the end of the Second World War, intellectuals around the world were faced with an unpredicted linguistic turmoil: For one, scientific research, which since the mid-19th century had largely been published in only three languages (English, French, and German, with the latter two decreasing rapidly after the First World War; cf. Viegand, 1999), now also appeared in publications in Russian, owing to the Soviet Union's rapidly enlarging scientific facilities. Second, former colonies in

Asia and Africa were uncoupled from their imperial contexts, which pointed public awareness to the question as to what the official languages of the former colonies should be—examples of postcolonial multilingual nation-states might be Jamaica, Sri Lanka, and Cameroon (Anchimbe, 2007; cf. also Weber, 2009). Concurrently, ideological differences were discursively interpreted as communication difficulties, especially in the areas that were torn between West and East: Stevenson (2002) collected catchy newspaper examples of a discourse on alleged linguistic problems of communication between East and West Germans that suggested that they may understand each other's words but they do not understand what each other is saying.

The solution for this linguistic confusion, as the quoted jokes already indicated, was sought in automatic processing of seemingly *universal* structures: Cybernetic concepts, which had emerged during the Second World War as an "interdisciplinary science of the structure of complex systems," had re-conceptualized any communication as "information processing" (Hartmann, 2008, p. 45). After the Second World War, cybernetics as a science emancipated itself from the concrete war context, promoted by utopian visions, political beliefs in feasibility and practicability, and a strong belief in scientific innovation (cf. Tanner, 2008, p. 377): Not only did cybernetics in the Western European countries represent and transport the ideology of a "technocratic objectivity" (Tanner, 2008, p. 412), but it also served at the same time as a meta-science, a bridge between the different academic disciplines (cf. Pongratz, 1978, p. 14) and across countries.[1]

With the cybernetic definition of information, in which it was understood as abstract, information was hence equally applicable to social and natural sciences, to all human beings and machines, likewise connecting to mathematical information theory (Tanner, 2008, p. 403).

A structural understanding of scientific disciplines and educational subjects was the most present in discourses in mathematics (cf. Lenz, Rohstock, & Schreiber, 2013; Schreiber, 2014): Cultivating specific mental dispositions, mathematics was deemed ideal to teach good thinking, and especially the new emerging mathematics with an emphasis on formal and abstract elements was believed to foster active scientific thinking. Abstract ways of organizing mathematics in sets, relations, operations, and structures such as modules, fields, vector spaces, and groups (Scholtus, 1971) gave the illusion of a uniform structural mathematics, linked by fundamental ideas common to all of them—per se one kind of thinking for all citizens and "one mathematics for the whole world" (Dieschbourg, 1975, p. 65).

This chapter will focus not on mathematics but on the allegedly "softer" school subjects instead, on language education, and will investigate what elements of mathematical and cybernetic information theories were integrated into concepts of language teaching and how the internationally changing educational understandings of linguistics were adapted to specific national contexts when they were integrated into the curriculum. More precisely, it will focus on the idea of a natural language that can be seen as an abstract structure to which mathematical techniques and operations can be applied and will investigate both its embeddedness in international language education policies and its implementation in national curricula, based on empirical evidence from Luxembourg.

In this chapter I want to make the thesis plausible that global educational similarities, like this idea of linguistic interdependence and universal grammatical relations in foreign language learning, as still promoted today within global policies of multilingualism and intercultural education, can be understood only in their concrete historical development, in this case the challenge to solve the communication and ideological problems of the Cold War, and in their national contexts, which differed significantly from these international aspirations. To do so, I will proceed in three steps: First, I will exemplify the educational and didactic implications of an assumption of somewhat universal linguistic structures that emerged from an international "Cold War culture" (Whitfield, 1996).

I then focus on one national case, Luxembourg, as an allegedly culturally "inherited" linguistic "melting pot at the heart of the European Union" (J.-P. Hoffmann, 1996, pp. 96f.) and one of the political centers where the European institutions are located; it is situated between two big neighboring countries, whose reputation as scientific role models in the world was rapidly declining. Based on this empirical study, I will investigate the Luxembourgian adaptations and demonstrate that Luxembourgian curricular negotiations took up the international discussions but supplemented them with other, explicitly national functions—namely, that of national integration and the persistence of idiosyncratic language learning. Based on this historical study, the chapter will offer some outlooks on post–Cold War language instruction in Luxembourg, which is widely based on the notion of multilingualism.

Within the overall topic of this book, this chapter considers these international and national language discourses a suitable example, as it addresses international policies within a field that was traditionally closely connected to constructions of national identity and nation-state citizenship rather than to construction of universally valid abstract forms.

Most nation-states in Western and Northern Europe were more or less monolingual constructions, in contrast to the multilingual Ancien Regimes, such as the Austro-Hungarian, Russian, and Ottoman Empires and the Holy Roman Empire of the German Nation. Especially the two dominant nation-states of 19th century continental Europe, France and Germany, identified their allegedly superior national characters with their respective natural languages (Tröhler, in press). Even states that were provisioned constitutionally as multilingual, such as Belgium and Switzerland, were linguistically organized along the principle of territorial monolingualism.

A structural understanding of language as an abstract phenomenon, in the context of the postwar period, alternatively offered new opportunities to uncouple the European languages from their nationalist connotations and from their respective historical cultural contexts, which prompted different reactions by educationalists in the respective countries. In Germany, Ludwig Pongratz (1978), for instance, deliberately and pejoratively talked about the *Geschichtslosigkeit* [absence of historicity] of all cybernetic structuralism. In the United States, in contrast, linguistics gained a reputation as the most advanced of all social sciences, based on its allegedly systematic and overall formal nature (Martin-Nielsen, 2012, p. 63). And yet, in terms of historiography, linguistics is one of the least-investigated social sciences of the postwar era (p. 63) and still a desideratum to be analyzed with regard to its educational implications in school curricula.

## Educationalizing the Search for Universal Language Structures: Competing and Complementary Approaches

It has already been indicated that U.S. politics fostered linguistics at the intersection with cybernetics, in order to, as Léon Dostert[2] expressed it in 1957, obtain "ready, un-delayed access to scientific information written in the languages of the several scientifically creative cultures of our day" (cited in Martin-Nielsen, 2012, p. 67): Even though the reference to the Soviet Union is not made explicit here, announcements like this have to be understood in the direct context of the launch of the Russian satellite Sputnik in the same year, which publicly formed a hardly ignorable and unmistakable symbol of Russian scientific progress. In the years after the Sputnik launch, educationalists and politicians stressed the need to increase foreign language capacity among students. Language knowledge grew into a highly valued *commodity* (Martin-Nielsen, 2010, p. 144).

Linguistic projects in the following years enjoyed great financial support in the United States, partially motivated by reported machine translation successes in the Soviet Union, such as English-to-Russian translation at the USSR Academy of Sciences in 1956 (Martin-Nielsen, 2012, p. 73). The two main objectives were fast (machine) translation and information retrieval. Both were syntax-based projects, and the work raised the awareness that the study of syntax was still in its infancy.

Language education in general was then promoted in the United States, and during the following years it was officially approved by the National Defense Education Act in 1958. Language became one of the main areas in which life was depicted as a permanent process of learning, thereby establishing the perception of language as a cognitive system. Since then, educational authorities in many parts of the world have made not only foreign language education but, more than that, communication skills training in general a part of their national curriculum (Block, 2008, p. 36).

Several competing linguistic perceptions have to be mentioned here that offered educational promises. The first was still a behaviorist one, which in the postwar period provided the ground for programmed instruction and the use of audiovisual media in education: The most prominent theory was presented by psychologist Burrhus Frederic (B. F.) Skinner (1957/1991) in *Verbal Behavior*, which described language as a system of verbal operants. Skinner's assumption was that children are born as blank minds; by slow and constant conditioning through schedules of reinforcement, language learning can be programmed. The main demand was that learning to *speak* a language would replace any abstract, mechanically learned grammatical knowledge.

Probably the most prominent and influential critique of Skinner's *Verbal Behavior* came from Noam Chomsky (1959). Chomsky's psycholinguistic theory, like Skinner's, assumed that children learn their mother tongue, the "internalized language," in early childhood yet not through conditioning solely but rather via their pre-programmed capacity to learn language in general: Chomsky's resulting transformational grammar was built on overall strong links between linguistic approaches and ancillary sciences, most of all electrical and computer engineering, computing, and mathematics. He and his followers elaborated the idea that internationally valid universal phenomena of the human mind underlie all language and that the grammars of individual languages were predicted as "permitted variants of this universal grammar" (Downes, 1984, p. 10).

Skinner's and Chomsky's concepts seem so different in their assumptions of a blank versus a pre-programmed mind that they were perceived as competing linguistic models, and there was no recognition that both approaches were variations of the same Cold War linguistic aspirations: Whether language knowledge is acquired by conditioning or intuition, both perceptions of language assume somewhat universal structures in language, and both approaches widely corresponded in their educational suggestions. The same holds true for rival syntactic theories that competed with Chomsky's *transformational grammar*, such as *stratificational grammar* and *constituency grammar*, which all aimed to explain the structure of natural language. As Martin-Nielsen (2010) argued, teachers in classrooms reassembled the different syntactic theories anyway into mixed tool-boxes suitable for the classroom setting (p. 146) and via international cooperation among teachers spread the following educational suggestions among language instructors throughout the world:

- Audio-lingual methods and "structural-global" methods of language learning were implemented that aimed to teach grammar (especially syntax) together with, and not separately from, the other aspects of communication in a foreign language. All aspects of speech in a foreign language—intonation, phonetics, vocabulary, grammar, and even non-verbal speech (gestures, mimicry, allusions, behavior)—should be taught to the student to come as close as possible to "real" situations.
- Accordingly, the need for active learner participation and for greater emphasis on communicative competences was stressed as a way of teaching students the communication skills and abstract logical structures behind language that—according to cybernetic thinking—were expressed in terms of circular causality, feedback mechanisms, and steering processes (Hartmann, 2008, p. 45).

- Other ideas included the use of new audio-visual media, sequential contrasting of language structures, programmed instruction as envisioned by Skinner (1957/1991) in the form depicted above, and the establishment of language laboratories (Urth, 1964).

Already in the 1950s, American schools had dealt with *structural grammar*. This approach to linguistics was an integral part of American structuralism: It assumed that language was imbued with systematic structural characteristics that could be determined through study. At professional association meetings and in journals and teaching newsletters, teachers debated the merits of applying theoretical linguistics in their classrooms. Even those who were concerned about the speed with which academic linguistic theories were changing were attracted by the tools they offered (Martin-Nielsen, 2010, p. 145). However, these educational suggestions were abstract and flexible enough to leave room for national idiosyncrasies. Cybernetics-inspired ideas in their understanding of language were flexible containers for varying meanings of national content per se; like most cybernetic notions they were "underdetermined concepts" (Tanner, 2008, p. 379).

## Adaptations in Luxembourgian Language Education

The Second World War and the German occupation had interrupted Luxembourgian school politics at a time of emotional reform debates, and the discussions reignited only slowly in the 1960s. The main reform of the direct postwar period was the reinstatement of the pre-war syllabi, with the aim to "reinstall" specifically Luxembourgian traditions, as the secondary school teachers' petitions tell us (Ministère de l'Education Nationale [MEN]-1145, 1947).

But the reignited reform discussions of the 1960s were perceived as presenting completely "new measures," or "unprecedented proposals," to put it briefly: an entire renewal of the education system to achieve a "school for the future," with a "modern spirit" (*d'Letzeburger Land*, May 26, 1961, p. 3; July 7, 1961, p. 1; September 21, 1962, p. 3), indicating also a significant change in the perception of education in general as "transformative" (Action familiale et Populaire, 1970, unnumbered foreword).

International organizations like UNESCO; further bilateral agreements with the United States and European countries such as Belgium, the Netherlands, the Federal Republic of Germany, Italy, and Switzerland; and various multilateral agreements supported the transnational exchange in education, resulting in Luxembourg's participation in international conferences, seminars, and teacher training. Indeed, harsh critics of cybernetic suggestions, as they existed for instance among (West) German peers who were concerned about the "cybernetic undermining of the idea of *Bildung*" (Pongratz, 1978, p. 255), could not be found among Luxembourgian educationalists. Supported by international policies, debates on scientification that seemed to challenge the previous supremacy of language instruction took place across all Luxembourgian newspapers and professional discourses. This "new scientific spirit" (*Luxemburger Wort*, February 6, 1968) was claimed to offer more social justice, overcome cultural bias, and provide new coherent ways of thinking and learning. The new scientific methods not only were considered to promote the innovative potential of deprived students but also were intertwined with the ideal of objectivity that was prominently placed in discussions about career chances and the social (in)justice of secondary schooling in Luxembourg, for which programmed instruction in particular seemed perfectly suitable. Even the potential of replacing all types of exams was attributed to programmed teaching. These ideas were also integrated into teacher training, when the *Normalschule* for primary school teachers established a seminar for programmed instruction and teaching machines in 1967 in close cooperation with scientists from abroad (*d'Letzeburger Land*, January 19, 1968, p. 3).

A new primary school syllabus in 1964 integrated cybernetic and structural thinking by explicitly stating "systematic progression" of all subject matter instead of single curricular knowledge as the basic principle of schooling (Ministère de l'Education Nationale, 1964, p. 5). Debates on the curriculum were explicitly about the intellectual discipline that future citizens would need (Ministère de l'Education Nationale, 1964). This notion assumed that behind every subject and behind the whole curriculum there stood a *system* of thinking, mirrored by the dictions of *Mechanismen* (mechanisms), *Aufbau* (setup), and *Struktur* (structure), and that students would only have to comprehend in order to move continuously from primary school to secondary school to higher education and between different school types.

The interpretation of the curriculum as "systematic progression" spread to the notion of language as a structural phenomenon with intelligent and transferable processes (e.g., Schloesser, 1974). To learn these processes, language laboratories seemed to be the perfect medium (Figure 12.1) (Urth, 1964; Hauffels, 1970; Legerin-Lambert, 1974). Syntax was addressed actively by means of integral teaching methods such as the *méthode structuro-globale* (*Luxemburger Wort*, October 11, 1969), which fostered primarily concrete conversational situations (e.g., Ministère de l'Education Nationale, 1975). For instance, French lessons were now oriented along concrete topics such as "the route," "contemporary events," "sports," and "adventures" (MEN-1136, 1971) to bring French to a "daily and concrete level" (MEN-1136, 1971). Spoken presentations and dialogues were considered to be of highest didactical value (Mathieu, 1968). In addition, French instruction no longer compiled vocabulary lists that were divided into word classes (e.g., Schilling, 1974) but instead grouped vocabulary by sentences and sense groups.

Nevertheless, teachers in Luxembourg were anxious to give a national quality to this scientific "renewal." In a very pragmatic understanding, the Luxembourgian discourses implemented the international suggestions in language education as a means to maintain the strong position of language education against reform attempts to increase the lesson time scheduled for other school subjects, especially

**FIGURE 12.1** Language laboratory at a Luxembourgian school. Picture taken by Tony Krier (Letzeburger Land, October 24, 1969). Permission for publication granted by the *Bibliothèque nationale de Luxembourg*.

for the sciences: Philologists made up 57.3% of all Luxembourgian teachers, and language education amounted to more than one third of all lessons in the vocational school tracks and more than one half in the secondary school tracks (MEN-1136, 1970). High school mathematics, biology, and geography teachers complained continuously about further reductions of classes in favor of language instruction that could strengthen what was already a "manifest disequilibrium" (MEN-1135, 1969). French, German, Luxembourgish, English, and Latin lessons, for instance, would add up to 43–45 hours (out of a total of 86 hours) after the three lower grades of the secondary school, whereas mathematics, biology, and geography had only 18 hours altogether: With this disparity between language and science education, the teachers declared, it would be impossible to follow the evolution that mathematics education had undergone in other countries (MEN-1158, 1967).

Language education was also exploited for another purpose that stood in no connection with the international policies and was not made explicit in the Luxembourgian discourse—namely, for the purpose of national integration. The following functions, which I examine further below, served this purpose:

- the construction of one coherent national school system through global language teaching methods
- the furthering of Luxembourgish as a spoken language
- the uncoupling of French and German from their cultural-historical roots in the neighboring countries, and their implementation as proxies of national narratives

- the veiling of intranational language hierarchies that distinguished the traditional *humanistic* secondary schools of the elite from the other schools.

## *Language to Construct Coherence*

In fact, Luxembourgian educational discourses of the 1960s and 1970s were faced with specific educational problems: There was criticism of the high intranational stratification that was mirrored in distinct curricular differences according to social status, region, father's profession, and gender (cf. Schreiber, 2014). Brochures that were distributed by private initiatives (Bollendorf, 1962) reveal that there was a rising awareness of "social inequalities" reflected in and/or created through the school system, which were perceived as hurdles for national unity.

In this context, methodological discussions on language education gained further importance, a fact that demonstrates the allegedly unifying (yet rather symbolic) potential of a coherent method rather than coherent topics (e.g., *Luxemburger Wort*, July 15, 1969, p. 3). Perspectives were to be chosen in language education in which children themselves appeared as *acting* persons (Ministère de l'Education Nationale, 1964, pp. 30f.).

The perspective shifted increasingly from a focus on the curriculum to a focus on (individual) learning progress and not on the matters taught, and the methodological focus on specific skills mirrored ongoing discourses on social justice and individual opportunities. The range of methods presented to promote specific skills of the democratic, critical, and active citizen within a more coherent national system was broad and included the direct method, the *méthode structuro-globale*, and global reading methods (e.g., *Luxemburger Wort*, July 15, 1969, p. 3). A chapter on audio-visual media was also included in the primary syllabus of 1964 (Ministère de l'Education Nationale, 1964, pp. 123–125). Particular importance was also attached to all methods that would foster the class as a group and strengthen cooperation among students to create a community that was working together—a function that had not been mentioned in any curricular document previously (*Luxemburger Wort*, October 15, 1968). Thoughts about group dynamics kept teachers-to-be busy in their educational theses (e.g., Hetto, 1967; Klemmer, 1969), and team teaching methods were integrated in English, French, and German lessons (e.g., Klemmer, 1969).

The discursive importance of specific *language skills* that should be fixed as provisions of the syllabus (speaking being the most prominent) left further room for curricular differences in how to achieve the envisioned aims, while stressing an alleged continuous *legato* process over different branches and instances of the school system, hence constructing a coherent nationwide school system, where the junctions between the different school forms and the distinctions between the national languages (French, German, and the Luxembourgian dialect) were blurred. With this, the professional discourses ignored the fact that the still existing structural transitions in the school system were always accompanied by *staccato* linguistic switches and that language learning hence was coupled to distinct curricular steps.

## Luxembourgish as an Informal Language

The educational focus on speaking and communication skills and universal linguistic structures provided additional legitimation for the development of Luxembourgish as an informal spoken language (instead of just a German dialect) and as a key symbol of the independent Luxembourgian nation. Although Luxembourgish was recognized as an official language only in 1984, language education in Luxembourg, which up to 1964 had been bilingual, became trilingual with the primary school syllabus of 1964 (Ministère de l'Education Nationale, 1964, p. 9). The construction of Luxembourgish as a language gained further momentum: Luxembourgish figured in the program as a proper school subject for the first time and was placed even before French and German. The aim was more of a representative (political) one than a specific educational added value: The official aspirations in the syllabus did not specify any more than that "our Luxembourgish language is the expression of our mental and cultural idiosyncrasy and has to have a place of honor in our school" (p. 9). Difficulties that resulted from the fact that a transparent and generally valid orthography did not yet exist were circumvented by handing the problem over to the teachers: If they graded achievement in written schoolwork, they were only allowed to grade content and choice of expressions but not the writing itself (p. 10).

## Language Structures and the Absence of Historicity

Along similar arguments, the emphasis on orthographic correctness in German lessons also diminished, continuing the trend of the language education reforms of the interwar period that aimed to open up German lessons also for Luxembourgish language particularities. International "vulgarized" methods were to familiarize children with the use of diverse languages as "vehicles" of thought. The study of grammar, syntax, orthography, and style followed only as a second step: The compartmentalization of German instruction comprised, first, object lessons; then, second, reading and writing; and, as a third subdiscipline, "free conversation" (Ministère de l'Education Nationale, 1964, p. 41). After that, the traditional subdisciplines of vocabulary and stylistics were taught and, only last, orthography and essay writing (p. 49). Luxembourgian evolving psycholinguistics had tried the same approach already since the First World War (Schreiber, Gardin, & Tröhler, in press). Not only did this blur the distinction between formal German and Luxembourgish, but the efforts also aimed at a language policy in favor of German, but a German distinct from the historical-cultural context of Germany.[3] By abstracting from the language itself to an extended methodological discussion on "How do I learn to read?," the syllabus of 1964, for instance, permitted all methods (synthetic, analytic, mixed, or *integral*) as equivalent (Ministère de l'Education Nationale, 1964).

To a lesser extent, this happened in French language education as well. The discourse emphasized the common, integral elements of language learning instead of differences between the languages and their cultural connotations. On the contrary, language was understood as a medium to shape students' intelligent problem solving capabilities and their structural and logical understanding. At a formal level French was strengthened as the language of official communication and as one of the most important school subjects in primary school and one on which the syllabus prescribed spending the most time (Ministère de l'Education Nationale, 1964, pp. 11–29). However, at the same time, the subject French was attached to the "breath of Old Luxembourg" (*Luxemburger Wort*, March 10, 1970). In French instruction, one can therefore also detect certain attempts to uncouple the language from its previous historical-cultural contexts as a formal language of French literature, which had been the role model for Luxembourgian elites since the 19th century: Knowledge of French grammar was no longer included as an aim per se (Ministère de l'Education Nationale, 1964, p. 11). In accordance with the emphasis on applied French language, teaching and learning themselves changed: Vocabulary was not learned according to formal aspects but as appropriate to the application. Sentences were learned as a whole, not as a conglomeration of vocabulary. The sentence as a *group of meaning* was linked to a projected audio-visual equivalent (*Luxemburger Wort*, October 11, 1969; Schilling, 1974). In secondary schools, the literature and textbooks provided for reading were also modernized: The programs integrated supplementary works of contemporary literature and youth literature (MEN-1135, 1969). Luxembourgian literature in French was likewise incorporated into the curriculum (Ministère de l'Education Nationale, 1975, pp. 45f.), although no literature of that kind was ever mentioned by the professors or program commissions regarding the practical conduct of language teaching.

Uncoupled in that way from their original cultural connotations, both German and French could function as propagators of national unity (MEN-1136, 1971). The German program in particular conveyed a new self-perception of the Luxembourgian state more than other school subjects did. It was used, for instance, to support the historical master narrative of its alleged 1,000 years of existence, although under foreign domination (Ministère de l'Education Nationale, 1964, p. 125).

## *Veiling Intranational Language Hierarchies*

The Luxembourgian educational system—with German being the language of instruction in the lower school tracks and French in the higher school tracks (MEN-1135, 1968)—adhered to an educational hierarchy that fixed German as the language of the whole nation, including the less educated,[4] and French as the language of the educated elite:

> One uses French within the bounds of possibility and German whenever indispensable, i.e., practically everywhere where it is necessary to make oneself assuredly understood by a less educated audience.
>
> (Zimmer, 1977, *p. 155*)

Numerous professors problematized the use of German as a teaching language in secondary education in general (MEN-1136, 1970), and others protested against "amputations" of French that would contradict the "tradition" and its "formative value" (MEN-1135, 1969).

The new language policies made these hierarchies invisible by blurring the contours between the learning and employment of the particular languages in abstract form, without changing the language hierarchies per se, not only between German and French but also between modern and classical languages.

New types of secondary education were added in the early 1960s. The traditionally humanistic secondary schools for the Luxembourgian elite, which had been built on a strong focus on the classical languages, were confronted with the probably highly complicated task of harmonization: to continue their humanistic school tradition but without abandoning the international orientation that they also counted as their tradition, and to fulfill what the reports of the curricular commissions called "the spirit of progress and realism" (MEN-1135, 1968). The ideal route for the classical secondary schools was assumed to be strong but gradual specialization into various secondary school sections with different options.

The questions at stake were foremost matters of principle: the equality and equivalence of the two educational orders, classical and modern,[5] to prevent "certain discrimination" (MEN-1135, 1968). New language sections were formed for "living languages." In addition to English, German, and French, courses in Italian and Spanish were offered by several schools on a voluntary basis in both the lower and the upper grades (e.g., Ministère de l'Education Nationale, 1975, pp. 65f.); this is another indicator of the conciliatory policy to allow for modernization of language education in Luxembourg. The reform of the duration of the secondary schools, limiting the classical sections to six years, assigned equal periods of study to the ancient language and modern language sections. The holistic language learning method was even adapted to Latin language instruction in form of *Assimil Latinum* (Liefgen, 1968), and through this, with some methodological and didactic effort, Latin professors managed to give Latin a modernized image (e.g., Weins, 1970). With measures like these, the notion of *Bildung* was established as one that was transferable to postwar educational practice (Koch, 1972). The notion of humanism was simultaneously stretched to include a realist dimension, so that it became compatible with new tendencies in the educational theory and societal discussions of the time. For instance, in a psychological interpretation, foreign language skills, in classical and modern languages alike, were considered to be an indicator of students' motivation (*Leistungswille*; e.g., Hierzig, 1978, p. 99).

But in the meantime, discourses among secondary teachers envisaged a revival of discussions on ancient values that could provide a moral, ethical, and aesthetic orientation, as expressed, for instance, in strong support for formal Latin-to-French translations (Schmit, 1973), stylistic finesse, and a choice of readings that favored ancient philosophical original works (Scheidweiler, 1965; Kohnen, 1967).

All these additional functions showed that the innovations in language education were strongly adapted to the purpose of national integration and were hence established only as flexible containers for persistent ways of linguistic reasoning. It is therefore not surprising that, even so, the reflections on an overarching language learning largely ended in talk during the 1970s: The last mention of language laboratories was in 1974, for instance (Legerin-Lambert, 1974).

## "Multilingual Luxembourgers at the Heart of Europe": Outlooks on Current Language Education

However, these discourses of the 1960s and 1970s loosely provided the ground for recent policies of multilingualism embedded in discourses on *globalization* that were only made possible by the ideas of Cold War linguistics. The basic idea is simple: Once humanity has understood the fundamental universal syntax of a structural language, then different languages are only different forms of expression for the same thing. Also providing the ground for this was the de-historicization of language, the relativization of languages' historical connotations as products of a specific culture.

Since the mid-20th century, UNESCO reports dedicated themselves to the definition of the relation between national languages as tokens of national identities and other languages that are used in specific financial, economic, or power contexts: "Now languages not only are signs of authentic national identities, they are also seen as commodities, the possession of which is a valued skill in the job market" (Block, 2008, p. 34).

Indeed, multilingualism became a defining part of national narratives of post–Cold War Luxembourg: The school system creating "multilingual Luxembourgers at the heart of Europe" (*d'Letzeburger Land*, October 27, 1989) was ever and anon lauded in research for its "highly complex, and admirable, path towards a truly European education" (C. Hoffmann, 1998, p. 159).

Yet several points are still not made explicit in Luxembourg's self-perception as a multilingual society:

- First, the Luxembourgian model of multilingualism still reveals language to be a medium of social distinction, not least because societal multilingualism in Luxembourg was in recent decades strongly dependent on material wealth (C. Hoffmann, 1998, p. 159). Trilingual language learning does not take place as a continuous *legato* process but through several language switches that are situated at certain stages of transition, depending on which school branch a student follows.
- Second, in contrast to the notion of multilingualism as the solution to social problems, in which it is ascribed the potential to bridge societal differences, it had exactly the opposite effect in Luxembourg, making it harder to talk across groups (cf. Schreiber, 2014); at the same time, it established a notion of the

"less educated" monolingual Luxembourgers, or even of multilingual ones who are equipped with the "wrong" multilingualism, as deficitary citizens (e.g., Willems & Milmeister, 2008, pp. 85f.)
- Third, Weber (2009) detected strategies of invisibilization of linguistic resources and needs that do not fit this ideal image, and also an invisibilization of children themselves: In Luxembourgian discourse, *multilingualism* and *multiculturalism* today are still frequently understood to refer to "the idealized model of individual Luxembourgish-German-French trilingualism," whereas the actual present-day multilingualism of Luxembourgian society is widely ignored (p. 16).
- At the same time, the secondary schools in particular continued and continue today to teach highly formal French. Up to now, the school system has not responded to the increasing number of students speaking vernacular French and contact language varieties (cf. Weber, 2009, p. 38).

Considering this context, one could speak of a postwar reconstruction of Luxembourg's education system along the lines of a purportedly national identity that (only at first glance contradictory) in turn led to an orientation towards international policies and vice versa. Suggestions for language education concerning linguistic interdependence and universal grammar that emerged from a specific international Cold War culture were combined with goals of national integration and even today have left their imprint on language education in Luxembourg.

## Notes

1. Cybernetics as a meta-science, for instance, addressed the mid-century debate on the relation between the natural/formal sciences as academic disciplines and the social sciences/humanities. One of these debates was the famous German positivism dispute of the 1960s between scholars like Karl Popper, Theodor Adorno, and Jürgen Habermas. The actuator was a debate at a conference held by the German Sociological Association in 1961, where invited speakers discussed differences between the social and natural sciences.
2. Colonel Léon Dostert's CV is the best example to illustrate how the career of linguistics in the United States originated in the context of the Second World War: Working as a translator for General Eisenhower during the war, Dostert became responsible for one of the biggest simultaneous translation projects in history, namely, the simultaneous translation of the Nuremberg trials. In 1949 Dostert, now a professor, was co-founder of the Institute of Languages and Linguistics at Georgetown University and would serve as director of the institute from 1949 until 1959 and also as chair of the Department of Foreign Languages in the School of Foreign Service. In 1954 Dostert was the main person responsible for the cooperation between Georgetown and the International Business Machine Corporation (IBM) on an experiment to produce the first mechanical transfer from one language to another, and he directed the Machine Translation Research Project of Georgetown University, established in 1955.

3. These discourses have to be understood in the context of the two occupations by Germany during the First and Second World Wars and in the context of German discourses that constructed a linguistic unity of Luxembourg and Germany.
4. The best example is special education: Ironically, disabled students, who had to cope the most frequently with the French-speaking authorities, were taught only German, which made them the only completely monolingual group and left them dependent on their environment.
5. After 1968 four rough distinctions were made (*latin-langues*, *latin-sciences*, *langues modernes*, *langues modernes-sciences*); as the choice of the sciences section distinguished further between a mathematical, scientific, or economic focus, there were eight options altogether.

## References

Action familiale et Populaire. (1970). *Schulen von heute, Schulen für morgen: petit guide de l'orientation scolaire*. Luxembourg, Luxembourg: Saint-Paul.

Anchimbe, E. A. (Ed.). (2007). *Linguistic identity in postcolonial multilingual spaces*. Newcastle, UK: Cambridge Scholars Publishing.

Block, D. (2008). Language education and globalization. In S. May & N. H. Hornberger (Eds.), *Encyclopedia of language and education: Vol. 1. Language policy and political issues in education* (2nd ed., pp. 31–43). New York, NY: Springer Science and Business Media.

Bollendorff, L. (1962). *Schulen für alle: petit guide de l'orientation scolaire*. Luxembourg, Luxembourg: Saint-Paul.

Budiansky, S. (1998). Lost in translation. *Atlantic Monthly, 282*(6), 80–84. Retrieved from http://www.theatlantic.com/magazine/archive/1998/12/lost-in-translation/377338/

Chomsky, N. (1959). A review of B. F. Skinner's *Verbal Behavior*. *Language, 35*(1), 26–58. doi:10.2307/411334

Dieschbourg, R. (1975). La mathematique nouvelle. *CLEC Bulletin, 7*, 65–70.

*d'Letzeburger Land. Unabhängige Wochenzeitung für Politik, Wirtschaft und Kultur*. (1954–). Luxembourg, Luxembourg: Imprimerie Bourg-Bourger (Imprimerie Centrale, Imprimerie Saint-Paul).

Downes, W. (1984). *Language and society*. London, UK: Cambridge University Press.

Hartmann, F. (2008). *Medien und Kommunikation*. Vienna, Austria: UTB.

Hauffels, P. (1970). *Le laboratoire de langues et l'enseignement de l'anglais*. Mémoire pédagogique. Archives Nationales de Luxembourg IP-2316.

Hetto, M.-P. (1967). *Die Klasse, eine Gruppe*. Mémoire pédagogique. Archives Nationales de Luxembourg IP-2364.

Hierzig, F. (1978). Beiträge zur Geschichte des Französischunterrichts in unseren Primärschulen. *École et vie, 4*, 98–99.

Hoffmann, C. (1998). Luxembourg and the European schools. In J. Cenoz & F. Genesee (Ed.), *Beyond bilingualism: Multilingualism and multilingual education* (pp. 143–174). Philadelphia, PA: Multilingual Matters.

Hoffmann, J.-P. (1996). Lëtzebuergesch and its competitors: Language contact in Luxembourg today. In G. Newton (Ed.), *Luxembourg and Lëtzebuergesch* (pp. 96–108). Oxford, UK: Clarendon.

Klemmer, R. (1969). *Le travail en groupes. Un moyen pour stimuler l'activité et l'intérêt des élèves dans l'enseignement des langues modernes*. Mémoire pédagogique. Archives Nationales de Luxembourg IP-2531.

Koch, R. (1972). *Der Bildungsbegriff und die pädagogische Praxis*. Mémoire pédagogique. Archives Nationales de Luxembourg IP-2546.

Kohnen, J. (1967). *Pour une réforme du cours d'auteurs grecs*. Mémoire pédagogique. Archives Nationales de Luxembourg IP-2558.

Legerin-Lambert, H. (1974). *Utilisation optimale du laboratoire de langues pour l'enseignement de l'anglais en classe deVIe*. Mémoire pédagogique. Archives Nationales de Luxembourg IP-2644.

Lenz, T., Rohstock, A., & Schreiber, C. (2013). Tomorrow never dies: A socio-historical analysis of the Luxembourgish curriculum. In W. F. Pinar (Ed), *International handbook of curriculum research* (2nd ed., pp. 315–328). New York, NY: Routledge.

Liefgen, Paul (1968). *Assimil Latinum. La méthode Assimil dans l'enseignement du latin*. Mémoire pédagogique. Archives Nationales de Luxembourg IP-2659.

*Luxemburger Wort. Für Wahrheit und Recht*. (1848–). Luxembourg, Luxembourg: Saint-Paul.

Martin-Nielsen, J. (2010). "This war for men's minds": The birth of a human science in Cold War America. *History of the Human Sciences, 23*(5), 131–155. doi:10.1177/0952695110378952

Martin-Nielsen, J. (2012). "It was all connected": Computers and linguistics in early Cold War America. In M. Solovey & H. Cravens (Eds.), *Cold War social science: Knowledge production, liberal democracy and human nature* (pp. 63–78). New York, NY: Palgrave Macmillan.

Mathieu, A. (1968). *Der mündliche Vortrag und das Klassengespräch im Französichunterricht auf der Quarta: Zu einer Reihe von praktischen Versuchen*. Mémoire pédagogique. Archives Nationales de Luxembourg IP-2730.

Ministère de l'Education Nationale (MEN): portfolio MEN. (1947). Fonds des ministères, administrations et institutions publiques. Archives Nationales de Luxembourg MEN-1135 to MEN-1163.

Ministère de l'Education Nationale. (1964). Plan d'Etudes pour les Ecoles Primaires du Grand-Duché de Luxembourg. *Courrier de l'Education Nationale* 1, Numéro Spécial.

Ministère de l'Education Nationale. (1975). *Enseignement Secondaire: Horaires et programmes 1975–1976*. Luxembourg, Luxembourg: Ministère de l'Education Nationale.

Pongratz, L. (1978). *Zur Kritik kybernetischer Methodologie in der Pädagogik: Ein paradigmatisches Kapitel szientistischer Verkürzung pädagogisch-anthropologischer Reflexion*. Frankfurt, Germany: Peter Lang.

Scheidweiler, G. (1965). *Faut-il, dans les lycées luxembourgeois, traduire le latin en allemand ou en français?* Mémoire pédagogique. Archives Nationales de Luxembourg IP-3065.

Schilling, R. (1974). *Die Behandlung des französischen Wortschatzes im Sekundarunterricht. Vorschläge zu einer Neuorientierung*. Mémoire pédagogique. Archives Nationales de Luxembourg IP-3082.

Schloesser, J. (1974). *La linguistique structurale dans l'enseignement*. Mémoire pédagogique. Archives Nationales de Luxembourg IP-3099.

Schmit, E. (1973). *Vorschläge zur Förderung des altsprachlichen Unterrichts und des antiken Gedankenguts*. Mémoire pédagogique. Archives Nationales de Luxembourg IP-3108.

Scholtus, F. (1971). *Einführung und Anwendung des Modulbegriffes im Mathematikunterricht der Prima*. Mémoire pédagogique. Archives Nationales de Luxembourg IP-3164.

Schreiber, C. (2014). *Curricula and the making of the citizens: Trajectories from 19th and 20th century Luxembourg*. Unpublished doctoral dissertation, University of Luxembourg, Luxembourg.

Schreiber, C., Gardin, M., & Tröhler, D. (in press). Curriculum unter Beschuss? Luxemburger Schulreformen im Kontext des Ersten Weltkriegs. In C. Roemer, B. Majerus, &

G. Thommes (Eds.), *Guerre(s) au Luxembourg 1914–1918/Krieg(e) in Luxemburg.* Luxembourg, Luxembourg: capybarabooks.

Skinner, B. F. (1991). *Verbal behavior.* New York, NY: Copley. Kindle Edition. (First published 1957)

Stevenson, P. (2002). *Language and German disunity: A sociolinguistic history of east and west in Germany, 1945–2000.* Oxford, UK: Oxford University Press.

Tanner, J. (2008). Komplexität, Kybernetik und Kalter Krieg: "Information" im Systemantagonismus von Markt und Plan. In M. Hagner & E. Hörl (Ed.), *Die Transformation des Humanen: Beiträge zur Kulturgeschichte der Kybernetik* (pp. 377–413). Frankfurt, Germany: Suhrkamp.

Tröhler, D. (in press). Curriculum history. In J. Rury & E. Tamura (Eds.), *Oxford handbook on the history of education.* Oxford, UK: Oxford University Press.

Urth, M. (1964). *Das Sprachlaboratorium und sein Anwendung im Luxemburger Unterricht.* Mémoire pédagogique. Archives Nationales de Luxembourg IP-3371.

Viegand, H. E. (Ed.). (1999). *Sprache und Sprachen in den Wissenschaften.* Berlin, Germany: De Gruyter.

Weber, J.-J. (2009). *Multilingualism, education and change.* Frankfurt, Germany: Peter Lang.

Weins, R. (1970). *Neue Methoden des Lateinunterrichts in der Sekundarschule.* Mémoire pédagogique. Archives Nationales de Luxembourg IP-3447.

Whitfield, S. J. (1996). *The culture of the Cold War* (2nd ed.). Baltimore, MD: Johns Hopkins University Press.

Willems, H., & Milmeister, P. (2008). Migration und integration. In W. Lorig & M. Hirsch (Eds.), *Das politische System Luxemburgs* (pp. 62–92). Wiesbaden, Germany: VS Verlag für Sozialwissenschaften.

Zimmer, R. (1977). Dialekt—Nationaldialekt—Standardsprache: Vergleichende Betrachtungen zum deutsch-französischen Kontaktbereich in der Schweiz, im Elsaß und in Luxemburg. *Zeitschrift für Dialektologie und Linguistik, 44*(2), 145–157.

# 13

# CONTESTING EDUCATION

## Media Debates and the Public Sphere in Luxembourg

*Thomas Lenz*

In Luxembourg a press system that perished in the rest of Europe some 80 years ago has survived until this day: Every political party still has its own affiliated press. This chapter shows how and why the press, the parties, and the state in Luxembourg are entangled, and why this system of interdependency survived national and international pressures. With the help of two concrete examples—namely, the international discussions on school reforms following the Sputnik "crisis" and the "shock" of the Programme for International Student Assessment (PISA)—it also demonstrates how international institutions put pressure on the political system and how the connections between the media, the political parties, and the administration turned this pressure into a particular policy for Luxembourg. The entanglement of the media, the parties, and the administration helped to transform international debates on school reform into national policies with a specific "Luxembourgish flavor."

## Theoretical Framework

In the European communication sciences and especially in the field of media sociology, the way of thinking about the public sphere is largely defined by a German and also, to a lesser degree, an American tradition—traditions that one can trace back to Talcott Parsons' structural functionalism, Niklas Luhmann's system theory, and Jürgen Habermas' notion of the public. As different as these concepts may be, they all view the public sphere as a professional, differentiated sub-system of society that works according to its own inner logic and that defines itself in more or less sharp contrast to the political, cultural, and economic system (Habermas, 1962; Parsons, 1970; Luhmann, 2004).

According to Luhmann, for example, the public—like any other social sub-system—is an answer to problems provided by the environment. It entails several interactive elements constituting a whole to reach the aim, problem solving. The very idea of a sub-system is that, once erected, it aims at self-preservation, but at the same time it is irritated by other sub-systems. This in turn means that sub-systems watch each other, and they react with resonance to any irritation from the environment. Against this background, educational reform movements "from outside" the educational system (whether from politics, the church, or any other interest group) are seen as disorganization, and their aims have to be "translated" into the pertinent form of communication of the sub-system. This, in turn, uses a lot of resources and hinders the sub-system from fulfilling its actual tasks.

This system-theoretical model has been considered to be fruitful, but at the same time it is criticized for its extremely abstract and fundamentally unhistorical character. The historical condition for this conception of a public sphere was the professionalization of the printed press, as the printed press was (and in a way still is) seen as the main arena in which something like a public sphere can build itself. But the idea of a public sphere that is largely decoupled from the political and economic system would not have been too convincing in the 19th century and at the start of the 20th century. The European printed press at that time was to a large extent an appendix of the bigger printing houses; there were also newspapers belonging to political parties. The emancipation process of the printing houses from the political parties started after the Second World War for most Western European papers, Luxembourg and Switzerland being the only exceptions. And the somewhat idealistic idea of a more or less pure public sphere stems to a large extent from this decoupling process.

In contrast to these somewhat sterile ideas of the media public, American communication scientists Blumler and Gurevitch (1995) developed a theory that sees the public as a combination of interdependent economic, political, and media spheres. In this perception the public is a fuzzy, somewhat messy concept that changes over time. Media, politics, and economics are entangled, interdependent, and not clearly separable. This idea of a "messy public" is formulated in sharp contrast to the continental and, most of all, the German discussion.

In Luxembourg the political party press of the 1920s is preserved as if it were under a cheese dome: Every party still has its own press. In the 1950s and the 1960s the public discussions were fairly clear-cut between the bigger Catholic, socially conservative Christian Social People's Party (CSV) and its newspaper, the *Luxemburger Wort*, and the Luxembourg Socialist Workers' Party (LSAP) and its newspaper, the *Tageblatt*. Nowadays, however, the differences between those big political camps, and especially between their newspapers, tend to blur. One important reason for this blurring, at least with regard to the newspapers, is economic pressure, a pressure that as we all know melts everything that is solid into air, even the Luxembourgish press.

In the following, I want to show in a first step how the media public in Luxembourg is structured and how and why the press, the parties, and the state are entangled. In a second step, I demonstrate with the help of two concrete examples—namely, the discussions on school reforms following the Sputnik crisis and the PISA shock—how far the media public in the 1960s was clearly divided and how this division has started to blur in more recent times. Today we can witness the slow decay of the political party press in Luxembourg. And this transformation is changing the conditions of the arena in which a discussion about school reform can take place.

## Media in Luxembourg

Three large media groups dominate the Luxembourgish media market: Saint-Paul, mainly owned by the Catholic Church and publishing the most influential daily paper, the *Luxemburger Wort*; Editpress, mainly owned by the Luxembourgish unions and publishing the second biggest daily paper, *Tageblatt*; and the RTL group, mainly owned by Bertelsmann, which does not publish a newspaper but dominates the radio and television market (Hirsch, 2002, pp. 420ff.).

The *Luxemburger Wort*, the largest daily newspaper (67,000 papers sold in 2012), belongs to the Saint-Paul Group, which is heavily influenced by the Catholic Church. The head of the administrative board is a moral theologist who was appointed directly by the archbishop and is considered to be distinctly conservative. The *Luxemburger Wort* also saw and still sees itself as belonging in some way to the conservative CSV party. The left-wing *Tageblatt* (14,000 papers sold in 2012) has several ties to the unions. For a long time it was the official paper of the socialist LSAP, and it has its roots especially in the south of the country—where the huge mines and smelteries were found. The smaller dailies are also more or less connected to political parties: The *Luxemburger Journal* is owned by a foundation controlled mainly by the liberal Democratic Party, and the *Zeidung vom letzeburger Vollek* is more or less the official paper of the Luxembourgish communist party (the two papers sold less than 4,000 papers each in 2012) (Hilgert, 2012).

The political discourse is chiefly dominated by the *Luxemburger Wort* and, to a much smaller degree, by the *Tageblatt*. The *Luxemburger Wort*, founded in 1848, is tellingly much older than the CSV party itself, and many editors of the paper became politicians within the party when it was founded in 1914. The *Luxemburger Wort* itself was founded as a by-product of the Saint-Paul print shop owned by the Catholic Church, and its first editors were all Catholic clergymen. The church, the CSV, the Saint-Paul Group, and the *Luxemburger Wort* are still heavily intertwined: Editors of the *Luxemburger Wort* belong to the managing board of the Saint-Paul Group, which still belongs to the Catholic Church, the church has a representative on the managing board of the *Luxemburger Wort*, and editors of the *Luxemburger Wort* are also delegates for the CSV. Until 1968 the office of the CSV was even located in the publishing house of the *Luxemburger Wort*. For a long time, one could say cynically that the church owned the Saint-Paul printing house, which owned the *Luxemburger Wort*, which in a way owned the CSV, which owned, or let us say ruled, Luxembourg itself. This is of course an improper reduction of the many ways in which these institutions were intertwined, coupled, and also in competition with each other, but it may make plausible why the socialist party LSAP used its brief governance of Luxembourg from 1974 to 1979 to introduce the "aide à la presse" law in 1976: This law established a huge subsidy system for the Luxembourgish press. So one can say that the diverse media landscape of today is possible only because the printed press is heavily subsidized by the state. In 2012 the state paid a total of 7.5 million euro in direct help to the printed press (Humprecht, 2012).

In the 1950s and 1960s the daily papers were more or less able to support themselves via their party affiliation, but these links became weaker in the 1960s and 1970s. The once close bonds between readers, parties, and newspapers began to deteriorate in all parts of the political spectrum, and the survival of especially the smaller daily papers was threatened. The greater commercial success of radio programs also put huge pressure on the printed press. The "aide à la presse" law of 1976—the decision of the socialist LSAP government to heavily subsidize the press—came just in time to save media diversity in Luxembourg (which was basically a relic from the 1920s), and in a way it petrified the status quo just before the media concentration processes that had already hit most other European countries could hit Luxembourg. It also stopped the decoupling process that had started to loosen the links between the political parties and "their" newspapers. One could argue that the party press so typical of the 1910s, 1920s, and 1930s somehow survived the 1950s and 1960s in Luxembourg to be set into stone in 1976. But in the 1980s and especially the 1990s, the papers started to lose their readership slowly but steadily. The advent of Luxembourgish television in 1984 and later of a Luxembourgish Internet scene increased the economic pressure on Saint-Paul and Editpress. The two publishing houses began to see themselves more and more as commercial media publishers and not so much as political entities. Their flagships, the *Luxemburger Wort* and the *Tageblatt*, had to find their readership beyond the classic party borders.

In the following, I show what this move from a political party press to a more neutral way of publishing can mean for the public discourse in Luxembourg, especially regarding the public debates on school policy.[1] I will try to exemplify this by showing how school reforms were discussed in the *Luxemburger Wort* and the *Tageblatt*, and I chose two events that were depicted within the media as shocks to the educational system: Sputnik and PISA.

Sputnik and PISA can in a way be seen as the two most prominent examples of events that were highly controversial and wildly discussed within the public media sphere and that triggered, or were used to trigger, political debate on educational and curricular reform (Tröhler, 2010). The fierce reactions to PISA in Germany, for instance, resulted from a cultural clash between the taken-for-granted national assumptions about education and the transnational agenda of an international organization such as the Organization for Economic Cooperation and Development (OECD). In Switzerland, where the schools are governed by the individual cantons and the school laws have to be approved in a referendum, educational reform proposals following an international agenda are turned down by local or regional authorities. Both Sputnik and PISA are also prime examples for scientification and internationalization of the debates on schooling.

## Examples: From Sputnik to PISA

### *The Sputnik Crisis and Its Perception in Luxembourg*

The Sputnik crisis in 1957 initiated heated debate on education and curriculum reform in the Western world, and Luxembourg was no exception. Sputnik symbolized a threat to the security of the Western world and a challenge to the belief in the superiority of science and technology in the United States and Western Europe. And it played a very important role in the educational reform movement, as many argued that the perceived "technology gap" between the Soviet Union and the "free world" could be bridged only with the help of better-educated students and especially with the help of better mathematics and science curricula (Rohstock & Lenz, 2012).

Although in the United States the educational debates of the 1950s and 1960s were already under way when Sputnik was launched by the Soviet Union, the technological challenge from a communist country found Western Europe largely unprepared. In the United States, far-reaching educational reforms were undertaken by educators, scientists, and mathematicians, with the public supporting their efforts, but the reactions in Western Europe were much more restrained. Nevertheless, the launching of the Soviet satellite did fuel the movement for curriculum reform in Europe and posed a challenge to the mostly conservative teachers and teachers' unions in the Grand Duchy of Luxembourg. Whereas many in the United States and also in Western Europe tried to use Sputnik as an event touching off curriculum revision and putting mathematics, technology, and the like on the educational agenda, conservative and more cautious educators in Luxembourg believed that the Sputnik debate would endanger their predominantly humanistic educational ideal.

The most important daily newspaper in Luxembourg, the conservative Roman Catholic *Luxemburger Wort*, saw Sputnik as a technologically superior product of a politically and ethically inferior system. Sputnik was the frightening symbol of a feat that a totalitarian country like the Soviet Union could accomplish simply because it was able to devote large amounts of resources to one aim only, whereas the "free Western world" was squandering its possibilities, not knowing exactly where to go. The conclusion for the *Luxemburger Wort* was clear: Western Europe had to find ways of working together more closely: "The signals from space have no other meaning for the free countries of Europe than: Unify, unify, unify!" (October 16, 1957, p. 3).[2]

School reform and curriculum reform in particular were seen as a means of, as the *Luxemburger Wort* put it, "intellectual self-defense" against the threat of Soviet "slavery" (November 11, 1957, p. 3). This intellectual self-defense did not mean that everybody should profit from educational reform but that mainly the higher branches of secondary education needed a complete overhaul. Whereas the American educational discussion quickly concentrated on the importance of new mathematics and science curricula, the Luxembourg debate was broader and less focused, and it tried to find a compromise between the notions of classical education (*Bildung*) and the need for new curricular concepts. The socialist *Tageblatt* stressed the importance of mathematics and science education, supporting curricular reforms similar to those in the United States (December 11, 1957, p. 8). The conservative *Luxemburger Wort*, on the other hand, demanded the teaching of ethics in schools, fearing that the ideal of humanist education was threatened by the "cult of technology" (February 10, 1958, p. 3). For the culturally and politically dominant conservative press, it was clear that technological and scientific progress in general raised new questions in the field of education, but they did not want to go the "American way." Instead, they stressed the dangers of new technologies and the importance of educating the future generation so that they could handle these technologies in a responsible way via the strengthening of ethics in the curriculum. In an editorial in the *Luxemburger Wort*, the minister of education, Pierre Frieden (a member of the conservative CSV), stressed the importance of ethical and religious education that would enable young people to cope with the challenges of the new times (February 10, 1958, p. 3). The conservative CSV made it clear that science education should become more important in Luxembourg; for example, Frieden proclaimed in another article in the *Luxemburger Wort* in 1958: "Those who have the best scientists will win the Cold War. Those who have the best scientists will win the economic war!" (February 27, 1958, p. 3). The influential editorials in the *Luxemburger Wort* saw the humanist ideal of *Bildung* as the main solution to the Sputnik crisis, and with a series of articles, the *Luxemburger Wort* managed to cool down the interest in a new curriculum that eventually bloomed within the more progressive parts of the CSV.

The socialist *Tageblatt* argued that the Soviet Union was so successful because it was able and willing to unleash the full intellectual potential of its peoples. One of the few big articles on Sputnik and science education in the *Tageblatt* was a reprint from the French newspaper *Le Monde*; spread over three issues of the *Tageblatt*, it stated:

> [O]ne of the biggest advantages of the Soviet school system compared to our Western bourgeois system is that it is completely for free and that it fosters the best students from all classes. It only relies on students' effort and talent and not on the wealth of their parents.
>
> *(December 12, 1957, p. 8)*

In a series of smaller articles, the *Tageblatt* emphasized the importance of government control over the scientific, military, and educational efforts, as only the government would be able to ensure the vigor needed to accomplish something like Sputnik.

Although the *Tageblatt* advertised a new scientific curriculum and many LSAP members raised their voices in the newspaper to support the idea of an education system that would include all classes and take the sciences more seriously, the party itself remained silent. The big parties CSV and LSAP were in a coalition in 1957, and they both decided not to change the Luxembourgish curriculum but to stay true to the notion of classic *Bildung*. It was their papers—the *Luxemburger Wort* and *Tageblatt*—that fought fiercely over the question of whether Luxembourg needed a new curriculum. Although the Sputnik debate was used by the powerful conservative representatives of the Luxembourgish press to promote a rhetoric of morality in an uncertain age of technology, it did not really change much within the political system of the country. The *Luxemburger Wort* and the CSV dominated the political discourse fairly clearly, and the LSAP followed more or less silently. Only the *Tageblatt* begged to differ, but its rhetoric of reform mainly remained unheard.

## PISA: The New Sputnik?

The PISA results of the year 2000 were publicly regarded as a second shock to the educational system in many Western European countries, with Luxembourg once again being no exception. The studies of student outcomes seemed to show that the Luxembourgish school system produced mediocre results at best (especially in mathematics) and that the language-oriented curriculum was a severe challenge for the large migrant population. This problem has been known for years, of course. But it took the PISA shocks—where Luxembourg found itself ranked below all of its fellow Europeans—to get a major discussion going.

Despite this discussion, and unimpressed by OECD pressure and recommendations, the Luxembourgish Parliament rejected the OECD-driven idea of a school system with a stronger differentiation between German and French. The government feared that a two-track system would endanger the nation's unity in the medium term (Geyer, 2009, p. 9).

Nevertheless, the Luxembourgish government used the PISA debate to initiate several reforms. The first reform of the (primary) school laws since 1912 came into force in 2009, a reform that probably would not have been realizable without the devastating PISA outcomes. In an interview with the *Luxemburger Wort*, the Rapporteur of the Commission de l'Education affirmed this assumption quite frankly in retrospect: "I won't hesitate to claim that the international comparisons paved the way for the reform of the school law from 1912" (January 20, 2009, p. 275). And as far-reaching as the reform was, it seemed non-controversial, at least at the beginning. It was mainly initiated by the LSAP ministry, but the CSV agreed to all of the big changes that the reform brought to the primary school. And in a sharp contrast to the ideological fights of former times, the *Luxemburger Wort* and the *Tageblatt* were both largely in favor of the proposed reform. The first editorial in the *Luxemburger Wort* on the reform was titled "In the Name of the Children" (January 20, 2009) and called it "the reform of the century." One day later, the

*Tageblatt* agreed and produced the headline: "This School Reform Is the Reform of the Century," (January 21, 2009) and one week later, another big editorial was titled "The Reform Is One Big Step Forward for Luxembourg" (January 26, 2009). There were certainly critical voices to be heard in the *Luxemburger Wort* as well as in the *Tageblatt*, but they were not picked up in editorials or comments.

What is remarkable is that, in contrast to the Sputnik discussion, this debate about a school reform in the context of the larger PISA debate took place largely without any huge ideologically driven editorial pieces in the *Luxemburger Wort* or the *Tageblatt*. Most of the news coverage is triggered by certain incidents like press conferences, demonstrations, and so on, and there are very few distinctly editorial pieces to be found. The *Tageblatt* tends to cover the teachers' unions more closely, whereas the *Luxemburger Wort* remains low key when it comes to the reform of 2009. The times of the big ideological fights seem to be over, but it also seems as though the two big daily newspapers do not know exactly where to go instead.

## Summary

At least to some degree, the Luxembourgish press can be seen as a relic from the early 20th century. The strong bonds between the daily newspapers and their respective political parties as well as the economic dependence on the state show fairly clearly that the public media sphere in Luxembourg cannot be seen as a professional, differentiated sub-system of society that works according to its own inner logic and that defines itself in more or less sharp contrast to the political, cultural, and economic system. It really is a sphere where politics, economics, the state, and the media are entangled and interdependent like nowhere else in Western Europe.

But the deterioration of the links between the newspapers and "their" political party, which was observable during the PISA discussion, can be described as a slow farewell to the party press. At the same time, the fact that the media debate on the educational consequences of the Sputnik crisis was much more ideologically loaded than the media debate on PISA is not only a result of the vanishing influence of the political parties on "their" press but also an example of the dominance of an internationalized language of education, as well as an example of a scientification process in the realm of the educational system that makes it hard for alternatives to be heard and discussed.

For the public debate on schooling in Luxembourg, this means that one could on the one hand be optimistic and hope that the cheese dome will be lifted from the media system, that the Luxembourgish press will turn away from its party roots, and that the debate on schooling and education will become less ideologically loaded. On the other hand, being a bit more pessimistic, we could expect a loss of variety in the Luxembourgish media system, and with it the loss of dissenting voices, leaving a press that discusses educational questions mainly within the internationalized language of education that is dominant right now.

## Notes

1. The discussion is based on my analysis of the complete editions of the *Luxemburger Wort* and the *Tageblatt* from mid-1957 to mid-1958 and from mid-2008 to mid-2009. For the first period, 331 articles in the *Luxemburger Wort* and 148 in the *Tageblatt* dealt with schooling, for the second period 233 in the *Luxemburger Wort* and 205 in the *Tageblatt*.
2. Quotations from the two newspapers are cited here by newspaper name, date of the article cited, and page number.

## References

Blumler, J., & Gurevitch, M. (1995). *The crisis of public communication*. London, UK: Routledge.

Geyer, F. (2009). *The educational system in Luxembourg: CEPS special report*. Luxembourg, Luxembourg: Centre for Population, Poverty and Public Policy Studies (CEPS).

Habermas, J. (1962). *Strukturwandel der Öffentlichkeit: Untersuchungen zu einer Kategorie der bürgerlichen Gesellschaft*. Neuwied, Germany: Luchterhand.

Hilgert, R. (2012). *Der zögerliche Abschied der Parteiblätter*. Retrieved from http://www.land.lu/2012/09/21/der-zogerliche-abschied-der-parteiblatter/

Hirsch, M. (2002). Das Mediensystem Luxemburgs. In Hans-Bredow-Institut (Ed.), *Internationales Handbuch Medien* (pp. 419–425). Baden-Baden, Germany: Nomos.

Humprecht, E. (2012). *Luxemburger Wort für Wahrheit und Recht*. Retrieved from http://www.mediadb.eu/forum/zeitungsportraets/luxemburger-wort

Luhmann, N. (2004). *Die Realität der Massenmedien*. Wiesbaden, Germany: VS Verlag.

Parsons, T. (1970). *The social system*. London, UK: Routledge & Kegan.

Rohstock, A., & Lenz, T. (2012). A national path to internationalization: Educational reforms in Luxembourg, 1945–70. In C. Aubry & J. Westberg (Eds.), *History of schooling: Politics and local practice* (pp. 108–126). Bern, Switzerland: Peter Lang.

Tröhler, D. (2010). Harmonizing the educational globe: World polity, cultural features, and the challenges to educational research. *Studies in Philosophy and Education, 29*(1), 7–29.

# 14

# GLOBALIZATION IN FINNISH AND WEST GERMAN EDUCATIONAL RHETORIC, 1960–1970

*Matias Gardin*

On May 18, 1972, UNESCO published a new report on education that summarized its political and cultural expectations from the past decade. By looking at the world's educational situation as a whole, the study's primary justification was "the existence of an international community which, amidst the variety of nations and cultures, of political options and degrees of development, is reflected in common aspirations, problems and trends, and in its movement towards one and the same destiny" (UNESCO, 1972, pp. 5–6). As part of this, the report argued that nations should tie their education policies closer to their governing structures, the welfare state in particular. Behind the message was an ambitious imperative: fundamental demands for global progress, democratization, and rationalization of the education sector, and optimization of international competitiveness and economic growth. At a European level, the effort was also to increase cooperation and mutual understanding and, by that, mutual adaptation (pp. 36–39). Increased cross-national comparisons of different education systems became popular in the press (Kuikka, 1992). It was predicted that domestic curriculum developments would become more prone to pressures and influences from abroad, enabled by the new international climate.

Based on the example of UNESCO's normative narrative, this chapter explores how education formed an integral part of the welfare state during the Cold War. By using the educational expansion in Finland and West Germany in the 1960s and 1970s as case studies, I argue that global actors (and their pervasive vocabularies) have played an essential role in the development of national education systems. How did Finland—a European hinterland and socioeconomically backward nation-state in 1945—develop into a paragon of egalitarian education? How did West Germany—a European laggard in education until the mid-1960s, shaken by its immediate past and destitute in 1945—become known once again as a respectable education society?

By merging the welfare state, Cold War, education, and global affinities, particular emphasis is also placed on the democratization of education from 1960 to 1970. As historian Thomas Mergel (2010) contends, "Even democracy as a political form had to be first laboriously learned, and this is what happened with a long-term effect only after the generation of 1945" (p. 23).[1] For my purposes, however, rather than viewing post-1960 political practices as purely national histories, I suggest that education policies were also affected by global rhetoric in this era, and in this sense they became increasingly centered around the Cold War ideological climate that demanded rapid investment in human capital via education (see, for example, Organization for Economic Co-operation and Development [OECD], 1973).

Methodologically, this study analyzes parliamentary debates surrounding five national education reforms from 1963 to 1972 and the ways they were conditioned and justified by supranational agendas. The chapter is divided into two parts: "Political Transformation of Mass Publics" focuses on the background rationale for the educational expansion of 1960–1970, and "Towards an Education Society" examines the crucial education reforms that took place in these countries during the same period, and how they were (at least partly) legitimized globally by domestic politicians. Placed in-between national (or regional) and international negotiations, this reflected the Cold War Finnish and West German welfare state developments as a whole, where the self (capitalist West) and other (communist East) were deliberately juxtaposed and reinforced.

## Political Transformation of Mass Publics

As education had previously embodied hierarchies and exclusions, widening access to education was one of the most innovative concepts in the development of the European nation-state after the Second World War (see Hadjar & Becker, 2009, pp. 9–19). It was part of a wider global movement, forming a component in the international skills competition, positioned against and influenced by the Cold War. Education thus also constituted one of the most heated debates in the Finnish (Eduskunta) and West German (Bundestag) parliaments in the 1960s. Whereas Germany had been the European leader in public education until the First World War, Finland's system remained underdeveloped and poorly resourced well into the 1940s (Alestalo & Uusitalo, 1986). However, although there was a strong push to invest in Finnish education in the immediate post-1945 era, the West German system remained largely untouched until 1960. Georg Picht (1964) famously termed the situation an "educational catastrophe" (*Bildungskatastrophe*), a situation that needed urgent restructuring under international pressure. Without restructuring, West Germany's "people would soon become the uneducated and unskilled labourers of Europe" (Geschka, 1991, p. 192).

Whereas discussions over the direction of education were still being conducted in Bonn, large-scale transformations had already been decided on and were taking place in Helsinki: The Finnish education system was being expanded, financed more adequately, internally restructured, and access to it made more egalitarian (Välimaa, 2004; Saarivirta, 2010). From 1950 to 1980 the increase in Finnish educational expenditure was eightfold. In 1981 education spending amounted to 4.9% of the Finnish gross domestic product (GDP) (Alestalo & Uusitalo, 1986, pp. 206–207, 217). In West Germany the percentage rose from 2.1% of the GDP in 1950 to likewise reach 4.9% in 1981 (Alber, 1986, p. 33). In both countries, upper mobility in the education system became an important prerequisite for a democratic order as demanded by the international community (UNESCO, 1972, pp. 21–27; see also OECD, 1973, pp. 35–40), that is, for a change from an elite to a mass system of participation.

Hadjar and Schlapbach (2009) link education to distinctive national values, party-political orientations, "compulsory" participation, and active citizenship. They found that education policies between 1960 and 1970 were characterized by three trends: (1) raising the educational level to increase productivity and economic prosperity, (2) reducing inequalities, and (3) improving democracy by increasing political participation (pp. 180–181). By the first, they refer to the aim to transform the mass public into a pool of advanced competences and skills. By the second, they mean that reducing inequalities would also imply utilizing "skill resources" in disadvantaged groups. By the third, they refer to the new role of education in enhancing the civil liberties of socially mature people. How was this knowledge production mobilized and placed in conversation with the political status quo and future socioeconomic order of Finland and West Germany? Education, which had previously been neglected in the nations' post-war state-building processes and which was regarded as a separate entity from social policy, now also entered Finnish and West German welfare state politics. Educational expansion came to lead the way towards societal value changes that increased social mobility and produced political stability. Yet what were the concepts that were developed to increase democratization and rationalization of education, international competitiveness, and economic growth and, thereby, also global progress?

In West Germany educational matters remained the sole competence of the federal states (*Länder*) until the 1950s, and thereafter many attempts to reform the fragmented system failed (Katzenstein, 1987, pp. 318–319; Lohmar & Eckhardt, 2013). In Finland the centralized state controlled the country's education system with increased rationality, especially regarding the inactive parts of the population (Kuusi, 1961, p. 41). In the Cold War context, education was viewed as a political mechanism for elevating members of the nation-state from passive to active participation. Inclusion, national success, improvements in health and well-being, and stability and unity through educational expansion became mediums to deal with the heated international framework.

On October 18, 1963, Chancellor Ludwig Erhard addressed the issue in the Bundestag by referring to societal cohesion, global skills competition, and economics: "Without strengthening its intellectual investments Germany would fall behind other cultural and industrialized countries. But that would mean not only risking economic progress and prosperity, but also social security"[2] (Bundestag, 1963a, p. 4201). Fritz Erler, a member of parliament (MP) from the Social Democratic Party, or SPD, criticized Erhard's parliamentary statement (*Bundestag Erklärung*) six days later. For Erler, the problem with the education system in West Germany lay in federalism. His idea was to combine federal and national forces to gain a more competitive edge internationally: "Regarding education and science policy, we should no longer allow fruitless arguments to take place around the principles of federalism. If we are to compete with nations, we need to combine our federal and state powers"[3] (Bundestag, 1963b, p. 4261).

Similar international comparisons, calls for progress, and global dimensions were present in Finland. Educational issues were located in world politics (Allardt, 1990; Kettunen, 2001). For example, MP Kuuno Honkonen (of the Finnish People's Democratic League, or SKDL) brought the issue to the Eduskunta on November 25, 1971. Promoting greater centralization, uniformity, and universalism in the Finnish education system, Honkonen concluded: "In Sweden and the Soviet Union, the state contribution towards educational funding is many times greater than in Finland. Globally speaking we are still lagging behind, even though the evolution in recent years promises a more positive future"[4] (Eduskunta, 1972a, p. 2981).

The main West German educational body was the Federal Ministry of Scientific Research (Bundesministerium für wissenschaftliche Forschung), which was renamed the Federal Ministry of Education and Science (Bundesministerium für Bildung und Wissenschaft) in 1969. This was accompanied by the Central Science Council (Wissenschaftsrat), the Education Council (Bildungsrat), and the Standing Conference of the Ministers of Culture (Kultusministerkonferenz), whose primary role was to plan, co-ordinate, and advise (Alber, 1986, pp. 34–35; Katzenstein, 1987, pp. 310–311, 328), whereas the individual *Länder* regained their independence in education policy, that is, in their respective parliaments. In contrast to the situation in West Germany, centralization, intensification, and revision of the educational administration were the norms in Finland, which moved from an unorganized towards a unified and standardized curriculum. The goal was to establish a homogeneous institutional setting that would activate the citizenry through the central empowerment of education. Tighter state control over education was fostered by the Ministry of Education (Opetusministeriö) and a semi-autonomous governmental body, the Finnish National Board of Education (Opetushallitus). The purpose was to bring together the fragmented education legislation under one single body, moving "from fragmentation to unity,"[5] as MP Erkki Tuomioja (of the Social Democratic Party, or SDP) summarized it on November 30, 1971 (Eduskunta, 1972a, p. 3069).

On December 9, 1964, MP Berthold Martin (of the Christian Democratic Union, or CDU) replied to Erler's interpellation (*Große Anfrage*) in the Bundestag:

> There is a deep-seated barrier among our people in Germany when it comes to education, a barrier which probably also has an ideological character. It derives

from a fatal relationship between education and wealth, and from the fact that education was once a matter of class war, which it no longer has to be.[6]
*(Bundestag, 1964b, p. 7440)*

Almost an identical observation was made by a Finnish MP, Magnus Kull (of the Swedish People's Party of Finland, or RKP), who emphasized structural educational (in)equality in the Eduskunta on November 15, 1966: "By law young students are classified into good and bad, depending on the destination of their degree [. . .] [C]hange in the law does not withdraw the disadvantages inherent in the system as such"[7] (Eduskunta, 1967, p. 883). There were thus similar causal factors driving for change behind the agendas of Finland and West Germany: The political transformation of mass publics into a pool of advanced competences was crucial for a dynamic future economy, global recognition, and increased equality of opportunities.

Against the background of the Cold War, social and political activism became key words for maintaining democracy (Hadjar & Becker, 2009, p. 11). Active political participation via education was vital to compete with communist territories.[8] By allying West Germany with market liberalism and a strong "Western" identity, this also provided a way to further distance the country from the German Democratic Republic. Regarding education, the idea was to compete with the East and offer a more progressive, attractive, and extensive welfare milieu than that provided by the German Democratic Republic, to show "that capitalism could deliver better welfare than socialism" (Pulzer, 1995, p. 64). As for Finland, the plan was to move away from the dysfunctions and authoritarian tendencies of the Soviet Union, for "education was seen as a basic requirement for maintaining a democratic society of politically mature people" (Hadjar & Schlapbach, 2009, p. 183).[9]

From 1960 to 1970 the slogan "science to serve people at a democratic university"[10] epitomized Finnish educational reforms (Heiskala, 2011, p. 93). Through state intervention, education became a catalyst for social policy expansion in which personal commitment gained equal importance with the increase in state power. As in West Germany, there was a genuine need for proactive political participation. This democratic activism was regarded as a personal obligation to the future knowledge/learning society, which was stressed by UNESCO in reference to global advancements: "They [modern states] appreciate that fresh progress is possible and desirable, by making the highest possible level of knowledge available to the greatest possible number of 'learners'" (UNESCO, 1972, p. 20). In Finland—positioned at the heart of the Cold War fronts—this created a fertile catalyst for post-war reconstruction (Kettunen, 2001). In West Germany, too, national education policies were seen as leading towards greater national stability—an important component in the democratization of the nation vis-à-vis the East—exemplified by the extensive government report on educational planning (*Bericht des Bundes über Bildungsplanung*) of 1966 (Bundestag, 1966). Similar to the Finnish rhetoric, education was highlighted globally as a democratic duty of all West European citizens: "To function, the prevailing West European democracy requires a certain amount of knowledge, an ability to judge, to understand, to be open towards binding community responsibilities"[11] (Bundestag, 1966, p. 11).

## Towards an Education Society

The education reforms that were introduced from 1960 to 1970 therefore took place in the context of a changing idea of social policy. Wider access to education was pursued as a national necessity, a conviction shared by all major political parties. Three law frames became landmarks in Finland: the University Development Act 1967–1981 of 1966 (Laki korkeakoululaitoksen kehittämisestä vuosina 1967–1981), the Education System Act of 1968 (Laki koulujärjestelmän perusteista), and the Study Allowance Act of 1972 (Opintotukilaki). As for West Germany, two similar national milestones were reached in the same timeframe: the Hamburg Agreement of 1964 (Hamburger Abkommen) and the Education and Training Assistance Act of 1970 (Das Erste Gesetz über individuelle Förderung der Ausbildung, or Bundesausbildungsförderungsgesetz, or BAföG).

With reference to internationalization at a rhetorical level, the education reforms mentioned above become relevant for three reasons: First, the law frames themselves as carriers of global socioeconomic ideals certainly contributed towards new paradigms in national curricula. Second, the timescale in which this took place varies between Finland and West Germany. In Finland the expansion of education began earlier. Along with health services, education was the first policy area to be rapidly improved in the 1950s (Nousiainen, 1990, p. 255). In West Germany similar reforms commenced only under the Grand Coalition of 1966–1969 (Alber, 1986, p. 14), and even then they often led to tension between regional and national cultures. Third, to include previously unknown objectives under "education"—human capital, universalism, and international economic competitiveness—became remarkably fashionable, which is an example of effective transnational framing.

In West Germany the Hamburg Agreement was approved by the 11 state minister presidents on October 28, 1964. This replaced the Düsseldorf Agreement of 1955 (Düsseldorfer Abkommen), which had given state ministries the power to provide guidelines for national standardization, which in turn was seen as a prerequisite for the dynamic internationalization of education. The agreement was the first serious attempt among the individual states to harmonize the fragmented education system in West Germany (Kultusministerkonferenz, 2011). It included nationwide education principles, such as the duration and structure of compulsory education, mandatory language studies, school dates and holidays, examinations, and grading scales. MP Heinrich Holkenbrink (of the CDU) explained the spirit of the agreement a month later in the Bundestag, stating it was vital "that the German Parliament carries a high degree of co-responsibility for the status and development of German culture"[12] (Bundestag, 1964a, p. 1). This was accompanied by the search for national cohesion, "because the preservation of cultural heritage and a transparent and continuous development in all areas of culture are the key means for achieving national unity amongst the German people"[13] (p. 1).

Meanwhile, in Finland, the University Development Act 1967–1981, a plan for quantitative and qualitative growth in Finnish university education for the following 15 years, was passed in the Eduskunta on March 29, 1966. The law entailed increases in university resources. The motivation behind the act was that higher education was in need of urgent and thorough improvement to keep up with global trends and technological advances; the key word was "indispensable" (*välttämätön*):

> Research and specialized training, and a general rise in the level of knowledge, are generally regarded as indispensable conditions for economic growth, and spiritual and social advancement. It is obvious that our country cannot be left behind in the development of research and higher training.[14]
> (Eduskunta, 1965, p. 1)

The Education System Act, which introduced the comprehensive school system in Finland (replacing the parallel schooling structure), was enacted on April 14, 1967. The law came into force the following year and provided extensive new benefits: free instruction and materials, free health services, free school meals, free transport and accommodation (if needed), and smaller class sizes (Eduskunta, 1968, pp. 20–28; Itälä, 1969). This stemmed from the need to further rationalize the education sector, which required the removal of external hindrances in common learning: "It is therefore essential that external obstacles in education be removed, first with regards to pupils in compulsory education, but as soon as possible also for students in upper secondary schools, vocational colleges, and higher education"[15] (Eduskunta, 1968, p. 2).

The West German Education and Training Assistance Act, the first law to introduce study allowances for students in post-compulsory education, went into effect in 1970. This followed the constitutional reform of May 13, 1969 (*Grundgesetzänderung des Artikels 74:13*), which had empowered the federal government to make legislation regarding educational allowances (*Finanzverfassungsreform*) (Bundestag, 2010, p. 61). On February 14, 1969, an ad hoc committee on educational assistance (*Ausbildungsförderung*) had been set up. The goal of the law was described as follows: "The design will draw on the area in the Basic Law that guarantees equal opportunities and a free choice of profession and training"[16] (Bundestag, 1969a, p. 3).

In Finland, the Study Allowance Act, an initial scheme for study allowances and loans in higher education, was passed on December 3, 1971. The law went into effect on July 1, 1972. It stated: "The aim should be the development of educational-social conditions in such a way that everybody has the chance to educate themselves in a socially and individually meaningful manner, regardless of social, economic, and regional factors"[17] (Eduskunta, 1972b, p. 1). And, perhaps most importantly, it stated that educational responsibilities should be shifted from families to society: "To develop a financial aid system for students is about the transfer of education costs to a larger degree from students themselves and their parents to society"[18] (p. 1). In Finland and West Germany, these five crucial education reforms thus provided new paradigms demanded by the international community: to contribute towards and broaden the concept of educational rationality, innovation, equality of opportunity, and economic growth (OECD, 1973).[19]

Yet, in Finland, all the agendas had a common motive—namely, "a systemic convergence" towards a standardized and universal model of education (Välimaa, 2004, p. 39). This runs contrary to the reform process in West Germany, where parliamentary debates were characterized by the issue of "whether or not the individual states want[ed] to grant the federal government a genuine right to participate in educational planning,"[20] as MP Martin put it in 1965 (Bundestag, 1965, p. 9355). Federal conflicts thus delayed and shaped the West German educational reform from the start. In Finland the agenda was set differently: The reform process was speedier and began earlier, and processing and implementing it seemed much more manageable. For instance, referring to the University Development Act 1967–1981, Prime Minister Johannes Virolainen (of the Center Party) had called in 1966 for the expansion of state power through education. Virolainen assessed the law as the great cultural-political achievement of 1960: "The Act does not decrease the opportunities of parliament or government to conduct appropriate and effective higher education policy. On the contrary, it increases these opportunities because it obliges the state to monitor these developments"[21] (Eduskunta, 1966, p. 2999).

Perhaps surprisingly, in West Germany the Kultusministerkonferenz regretted that the standardization of the German curriculum had not gone far enough and that it had not been initiated earlier, but, still, "they could not be expected to concede publicly that the tussle of *Land* politics often obstructed agreement" ("West Germany: Marks for Teachers," 1964). Therefore, the Finnish and West German educational expansions of the 1960s, albeit quite different in many respects, provide interesting examples in which the structural context, timing, rhetoric, and tactics proved crucial. In this sense, as a model of global collectivity or communality in the face of international scientific and technological revolutions (see UNESCO, 1972, pp. 32–34), the concept of an "education society" employed by Finnish and West German politicians seems especially appealing here: "The University Development Act 1967–1981 is the great cultural-political achievement of this decade. [. . .] It will set the new foundation for an *education society*"[22] (Eduskunta, 1965, p. 2999). As opposed to alienation, "individualization" was also framed as positive, as an imperative in the highly competitive future world: "Bit by bit, this law [the Education and Training Assistance Act of 1970] must be developed into a major piece of legislation that enables the individual to meet the requirements of a modern *achievement-oriented society*"[23] (Bundestag, 1969b, p. 13580; italics added). By the same token, in his 1967 speech, Willy Brandt (of the SPD) expounded: "The battles of the future will be fought in schools, workshops, laboratories, and lecture halls"[24] (SPD, 1967, p. 5).[25]

However, stressing education as a national project led to tension with German federalism. For example, *The Times* reported on November 7, 1965, on the multifarious federal interests vis-à-vis the growing national economic necessities of the West German education system:

> The reformers want a political decision, across the *Länder* frontiers [. . .] aimed at ironing out regional differences [. . .] based less on German nineteenth-century ideals [. . .]. But, in a materially so successful country, the reformers still have to convince the public that more education is part of social justice as well as a growing economic necessity.
> *("Reformers' Demand," 1965)*

It is again here that Finland parts company with West Germany. In contrast to the above, key attributes of education in the Finnish Study Allowance Act of 1972, for instance, were to be as universal (*yleinen*), cohesive (*yhtenäinen*), holistic (*kokonaisvaltainen*), rational (*järkiperäinen*), and precise (*täsmällinen*) as possible (Eduskunta, 1972a, pp. 2979–2981, 3071). Nonetheless, in the second half of the 1960s it became more apparent that it was also the duty of West Germany to produce sophisticated individuals at a national level. This was regarded as an obligation also *beyond* national borders, to maintain the country's international reputation, as Brandt framed it: "This country, this Federal Republic of Germany, has the task to produce heads, for ourselves and for the rest of the world"[26] (SPD, 1967, p. 6).

## Conclusion

Globally speaking, the mid-20th century has often been referred to as "the human capital century" (Saarivirta, 2010, p. 355), having the aim of "improvement of the economic conditions of individuals" (Hadjar & Becker, 2009, p. 12). In particular, 1960–1970 as the end of the "golden age" of European capitalism—*Les Trente Glorieuses*, three decades of continuous economic prosperity from 1945 to 1975—was characterized by dramatic social expenditure expansion, almost full employment, and extraordinary economic growth (Lane & Ersson, 1987). Optimistic international objectives were to bring technological, economic, and societal advantages (OECD, 1973). In this sense, it was in the 1960s and 1970s that Finland and West Germany took bold and decisive steps to democratize the field of education, to bring their systems into line with "international standards." For example, the number of students at Finnish universities increased from a relatively low 25,303 in 1960 to a staggering 60,692 in 1970 (Allardt, 1990, p. 622). The same figures for West Germany were 240,000 and 410,000 (Studis Online, 2010).

But whereas the Finnish education system was radically altered by the Education System Act of 1968, that is, a change from a stratified to a unified and standardized system and curriculum, numerous attempts to reform the fragmented West German system proved unsuccessful. Education reforms progressed at a much slower speed in West Germany with distinct regional variations and disputes between the different levels of administration, that is, federal versus *Länder* governments, but in Finland speedy progress was made possible by centralization and comprehensiveness. The West German Education Council (Bildungsrat), which characterized and symbolized the united education front, was finally dissolved in 1975 after its targets became impossible to realize. Despite dynamic politicians across the political spectrum, and their genuine willingness to reform the system from above, pluralism continued in education, where, for instance, the three-tier stratified schooling structure acted as a barrier to the more general "global" objectives of the 1960s.

The revolutionary education reforms in Finland and West Germany thereby emerged alongside and, I suggest, as part and parcel of the attraction to (or partial rejection of) global affinities and dynamic internationalization, with the effect of providing precisely a space for the new role of state and individual, optimization of competitiveness, economic growth, and a national knowledge base. The educational revolution of the 1960s should thus be viewed not only as a victory of the political left (Alber, 1986, p. 14; Alestalo & Uusitalo, 1986, pp. 246, 253–257) but also as a result of tactical moves made by all political parties, a skillfully controlled system of governance that altered the relationship between domestic (or regional) and global. The debate on crucial education reforms in West Germany and Finland was about how to plan a successful program that would reconcile the pressing needs of post-war societies, and to reassess the educational goals demanded by the new industrial and technological forces above and beyond the nation-state.

The juxtaposition between national and international has thus functioned as a comparative element throughout this chapter. In both the Finnish and West German parliaments, education entered social policy thanks to the positive and inspirational rhetoric and framings presented by skillful politicians and other policy bodies. All this also had a deeper international goal, "that of educating the complete man [. . .] which may be common to all educational systems, in terms of objectives adapted to each country" (UNESCO, 1972, pp. 6–7). It was this continuous, demanding, and pervasive narrative—a message of boundless optimism and progression, of global interconnectedness—that exerted strong pressure on national education systems and their curricula. At a rhetorical level, education policies were rendered national in a way that was meant to foster increased social mobilization and equality among the Finnish and West German publics, but they also brought everything back to international questions on how to rationalize the welfare state and the educational sector, optimize economic growth, and improve the usefulness of individuals during the chills of the Cold War.

## Notes

1. "Auch die Demokratie als politische Form musste erst mühsam gelernt werden, und das geschah mit Langzeitwirkung erst in der Generation nach 1945." All translations from German, Finnish, and Swedish in this chapter are my own.
2. "Ohne Verstärkung der geistigen Investitionen müßte Deutschland gegenüber anderen Kultur- und Industrieländern zurückfallen. Das aber hieße, nicht nur den wirtschaftlichen Fortschritt und Wohlstand, sondern auch die soziale Sicherheit aufs Spiel setzen."
3. "Einen unfruchtbaren Prinzipienstreit über den Föderalismus in der Bildungs- und Wissenschaftspolitik sollten wir uns nicht länger gestatten. Wir müssen die Kräfte von Bund und Ländern zusammenfassen, wenn wir im Wettbewerb der Nationen bestehen wollen."
4. "Niin Neuvostoliitossa kuin Ruotsissakin valtion panos opintojen rahoituksessa on moninkertaisesti suurempi kuin Suomessa. Kansainvälisesti katsoen olemme siis edelleen jäljessä, jos kohta kehityksen vauhti viime vuosina lupaakin myönteisempää jatkossa."
5. "Hajanaisesta yhtenäiseen."
6. "Es steckt darin eine tiefsitzende Sperre bei unseren Menschen in Deutschland gegenüber der Bildung, eine Sperre, die wahrscheinlich auch ideologischen Character hat. [. . .] Sie kommt aus der fatalen Gleichsetzung von Besitz und Bildung und aus der Tatsache, daß Bildung einmal eine Klassenkampfsache gewesen ist, die sie nicht mehr sein darf."
7. "Den studerande ungdomen klassificeras i lagen i bättre och sämre, beroende på vilken examen som är slutmålet [. . .] lagändringen undanskaffar inte de olägenheter som vidlåder systemet som sådant."
8. In this context Finland was sometimes also highlighted as specifically in line with the "Nordic" model, influenced by Scandinavia (most notably Sweden), which claimed that it did not belong to either the Western or Eastern camp (see, for example, Kettunen, 2001, p. 234).
9. In West Germany this was manifested also in the expansion of second-chance education from the mid-1960s onwards. For instance, in Helmut Belser's *Zweiter Bildungsweg: Das Problem eines berufsbezogenen Bildungsganges zur Hochschulreife*, it was made evident that "[i]ts development and implementation are occurring—not least because of the ideological, social, and economic competition with the East" ("Seine Entwicklung und Durchsetzung kommt—nicht zuletzt wegen des ideellen, sozialen und wirtschaftlichen Wettbewerbs mit dem Osten") (Belser, 1960, p. 11).
10. "Tiede kansaa palvelemaan demokraattisessa yliopistossa."
11. "Die in Westeuropa vorherrschende Demokratie setzt, soll sie funktionieren, ein bestimmtes Grundwissen und ein geschultes Urteilsvermögen sowie Verständnis und Aufgeschlossenheit für die verpflichtenden Gemeinschaftsaufgaben voraus."
12. "daß der Bundestag eine hohe Mitverantwortung für den Stand und die Entwicklung der deutschen Kultur trage."
13. "weil die Bewahrung des kulturellen Erbes und eine klare und kontinuierliche Entwicklung in allen Bereichen der Kultur die entscheidenden Mittel zur Behauptung der nationalen Einheit des deutschen Volkes sind."
14. "Tutkimusta ja erikoiskoulutusta sekä yleensä tiedon tason nousemista pidetään yleisesti yhteiskunnan taloudellisen kasvun sekä sen henkisen ja sosiaalisen edistämisen välttämättömänä edellytyksenä. On selvä, ettei oma maamme voi jättäytyä tutkimuksen ja ylimmän opetuksen kehittämisessä jälkeen [. . .]."

15. "Sen vuoksi on välttämätöntä, että koulunkäynnin ulkonaiset esteet saadaan poistetuksi, aluksi oppivelvollisuusikäisten osalta, mutta mahdollisimman pian myös lukion, ammatillisten oppilaitosten ja korkeakoulujen opiskelijain osalta."
16. "Der Entwurf will für diesen Bereich die im Grundgesetz garantierte Chancengleichheit und die freie Wahl von Beruf und Ausbildungsstätte ermöglichen."
17. "Tavoitteena tulee olla opintososiaalisten olosuhteiden kehittäminen siten, että kaikilla on mahdollisuus sosiaalisista, taloudellisista ja alueellisista tekijöistä riippumatta kouluttaa itsensä sekä yksilön että yhteiskunnan kannalta tarkoituksenmukaisella tavalla."
18. "Opintotukijärjestelmän kehittämisessä on kysymys koulutuskustannusten entistä suuremman osuuden siirtämisestä koulutettavilta itseltään ja heidän vanhemmiltaan yhteiskunnalle."
19. On unexpected consequences of the educational expansion, see also Hadjar & Becker, 2009, p. 10.
20. "ob die Länder dem Bund eine echte Mitwirkung in der Bildungsplanung einräumen woll[t]en oder nicht."
21. "Laki ei vähennä eduskunnan tai valtioneuvoston mahdollisuuksia harjoittaa tarkoituksenmukaista ja tehokasta korkeakoulupolitiikkaa. Päinvastoin se lisää näitä mahdollisuuksia, koska se velvoittaa valtiovaltaa kehityksen seuraamiseen [. . .]."
22. "Laki korkeakoulujen kehittämisestä vuosina 1967–1981 on tämän kymmenluvun suuri kulttuuripoliittinen saavutus. [. . .] se laskee uudenaikaisen *koulutusyhteiskunnan* [italics added] perustan."
23. "Nach und nach muß dieses Gesetz [BAföG] zu einem großen Gesetzeswerk ausgebaut werden, das zu einem Instrument wird, das den einzelnen befähigt, den Anforderungen einer modernen *Leistungsgesellschaft* [italics added] zu genügen."
24. "Die Schlachten der Zukunft werden in den Schulen, in den Werkstätten, in den Laboratorien und in den Hörsälen geschlagen."
25. A headline in the SPD newspaper *Vorwärts* on February 26, 1964, stated that West Germany was now truly and fully "on the way towards the education society" ("Auf dem Wege zur Bildungsgesellschaft," 1964). As for Finland, Martti Kuikka (1992) also reflected on how in the early 1970s there was talk about a new type of social model that was called "a learning society" (*oppimisen yhteiskunta*) (p. 117).
26. "Dieses Land, diese Bundesrepublik Deutschland, hat die Aufgabe, Köpfe zu produzieren, für uns selbst und für die Welt."

## References

Alber, J. (1986). Germany. In P. Flora (Ed.), *Growth to limits: The Western European welfare states since World War II: Vol. II* (pp. 1–114). Berlin, Germany: Walter de Gruyter.

Alestalo, M., & Uusitalo, H. (1986). Finland. In P. Flora (Ed.), *Growth to limits: The Western European welfare states since World War II: Vol. I* (pp. 197–266). Berlin, Germany: Walter de Gruyter.

Allardt, E. (1990). Tieteen Ja Korkeakoululaitoksen Kehitys Keskeiseksi Yhteiskunnalliseksi Laitokseksi. In O. Riihinen (Ed.), *Suomi 2017* (pp. 615–633). Jyväskylä, Finland: Gummerus.

Auf dem Wege zur Bildungsgesellschaft. (1964, February 26). *Vorwärts*.

Belser, H. (1960). *Zweiter Bildungsweg: Das Problem eines berufsbezogenen Bildungsganges zur Hochschulreife*. Weinheim, Germany: Julius Beltz.

Bundestag. (1963a). *Verhandlungen des Deutschen Bundestages*. Bonn, Germany: Bonner Universitäts-Buchdruckerei: 4. Wahlperiode, 90. Sitzung, 18 Oktober.

Bundestag. (1963b). *Verhandlungen des Deutschen Bundestages*. Bonn, Germany: Bonner Universitäts-Buchdruckerei: 4. Wahlperiode, 92. Sitzung, 24 Oktober.

Bundestag. (1964a). *Schriftlicher Bericht (Betr. Förderung der Wissenschaftlichen Forschung und Aufgaben der Bildungsplanung): Drucksache IV/2773*. Bonn, Germany: Bonner Universitäts-Buchdruckerei.

Bundestag. (1964b). *Verhandlungen des Deutschen Bundestages*. Bonn, Germany: Bonner Universitäts-Buchdruckerei: 4. Wahlperiode, 151. Sitzung, 9 Dezember.

Bundestag. (1965). *Verhandlungen des Deutschen Bundestages*. Bonn, Germany: Bonner Universitäts-Buchdruckerei: 4. Wahlperiode, 186. Sitzung, 21 Mai.

Bundestag. (1966). *Bericht des Bundes über Bildungsplanung: Drucksache V/2166*. Bonn, Germany: Bonner Universitäts-Buchdruckerei.

Bundestag. (1969a). *Schriftlicher Bericht (des Ausschusses für Familie- und Jugendfragen): Drucksache V/4377*. Bonn, Germany: Bonner Universitäts-Buchdruckerei.

Bundestag. (1969b). *Verhandlungen des Deutschen Bundestages*. Bonn, Germany: Bonner Universitäts-Buchdruckerei: 5. Wahlperiode, 243. Sitzung, 26 Juni.

Bundestag. (2010). *Grundgesetz für die Bundesrepublik Deutschland*. Berlin, Germany: Deutscher Bundestag.

Eduskunta. (1965). *Hallituksen Esitys Eduskunnalle Laiksi Korkeakoululaitoksen Kehittämisestä Vuosina 1967–1981: He 141/1965*. Helsinki, Finland: Valtion Painatuskeskus: asetuskokoelma: 228/1966. 12. marraskuuta.

Eduskunta. (1966). *Valtiopäivät 1965: Pöytäkirjat III*. Helsinki, Finland: Valtioneuvoston Kirjapaino.

Eduskunta. (1967). *Valtiopäivät 1966: Pöytäkirjat I*. Helsinki, Finland: Valtion Painatuskeskus.

Eduskunta. (1968). *Hallituksen Esitys Eduskunnalle Laiksi Koulujärjestelmän Perusteista: He44/1967*. Helsinki, Finland: Valtion Painatuskeskus: asetuskokoelma 467/1968. 14. huhtikuuta.

Eduskunta. (1972a). *Valtiopäivät 1971: Pöytäkirjat II*. Helsinki, Finland: Valtion Painatuskeskus.

Eduskunta. (1972b). *Valtiopäivät 1971: Pöytäkirjat III*. Helsinki, Finland: Valtion Painatuskeskus.

Geschka, O. (1991). Participation and disadvantage: Women in the educational system. In E. Kolinsky (Ed.), *The Federal Republic of Germany: The end of an era* (pp. 189–198). New York, NY: Berg.

Hadjar, A., & Becker, R. (Eds.). (2009). *Expected and unexpected consequences of the educational expansion in Europe and the US: Theoretical approaches and empirical findings in comparative perspective*. Stuttgart, Germany: Haupt.

Hadjar, A., & Schlapbach, F. (2009). The 1968 movement revisited: Education and the distinction in values, political interest and political participation in West Germany. *German Politics, 18*(2), 180–200. doi:10.1080/09644000902870867

Heiskala, R. (2011). Suomalainen yliopisto II maailmansodan jälkeen. *Yhteiskuntapolitiikka, 76*(1), 92–97.

Itälä, J. (1969). *Koulusuunnittelu*. Helsinki, Finland: Tammi.

Katzenstein, P. (1987). *Policy and politics in West Germany: The growth of a semi-sovereign state*. Philadelphia, PA: Temple University Press.

Kettunen, P. (2001). The Nordic welfare state in Finland. *Scandinavian Journal of History, 26*(3), 225–247. doi:10.1080/034687501750303864

Kuikka, M. (1992). *Suomalaisen koulutuksen vaiheet*. Helsinki, Finland: Otava.

Kultusministerkonferenz. (2011). *Abkommen zwischen den Ländern der Bundesrepublik zur Vereinheitlichung auf dem Gebiete des Schulwesen*. Retrieved from: http://

www.kmk.org/fileadmin/veroeffentlichungen_beschluesse/1964/1964_10_28-Hamburger_Abkommen.pdf

Kuusi, P. (1961). *60-luvun sosiaalipolitiikka*. Helsinki, Finland: WSOY.

Lane, J.-E., & Ersson, S. (1987). *Politics and society in Western Europe*. London, UK: Sage Publications.

Lohmar, B., & Eckhardt, T. (2013). *The education system in the Federal Republic of Germany 2011/2012*. Bonn, Germany: Secretariat of the Standing Conference of the Ministers of Education and Cultural Affairs (KMK).

Mergel, T. (2010). *Propaganda nach Hitler: Eine Kulturgeschichte des Wahlkampfs in der Bundesrepublik 1949–1990*. Göttingen, Germany: Wallstein.

Nousiainen, J. (1990). Poliittisen Järjestelmän Hiljainen Kehitys. In O. Riihinen (Ed.), *Suomi 2017* (pp. 249–266). Jyväskylä, Finland: Gummerus.

Organization for Economic Co-operation and Development (OECD). (1973). *Recurrent education: A strategy for lifelong learning*. Washington, DC: OECD Publications.

Picht, G. (1964). *Die deutsche Bildungskatastrophe: Analyse und Dokumentation*. Freiburg, Germany: Walter.

Pulzer, P. (1995). *German politics 1945–1995*. Oxford, UK: Oxford University Press.

Reformers' Demand for Wider Opportunities. (1965, November 7). *The Times*.

Saarivirta, T. (2010). Finnish higher education expansion and regional policy. *Higher Education Quarterly, 64*(4), 353–372. doi:10.1111/j.1468–2273.2010.00455.x

Sozialdemokratische Partei Deutschlands (SPD). (1967). *Jugendpolitische Leitsätze der Sozialdemokratischen Partei Deutschlands*. Bonn, Germany: Vorwärts-Druck.

Studis Online. (2010). *Die BAföG-Story*. Retrieved from: http://www.bafoeg-rechner.de/Hintergrund/geschichte.php

UNESCO. (1972). *Learning to be: The world of education today and tomorrow*. Paris, France: Offset Aubin.

Välimaa, J. (2004). Nationalisation, localisation and globalisation in Finnish higher education. *Higher Education, 48*(1), 27–54. doi:10.1023/b:high.0000033769.69765.4a

West Germany: Marks for Teachers. (1964, April 11). *The Economist*.

# PART IV
Recent Developments

# 15
# CALLING FOR SUSTAINABILITY
## WWF's Global Agenda and Teaching Swedish Exceptionalism

*Malin Ideland and Daniel Tröhler*

> To be perfectly honest with you, teachers are quite possibly our #1 customers. It is through you—what you teach, how you teach—that we can quite possibly have the biggest impact on our combined efforts to conserve the majesty of our one and only planet.
> *(WWF, 2014)*

The search for educational solutions to societal problems is a well-rooted social practice. In the quote above, the future of the planet is put into the hands of teachers and, ultimately, their students. This phenomenon has been labeled "educationalization," and it describes a cultural reflex situated at the core of modernity. It is characterized by the translation of perceived social problems (which are not educational problems per se) into an educational problem: a problem in which individual teachers and students are made responsible for the solution, in this case, a sustainable future (Scott & Gough, 2003).

One of the most well-known examples of this cultural reflex called educationalization is found in the reaction of the United States to the launch of Sputnik by the Soviet Union in 1957; political and military leaders fearing communist doctrine blamed the school system for its poor performance. As a consequence, in 1958 the U.S. Congress passed its very first national law on education, the National Defense Education Act. A second well-known example is the report *A Nation at Risk*, published in 1983 by a national commission set up by President Ronald Reagan (National Commission on Excellence in Education, 1983). This commission was required to examine the broader causes of the long economic decline of and inflation in the U.S. economy. Again, the conclusions in 1983 were the same as in 1958; the education system was to be blamed for the economic misery, and, consequently, major educational reforms were put into place. In politics, education seems to be regarded as a strong determiner of national success or even redemption. Ironically, this educationalized national agenda is to be found in all modern nation-states. Despite national performances, it is a global phenomenon and is interpreted as part of a global narrative.

Environmentalism and sustainability are no exception to the strong belief in education for sustainable development (ESD) as a prime mover. The argument for promoting sustainability perspectives in education is not based on economic or military success but rather the desire to make the world a better (more sustainable) place for all species throughout the world, now and in the future. This is exemplified in the WWF quote above: "to conserve the majesty of our one and only planet." ESD is, in other words, a globally educationalized phenomenon of perceptions of the problem that human behavior harms nature and, as a consequence, the living conditions for all species.

ESD has often been described as a complex and interdisciplinary field that is difficult to fit into established cultural patterns and curricular structures in school (Stevenson, 2007; Hasslöf & Malmberg, 2014). This "misfit" might be one of the reasons why environmental non-governmental organizations[1] (NGOs) have become important educational agents during the last decades. For instance, Agenda 21, a declaration and action program of the United Nations (UN) (1992), clearly expresses the need for collaboration between formal educational institutions and NGOs, which provides a kind of gold standard for how to transform complex environmental issues into engaging and concrete lesson plans. In other words, ESD is a globally harmonizing educational practice in line with the reports from the Organization for Economic Cooperation and Development (OECD)'s Programme for International Student Assessment (PISA), UNESCO educational initiatives, and more (Rizvi & Lingard, 2006; Tröhler, 2010).

One of the most influential actors in the field is the World Wide Fund for Nature, or WWF.[2] In this chapter, the example of WWF serves to illustrate the educationalization of environmental problems and to show how this globally harmonized practice takes on national(ist) expressions when transformed through the national environmental and educational culture. WWF has a strong international agenda, with international headquarters as well as a number of national organizations that work locally in fundraising, activity planning, and development of teaching materials. WWF Sweden refers to itself one of the most prominent national WWF organizations when it comes to educational issues, and it will be the focus of our analysis in this chapter. Since the late 1990s, WWF Sweden has had employees working exclusively on education and the development of methods and materials for educational contexts in Sweden and in other parts of the world.

This chapter explores to what extent the global agenda of ESD is an imagined global agenda or, in fact, an extrapolated cultural agenda that imposes culturally imprinted views of the world as a whole, including the framing of its bearers (the sustainable eco-citizens). Two questions are of interest here: How did environmentalism become simultaneously globalized and educationalized? What happens when this practice, justified as a global movement, is translated into a specific national culture? We illustrate this by referring to the example of WWF and WWF teaching materials for ESD that were developed in the specific Swedish context. Our intention is to reconstruct this national performance of a global agenda in three steps. Following this introduction, in the first step we present an overview of how WWF International has grown, changed, and contributed to a more educationalized world culture, fabricating world citizens. In the second step, we analyze how the internationalization of WWF educational programs can be seen as epistemological imperialism operating in a construction of Swedish exceptionalism. Under the headings "Helping to Learn" and "Learning to Help," we examine how educational efforts to foster world citizens with the joint mission of saving the world take on national(ist) features. This is done through an analysis of documents produced by WWF Sweden aimed at educating people "somewhere else" (in Africa and Asia), as well as documents prepared for teachers and students in Sweden. In the third and last step, we suggest that the internationalization of ESD/environmentalism (ironically) becomes a foundation for a new kind of white national pride, which in this case is labeled "Swedish exceptionalism."

## The Rise of Environmental NGOs

As an international NGO, WWF is embedded in a broad movement that dates back to the late 19th century. The number of environmental NGOs increased considerably (but not steadily) over the last century, in three major waves: The first wave was around 1945, after the end of the Second World War and the founding of the UN. The second was in the early 1970s, after the establishment of the UN Environment Program,[3] which is a specific agency of the UN, and the third was in the wake of the Rio Conference on Environment and Development, the Earth Summit, in 1992 (Frank, Hironaka, Meyer, Schofer, & Tuma, 1999, pp. 84f.). The UN's commitment to the movement to save nature via education has become so striking that it has been described as colonizing the arena for environmental education and ESD (Gough, 1999; Jickling & Wals, 2008) because of its outstanding opportunities to spread the word "through a myriad of widely circulated reports, agendas and charters" (Galvin, 2009, pp. 2f.). Agenda 21 (UN, 1992), which resulted from the Earth Summit in Rio, may be described as a pivotal historical point when education and sustainability were indissolubly co-constructed—education as essential for sustainable development, but sustainable development as a condition for equal education around the world.

The increase in interest and concern for environmental issues has been impressive. By 1990 some 543 environmental NGOs had been identified, and the number of their members can only be estimated. WWF membership increased from 570,000 in 1985 to over 5,200,000 in 1995, an increase of almost 900% in a single decade (Frank et al., 1999, pp. 86f.); however, this number has remained quite steady since then (not including followers on social media, e.g., Facebook, which is a new kind of commitment). These figures and trends have been interpreted by scholars as advocating the onset of a world culture or world polity over the last two decades, depicting "a world-level rationalized discourse around nature" and therefore "requiring little justification or defense by those active in the environmental arena" (p. 99). In other words, engaging in the common good of the planet means that people fulfill cultural benchmarks for the citizen and "feel good" (Ahmed, 2011). One could argue that in a historical, rural society, commitment to nature was something taken for granted and thus not an obvious identity marker. However, over the last decades, one can see a change in the characteristics of "environmental citizenship," a change from being involved in the practical care of nature in local society to an individualistic approach to global issues of sustainable development (Hillbur, Ideland, & Malmberg, in work). McKenzie (2012) describes the shift as originating from "local good sense" to "global common sense" (p. 165).

This global agenda—the European share in environmental INGOs decreased from 77% in 1935 to 31% in 1990 (Frank et al., 1999, p. 86)—indicates how environmental concern has globally spread a "world citizenship" (p. 86). This world citizenship does not come for free, just as with any other idea of citizenship. The particular normative vision of the environmentally sensitized citizen fundamentally expresses the educationalized vision: citizens who are not born but made, for instance, through educational programs and means. To assess the range of this environmentally sensitized, rational, global citizenship, WWF as a successful environmental NGO may be an ideal field of research. In the beginning of WWF, global and educational aspirations may not have been excluded, but they were not at the forefront of the legitimating discourse. Instead, the main concern was the fate of popular national parks in the context of the decolonization of Africa around 1960. The particular fear that the departing authorities had was that the now-independent colonies would not be able to maintain nature's richness and beauty but would instead exploit those paradises. In 1960—the year when the largest number of former colonies (18) became independent states[4]—a German veterinarian, Bernhard Grzimek, started a popular magazine, *Das Tier* [The animal], a year after he had written and directed his Oscar-winning documentary, *Serengeti Shall Not Die* (1959). The concern was clear: The natural paradises of Africa would be destroyed "by these sort of people [the indigenous]" (Grzimek, cited in Schwarzenbach, 2011, p. 44). To raise funds for preserving nature in Africa, shocking pictures and "wildlife stories of particular drama and intensity" were published in European newspapers with the aim to "encourage children to develop a love and understanding of wildlife" (Grzimek, cited in Schwarzenbach, 2011, p. 51).

Although there was a global and educational aspect, the target was "somewhere else." The "endangered paradises" and the educational aspect that aimed at developing love of and understanding for nature were in the realm of ennobling feelings for others in "other places." A comprehensive and "holistic" understanding of the notion of an ecosystem was not yet in sight, even though the environment was becoming an increasingly crucial issue in the West in the wake of the 1960s. The book *Silent Spring* (Carson, 1962) triggered an environmental movement that challenged the idea of a mechanical and technological world order and linear notions of progress (Tröhler, 2014). At the same time, a more holistic mode of thinking about the world arose wherein people, fauna, and flora were understood as interdependent parts of an overall "system." These ideas had, in principle, been formulated by biologists much earlier and by cybernetics at the end of the Second World War (Wiener, 1948). With the advent of the computer, which was able to process infinite amounts of data, a specific systems approach was universalized (Hughes & Hughes, 2000) and became the dominant mode for understanding the world as a whole.[5] Towards the end of the 1970s, endangered natural habitats had turned into a complex ecological issue, with human beings pinpointed as those endangering part of this system. It was then that the ecology underwent a fundamental educational turn, shifting from care towards action, as expressed in the title of the book *From Care to Action: Making a Sustainable World* (Holdgate, 1996).

WWF played an important role in this educational shift, and encouraged it to continue along this line, as a report from 1989 emphasized. According to this record, WWF initiatives in the realm of "threatened species management" had a success rate of (only) 55%, whereas the WWF "education and awareness projects had been "remarkably successful" at 100 per cent" (Schwarzenbach, 2011, p. 264). This difference indicates a shift in which WWF transformed itself from a "grant-making" organization to a "project executing environmental organization," not limited to "some isolated projects" but focusing on a more holistic world vision: "a future in which humans live in harmony with nature" (pp. 265ff.). The targets of intervention activities were not simply specially selected animals or forests but "ecoregions" (p. 267).

This shift included the transformation of human beings into agents who would understand themselves not only as those called on to solve the problems of others but also as part of the problem itself. To evaluate the educational strategies, WWF contracted scholars from the University of Bath and Griffith University, who concluded:

> Across the WWF network, education is gradually coming to be recognized as one of the social strategies that . . . are vital if people are to acquire the knowledge, skills, attitudes and values that they will need if they are to change the way they live in relation to conservation, biodiversity and other issues of sustainability.
>
> *(Fien, Scott, & Tilbury, 1999, p. 27)*

What is interesting in this particular context is how these efforts to foster world citizens offer a specific perspective on the world and on power relations in terms of which people are the norm for a sustainable life and which people are pointed out as needing to change their way of living. Some scholars have called attention to how this educational movement may be seen as modern, Western imperialism, promoting a "culturally-blind isomorphism" (Chan-Tiberghien, 2004; Sauvé, Berryman, & Brunelle, 2007). Against this background, we intend to show how this cultural imperialism is taking place in contemporary educational contexts through the good intentions of educating people towards a sustainable world. We argue that the schooling of well-informed, engaged, and environmentally friendly "world citizens" ironically constructs images of national exceptionalism and racist differentiations of "us" and "them"; the communication of globalism fosters nationalism (cf. Pinar, 2003; see also the introduction in this volume). The good intentions of a just world actually operate in the opposite direction owing to established power structures. To be clear, this does not mean that good intentions, educational aid, or environmental work is "bad" or "useless" and that we should reject them (cf. Brown, 2006, p. 11). Rather, it means that we need to see them in another light and to learn about the unintended effects of these good intentions.

## Helping to Learn

As mentioned above, the language of WWF is characterized by globalism and symbols of a common world. Orangutans, tigers, and the WWF's famous symbol, the giant panda, are objects for care and salvation in Sweden, Indonesia, and the United States. The brand of the organization emphasizes how WWF is distributed all over the world, involving people of different nationalities, cultures, and races who strive towards a common, globally sustainable lifestyle. One contemporary example of this "globalism" that emphasizes fostering world citizens is WWF's annual campaign, Earth Hour. During the latest Earth Hour (March 2014), "millions of people across the world switched lights off for one hour—to celebrate their commitment to the planet" (http://www.earthhour.org/about-us). In other words, togetherness is a central theme, and it is represented by images of different places and people all over the world, but the people and places are represented in different ways, as shown in Figure 15.1.

In these images, the only person in need of help (the woman up in the middle, photographed from above) is also the only non-white person (except for the red Spider-Man at the bottom). White people (photographed from an equal position) are the ones who help in different ways. Aside from communicating togetherness, the rhetoric enhances otherness, in a double gesture of helping and also defining who is in need of help (cf. Popkewitz, 2008). The double gesture of inclusion/exclusion operates through the best of intentions, but this good intention "nevertheless produces and positions subjects, orchestrates meanings and practices of identity, marks bodies, and conditions political subjectivities" (Brown, 2006, p. 4).

FIGURE 15.1  Earth Hour 2015. Retrieved from http://www.earthhour.org/

This double gesture becomes even more evident when we look at material produced by WWF Sweden with the aim of educating people in other countries. The people who are to be helped are all situated in Asia and Africa and not in, for example, North America, Australia, or China, even though those countries are often described as heavy environmental polluters. In a 116-page booklet, *From Vision to Lesson: Education for Sustainable Development in Practice* (Östman, Svanberg, & Aaro-Östman, 2013), WWF Sweden reports and elaborates on ESD projects in countries around Lake Victoria in East Africa and in Mongolia, India, and the Malaysian area of Borneo—the same areas where "endangered paradises" were considered in need of protection when WWF was founded. Education is described (and justified) here as the golden way to sustainable development (SD):

> The importance of education when dealing with SD challenges is obvious. If we take into account that pupils communicate what they have learned in school to their parents and relatives, the estimation is that between 50–70% of a country's population can be reached.
>
> (p. 6)

WWF Sweden follows a tradition of Swedish educational aid in Africa, and in this discourse white Swedes are situated as those who teach or even help others to learn, whereas indigenous Africans are those in need of education (Nordvall & Dahlstedt, 2009). The *From Vision to Lesson* report quotes teachers in various countries, emphasizing how they have developed. For example, it offers a quote from Indonesia: "Teachers expressed their satisfaction at having developed a new role as teachers: Now we can explain things as knowledgeable resource persons" (Östman et al., 2013, p. 71), as well as a similar statement from Mongolia: "We have developed the ability to practice this knowledge in our teaching" (p. 71).

It must be said that the projects reported on by Östman et al. (2013) in many ways appear to be an attempt to escape epistemological imperialism (cf. Gough, 2002), and the authors express awareness of the power relations between the educating Swedes and the non-Swedes in need of help to learn. Nevertheless, this illustrates the core of the difficulties of escaping the colonial gaze in globalized efforts to harmonize education—the ESD practice is stuck in an "otherness machinery" (Ideland & Malmberg, 2014). Through this machinery, differences between us and them are (re)constructed within a colonial power structure (McClintock, 1995) in which the represented Other lacks a voice and agency. It is worth noting that all projects described in *From Vision to Lesson* were carried out and reported on by three white Swedish experts, paid for by Swedish government agency Sida, and organized by WWF Sweden, not by WWF India or Uganda. The experts from Sweden are the interpreters of problems to be solved through education, as well as the people who know how to do it. As stated in the previous quotes, the participants feel they have been "developed" as knowledgeable persons, and even in the ambitious development of locally relevant ESD, the colonial gaze organizes the work. Whereas the content of the lessons is locally situated (e.g., fishing in Lake Victoria), the ESD teaching methods described are the same as in Swedish schools. Hands-on activities, group work, exercises with moral dilemmas, and role playing are examples of established and preferred teaching methods (within Swedish ESD culture). They express a globalized view (from the North and/or West) of how educational solutions can be transferred from one culture to another in line with other efforts to harmonize national educational systems.[6]

We have to recognize that we do not know anything about what happens in the schools addressed by WWF Sweden and in what ways the standards are locally negotiated, but what we can see is how a Swedish national identity or even a discourse of Swedish exceptionalism (cf. Stråth, 2000) is strengthened by exporting ESD. Using Nordvall and Dahlstedt's (2009, p. 43) notion of a "paradox of solidarity," we can see that WWF Sweden's good intention of sharing knowledge and helping the Other to learn is orchestrated by the idea of Swedes defining the conditions for, and interpretations of, successful ESD—golden standards for how to save the world. This is not unique in WWF material; rather, it is included in a traditional, colonial separation of the West from the Rest (Hall, 1992) in which white people from the West are socially constructed in terms of civilization, as in urbanization, enlightenment, and technological competence, while black people from the Rest are constructed as uncivilized, for example, rural, mystical, and, not least, technologically underdeveloped (see, for example, Dyer, 1997; Young, 2004). The idea of uncivilized (non-enlightened) people destroying paradise organizes the environmental discourse in the same way that it did in the 1960s (as described above). The normalizing power of this discourse, which defines what knowledge counts as reason and who counts as knowledgeable or reasonable (Popkewitz, 2008), makes epistemological imperialism possible and unquestioned. In the next section, we outline how Swedish children learn to identify with this national self-image of exceptionalism in ESD.

## Learning to Help

With regard to teaching globalism, the Swedish curriculum has an ambitious goal for students: "to form a personal position with respect to overarching and global environmental issues" (Skolverket, 2011, p. 12). This can be compared to the 1960s type of environmental education that was focused on local issues and practical care for nature (Hillbur et al., in work). The Swedish curricula and WWF teaching material have followed the global turn in environmentalism from local care to holistic understanding. In the case of WWF, we see that the educational material has gone from featuring Swedish nature and local problems in the 1990s (e.g., Eco-watchers: WWF, 1997) to using a more recent "globalized" approach including ecological footprints, deforestation of rain forests, and climate change (e.g., Earth Hour; "schooling in a sustainable way," WWF, 2010). These issues are said to be relevant for the planet's ecological system, and they thus respond to the globally harmonizing standards for ESD.

Through this global approach to environmental issues, the world citizen is normalized and thus constructed as desirable—a person willing and able to engage in issues far outside one's own personal sphere. This construction of desirable attributes among teachers and students works as a governing technology also in the fostering of the *Swedish* world citizen, a specific kind of human being embodying a national identity in the globalized world. The following story from a WWF (2010) publication about one of WWF's "model schools"[7] in Sweden nicely illustrates the core in this national identity:

### Keeping South Africa alive in Falun:

Hosjöskolan (Hosjö school) in Falun has for 10 years collaborated with two school classes in South Africa. They keep in touch via sms [text messages], Facebook, and sometimes letters. In connection with Earth Hour in March 2010, the Hosjö class sent letters and drawings in which they described what one can do to not negatively affect the environment. It was exciting for the kids to learn that countries in different continents think similarly and feel the sense of community—we are strong together! A headmaster in South Africa wrote: "I love to work with you in Sweden since everything we do with you turns into gold!" One of the African schools is lacking resources and therefore finds it difficult to answer the letters. It doesn't matter that much, since the pupils at Hosjö school instead then develop the ability to "give." The other school, with almost only white students and teachers, is always contributing with their thoughts and works. It is important for them to know that schools in Sweden are there for them and that the contact remains.

*(WWF, 2010, p. 74)*

Through this account, WWF simultaneously fabricates a world citizen and Swedish (white) exceptionalism. On the one hand, "togetherness" and equity are emphasized, in reference to being strong together and a sense of community. Nevertheless, differences (and power relations) between Sweden and South Africa, white and black, orchestrate the story. Constructions of blacks as non-developed and poor are made through telling the reader about a probably black (skin color is not explicitly stated) South African school that lacks resources. The white school, on the other hand, is described as a little bit more equal to the Swedish school, though, and they contribute with their work. Skin color becomes a boundary marker, carrying beliefs about possibilities, enlightenment, competence, and technological development.

Furthermore, national differences are fabricated through the quote from the African headmaster about Sweden turning things into gold, as well as the last lines showing the South Africans' need for contact and knowing that "schools in Sweden are there for them." The opposite is not mentioned. Finally, Swedish exceptionalism is emphasized in the mention of how the pupils learn to give and help—a marker for a civilized society with modern, competent citizens (cf. Brown, 2006).

Through an analysis of constructions of "competent children" in Danish schools, Gitz-Johansen (2004) showed how Danish children represent modernity, and ethnic-minority children represent the "problems of modernity": "In this way even the majority children's 'deficits' are represented as more appropriate in modernity than the minority children's 'deficits'" (p. 207). Related to environmental issues, the (civilized) Swedish children's "deficits," such as polluting (accompanying their modern technological development), become, in a way, less problematic than the (uncivilized) South African children's lack of development and modern facilities (which are, most likely, less polluting). Ironically, the worse environmental polluters are also the norm for the environmentally friendly person, constructed through a specific kind of modern competence, including engagement and enlightenment (Popkewitz, 2008). This norm operates in many different ways, governing educational systems as well as individuals, separating those who know from those in need of learning, and thus reproducing skewed power relations.

Ahmed (2011) helps us to see how these good intentions to help, give, and, for example, be anti-racist are, in fact, opening up a new kind of white national pride. An imagined globalization has not decreased the importance of the nation; on the contrary, national borders have become even more important in cultural definitions of differences (Popkewitz, 2008, p. 174). The nation and its inhabitants are an imagined community (Anderson, 1983) in the globalized discourse and thus also in the educational culture. Most likely, the globalization approach believes in the construction of cosmopolitical world citizens, enlightened and rational but also willing to engage and help others (Popkewitz, 2008). However, as the analysis shows, globalization strengthens nationalism rather than displacing it and situates world citizens as reflections of the Other. The cultural production of togetherness also produces otherness; therefore, it might not be surprising that a strong Swedish identity is fabricated in teaching material about globalized issues such as sustainable development. Through a cultural transformation of the globalized ESD discourse, environmental knowledge and engagement become virtues in the construction of "Swedishness." The norm is established through representations of people who are in need of being helped, tolerated, and/or enlightened; the Other becomes an "abject," the one who privileged social groups reject but cannot live without (McClintock, 1995, p. 72). Without someone to help or tolerate, someone who represents the problematic Other, "we" cannot picture "ourselves" as good.

## The National(istic) World Citizen

To summarize, we can see that WWF has grown as an educational organization. In line with an educationalized world culture, conservation of exotic paradises was believed best done through education, first addressed to "indigenous people" but later to "everyone," all in regard to a more holistic understanding of the environment. Educationalization of environmental problems, as well as making everyone responsible for problems everywhere, is not unique to WWF but is a discourse operating in UN documents such as Agenda 21 and in national curricula and teaching materials. This discourse has opened up space for NGOs to take the role of central actors in formal education systems as a certain type of expert on "how to save the world." In Sweden, WWF grew as an educational organization, building on long traditions of educational aid to developing countries; however, via its good intentions to teach other countries, a Swedish model for ESD and an image of Swedish exceptionalism concerning ESD was constructed. Speaking with Ahmed (2011), we learn that white national pride is hidden behind good intentions to help (and teach Swedish students to help) people in foreign, developing countries. Nationalism is constructed through globalism. The culturalized features of the globally communicated togetherness can, ironically, be understood as nationalism, differentiating Swedes from Others, white from black.

Bourdieu (2003) suggests that globalism should be seen as performative, "a pseudo-concept, at once descriptive and prescriptive" (p. 85). Describing a common world with common environmental problems and common solutions evokes specific behavior and, of course, educational strategies. In a Swedish context, globalism in the environmental education discourse ironically performs a

Swedish exceptionalism; education still works towards nationalist ends. One can argue that globalism or a globalized society indicates a universal "everything" in rhetoric about the economy, education, and environmentalism. At the same time, at an empirical level, it turns out to be a national endeavor in the guise of universalism. In other words, the hope for a world citizen with global responsibility is transformed through educational means into a colonial gaze on the world.

## Notes

1. Agenda 21 mentions NGOs as well as INGOs, international non-governmental organizations. WWF is an INGO, but to avoid using too many different acronyms, we use NGO to discuss its role in global educational movements.
2. WWF was originally called the World Wildlife Fund, a name that is still being used by the two North American sections.
3. This was created during the UN Conference on the Human Environment initiated by the Swedish government in 1972.
4. The 18 states include Cameroon, Togo, Mali, Madagascar, Dahomey (renamed Benin in 1975), Niger, Upper Volta (renamed Burkina Faso in 1984), Ivory Coast, Chad, Central African Republic, Republic of the Congo (Brazzaville), and Mauritania.
5. One effect of this computer-based interpretation of the world as a system was the famous report for the Club of Rome, *The Limits to Growth* (Meadows, Meadows, Randers, & Behrens, 1972), published the same year that the UN Conference on the Human Environment took place in Stockholm in 1972.
6. Another example of the export of the Swedish model through emphasizing the local is the booklet *Handbook in Entrepreneurship: How to Start an Eco-Friendly Small-Scale Business* (WWF, 2013). This booklet is produced by WWF Sweden and published for various countries (in need) with exactly the same content but with culturally customized images. Emphasizing the local becomes a tool in governing the global through promoting a certain set of ideologies (Martin, 1996).
7. WWF Sweden has an established collaboration with 10 Swedish schools under the label "model schools." These schools have a special focus on sustainability issues. This model has been exported to other countries (WWF, 2010).

## References

Ahmed, S. (2011). *Vithetens hegemoni*. Hägersten, Sweden: Tankekraft förlag.
Anderson, B. (1983). *Imagined communities: Reflections on the origin and spread of nationalism*. London, UK: Verso.
Bourdieu, P. (2003). *Firing back: Against the tyranny of the market*. London, UK: Verso.
Brown, W. (2006). *Regulating aversion: Tolerance in the age of identity and empire*. Princeton, NJ: Princeton University Press.
Carson, R. (1962). *Silent spring*. Houghton, MA: Mifflin.
Chan-Tiberghien, J. (2004). Towards a "global educational justice" research paradigm: Cognitive justice, decolonizing methodologies and critical pedagogy. *Globalization, Societies and Education, 2*(2), 191–231.

Dyer, R. (1997). *White*. New York, NY: Routledge.
Fien, J., Scott, W., & Tilbury, D. (1999). *Education and conservation: An evaluation of the contributions of educational programmes to conversation within the WWF Network*. Washington, DC: World Wildlife Fund.
Frank, D. J., Hironaka, A., Meyer, J. W., Schofer, E., & Tuma, N. B. (1999). The rationalization and organization of nature in world culture. In J. Boli & G. M. Thomas (Eds.), *Constructing world culture: International nongovernmental organizations since 1875* (pp. 81–99). Stanford, CA: Stanford University Press.
Galvin, K. (2009). *Environmental education from a postcolonial perspective: Analyzing the influence of UNESCO's discourse on the Ontario elementary science curriculum*. Ottawa: Faculty of Education. Master thesis.
Gitz-Johansen, T. (2004). The incompetent child: Representations of ethnic minority children. In H. Brembeck, B. Johansson, & J. Kampmann (Eds), *Beyond the competent child: Exploring contemporary childhoods in the Nordic welfare societies* (pp. 199–228). Roskilde, Denmark: Roskilde Universitetsforlag.
Gough, N. (1999) Globalization and school curriculum change: Locating a transnational imaginary. *Journal of Education Policy, 14*(1), 73–84. doi: 10.1080/026809399286503
Gough, N. (2002). Thinking/acting locally/globally: Western science and environmental education in a global knowledge economy. *International Journal of Science Education, 24*(11), 1217–1237. doi:10.1080/09500690210136620
Hall, S. (1992). The West and the rest: Discourse and power. In S. Hall & B. Geiben (Eds.), *Formations of modernity* (pp. 15–30). Cambridge, UK: Polity Press.
Hasslöf, H., & Malmberg, C. (2014). Critical thinking as room for subjectification in education for sustainable development. *Environmental Education Research*, e-pub ahead of print, 1–17. doi:10.1080/13504622.2014.940854
Hillbur, P., Ideland, M., & Malmberg, C. (in work). Response and responsibility: Fabrications of eco-certified citizens in Swedish curricula 1962–2011. Manuscript submitted for publication.
Holdgate, M. (1996). *From care to action: Making a sustainable world*. Washington, DC: Taylor & Francis.
Hughes, A. C., & Hughes, T. P. (2000). *Systems, experts, and computers: The systems approach in management and engineering, World War II and after*. Cambridge, MA: MIT Press.
Ideland, M., & Malmberg, C. (2014). "Our common world" belongs to "Us": Constructions of otherness in education for sustainable development. *Critical Studies in Education, 55*(3), 369–386. doi:10.1080/17508487.2014.936890
Jickling, B., & Wals, A. (2008). Globalization and environmental education: Looking beyond sustainable development. *Journal of Curriculum Studies, 40*(1), 1–21. doi:10.1080/00220270701684667
Martin, P. (1996). A WWF view of education and the role of NGOs. In J. Huckle & S. Sterling (Eds.), *Education for sustainability* (pp. 40–51). London: Earthscan.
McClintock, A. (1995). *Imperial leather: Race, gender and sexuality in the colonial contest*. New York, NY: Routledge.
McKenzie, M. (2012). Education for Y'all: Global neoliberalism and the case for a politics of scale in sustainability education policy. *Policy Futures in Education, 10*(2), 165–177.
Meadows, D. H., Meadows, D. L., Randers, J., & Behrens, W. W. (1972). *The limits to growth: A report for the Club of Rome's project on the predicament of mankind*. Washington, DC: Potomac Associates.
National Commission on Excellence in Education. (1983). *A nation at risk: The imperative for educational reform*. Washington, DC: U.S. Department of Education.

Östman, L., Svanberg, S., & Aaro-Östman, E. (2013). *From vision to lesson: Education for sustainable development in practice*. Stockholm, Sweden: WWF.

Pinar, W. F. (2003). *The internationalization of curriculum studies*. Retrieved from http://www.riic.unam.mx/01/02_Biblio/doc/Internationalizaton_Curriculum_W_PINAR_(MEXICO).pdf.

Popkewitz, T. (2008). *Cosmopolitanism and the age of school reform: Science, education and making society by making the child*. New York, NY: Routledge.

Rizvi, F., & Lingard, B. (2006). Globalization and the changing nature of the OECD's educational work. In H. Lauder, P. Brown, J. Dillabough, & A. H. Halsey (Eds.), *Education, globalization and social change* (pp. 247–260). Oxford, UK: Oxford University Press.

Sauvé, L., Berryman, T., & Brunelle, R. (2007). Three decades of international guidelines for environment-related education: A critical hermeneutic of the United Nations discourse. *Canadian Journal of Environmental Education (CJEE), 12*(1), 33–54.

Schwarzenbach, A. (2011). *Saving the world's wildlife: WWF—the first 50 years*. London, UK: Profile.

Scott, W., & Gough, S. (2003). Rethinking relationships between education and capacity-building: Remodelling the learning process. *Applied Environmental Education & Communication, 2*(4), 213–220. doi:10.1080/15330150390241409

Skolverket. (2011). *Curriculum for the compulsory school, preschool class and the recreation centre 2011*. Stockholm, Sweden: Skolverket.

Stevenson, R. B. (2007). Schooling and environmental education: Contradictions in purpose and practice. *Environmental Education Research, 13*(2), 139–153. doi:10.1080/13504620701295726

Stråth, B. (2000). The Swedish image of Europe as the other. In B. Stråth (Ed.), *Europe plurielle/Multiple Europes:Vol. 4. Europe and the other, Europe as the other* (pp. 359–384). Brussels, Belgium: P.I.E.-Peter Lang.

Tröhler, D. (2010). Harmonizing the educational globe: World polity, cultural features, and the challenges to educational research. *Studies in Philosophy and Education, 29*(1), 5–17.

Tröhler, D. (2014). The medicalization of current educational research and its effects on education policy and school reforms. *Discourse: Studies in the Cultural Politics of Education, 35*, 1–16. doi:10.1080/01596306.2014.942957

Wiener, N. (1948). *Cybernetics or control and communication in the animal and the machine*. New York, NY: Technology Press.

WWF. (1997). *Eco-watchers*. Stockholm, Sweden: WWF.

WWF. (2010). *Skola på hållbar väg—skolors arbete inom hållbar utveckling* [Schooling in a sustainable way: School work in sustainable development]. Stockholm, Sweden: WWF.

WWF. (2013). *Handbook in entrepreneurship: How to start an eco-friendly small-scale business*. Kolkata, India: WWF.

WWF. (2014). A collection of articles, ideas and links for lesson planning? Retrieved from http://wwf.panda.org/about_our_earth/teacher_resources/.

Young, R. (2004). *White mythologies*. New York, NY: Routledge.

# 16

# FROM THE LITERATE CITIZEN TO THE QUALIFIED SCIENCE WORKER

## Neoliberal Rationality in Danish Science Education Reforms[1]

*Jette Schmidt, Peer Daugbjerg, Martin Sillasen, and Paola Valero*

> It is crucial that our children and young people learn something that they can use. Therefore, we have introduced mandatory aims for what students should know at certain years in school. And we will give schools a better opportunity to test whether the objectives are achieved.
>
> *(Prime Minister Anders Fogh Rasmussen, speech at the opening of Parliament, October 5, 2004)*

> Denmark needs more young people who want to be engineers, biotechnologists, and science teachers. We need many of them to choose a career in the scientific and technological areas. Much of Denmark's prosperity and competitiveness are built on these areas. Therefore, public as well as private companies are completely dependent on the availability of a qualified workforce in science and technology, now and in the future.
>
> *(Haarder, 2009)*

The above statements by the liberal-conservative government in power in the 2000s illustrate the political desire for a new direction in Danish education. With the government distancing itself from the social-democratic idea of "education for the many," a new era of making efficient one of the most expensive education systems in the world had arrived. A well-regulated education system was to contribute to Denmark's place as a leading nation in a global competitive economy. The scientific training/qualification of the population would be the motor of a knowledge-intensive economy. Competitiveness and social welfare were to be combined and become the banners for opening Denmark to a new, globalized world (Regeringen, 2006).

An analysis of science education reforms in Denmark since 1993, with a special focus on the years 2001 to 2009, shows how local educational reforms link to a global neoliberal rationality. By tracing the policy texts of procedures of government such as individualization, competence, and accountability, we can illustrate how the agendas of institutions such as the Organization for Economic Co-operation and Development (OECD) became incorporated into Danish educational policy, which led to the particular formation of curricular guidelines for primary school science education. This analysis is of relevance to the intention of this book—namely, to challenge the apparent tendency toward unification of education systems through the examination of differences in the national fabric of educational traditions and rationalities. We contribute in particular by showing how an area of the curriculum like science education is also part of the national effort to steer education toward the creation of entrepreneurial, competitive, and science-literate citizens. We argue that the global neoliberal rationality has played a salient role in transforming the purpose of schooling in Denmark and the Danish science education curriculum from forming literate citizens to training qualified science workers.

## The Neoliberal Rationality in Science Educational Discourses

The increasing neoliberalization of education around the world in the last two decades has been widely discussed. Conceptualized as a particular rationality of government, neoliberalism is deployed in political strategies for inserting individuals into the logic of the market. It is not, as Read (2009) would argue, "an ideology in the pejorative sense of the term, or a belief that one could elect to have or not have, but is itself produced by strategies, tactics, and policies that create subjects of interest, locked in competition" (p. 30). The fabrication of the competitive, entrepreneurial, self-regulated, and self-supporting citizen is one of the power effects of neoliberal rationality (Lemke, 2001).

Following Rose (1996), the analysis of neoliberal forms of government could focus on the strategies, techniques, and procedures through which the conduction of conduct is being orchestrated. The neoliberal rationality is presented as an unavoidable state of affairs that no government can resist (Peters, 2001). The associated strategies of government are thus justified as non-political, as simple matters of rational, technical management and administration (Ong, 2006). Therefore, whereas national reform processes unfold in local circumstances, there appears to be a homogenization of the reform mechanisms internationally (Lundahl, 2006).

Neoliberalism permeates educational technologies for governing the conduct of teachers and children alike. Educational reforms steer the curriculum, setting in place the procedures for achieving the fabrication of the desired child. In the literature on the impact of neoliberalism on education (e.g., Ranson, 2003; Bascia, 2005; Mayo, 2009), three particular procedures are highlighted:

- *Individualization* as the procedure that creates individuals as movable units in a competitive, flexible, and international labor force.
- *Development of individuals' competences* as a procedure whereby individuals acquire market value through the development of skills and knowledge that can be treated as a commodity.
- *Development of individual accountability* as a procedure establishing a clear relationship between individuals and their responsibility for their actions.

It is precisely the tracing of the assertions concerning these three procedures that guides our analysis of neoliberal rationality in the recent history of Danish education. International policy texts, Danish political speeches, Danish educational policy debates and texts, and the Danish primary science education guidelines are the documents studied. Political and policy statements display strategies to justify and imagine the desired future of education. At the same time, some of these texts delineate the techniques for governing through educational practices. Tracing assertions on individualization, competence, and accountability in the primary science curriculum (Grades 1 to 6), in particular in the topic of "the weather and seasons," allows us to show how the aims of a single topic have changed discursively over the years from an open formulation of aims to a standardized, mandatory formulation of competence-based aims. We provide evidence to support the argument that an international neoliberal rationality has contributed to shaping the changes in the school science curriculum in Denmark, effecting the move toward the fabrication of the desired scientifically competent workers for a national competitive economy.

Table 16.1 presents an overview of the changes in the curricular policy texts. In the following, we consider the arguments and analysis.

**TABLE 16.1** Overview of the discursive changes in the Danish curriculum, 2009–2011

| Year | Changes |
|---|---|
| 1993 | In The Public School Act of 1975 there was a sentence about responsibility for solving common tasks. This sentence disappeared in the Act of 1993. Retained from former school acts was, however, the dual purpose of ensuring <br> (a) versatile and personal development of students, and <br> (b) pupils provided with knowledge and skills to benefit society. <br><br> *Core Knowledge and Skills (CKS)* were defined in all school subjects at a national level, but the concrete aims for teaching were formulated at a municipality level or a school level. <br> For the topic of "the weather and seasons," the curriculum document read:" <br> The pupils shall work with: <br> Phenomena associated with weather and seasons" (CKS). |

*(Continued)*

**TABLE 16.1** (Continued)

| Year | Changes |
|---|---|
| 2002 | *CKS* was changed to what was called *Clear Aims*, which ensured a common state school where all pupils should have the opportunity to acquire the same knowledge and skills.<br><br>Examples of aims in primary science are "The education shall ensure that pupils have acquired knowledge and skills which enable them to explain the phenomena associated with the weather and the seasons" (Undervisningsministeriet, 1994) |
| 2004 | *Clear Aims* was changed to *Common Aims*.<br><br>It became mandatory for all municipalities and all schools to meet the same national aims (Undervisningsministeriet, 2004)<br><br>Examples of aims in science (*Nature/Technology*):<br><br>Education shall ensure that students acquire knowledge and skills that enable them to:<br><br>*After year 2:*<br><br>Know what conditions characterize the different seasons.<br><br>Investigate simple aspects of the weather.<br><br>*After year 4:*<br><br>Use simple technical terms in the description of weather observations.<br><br>Use simple measuring instruments to monitor the weather.<br><br>*After year 6:*<br><br>Compare own observations with a forecast.<br><br>Talk about phenomena related to the different seasons. |
| 2006 | *Individual study plans* were introduced. All students in primary and lower secondary schools must have a written study plan. A study plan consists of one or more physical or electronic documents developed at a primary or lower secondary school for each student (Dupont and Holm-Larsen, 2006). |
| 2009 | In 2009 *New Common Aims* were introduced in accordance with the Public School Act of 2006 (Undervisningsministeriet, 2008). The *Common Aims* of 2009 are more prescriptive with regard to which scientific concepts are taught and learned than the *Common Aims* of 2004.<br><br>For the topic of "the weather and seasons," the curriculum document reads:<br><br>Education shall ensure that pupils have acquired knowledge and skills that enable them to:<br><br>*After year 2:*<br><br>Connect the different seasons with important events in nature.<br><br>Investigate simple aspects of weather, including temperature and precipitation.<br><br>*After year 4:*<br><br>Use simple technical terms in the description of weather observations, including temperature, wind speed, rainfall, and visibility.<br><br>*After year 6:*<br><br>Compare their own data with a weather forecast. |

## Individualization

In neoliberal philosophy, individualism is a renewal of the classical economic liberalism: "It asserts that all human behavior is dominated by self-interest" (Peters, 2001, p. 118). The neoliberal philosophy of individualism provides the foundation for an extreme form of economic rationalism that focuses on individuals' knowledge and skills as a dominant commodity. This economic rationalism justifies standardization in education systems at the expense of self-development (Peters, 2001). In business and in government there is a belief in the existence of a hierarchy in people's knowledge and skills. Exams guarantee the maintenance and clear identification of these (Bourdieu & Gustavsson, 1998); thus, individualization as a procedure is supported.

*Education and the Economy in a Changing Society* (OECD, 1989) stated that the role of education is to develop individuals' capacity, flexibility, and quality to meet the demands of the labor market. The role of the OECD in education was stated as that of a catalyst in the process of aligning educational and economic outcomes. A key concept was the self-intended individual (Rubenson, 2008).

An integrated science and technology subject for primary school called *Nature/Technology* was established in connection with the National Danish School Act of 1993 to strengthen science education (Veje, 2001). Already in this act, individualization entered into the formulation of aims. A sentence from the School Act of 1975 about the importance of children's joint responsibility for solving common tasks disappeared. According to the School Act of 1993, education should contribute to the personal development of the individual student (Undervisningsministeriet, 1993). This was expressed by Bertel Haarder, the minister of education from 1982 to 1993 and from 2005 to 2010, as follows: "If there are 25 pupils in a class, they must be taught as 25 individuals" (cited in Hermann, 2007, p. 109). In 1993 the process of individualization in schools became more important than learning to solve tasks collaboratively.

It was in 2001, however, that the process of individualization really gained momentum in the primary and lower secondary schools. A reform process started in which the science curriculum was changed several times. These changes were justified based on the poor Danish results in the Programme for International Student Assessment (PISA) surveys in 2001 and 2003. Although it was a social-democratic/liberal government that supported Danish participation in PISA in 1997, the first PISA results in science education were published just before a liberal-conservative government took power in 2001. The PISA surveys then became a key source of leverage in the strategic plan of the liberal-conservative government (Regeringen, 2001). The resonance between the OECD's recommendations and the process of individualization in the Danish education system became more evident. Against the backdrop of various OECD reports, the liberal-conservative Danish government strengthened individualization in the education system.

This was also seen in an expert panel report from 2003 (Andersen, 2003). Among other things, the expert panel discussed the challenge of recruiting young people to study science at the tertiary level. Assertions about how studying science or technology leads to secure, well-paid jobs would encourage more young students to make the rational choice of enrolling in science, technology, engineering, and mathematics (STEM) education programs. This relates to the emphasis that the present discourse in Denmark places on the individual's ability to do well at work and be prepared for further study within science and technology.

In line with the PISA studies, which are based on individual, standardized tests, the Danish government in September 2005 abolished group examinations at all levels, taking effect from 2007. Furthermore, in 2006 individual study plans—an individually fitted learning plan that teachers had to tailor for each student in Grades 1 to 9—were introduced as a strategy to secure the focus on suitable instruction for each student. The decision to abolish group examinations had its origin in the government's strategic plan of 2005, where it is stated: "Each pupil must be evaluated against measurable, transparent criteria. Group examinations will be abolished. And it will be ensured that every student has a right to go to the individual exams and obtain an individual assessment" (Statsministeriet, 2005). Thus, group examinations were no longer allowed, and individual study plans were to ensure that each student could achieve the expected level of attainment in individual examinations. Even though the neoliberal influence in the Danish school system is quite ambiguous because it is not simply a right-wing strategy of government, the quotation above shows how equality and democracy were being transformed from concepts based on the well-being of the collective to concepts based on the optimal performance of individuals, secured by mechanisms such as individual study plans and individual examinations.

In the science curriculum the consequence of that move is that biology, physics/chemistry, and geography were mandated to conclude with individual examinations and individual national tests. Teachers are required to make a study plan for each student every year. The Danish school system moved step by step toward an increased focus on individualized learning and individual capacity building (OECD, 1989). The reforms in the education system are built on a hierarchy of skills guaranteed by exams and study plans, with individualization as the process that matches each pupil to the acquisition of measurable skills.

## Developing Individuals' Competences

The process of individualization went hand in hand with a focus on individuals' competence-based learning. Competence is a construct that combines acquired knowledge and skills with a capability to act in specific contexts (Wedege, 2003). In a neoliberal rationality, procedures of competence development are related to entrepreneurship, competitiveness, and mobility of capital and the workforce. Education should be competence-based so as to strengthen the competitiveness of private enterprise. This is justified by the idea that society and the private sector demand specific competences that help generate value (Wedege, 2003; Mayo,

2009). In this sense, competence is outcome-based, and the education system must ensure that individuals become more valuable in the international labor market.

The OECD has played a key role in promoting the concept of competence as a tool to characterize knowledge in education systems normatively. As part of its education reforms and international coordination, the OECD in 1996 described key competences in planning, steering, and control. The OECD competences made it possible to compare student outcomes at a national and international level (Durand-Drouhin, 1996). The OECD ended the project *Definition and Selection of Key Competences* (DeSeCo) in 2003 with the report *Key Competencies for a Successful Life and a Well-Functioning Society* (Rychen & Salganik, 2003). Later, the OECD selected and defined competences that would be crucial to successful societal development after the millennium (Hermann, 2007). This work was intended to formulate the competences that are vital for individual prosperity and well-functioning societies (DeSeCo, 2008).

The notion of competence entered Danish thinking on education when it was endorsed by Margrethe Vestager, minister of education in the social-democratic/liberal government in office from 1998 to 2001. Three expert commissions were set up to propose what a "competence-based" education would mean in the three key areas of the school curriculum: mathematics (Niss & Jensen, 2002), Danish language (Arbejdsgruppen Fremtidens danskfag, 2003), and science (Andersen, 2003). The introduction of a competence-based curriculum emphasized development of individuals' ability to act competently in different situations by applying knowledge acquired through education (Hermann, 2007). For science education, the plans to introduce a competence-based curriculum were formulated in the strategy proposal *Science Education in the Future* (Andersen, 2003). The Danish Ministry of Education used this proposal to initiate a reform of the science curriculum in primary and secondary schools that sought to introduce competence-based aims.

Table 16.1 shows how the process of implementing competence-based aims in the science curriculum has undergone several revisions since 2002. According to the government's education strategy, the continuous revision of these competence-based aims is necessary, because the education system has to adapt constantly to the needs of the commercial sector:

> The fundamental common, social, cultural, and personal competencies shall be considered, and the demands and levels of subject matter knowledge and relevant competencies shall constantly be under development. The educational supply shall constantly adapt to the structurally determined competence needs in Danish commercial life.
>
> *(Regeringen, 2001, ch. 1)*

The science curriculum part of the government's Common Aims (Undervisningsministeriet, 2004) illustrates that the political focus on developing individuals' competences in the education system is a core issue. For the topic "the weather and the seasons," the curriculum states that the education shall ensure that pupils have acquired knowledge and skills that enable them to "connect the different seasons with important events in nature" (after Grade 2), "use simple technical terms to describe weather observations" (after Grade 4), and "compare their own data with weather reports" (after Grade 6). According to these aims, pupils' acquisition of science concepts is not the only purpose of teaching science. The pupils should also learn to use the acquired scientific concepts competently in different situations.

The development of competence-based aims in the science curriculum can be understood as the Danish government's response to the OECD's recommendations on implementing key competences as descriptive and normative tools in education systems worldwide. The political challenge of implementing competence-based aims was politically unproblematic, as justifications were taken from OECD reports on the necessity of standardizing education systems by using a competence-based approach (Durand-Drouhin, 1996; Rychen & Salganik, 2003). The experts in the project on the core science curriculum substantiated the argumentation of the government in power at that time, as they emphasized that the competences and skills of future generations are vital for the wealth, growth, and welfare of Danish society (Andersen, 2003). The competences for science education do not address the overall purpose of the school system, as they leave out the contribution of science to the versatile development of the pupil, including social skills.

The PISA studies and the implementation of key competences as developed by the OECD (DeSeCo, 2005) in the science curriculum since 2002 have made it possible to compare pupils' outcomes at a national and international level. This situation aligns the possibility of assessing pupils' educational outcomes from a utilitarian perspective with the neoliberal rationality that pupils' acquired competences are to be understood as a commodity.

## Developing Individuals' Accountability

Accountability is a concept that is difficult to translate into Scandinavian languages, and so it is often used without translation. Even in English it contains multiple layers (Ranson, 2003). These include responsibility, on the one hand, and bookkeeping, on the other (Schedler, 1999). This means that if a person is accountable for certain actions, there has to be a transparent match between the person's actions and the justifications for them. The correspondence between the former and the latter has to be made explicit to politicians and citizens alike. Accountability is indeed related to power and the distribution of power and, in public service, to forms of governance. Within a neoliberal rationality, accountability is granted authority through calculation and instrumentalization with a main focus on individualism, competitive advantage, control of input/output, and profit (Ranson, 2003). As we will show, the development of accountability affects both teachers and pupils.

In the 1970s, education was already changing from an autonomous profession detached from public scrutiny to a public concern faced with demands for public accountability, which included standards for achievement, appropriate teaching methods, and core curricula (Donnelly & Jenkins, 2001; Ranson, 2003). Neoliberal accountability has generated a series of changes from professional judgment to market competition, from specialist knowledge to consumer choice, and from internal reports to public data (Ranson, 2003). Public data (e.g., exam results) are standardized, so that they are comparable. This in turn places increased focus on standardization and assessment procedures based on education outcomes. The capacity to provide expert comparative knowledge according to accountability has given the OECD a discursive advantage with respect to other supranational organizations (Mayo, 2009).

In 2002 the minister of education, Ulla Tørnæs (in office from 2001 to 2005), explained the change from Core Knowledge and Skills (CKS) to Clear Aims as follows:

> Enhanced professionalism in teaching goes hand in hand with the development of pupils' versatile skills. The new subject descriptions contain more detailed core knowledge and skill areas (CKS) and indicative aims and constitute the backbone of the initiative, Clear Aims, which supports the government's policy of increased openness and transparency in the education sector.
>
> *(Undervisningsministeriet, 2002, p. 5)*

The statement illustrates how procedures such as accountability and transparency resonate with the changes within education in Denmark. The 1993 curricular documents state that pupils will work with "phenomena associated with weather and seasons," leaving the teacher and the pupils to decide how the pupils must work and with what elements of the weather and seasons. This means that the pupils and the teacher are mutually accountable for how the work is performed in the classroom. The 2009 curriculum states: "Education shall ensure that students have acquired knowledge and skills that enable them to . . ." (Undervisningministeriet, 2008, p. 14). This statement makes a demand of the teacher as well as the pupils. The teacher is accountable for the effect of her/his teaching on the pupils, and after receiving this education, the pupils are responsible for fulfilling the stated aims. It is the pupils' knowledge of the weather and seasons and their ability to apply this knowledge to daily weather and seasonal phenomena that determines whether (1) the pupils have met their obligations within primary science learning and (2) the teacher has met her/his obligations within primary science teaching.

In relation to the introduction of the Common Aims, Prime Minister Anders Fogh Rasmussen (in office from 2001 to 2009) stated:

> Some would call it a little reform, but I don't think of it like that, because by introducing a new scale, we promote a new mindset: You get focused on the idea that children should learn something at school, and we are giving parents a tool to hold schools responsible, if children do not learn enough.
>
> *(Larsen & Rasmussen, 2003, p. 301)*

Both responsibility and bookkeeping became part of the teacher's role. The teacher was accountable for students learning "something" in the school, and this "something" became more and more detailed and prescriptive in 2002, 2004, and 2009, as illustrated in Table 16.1. The frequent need for revision of the curriculum indicates a lack of political confidence in the school system to achieve the aims. Politicians have argued that more detailed and precise aims tend to make the schools more accountable, and they hope that reform will restore the general public's trust in the school system. However, according to Ranson (2003), who analyzed the education system in the United Kingdom:

> This regime of neo-liberal accountability, designed to restore trust to public service has, however, had unintended consequences of further eroding public trust in the stewardship of public services because it has embodied flawed criteria of evaluation and relations of accountability.
>
> *(p. 470)*

Regarding accountability, the situation in the United Kingdom is far beyond that in Denmark. Still, the political argument for more accountability illustrates a resonance between the developments in the two countries.

From 2001 to 2009 centralization of educational content took place. All schools had to implement the same aims in their curricula. The prime minister's statements above illustrate that the move was intended to foster transparency and control of teachers' work. The pupils' study plans and the prohibition of group examinations would further improve the transparency of the individual outcomes in the education system, which is part of the procedures of accountability for individual pupils' learning and teachers' work. In the neoliberal discourse, in science education children are molded into individuals who will perform well on standardized tests, and if they become good at science, they will be very valuable to the future labor market.

## Neoliberal Rationality and International-National Resonance

In this article we have examined individualization, competence, and accountability as important procedures in the neoliberal rationality of government. These procedures initiated practices and forms of thinking about children and teachers in ways that regulate people's conduct. We showed how the strategies, techniques, and procedures of a neoliberal rationality in government penetrate school science education through their insertion into the description of aims and topics in the Danish science curriculum. OECD reports and recommendations have caused individualization, development of individuals' competences, and accountability to permeate Danish education policy. The changes toward more detailed competence-based aims for primary and lower secondary schools make it easier to hold the individual teacher and pupils accountable. Successive governments in Denmark have ensured that education increasingly resonates with an international neoliberal rationality in which education is no longer conceived as an activity to secure a collective sense of human life and has started to promote a greatly reduced view of education as training for a competitive career.

Regarding the primary science education curriculum, we showed that individualization through individual exams and study plans has become mandatory, supported by a compulsory competence-based science curriculum description that establishes clearer demands for accountability among both pupils and teachers. By ensuring measurable individual competence-based outcomes, teachers and pupils can eventually be held accountable for their contribution to the overall national economic competitiveness. The competences promoted are those of general value in an international career within science and technology rather than competences that are of value in everyday life.

In the current political context it is common sense that science education realizes the promised future in developed societies. It is important to question the ways in which these naturalized ideas have entered recent national curricular changes within a growing neoliberal rationality. According to Popkewitz (2004), the good student is easily turned into a scientific problem-solving child, but this also creates a group of pupils who fall short of reaching the detailed competence-based aims. These pupils are in an individualized education system and are left alone with the distress of not meeting the standards of society (p. 3). For education research as well as research in science education, it is important to understand the politics of education in fields that, owing to their association with scientific neutrality and progress, are shaping the desired citizens of the future. Our analysis shows that, currently, science education in Denmark is, at least in terms of policy, ready to mold science-competent workers for now and the future. The question remains as to whether such a fabrication of children is most desirable for society.

## Note

1. The research in this chapter was funded by VIA University College, University College Northern Denmark, and Aalborg University. It is part of the activities of the Nordic Centre of Excellence JustEd—Justice Through Education in the Nordic Countries.

## References

Andersen, N.O. (2003). *Fremtidens naturfaglige uddannelser: Naturfag for alle—vision og oplæg til strategi* [Science education in the future: Science for all—visions and possible strategy]. Copenhagen, Denmark: Undervisningsministeriet [Danish Ministry of Education].

Arbejdsgruppen Fremtidens danskfag [Working group for the future of Danish as a school subject]. (2003). *Fremtidens danskfag—en diskussion af danskfaglighed og et bud på dens fremtid* [The future Danish—a discussion of the school subject and a proposal for its future]. Copenhagen, Denmark: Undervisningsministeriet [Danish Ministry of Education].

Bascia, N. (2005). *International handbook of educational policy*. Dordrecht, the Netherlands: Springer.

Bourdieu, P., & Gustavsson, B. (1998). *Moteld: Texter mot nyliberalismens utbredning* [Texts against the propagation of neoliberalism]. (B. Gustavsson, Trans.). Eslöv, Sweden: Bo Östlings bogforlag.

DeSeCo. (2005). *The definition and selection of key competencies*. Retrieved from http://www.deseco.admin.ch/bfs/deseco/en/index/02.parsys.43469.downloadList.2296.DownloadFile.tmp/2005.dskcexecutivesummary.en.pdf

DeSeCo. (2008). *Introduction to DeSeCo*. Retrieved from http://www.deseco.admin.ch/bfs/deseco/en/index.html

Donnelly, J.F., & Jenkins, E.W. (2001). *Science education: Policy, professionalism, and change*. London: Poul Chapman.

Dupont, K., & Holm-Larsen, S. (2006). *Folkeskoleloven 2006: Sammenstilling, bemærkninger og gennemførelsesbestemmelser m.v.* [Public School Act 2006: Commented]. Vejle, Denmark: Kroghs Forlag.

Durand-Drouhin, M. (1996). *Assessing and certifying occupational skills and competences in vocational education and training*. Paris, France: Organization for Economic Co-operation and Development.

Haarder, B. (2009). Naturfag er almen dannelse [The natural sciences are a liberal education]. In Undervisningsministeriet [Danish Ministry of Education] (Ed.), *Natur, teknik og sundhed. For alle og for de få, i bredden og i dybden* [Science, technology and health education: For all and for the few, in breadth and depth] (pp. 8–13). Copenhagen, Denmark: Undervisningsministeriet [Danish Ministry of Education].

Hermann, S. (2007). *Magt & oplysning: Folkeskolen 1950–2006* [Power and information: The public school, 1950–2006]. Copenhagen, Denmark: Unge Pædagoger.

Larsen, T., & Fogh Rasmussen, A. (2003). *Anders Fogh Rasmussen: I godt vejr og storm* [Anders Fogh Rasmussen: In good weather and storm] (3rd ed.). Copenhagen, Denmark: Gyldendal.

Lemke, T. (2001). "The birth of bio-politics": Michel Foucault's lecture at the College de France on neo-liberal governmentality. *Economy and Society, 30*(2), 190–207. doi:10.1080/03085140122085

Lundahl, L. (2006). Swedish, European, global: The transformation of the Swedish welfare state. In B. Lingard & J. Ozga (Eds.), *The RoutledgeFalmer reader in education policy and politics* (pp. 117–130). London, UK: Routledge.

Mayo, P. (2009). The "competence" discourse in education and the struggle for social agency and critical citizenship. *International Journal of Educational Policies, 3*(2), 5–16.

Niss, M., & Jensen, T.H. (2002). *Kompetencer og matematiklæring. Ideer og inspiration til udvikling af matematikundervisning i Danmark* [Competencies and mathematics learning:

Ideas and inspiration for the development of mathematics teaching in Denmark]. Copenhagen, Denmark: Undervisningsministeriet [Danish Ministry of Education].
Organization for Economic Co-operation and Development (OECD). (1989). *Education and the economy in a changing society*. Paris, France: OECD.
Ong, A. (2006). *Neoliberalism as exception*. Durham, NC: Duke University Press.
Peters, M. A. (2001). *Poststructuralism, Marxism, and neoliberalism: Between theory and politics*. Lanham, MD: Rowman & Littlefield.
Popkewitz, T. (2004). The alchemy of the mathematics curriculum: Inscriptions and the fabrication of the child. *American Educational Research Journal, 41*(1), 3–34. doi:10.3102/00028312041001003
Ranson, S. (2003). Public accountability in the age of neo-liberal governance. *Journal of Education Policy, 18*(5), 459–480. doi:10.1080/0268093032000124848
Read, J. (2009). A genealogy of homo-economicus: Neoliberalism and the production of subjectivity. *Foucault Studies, 6*, 25–36. Retrieved from http://rauli.cbs.dk/index.php/foucault-studies/article/view/2465/2463
Regeringen [Danish Government]. (2001). *Vækst, velfærd, fornyelse: Regeringsgrundlaget 26. november 2001* [Growth, welfare and renewal: Government strategic plan, November 26, 2001]. Copenhagen, Denmark: The Danish Government.
Regeringen [Danish Government]. (2006). *Fremgang, fornyelse og tryghed: Strategi for danmark i den globale økonomi* [Prosperity, innovation and security: Strategy for Denmark in the global economy]. Copenhagen, Denmark: The Danish Government.
Rose, N. (1996). Governing "advanced" liberal democracies. In A. Barry, T. Osborne, & N. Rose (Eds.), *Foucault and political reason: Liberalism, neo-liberalism and rationalities of government* (pp. 37–64). London, UK: UCL Press.
Rubenson, K. (2008). OECD education policies and world hegemony. In R. Mahon & S. McBride (Eds.), *The OECD and transnational governance* (pp. 242–259). Vancouver, Canada: University of British Columbia Press.
Rychen, D.S.E., & Salganik, L.H.E. (Eds.). (2003). *Key competencies for a successful life and a well-functioning society*. Göttingen, Germany: Hogrefe & Huber.
Schedler, A. (1999). Conceptualizing accountability. In A. Schedler, L. Diamond, & M. F. Plattner (Eds.), *Power and accountability in new democracies* (pp. 13–28). Boulder, CO: Lynne Rienner.
Statsministeriet [Danish Ministry of State]. (2005). *Nye mål, regeringsgrundlaget 2005* [New aims, government strategy 2005]. Retrieved from http://www.stm.dk/publikationer/reggrund05/index.htm
Undervisningsministeriet [Danish Ministry of Education]. (1993). *Lov om folkeskolen* [National Danish School Act]. Retrieved from http://inet.dpb.dpu.dk/ress/skolelove/folkeskole/30.06.1993.html
Undervisningsministeriet [Danish Ministry of Education]. (1994). *Formål og centrale kundskabs- og færdighedsområder—folkeskolens fag* [Purpose and core knowledge and skills in public schools]. Copenhagen, Denmark: Undervisningsministeriet [Danish Ministry of Education].
Undervisningsministeriet [Danish Ministry of Education]. (2002). *Klare mål—fysik/kemi* [Clear aims—physics/chemistry] (1st ed.). Copenhagen, Denmark: Undervisningsministeriet [Danish Ministry of Education].
Undervisningsministeriet [Danish Ministry of Education]. (2004). *Fælles mål—natur/teknik* [Common aims—nature and technology] (1st ed.). Copenhagen, Denmark: Undervisningsministeriet [Danish Ministry of Education].

Undervisningsministeriet [Danish Ministry of Education]. (2008). *The aims of the folkeskole*. Retrieved from http://eng.uvm.dk/Uddannelse/Primary%20and%20Lower%20Secondary%20Education/The%20Folkeskole/The%20Aims%20of%20the.aspx

Veje, C. J. (2001). *Natur/teknik i folkeskolen: Hvorfor og hvordan* [Nature and technology in the public school: Why and how] (1st ed.). Copenhagen, Denmark: Alinea.

Wedege, T. (2003). *Kompetence(begreber) som konstruktion* [Competencies as a construction]. Roskilde, Denmark: Center for forskning i matematiklæring.

# 17

# THE EUROPEAN EDUCATIONAL MODEL AND ITS PARADOXICAL IMPACT AT THE NATIONAL LEVEL

*Lukas Graf*

This chapter looks at developments between the national and the European level, taking as examples two relatively similar education systems. Within the European Union, Austria and Germany are best known for their extensive systems of vocational education and training and especially their long-term institutionalization of the dual training principle. This means that a significant proportion of young people are enrolled in programs at the upper-secondary level that combine in-firm training with theoretical learning at a vocational school. However, in both countries, the dual-track vocational education and training is institutionally separated from general academic education at the upper-secondary level (the *Gymnasium* type of school) and also university-level education. This institutional divide, which Baethge (2006) has called the "educational schism," leads to a lack of permeability between the two major sectors in the German and Austrian national education systems—namely, between vocational education and training (VET) and higher education (HE).

In both Austria and Germany, this lack of permeability has been increasingly problematized since the late 1960s. For example, this institutional separation limits the social mobility of individuals and thus fails to acknowledge the rising educational aspirations of young people (e.g., Powell & Solga, 2010). Furthermore, it neglects the ongoing shift from the manufacturing sector to the service and knowledge sectors of the economy, a shift that brings with it a growing demand for general academic skills (e.g., Streeck, 2012). However, dissolving the institutional divide between the fields of VET and HE is a challenging task, given that both fields are strongly path dependent and organized according to distinct educational ideals, standards, and laws. Most importantly, each of the two fields falls within the sphere of responsibility of different political actors. For instance, the field of VET is one of the few areas in which the social partners—that is, the interest organizations of employees and employers—still have a far-reaching influence on public policy. In contrast, the field of HE is strongly shaped by the interests of the educated elites (*Bildungsbürgertum*) and various state actors.

Interestingly, given the institutional stasis in these two fields, institutional innovation took place in a niche between VET and HE. More specifically, hybrid organizational forms that combine institutional elements from VET and HE have expanded rapidly since the late 1960s (Graf, 2013). These hybrids have succeeded in satisfying the demands of both employers and young people for programs that promote both detailed practical experience and high-level academic general skills. In Germany, dual study programs are the key example for hybrids of this kind, and in Austria, it is the *Berufsbildenden Höheren Schulen* (BHS) (higher vocational schools with HE entrance qualification). By promoting institutional permeability, these hybrids offer idiosyncratic solutions to a challenge that both countries face—namely, the institutional divide between VET and HE that has evolved historically.[1]

Yet it should be noted that these hybrids were not established as part of a top-down strategy by educational policy makers. Instead, they were developed by actors who circumvented the institutional stasis in the traditional organizational fields of VET and HE. As a consequence of this "unplanned" development, which took place within a gray zone at the margins of two established fields (i.e., VET and HE), the hybrids were not smoothly integrated into the given national institutional configurations of the education systems. In fact, an empirical analysis based on organizational institutionalism (see below) shows that the maintenance of hybrid organizational forms relies on a significant degree of loose coupling in relation to traditional educational pathways in Austria and Germany.

In view of the above-mentioned idiosyncratic developments at the national level, this chapter examines the impact of the growing European influence on the Austrian and German education systems. Over the last few decades the international dimension of education has evolved into one of the key reference frames in education development worldwide (e.g., Lanzendorf & Teichler, 2003, p. 220). Within the European Union and, indeed, in Europe more generally, one key way in which this international dimension has materialized is increasing European integration.[2] Ever since the Treaty of Rome, which established the European Economic Community in 1957, what is called the readability (or the transparency) of qualifications has been part of the European integration process (Bouder, Dauty, Kirsch, & Lemistre, 2008). However, it was only in the late 1990s that European educational policies gained their current influence on the national discourse on educational reform. In that context, one key innovation was the implementation of soft governance and the open method of coordination, whereby "[s]oft governance leaves room for multilevel games and creates opportunity structures enabling domestic actors to use EU initiatives to overcome domestic veto-points and veto-actors" (Powell & Trampusch, 2012, p. 289). In 1999 the Bologna Declaration was signed by 29 European education ministers with the aim of establishing a Europe-wide HE area. The key instrument developed in the Bologna Process was the two-tiered degree structure (bachelor's degree and master's degree) defined in terms of learning outcomes and measured by the European Credit Transfer and Accumulation System.

The Bologna Process provided the initial impetus for a range of other European educational policies. Ever since, European education and training reforms have been gaining in strength incrementally but forcefully and have also demanded greater mobility between VET and HE. In 2002 the Copenhagen Declaration was signed by 31 ministers with the intention of enhancing European cooperation in VET. For this, one of the key tools is the European Qualification Framework (EQF), which was formally adopted by the European Parliament and Council in April 2008. One of the basic goals of the EQF is to increase permeability between VET and HE, as it subsumes both under one qualification framework on the basis of a review of all qualifications available within a national education system by the relevant national stakeholders. That is, based on nonbinding recommendations, member states voluntarily commit themselves to developing a national qualification framework (NQF) that will later be linked to the EQF. The principal goal of the EQF, with its eight reference levels, is to diffuse and promote lifelong learning and to make national qualification systems more readable and understandable within and across different countries to facilitate national and international mobility.[3] Under the banner of lifelong learning as an ideal, the "diffused" norms, standards, and regulations include increased international transparency, a learning-outcome orientation, and enhanced permeability with regard to all types of education.

Thus, both the Bologna Process and the Copenhagen Process propose instruments to overcome the institutional divide between VET and HE. This is especially relevant for Austria and Germany, given that these countries represent "hard cases" for these reforms owing to their institutional divide between VET and HE. How do the relatively similar skill formation systems of Austria and Germany deal with this challenge, and what are the implications for the hybrid organizational forms mentioned earlier?

The next section presents the methods and data in brief. The subsequent section describes the hybrid organizational forms in Austria and Germany. After that, relevant theoretical concepts from organizational institutionalism are introduced and applied to understand how hybrids achieve relative stability despite their otherwise precarious status within the national education system. An analysis of the impact of current Europeanization processes on these hybrids then follows. The final section summarizes the key findings.

## Methods and Data

The case studies cover the time period from the genesis of the hybrid organizational forms—from roughly the late 1960s up to 2013 but with a focus on the "Bologna era" starting in 1999. As far as organization theory is concerned, my chapter is sympathetic to organizational heterogeneity. In fact, since the late

1970s, theories of organizations have generally moved away from organizational heterogeneity, as most scholars in organization theory have prioritized "abstraction over contextual specificity" and focused on explanations of homogeneity (King, Felin, & Whetten, 2009, p. 4). In contrast, my comparison aims to look at spatial and temporal variation to explain specific national patterns of organizational development (see Aldrich, 1999) at the nexus of VET and HE and with regard to hybrid organizational forms. Educational organizations can mean very different things in different countries, even if the titles they grant and their positioning within international qualification frameworks may suggest equivalence. Therefore, a dense description of the relevant organizations and their institutional embeddedness is essential if we are to compare them. For this purpose, my most important data source is the semi-structured interviews that I conducted in Vienna, Bonn, and Berlin with 48 key experts in VET and HE in the past few years. My goal was to arrive at a representative sample of important stakeholders in each country (state agencies, employer associations, employee organizations, and educational organizations). In addition to the expert interviews and available secondary sources, I analyzed official documents by national stakeholders, including statements by state ministries, political parties, social partners, and the educational organizations themselves. I will now describe the hybrid organizational forms in Austria and Germany.

## Hybrid Organizational Forms at the Nexus of VET and HE in Austria and Germany

### Austria: Hybrid Higher Vocational Schools With HE Entrance Qualification (BHS)

In comparison with Germany, Austria has the stronger tradition of full-time vocational schooling. The rapid expansion of the BHS since the 1970s builds on this tradition (Graf, Lassnigg, & Powell, 2012, pp. 162–165). The BHS takes one year longer than the general academic secondary school (the Austrian *Gymnasium*). In five years, it leads to the double qualification of a VET diploma and an academic baccalaureate (*Diplom- und Reifeprüfung*): The academic baccalaureate offers access to HE, and the VET diploma provides the right to practice higher-level occupations (*Berechtigung zur Ausübung gehobener Berufe*).[4] Currently, approximately 26% of all students in Grade 10 are enrolled in a BHS (Tritscher-Archan & Nowak, 2011). The BHS programs cover the fields of engineering, arts and crafts, business administration, the management and service industries, tourism, fashion, design, and agriculture and forestry.

After three years of relevant professional experience, graduates from most BHS institutions of engineering, arts and crafts, and agriculture and forestry can apply for the official title "engineer" (*Standesbezeichnung Ingenieur*) from the relevant ministry. Although these engineering titles are not official academic degrees, they nevertheless enjoy a very high reputation in the Austrian labor market. In fact, many BHS graduates choose to *not* access HE but to enter the labor market directly.

The BHS is recognized as enabling students to acquire skills beyond the upper-secondary level. Job advertisements frequently do not distinguish between BHS graduates and graduates of universities of applied sciences with bachelor's degrees (e.g., Lassnigg, 2013, p. 130). One major reason why some employers prefer graduates from a BHS over holders of bachelor's degrees is the higher proportion of practical training that the BHS offers, which is often very effective at meeting the skill demands of the small and medium-sized firms that dominate the Austrian economy.

The BHS systematically links curricular contents from vocational training and academic education, for example, in the training companies that are an integral learning site of the BHS institutions of business administration. The BHS provides an attractive educational pathway, especially for children from families with no previous history of HE participation. The decision to study at a BHS, typically made at the age of 14, is attractive to this group, as it keeps open two different educational and career pathways, reducing the risk of academic dropout. In this way, an important condition for social mobility is institutionally supported.

In terms of governance, the responsibility for the BHS lies with the Austrian Federal Ministry for Education, Arts and Culture but with the involvement of the social partners. For instance, the BHS is part of the system of VET governance, as it offers a VET diploma as part of the above-mentioned double qualification. Thus, the BHS is subject to the Vocational Training Act as far as access to formally regulated occupations or wage scale classifications are concerned.

In sum, the BHS represents a hybrid organizational form: First, it combines learning processes from both VET and HE. This combination manifests itself, for example, in the BHS double qualification, the BHS diploma thesis, and (in some cases) the possibility of being awarded an engineering title. Second, the BHS straddles the boundary between upper-secondary (VET) and post-secondary education (HE). This is also reflected in the high recognition of the BHS on the labor market and in the possibility for BHS graduates to receive credits for their prior learning if they enter HE. Third, the BHS sector is not solely subject to traditional academic school governance but integrates aspects of governance typical for the dual VET sector. For these three reasons, the hybrid BHS leads to increased institutional permeability between VET and HE.

## *Germany: Hybrid Dual Study Programs*

Dual study programs combine two distinct learning environments—namely, academic institutes and a workplace. In about a third of the dual study programs, the vocational school is integrated as a third location (Waldhausen & Werner, 2005). In dual study programs, students and firms are usually bound by training, part-time, practical training, traineeship, or internship contracts. Dual programs usually lead to a bachelor's degree in three to four years (dual studies at the master's level are still rare) and connect two didactic principles—namely, practical training and scientific grounding. For example, the teaching staff is composed of lecturers (at universities of applied sciences, vocational academies, or universities), trainers from industry, and sometimes vocational school teachers. Dual study programs combine institutional and organizational elements from the fields of VET and HE, for example, with regard to their curricula, teaching staff, or funding structures. Furthermore, dual study programs integrate the classroom and the workplace as two complementary learning settings. The original type of dual study programs, the *ausbildungsintegrierende* (training-integrated studies) type, leads to an official vocational certificate from the field of vocational training (upper-secondary level) as well as a bachelor's degree from the HE sector (post-secondary level) (see Graf, 2013, pp. 95–102 for a description of all available types).

The rise of the dual study programs supports the argument that the dual principle has "extended" and moved up to the HE sector (e.g., Sorge, 2007, p. 240). In April 2013 the Federal Institute for Vocational Education and Training (Bundesinstitut für Berufsbildung, BIBB) counted 1,461 dual study programs and more than 64,358 study places (BIBB, 2014). Compared to April 2008, this signifies a growth of 46% in registered study places (BIBB, 2008, 2014). Dual study programs are offered by German universities of applied sciences (59%), the Baden-Württemberg Cooperative State University (20%), vocational academies (15%), and universities (6%) (BIBB, 2014, p. 28). In total, around 27,900 cooperative arrangements exist between firms and various educational providers within the dual studies framework (Kupfer & Stertz, 2011, p. 29). Dual study programs are most commonly offered in engineering sciences, law, economics and business studies, and math and natural sciences. The profile of a dual study program is largely determined by internal negotiations and a cooperation agreement between the training firm and the organizational provider (Mucke & Schwiedrzik, 2000, p. 15). There is a significant degree of flexibility in the specific forms of coordination between firms and educational organizations (e.g., loose or tight) (e.g., Reischl, 2008). It is important to note that there is no federal standard with regard to the salaries of students enrolled in dual study programs. However, in the case of the *ausbildungsintegrierende* dual study programs, it is decreed that the student should receive at least the same payment that a regular apprentice (at the upper-secondary level) would receive.

To sum up, dual study programs are hybrid organizational forms and as such support institutional permeability between VET and HE for three reasons: First, they combine learning processes from both VET and HE, and the curricula usually stress the equal importance of academic and firm-based learning. Second, they link upper-secondary VET and post-secondary HE, for example, through the double qualification granted by the *ausbildungsintegrierende* programs. Third, these programs are not solely subject to either traditional HE governance or traditional VET governance but rather to a mix of both.

## Hybrid Organizational Forms, Stability, and Loose Coupling

The previous section described the two specific hybrid organizational forms that have developed at the nexus of VET and HE in Austria and Germany and have succeeded in overcoming the institutional divide between VET and HE. This section shows that the status of these hybrids is precarious for two reasons: because they are located in a gray zone between the traditional fields of VET and HE and because they draw on institutional elements from these two traditional fields, leading to some degree of functional overlap and potential friction. Based on theoretical considerations from organizational institutionalism, this section explains how these hybrids have nevertheless managed to achieve stability and have in fact expanded rapidly.

### *Some Theoretical Considerations*

According to organizational institutionalists, the survival of organizations is, beyond organizational efficiency, conditional on organizational conformity with dominant institutional myths present in their environment (Meyer & Rowan, 1977). Thus, organizations are constantly seeking legitimacy so as to acquire social acceptability and credibility (see Scott, 2008). However, the dominant myths in a given society or institutional context are not always consistent. To cope with these incompatible structural elements, which may lead to internal and boundary-spanning contingencies (Meyer & Rowan, 1977), organizations often rely on loose coupling between "frontstage" standardized, legitimate external practices and formal structures and "backstage" practical considerations and internal organizational behavior (DiMaggio & Powell, 1983; Meyer & Rowan, 1977). Tight coupling usually occurs when an issue supports the status quo, and uncoupling is more likely when an issue challenges the status quo (Lutz, 1982). However, it is also important to note that loose coupling is not always used strategically for "rational" organizational purposes but rather is applied as a result of organizational routines or because of perceived appropriateness (e.g., Hasse & Krücken, 2005). Orton and Weick (1990) discuss a number of ways in which such loose coupling has an impact on organizational performance. For example, it is often seen as creating persistence (e.g., in terms of a particular organization's reduced responsiveness to environmental changes). Another, related example is that loose coupling can have a buffering effect. That is, loose coupling can reduce conflicts within and between organizations and organizational fields and hence isolate problems and prevent their spread.

The following empirical illustrations from the Austrian and German cases indeed show that loose coupling helps to reduce conflicts resulting from the functional overlaps between the hybrid organizational forms and more traditional non-hybrid organizational forms within the national education system. The argument, illustrated in the following section using one key example each from the Austrian and the German cases, is that loose coupling is central to the maintenance of hybrid organizational forms, which are otherwise unstable. This is because key actors in the traditional fields of VET and HE tend to perceive these hybrids as competitors and would like to either integrate them into their respective organizational field, which would strengthen their "monopoly," or push them far into the other field, which would reduce direct competition.

## Austria: The Functional Overlap Between the BHS and Universities of Applied Sciences

The BHS converts key institutional elements from the fields of VET and academic education and blends them within its hybrid organizational structure. However, the expert interviews reveal that there is a significant functional overlap between the BHS and the universities of applied sciences. For example, studying at a BHS or a university of applied sciences often leads to similar positions in the labor market, even though the BHS is formally located within the upper-secondary education sector and the university of applied sciences within the post-secondary education sector. However, this did not initially lead to major frictions between the universities of applied sciences and the BHS (or to the collapse of the hybrid BHS), because the two organizations were instead decoupled from each other. In fact, the creation of the universities of applied sciences, which took place in the early 1990s, was only able to go forward precisely because of this decoupling, since BHS stakeholders insisted on their special status being maintained. The key policy makers in the Austrian skill formation system, rather than trying to make the hybrid BHS fit the logic of either VET or HE, have allowed a loosely coupled relationship between the BHS and the universities of applied sciences to prevail, in this way enabling the maintenance of the hybrid BHS. Furthermore, the state is willing to finance both organizations.

## Germany: The Functional Overlap Between Dual Studies and Traditional Dual Apprenticeship Training

Dual study programs blend HE elements with the dual apprenticeship principle. For instance, the HE institute and the participating firm are responsible for coordinating the study program. Thus, hybrid dual study programs signify a layer located in a niche between VET and HE. Nevertheless, although greater institutional permeability between VET and HE is promoted within dual study programs (e.g., as they transfer the dual principle to HE), the educational schism continues to exist at the system level. That is, the classic dual apprenticeship training still remains largely isolated from the world of HE.[5] Yet the co-existence of dual studies and dual apprenticeship training leads to a functional overlap, especially in regulated occupations that are offered both in the dual apprenticeship training system and in the form of dual study programs.[6] This implies potential friction at the system level, for example, considering that individuals with the same entrance qualification (i.e., a

HE entrance qualification) end up in programs at different educational levels (i.e., the upper-secondary level in the case of dual apprenticeship training and the post-secondary level in the case of dual studies). Yet, in practice, the actors and regulatory authorities have been largely unconcerned with or unaware of these functional overlaps. As a consequence, they enabled the loose coupling of institutional structures and, with that, the expansion of dual studies, despite their positioning in a gray zone between the strongly institutionalized fields of VET and HE.

In view of these locally specific institutional solutions, the next section analyzes the influence of current Europeanization processes on the stability of hybrid organizational forms in Austria and Germany.

## Europeanization Reduces the Scope for Routines of Loose Coupling

The current Europeanization processes push for standards for the categorization of different kinds of educational programs and qualifications throughout Europe, with one key goal being to create greater transparency and permeability in European skill formation (see Powell, Bernhard, & Graf, 2012). This chapter, however, argues that the key tools of educational Europeanization, that is, the introduction of bachelor's and master's degrees and the EQF, fail to acknowledge the organizational specificities of hybrids. The comparison of the Austrian and German cases shows that a main effect of Europeanization is a reduction in the scope for loose coupling, a mechanism essential for the maintenance of hybridity. In this section, I first illustrate how the location of the respective hybrid organizational forms within the education system matters with regard to the impact of Europeanization. In this context, second, I compare the cases of Austria and Germany. Third, I discuss the influence of current Europeanization processes on the institutional permeability that the two hybrid organizational forms at the nexus of VET and HE represent.

### *The Location of Hybrid Organizational Forms Matters Regarding the Impact of Europeanization*

The specific location of the hybrid organizational forms within the national education system plays a significant role in determining the dynamics of hybridization. Both hybrids span the boundary between the upper- and post-secondary levels. However, each of them calls either the upper- or the post-secondary level its home domain. The core location of the Austrian BHS is the upper-secondary level (VET), integrating elements of post-secondary HE (e.g., access to an engineering title). In contrast, the core location of the German dual study programs is the post-secondary level (HE), although the programs also integrate the upper-secondary level (VET) (e.g., the possibility to obtain a formal occupational certificate from the dual system). Given that the core location of the German dual study programs is the post-secondary level (HE), the Bologna Process, involving the introduction of the bachelor's degree at the post-secondary HE level, matters more than the Copenhagen Process in this case. In the case of the Austrian BHS, it is the Copenhagen Process in the form of the EQF, which is intended to cover all qualifications within an education system, that has had the greatest impact on hybridity. Therefore, the following illustrations focus on the impact of Bologna and Copenhagen on hybrid dual study programs in Germany and the impact of the EQF on the hybrid BHS in Austria.

### The Austrian Case: The NQF Reduces Scope for Ambiguity and Loose Coupling

The Austrian case shows that the implementation of the EQF reduces the scope for hybrid organizational forms. The hybrid status of the BHS relies on the way in which it overcomes traditional institutional barriers between VET and HE and between upper-secondary VET and post-secondary HE. This is possible owing to a significant degree of informality and scope for loose coupling in its institutional environment. However, the implementation of the EQF has tended to diminish the scope for such ambiguities within the institutional environment. In fact, the EQF is mainly interpreted as a rigid classificatory matrix, which contradicts the nature of hybrid organizational forms. The consultation process regarding the NQF in Austria is exerting regulative pressure to formalize the position of the BHS double qualification, but it does not allow for an adequate mapping of the overlaps between the different qualification levels that it represents. In other words, the NQF reduces the previously available degrees of freedom that allowed the hybrid BHS to flourish. For instance, the NQF has strengthened the competition between the BHS and the universities of applied sciences. This is because the NQF increases the interaction and competition between organizational forms that previously stood in a rather loosely coupled relation to each other. This new, more competitive environment has been a source of friction between the BHS and the universities of applied sciences. The representatives of the universities of applied sciences regard the successful BHS institutions as competitors. As a consequence, in the NQF consultation process they have argued against BHS qualifications being associated with the three highest NQF levels, 6–8, which they see as reserved for bachelor's, master's, and PhD degrees respectively (Fachhochschulrat, 2008; Österreichische Fachhochschul-Konferenz, 2008). As a consequence, the BHS is losing some of its attractiveness as it is indirectly "downgraded" relative to the Austrian universities of applied science. In turn, this is detrimental to the degree of institutional permeability that the BHS represents as a result of its hybrid VET-HE status.

### The German Case: The Bologna Process Leads to Academic Drift

In the German case the introduction of bachelor's degrees in dual study programs has especially increased competition with dual apprenticeship training. The introduction of bachelor's degrees was a vehicle for the providers of dual study programs to further establish themselves within the HE sector. The dual study programs took up the bachelor's degrees rather quickly. Thus, in terms of their academic reputation, they became more similar to the traditional HE organizations. In this way, Bologna further legitimizes dual study programs as belonging to HE. Yet this drift towards traditional HE is not beneficial for institutional permeability. More precisely, because they are approximating universities of applied sciences and universities, the dual study programs have been losing some of their connections to VET at the upper-secondary level. Although dual study programs are located in a gray zone between VET and HE, with sufficient scope for the creative blending of institutional elements from both organizational fields, the implementation of the bachelor's degree standard has reduced this boundary-spanning capacity. For example, dual study programs now go through a formal accreditation procedure like other bachelor's degree programs, but accreditation is biased towards general academic learning. Furthermore, as the dual study bachelor's programs now last only three to four years (similar to dual apprenticeship training, which usually lasts three years) and as high-end dual apprenticeship programs and dual study programs compete for the same target group of students, the structural friction between dual study programs and traditional dual apprenticeship training is intensifying.

## Comparing the Impact on Hybrid Organizational Forms and the Degree of Institutional Permeability

What is the impact of these developments on the hybrid organizational forms and the institutional permeability that they represent through their combination of elements drawn from the otherwise largely separate organizational fields of VET and HE? In this context, I distinguish between the impact of Europeanization on (1) the hybrid organizational forms as such, (2) the degree of hybridity and institutional permeability, and (3) the potential friction between the hybrid organizational forms and closely related non-hybrid organizational forms:

1. The Bologna Process and the Copenhagen Process signify a drift in the institutional environment governing skill formation, but the two processes have affected the hybrid organizational forms differently depending on their core location. The Europeanization processes have tended to have unfavorable consequences for the organizational maintenance of the Austrian BHS, but the German dual study programs seem to have benefited from these processes. Here, it is especially relevant that the German hybrid is now directly linked to the bachelor's degree cycle, which has become the "hegemonic" global standard for undergraduate studies. In contrast, the BHS in Austria is more affected by the EQF, which, however, leads to increased organizational competition between the universities of applied sciences and the BHS and a relative downgrading of the latter.

2. In all three cases, the current Europeanization processes—or at least their national interpretations—have the unintended consequence of reducing the scope for loose coupling as a condition for hybridization at the nexus of VET and HE. In this way, the national interpretations of Bologna and Copenhagen reinforce the divide between upper-secondary and post-secondary education and between VET and HE, reducing the potential of the hybrid VET-HE organizational forms to increase institutional permeability.
3. What contributes to this dynamic is that both Bologna and Copenhagen have created an environment that to some extent drives closely related organizational forms further apart. This point refers mainly to the relationship between the BHS and the universities of applied sciences in the Austrian case and the relationship between dual studies and high-level dual apprenticeship programs in Germany.

## Summary

Although the focus of European educational processes on soft governance, outputs, comparability, and permeability appears neutral, it has had unintended consequences, in that it has reduced the scope for the loose coupling on which the hybrid organizational models rely for their continued reproduction. This holds both for the introduction of bachelor's degrees and for the EQF. For example, in Germany the introduction of bachelor's degrees has resulted in academic drift of the dual study programs, whereas in Austria debates on the EQF have tended to push the BHS out of the post-secondary level (to which they informally extend) in the direction of the upper-secondary level of education. Thus, although one of the central goals of the Europeanization of skill formation is to increase permeability between VET and HE, the rigid interpretation of the two-tiered degree structure (bachelor's and master's degrees) and the EQF has had the effect of reducing the level of loose coupling, while loose coupling is required for further hybridization. In this sense, these Europeanization tools have had the paradoxical result that they negatively affect some of the underlying conditions fostering further hybridization and thus institutional permeability at the nexus of VET and HE.

In conclusion, if European educational policy makers want to optimally promote permeability between VET and HE, then more attention needs to be paid to the complexity of national and local institutional conditions and to established innovative organizational solutions, such as hybrid organizational forms that straddle the boundaries between otherwise institutionally separated educational sectors.

## Notes

1. Please note that this analysis focuses mainly on permeability in terms of the rules, standards, and ideas that define the relationship between VET and HE—that is, institutional permeability—rather than a measure of actually realized individual social mobility.

2. On the complex (inter-)relationship between globalization, internationalization, and Europeanization in the field of education, see, for example, Altbach (2006, p. 123), Graf (2009), and Tröhler and Lenz in this volume.
3. In the EQF matrix the eighth level corresponds to the highest level of knowledge, skills, and competences.
4. The BHS differs, for example, from specialized academic upper-secondary schools (*berufliche Gymnasien*) in Germany. The latter are three-year, full-time programs that include vocationally oriented intensive courses but lead "merely" to a general academic HE entrance qualification. That is, the German specialized academic upper-secondary schools do not offer a vocational qualification but typically prepare for studies at a HE institute or a vocational program.
5. Despite several initiatives to build linkages from dual apprenticeship training to HE training.
6. In Germany, in a number of popular and high-end dual apprenticeship programs (e.g., bank clerk, industrial clerk, insurance and financial services broker, tax clerk, information technology specialist) the proportion of apprentices with a new training contract and a HE entrance certificate is well over 50% (see Graf, 2013, p. 113).

## References

Aldrich, H. E. (1999). *Organizations evolving*. Thousand Oaks, CA: Sage.

Altbach, P.G. (2006). Globalization and the university. In P.G. Altbach & J.J.F. Forest (Eds.), *International handbook of higher education* (pp. 121–140). Dordrecht, the Netherlands: Springer.

Baethge, M. (2006). Das deutsche Bildungs-Schisma: Welche Probleme ein vorindustrielles Bildungssystem in einer nachindustriellen Gesellschaft hat. *Soziologisches Forschungsinstitut—Mitteilungen, 34*, 13–27.

Bouder, A., Dauty, F., Kirsch, J.-L., & Lemistre, P. (2008). *Readability of qualifications: A question as old as Europe*. Thessaloniki, Greece: European Centre for the Development of Vocational Training (CEDEFOP).

DiMaggio, P. J., & Powell, W. W. (1983). The iron cage revisited: Institutional isomorphism and collective rationality in organizational fields. *American Sociological Review, 48*(2), 147–160. doi:10.2307/2095101

Fachhochschulrat (FHR). (2008). *Stellungnahme des Fachhochschulrates zum Konsultationspapier Nationaler Qualifikationsrahmen für Österreich*. Vienna, Austria: FHR.

Federal Institute for Vocational Education and Training (BIBB). (2008). *Projekt AusbildungPlus. Jahresbericht*. Bonn, Germany: BIBB.

Federal Institute for Vocational Education and Training (BIBB). (2014). *AusbildungPlus in Zahlen. Trends und Analysen 2013*. Bonn, Germany: BIBB.

Graf, L. (2009). Applying the varieties of capitalism approach to higher education: Comparing the internationalization of German and British universities. *European Journal of Education, 44*(4), 569–585. doi:10.1111/j.1465-3435.2009.01401.x

Graf, L. (2013). *The hybridization of vocational training and higher education in Austria, Germany and Switzerland*. Opladen, Germany: Budrich UniPress.

Graf, L., Lassnigg, L., & Powell, J.J.W. (2012). Austrian corporatism and gradual institutional change in the relationship between apprenticeship training and school-based VET. In M. R. Busemeyer & C. Trampusch (Eds.), *The political economy of collective skill formation* (pp. 150–178). Oxford, UK: Oxford University Press.

Hasse, R., & Krücken, G. (2005). *Neo-Institutionalismus* (2nd ed.). Bielefeld, Germany: Transcript-Verlag.

King, B. G., Felin, T., & Whetten, D. A. (2009). Comparative organizational analysis: An introduction. *Research in the Sociology of Organizations, 26*, 3–19. doi:10.1108/s0733-558x(2009)0000026002

Kupfer, F., & Stertz, A. (2011). Dual courses of study: The supply and demand situation. *BWP Special Edition*, 29–30.

Lanzendorf, U., & Teichler, U. (2003). Globalisierung im Hochschulwesen: Ein Abschied von etablierten Werten der Internationalisierung? *Zeitschrift für Erziehungswissenschaften, 6*(2), 219–238. doi:10.1007/s11618-003-0024-3

Lassnigg, L. (2013). Berufsbildung, akademische Bildung, Akademisierung der Berufswelt. In E. Severing & U. Teichler (Eds.), *Akademisierung der Berufswelt?* (pp. 109–141). Bielefeld, Germany: Bertelsmann.

Lutz, F. W. (1982). Tightening up loose coupling in organizations of higher education. *Administrative Science Quarterly, 27*(4), 653–669. doi:10.2307/2392536

Meyer, J. W., & Rowan, B. (1977). Institutionalized organizations. Formal-structure as myth and ceremony. *American Journal of Sociology, 83*(2), 340–363. doi:10.1086/226550

Mucke, K., & Schwiedrzik, B. (2000). *Duale berufliche Bildungsgänge im tertiären Bereich.* Bonn, Germany: Federal Institute for Vocational Education and Training (BIBB).

Orton, J. D., & Weick, E. K. (1990). Loosely coupled systems: A reconceptualization. *The Academy of Management Review, 15*(2), 203–223. doi:10.5465/amr.1990.4308154

Österreichische Fachhochschul-Konferenz (FHK). (2008). *Stellungnahme der Österreichischen Fachhochschulkonferenz zum Konsultationspapier Nationaler Qualifikationsrahmen für Österreich.* Vienna, Austria: FHK.

Powell, J. J. W., Bernhard, N., & Graf, L. (2012). The emerging European model in skill formation: Comparing higher education and vocational training in the Bologna and Copenhagen Processes. *Sociology of Education, 85*(3), 240–258. doi:10.1177/0038040711427313

Powell, J. J. W., & Solga, H. (2010). Analyzing the nexus of higher education and vocational training in Europe: A comparative-institutional framework. *Studies in Higher Education, 35*(6), 705–721. doi:10.1080/03075070903295829

Powell, J. J. W., & Trampusch, C. (2012). Europeanization and the varying responses in collective skill systems. In M. R. Busemeyer & C. Trampusch (Eds.), *The comparative political economy of collective skill systems* (pp. 284–316). Oxford, UK: Oxford University Press.

Reischl, K. (2008). Bestandaufnahme der bisher in Deutschland akkreditierten dualen Studiengänge. In BLK (Ed.), *Tagungsband zur Fachtagung des BLK-Projektes* [CD-ROM]. Bonn, Germany: Bund-Länder-Kommission für Bildungsplanung und Forschungsförderung (BLK).

Scott, W. R. (2008). *Institutions and organizations: Ideas and interests.* Thousand Oaks, CA: Sage.

Sorge, A. (2007). Was ist von einer produktiven Wissengesellschaft durch nachhaltige Innovation und Berufsbildung zu erwarten? In J. Kocka (Ed.), *Zukunftsfähigkeit Deutschlands* (pp. 229–249). Berlin, Germany: Sigma.

Streeck, W. (2012). Skills and politics: General and specific. In M. R. Busemeyer & C. Trampusch (Eds.), *The political economy of collective skill formation* (pp. 317–352). Oxford, UK: Oxford University Press.

Tritscher-Archan, S., & Nowak, S. (Eds.). (2011). *Country report Austria.* Vienna, Austria: ReferNet Austria.

Waldhausen, V., & Werner, D. (2005). *Innovative Ansätze in der Berufsbildung: Höhere Durchlässigkeit und Flexibilität durch Zusatzqualifikation und duale Studiengänge. Forschungsbericht IW No. 12.* Cologne, Germany: Deutscher Instituts-Verlag.

# 18

# ACCELERATED WESTERNIZATION IN POST-SOVIET RUSSIA

## Coupling Higher Education and Research

*Viktoria Boretska*

> Did not Europe develop the ultimate form of human culture, which can only spread across the face of the earth bringing happiness to all tribes and peoples?
>
> *(Danilevsky, 1869/1995, p. 56)*

In the late 1800s, the Russian Slavophile and naturalist Nikolay Danilevsky was challenging the readers of the journal *Zarya* with articles, which were further compiled into his book *Russia and Europe* (Danilevsky, 1869/1995), referred to by his peer Fyodor Dostoyevsky (1869/1986) as a "future handbook of every Russian for all times" (p. 30). Danilevsky developed a theory of cultural-historical types and introduced a civilization approach to Russian history. He was convinced that Slavic[1] and Romano-Germanic (European) civilizations were "units of unequal order" (1869/1995, p. 55). It would be pointless, he concluded, to imitate the West: Every civilization has its own development phases (p. 77), progress is possible beyond the path of the rather one-sided European civilization (p. 56), and, for the equilibrium of world forces, Russia should chair an all-Slavic union with its center in Constantinople (p. 337).

Labeled as panslavistic, some of Danilevsky's questions and answers regarding the place and "mission" of Russia in a fast-changing world traveled through time. Reinforced by a new reading of Danilevsky, a strong spirit of exceptionalism could be traced in Russia's socialist choice of the 20th century that gave birth to the Soviet Union. Despite the idea of Russia's otherness, Russia aspired to build a sphere of importance roughly similar to that of the West: Lenin envisioned Russia as a "spark"[2] for lighting up revolutions throughout Europe, with Russia becoming its socialist leader; this was partly accomplished by Stalin's post-war ideological domination of Eastern and Central Europe, during which European models on industrial progress were actively adopted. Khrushchev, in turn, during the Cold War, accentuated a strong Soviet potential to overtake Europe and the United States.

Nevertheless, through the complexity of such domination and imitation relations and the fierce political, economic, and social competition during the Cold War, both socialist Russia and the democratic West could presume to stand on the same level, speaking the same language of freedom, equality, and material well-being. However, the disintegration of the USSR brought about a widening gap between the two poles of the Cold War and threw Russia far back in time to Danilevsky's definition: Slavic and European civilizations became "units of unequal order" again. In the well-known book *The Clash of Civilizations*, Huntington (1996) remarks fairly: "A Western democrat could carry on an intellectual debate with a Soviet Marxist. It would be impossible for him to do that with a Russian Orthodox nationalist" (p. 142).

The 1991 fall of the USSR, resulting in Russia's uncertain rebirth, in a general equilibrium, allowed for hopeful confidence in the West. Liberal democracy was legitimated by Fukuyama (1992) as the final form of human governance, leading to the end of ideological evolution and the end of history as a continuous process of evolution (p. xii). According to Fukuyama's prophecy, liberal democracy as an ultimate soundly functioning human environment would become an envisioned destination point of Russia's Titanic, too. In fact, Western-tuned "democratization" had already commenced shortly before the fall of the Soviets in the policy of its last leader Mikhail Gorbachev. Russia's aspirations of otherness dissolved completely together with the disintegration of the USSR: The Iron Curtain fell, and the world theater became more involved.

Russia commenced on a rocky path of utter modernization, defined as a *catching-up modernization model*. Particularly, Fedotova (1997), a social development and modernization scholar at the Russian Academy of Sciences, advocated this model of development in her monograph *Modernization of the "Second" Europe*[3] as indispensable and the only possible approach (p. 57). It had two phases: Modernization was at first equivalent to Westernization, and then, through further interaction within a dialogue between the Western "global" and the Russian local, modernization acquired culture-specific features, *dewesternizing*. "Westernization" is defined as the process of transition from traditional societies to modern ones through the direct transfer of structures and technologies from Western societies (p. 50).

Within these developments, a special role was assigned to education: Just as at the beginning of the century Russia was massively educated into socialism, at the end of the century it could as well be educated into liberal democracy. It was at this time that an educational policy was elaborated, a 10-year accelerated plan directive called "The Concept of Modernization of Russian Education up to 2010."[4] Education was delicately mandated with the responsibility for Russia's "transition to a democratic constitutional state and market economy, and control over the hazard of lagging behind the world trends of economic and social development" ("Kontseptsija modernizatsiji," 2001, p. 263). Because of the catching-up modernization model, Russia would start by importing Western schemes, referred to in the "Concept of Modernization" as "general trends in global developments that would shape changes in Russian education" (p. 263).

This chapter will generally examine Russia's path of catching-up modernization, based on the "Concept of Modernization of Russian Education" as a document illustrating the Western direction in educational transformations, and will look at its two main phases: (1) Westernization, or the injection of "global" trends; and (2) *dewesternization*, or the internal adoption or rejection, transformation, and conversion of these trends. To illustrate this, a model of vertical integration of higher education and research will be discussed. First, the channels of dissemination such as institutional and individual ties will be considered to describe international agency and national involvement in transporting this model. Second, I will attempt to place the model within a particular historical and cultural context of Russia in order to understand the dialogue between the "global" and local.

## The "Concept of Modernization of Russian Education" in the Making: Direction "West" on the Compass

The "Concept of Modernization of Russian Education" as "a political and national task" was accepted by the newly elected government of Vladimir Putin. It described the priorities and measures for fulfilling the general strategic program for the upcoming decade, which was called "modernization of education" ("Kontseptsija modernizatsiji," 2001, pp. 263, 266). After the laissez-faire decade of the 1990s, the state manifested its glorious return to the educational field: It now agreed on a need to "develop the optimal model of education governance" to fulfill the education modernization project (p. 278). The Western direction of Russia's educational transformations resides in numerous aspects of the priorities that the "Concept of Modernization" outlines: They may be effectively reduced to large-scale markers such as *quality*, *equality*, *commercialization*, and *control*. Within these markers, the transfer of particular organizational and structural models of the Western best practices in education was launched. In terms of both content and organization, education was subjected to a thorough reform, and the vocabulary for this reform was borrowed from the West.

The political climate at the turn of the century was particularly apt for this reform. Vladimir Filippov, minister of education in Russia from 1999 to 2004 and a Soviet-grown mathematician, was a passionate promoter of Westernization. The Peoples' Friendship University of Russia (PFUR), Filippov's alma mater and workplace, where he had been working loyally as a rector for almost two decades, became a promoter of Westernization as well. Filippov was educated as a mathematician; his dissertation on non-potential operators proved to the world how effectively physics questions could be answered with the at that time very promising math analysis approach. In 1984 he spent 10 months at the Free University of

Brussels and presented his report to the Royal Academy of Sciences in Belgium with the assistance of the famous Russian-origin physicist and Nobel Laureate Ilya Prigogine. At the Free University of Brussels, Prigogine chaired a physics research department for which Filippov's work was particularly valuable. In 1989 the American Mathematical Society published a monograph by Filippov in the United States (Filippov, 1989).

Filippov had already been actively involved in the governance of higher education since the early 1990s: He had become a dean of the PFUR Faculty of Mathematics, Physics, and Natural Sciences. Putting his scholarly career on hold, Filippov (1993) published *Practical Experience in Organization and Functioning of Universities in the Conditions of a Market Economy*, foreshadowing his own future experience. In the book, Filippov described organizational aspects of higher education in the West and included detailed descriptions of 20 specialized study plans from Western European and American universities (e.g., the Free University of Brussels, Belgium; George Washington University, United States; University Toulouse-3, France). Filippov wrote: "Integration of Russia into the world society demands the accordance of our educational system with world approaches in this field," and he argued that Russia's transition to a market economy posed principal problems to the organization of Russia's higher education (p. 4). In the same year, 1993, Filippov was elected rector of the PFUR, which became one of the first institutions to promote the Westernization of higher education in Russia and which established in 2000 the Department of Comparative Educational Policy (UNESCO Chair in Policies of Higher Education).

Also in 1993, UNESCO founded the World Commission on Culture and Development, with Prigogine becoming an honorary member. The General Conference in Paris was permeated by one harmonizing thought:

> After three decades of development, how far have we got? The world is still divided in two. Far from being filled, this gap between the wealthiest and the most destitute nations is widening. Inside individual countries themselves, both in the North and the South, the gulf is expanding between those who are excluded and those who have access to knowledge and well-being and to the forms of culture related to educational and scientific investment and to technology.
>
> *(UNESCO, 1993, p. i)*

In 1995 the World Commission on Culture and Development published a report, *Our Creative Diversity*, containing recommendations for further *culture-specific* development policy making, based on the argument that imported models for development collapsed because they neglected cultural aspects. Despite the commission's attention to cultural idiosyncrasies, in a rather contradictory way the vision of UNESCO still rested on a general belief in a wealthy, *united* globe, with the West disseminating its structures and leading the others. Filippov, in turn, was particularly interested in taking Russia's last train to this united, harmonious place and was absorbed by the idea of effective integration of Russian education in the world educational community.

In 1998, just as Filippov became the minister of education, he participated in the UNESCO World Conference on Higher Education in Paris, called "the largest international gathering on higher education held in the century" (UNESCO, 1998, p. 1). The conference adopted two documents of historical significance: the *World Declaration on Higher Education for the 21st Century* (p. 19) and *Framework for Priority Action for Change and Development in Higher Education* (p. 29). These documents, charged with the spirit of international unity and mutual responsibility within a globalized world on the edge of entering the second millennium, may be defined as belonging to a larger mechanism of constructing and disseminating world cultural blueprints (Chabbott, 2003). UNESCO, in particular, rose (and rises) up as one of the largest perpetual motion engines in maintaining and spreading the belief in a global society and world culture, and, particularly, in constructing education globally for the sake of development.

The *Framework for Priority Action for Change and Development*, accepted in 1998, called for a variety of "globally recognized" models in higher education to be adopted internationally for the sake of development and modernization. Here, among others, a particular model of integrated higher education and scientific research was fostered. The advancement of knowledge through research was called to be "an essential function of all systems of higher education. Of *special* importance is the enhancement of research capacities in higher education research institutions" (UNESCO, 1998, p. 23). Because of the *Priority Action* framework, "support mechanisms at national and international level to stimulate and sustain research groups in less developed systems of higher education should be strengthened in order to support institutional development" (p. 67).

Conventional in the West but alien to Russia, the coupling of education and research could seem to be a rather cosmetic transformation, yet it meant a fundamental shift that challenged national research policy even more ruthlessly than educational policy. Historically, Russia's research was concentrated in the Academy of Sciences, and the concept of research universities, initially developed by Alexander von Humboldt, was an inherently Western one. Lately, owing to the neo-institutional approach, among other factors, universities have largely been viewed through the prism of their "third mission" as entrepreneurial institutions for research commercialization and active participation in socio-economic development (Etzkowitz et al., 2008).

The relationship between higher education and research seemed to be crucial in constructing the knowledge society (Etzkowitz et al., 2008, p. 684). Developed in the 1990s, the Triple Helix concept of university-industry-government relationships was believed to form the DNA of aspired innovation for constructing the knowledge society (Etzkowitz & Leydesdorff, 1997). Of these three institutions, the university was already drawn as an active center of research, through which it created strong communication ties with industry, which, in turn, would produce demand for the research. These well-tuned feedback mechanisms of the Triple Helix elements, designed to understand and foster innovation for the sake of the knowledge society, were an area of great divergence from the post-Soviet legacy of Russia, where research was largely steered by state tasks.

The Western model of coupling education and research, as a fundament of the whole innovation mechanism, which rested on it, appears particularly interesting in the context of Russia's aspiration to adapt it to the post-Soviet environment. Not least, adoption of this model would be responsible for the principal course of Russia's modernization, as an aspiring market economy, knowledge society, and strong state. We will see how national and international initiatives brought this model to Russia and, ultimately, what reactions it triggered in a dialogue between the local and the global.

## Introducing Research to the University: Cooperative Effort

Higher education, in the course of Russia's catching-up pace of modernization, was a subject of principal structural and institutional reorganization, as it had a straightforward connection with Russia's economic and social conversion. Based on the "Concept of Modernization of Russian Education," the effectiveness of this connection was supposed to be achieved by "integration of university, academic, and industrial scientific research" ("Kontseptsija modernizatsiji," 2001, p. 280). Combining the three aspects of education, research, and external ties, as illustrated in Figure 18.1 and mentioned in the "Concept of Modernization," reflected a particular "globally" recognized vision that was reinforced by international organizations worldwide as the ultimate best model for research organization and innovation.

In 1994 a World Bank report stated:

> In most developed countries universities usually account for a significant proportion of national research expenditures and employ the bulk of

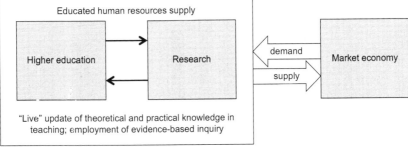

**FIGURE 18.1** The cycle of interaction in the integrated education-research model

scientists engaged in research and development work. Many countries have failed to utilize their potential for advanced scientific training and research . . . When Eastern and Central Europe were under communist regimes, the separation of scientific research from advanced scientific training was a major obstacle to their ability to contribute to the economy.

*(pp. 21–22)*

While the coupling of research and education was considered to be an attribute of a developed society, in Russia research was traditionally conducted at numerous institutes of the Russian Academy of Sciences (RAS) (from 1925 to 1991 named the Academy of Sciences of the USSR). A dedicated Russian science historian, Loren Graham, emphasized that "no other academy, society, university, or research foundation dominates the field of science in its country to the degree the academy of sciences in the Soviet Union does Russian science" (1967, p. vii). As it had been working for the sake and well-being of one system, after the fall of the Soviets the RAS was instantly disqualified as too centralized, too elitist, and too non-responsive to the demands of the time and the hunger for innovation.

UNESCO and the World Bank were and are carrying out the mandate of recognizing such dysfunctionality and suggesting the unquestionable solution. These international organizations became long-lasting stakeholders in the transformations that Russian higher education and, even more, the research tradition were facing. Integration of higher education and research has been one of those spicy topics at UNESCO conferences and in World Bank recommendations for Russia since the mid-1990s, to ensure that Russia chooses the right, that is, correct, path.

The 1994 World Bank report *Higher Education: The Lessons of Experience* suggested that these unique policy comparisons and analyses make up the part of the World Bank's unquestionable knowledgeability in the field. The World Bank's global expertise promoted trust, and its financial injections led to obligations; it became both advisor and donor for Russia's educational and scientific rebirth. In 1998 the World Bank co-funded "probably the most influential effort" of folding teaching and research together, a pilot project called Basic Research in Higher Education (BRHE), a product of international initiative and both national and international cooperation (Graham & Dezhina, 2008, p. 116). The mission of this program was to be accomplished through establishing research and education centers (RECs), in thorough imitation of the practices of Western universities. The RECs were to encourage combining scientific research and education while immediately establishing external ties with enterprises or organizations (p. 117).

The BRHE program was introduced as a joint responsibility of the Russian government and U.S. foundations, which provided external financial support: The program was administered by the Civilian Research and Development Foundation (CRDF) and additionally funded by the MacArthur Foundation (later also by the Carnegie Foundation), but the Russian government had to cover a remaining 50% of the program costs (p. 117). These costs were provided through a specific

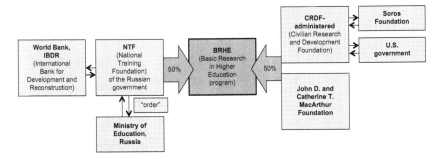

**FIGURE 18.2** BRHE program funding mechanism

*Sources*: Based on material from two Russian sources and one English source: (1) Chistokhvalov, V. N. (2010). *Osobennosti modernizatsii rossijskogo i evropejskogo vysshego obrazovanija v 1991–2005: istoriko-sravnitelnyj analiz* [Peculiarities of modernization in Russian and European higher education, 1991–2005: Historical comparison]. Moscow, Russia: Peoples' Friendship University of Russia (PFUR); (2) Dneprov, E. D. (2002). *Modernizatsija rossijskogo obrazovanija: Dokumenty i materialy* [Modernization of Russian education: Documents and materials]. Moscow, Russia: State University "Higher School of Economics"; and (3) Graham, L., & Dezhina, I. (2008). *Science in the new Russia: Crisis, aid, reform.* Bloomington: Indiana University Press.

mechanism of credit from the World Bank, in particular its International Bank for Development and Reconstruction, to the Russian National Training Foundation (NTF) (Chistokhvalov, 2010, p. 163). Under these circumstances, the program was carried out through administration by the CRDF and moderation by the NTF, in strict conformity with the rules and procedures of the International Bank for Development and Reconstruction, on one side, and consultations with the Ministry of Education and Science in Russia, which was the actual "client" of the projects under realization, on the other (p. 164).

Figure 18.2 introduces the funding mechanism of the BRHE project and illustrates the national and international involvement in the program design and execution. On the part of the U.S. foundations, as well as on the part of Russian government interaction with the World Bank, the BRHE program represented a pan-vision of a globally recognized and advocated model of integrating research into higher education.

In the realization of this model, as well as in further strong dedication to implementing the coupling of research and education, Irina Dezhina and the Russian Institute of Economy in Transition, Dezhina's workplace for 12 years (1995 to 2007), may be considered the individual and institutional receivers of the international organizations' dissemination channel. Starting from the launch of the BRHE project, Dezhina was a consultant at CRDF, having had previous international experience as a Fulbright scholar in the MIT Science, Technology, and Society Program. In 1998–1999 Dezhina studied the idea of vertical education–research integration, first as a science policy analyst at SRI International in the United States and then as a consultant at the Organization for Economic Co-operation and Development and the World Bank.

Since 1994 the World Bank's advisory activity in higher education in developing countries has been framed in joint projects with UNESCO: *Higher Education in Developing Countries: Peril and Promise* (World Bank, 2000), *Constructing Knowledge Societies: New Challenges for Tertiary Education* (World Bank, 2002), and, most applicable to the current topic, *From Knowledge to Wealth: Integrating Science and Higher Education for the Development of Russia* (World Bank & NTF, 2006). The latter project, prepared jointly by the World Bank and NTF in Russia, held to an already familiar line of argument, expressed in Recommendation No. 8: "To strengthen the support in integrating science, higher education, and business, in order to enhance the processes of innovation and full utilization of universities' potential in the innovation system" (p. 86). The mechanisms of state support to higher education should be focused on funding system projects on the integration of business, higher education, and science, the report authors highlighted.

Along with BRHE initiative launched in 1998, the early 2000s also saw some governmental involvement in the mission of modernizing the field of education and research. Adopted in 2001, the federal program for integration was foreseen to unfold from 2002 to 2006 and was aimed at training new specialists for the market economy through the mechanism of interaction between higher education, research, and industry. From 2007 on, amendments to the Federal Law on Higher and Postgraduate Education bear a prevailing theme of the integration of education and research: The forms of integration are thoroughly described in the Federal Law, but the executive procedure is still vague.

In an article on the BRHE program, Dezhina (2007) pointed out that education–research integration in Russia was hindered by a number of legal limitations: "There is no legislative definition for either the forms of integration that traditionally existed in Russia (e.g. Fundamental Research Laboratory) or progressive forms (e.g. Research University)" (p. 50). In that same year, the Russian government introduced the aim of developing a network of particular federal universities by 2016, carrying out a mission of fostering science and innovation (Dezhina, 2008, p. 48). In 2009 the status of the research university was finally fixed by law. The status of national research university would be granted for a 10-year period and result from competitive selection based on applicants' research and development programs (set out in Article 21 of the Federal Law on Higher and Postgraduate Education).

Thus, in its long path towards integrating education and research, Russia was eagerly accompanied by global agents like UNESCO and the World Bank. Through providing recommendations for development and financial aid for project realization, they greatly contributed to the vision of education as a global phenomenon, which Russia was invited to join by adopting Western best practices. Through international and national efforts, the Western three-fold model of education, research, and external ties was imported to Russia as a signal of the first stage of Russia's catching-up modernization. The conversion of this model within the second stage, *dewesternization*, as a dialogue between the Western global and the Russian local, will be considered in the next section.

## The Western Model in Interaction With Russian History and Reality

After almost a decade of cooperative international and national undertakings—the BRHE program and its 20 established RECs at universities across Russia, the elimination of legislative limits, and the stimulation of initiatives by the national government—there was still a considerable lack of integration between education, science, and business (World Bank & NTF, 2006). The 2006 joint report by the World Bank and the NTF specifically dedicated to the integration of education and research in Russia concluded:

> Russia has to overcome the cumbersome legacy of the past—institutional inflexibility and an ineffective organizational system. One can tell that the existing scientific and technical capital is so burdened with aged institutional frameworks and ineffective infrastructure that it can but only be of low liquidity.
>
> *(p. 11)*

By definition, as mentioned above, the archaic institutional structure as an obstacle to effective integration of research and education pointed to one of the historically oldest structures in Russia, the RAS.

During the 20th century the RAS, established in 1724 by Peter the Great, was invited to fall in and out of love with the Soviet order, and it did so successfully, becoming a cradle of Soviet science culture. Research, traditionally conducted at the numerous institutes of the RAS, was essential to the overall existence of the Soviet Union: It provided the Soviet apparatus with both its ideological (philosophy of dialectic materialism) and its economic (industry, defense, etc.) raison d'être. At its heyday, the RAS counted up to 220,000 workers, of which around 60,000 scientists worked tirelessly at 330 institutes and research establishments in pursuit of ideal communism: Research thus provided solutions to one particular system, and it was believed to be as much centralized in the RAS as the system it maintained. The president of the RAS, Yurij Osipov (1999), who chaired it from the collapse of the Soviet Union up to 2013, wrote that no major Soviet issue could be solved without thorough scientific research conducted by the RAS.

Thus, the RAS and its researchers constituted a powerful institution, any encroachment on which could be considered a disruption of the Russian world order: A common belief in scientific progress that the RAS embodied did not accord with the Western model of integrating research and education. Particularly, adopting the Western model of coupling education and research would imply a profound reorganization of the RAS. In the following, I will attempt to present some of the discussions triggered by implementation of the Western research organization model and relate them to the specific historical and cultural context of post-Soviet Russia.

## Policy Versus Public Discussion

Once the attempt at transferring the Western model was established, the policy makers, academicians, and broader public entered into an uncompromising debate on the pros and cons of reforming one of the historically oldest structures in Russia. A common argument used by international organizations and then immediately adopted by Russian government officials was that of the RAS's ineffectiveness and inefficiency: In the foreword to the World Bank report, the vice-minister of education and science in Russia, Dmitri Livanov, mentioned that the Soviet research system was destructive for the science that was still left in Russia (World Bank & NTF, 2006, p. i).

Dezhina (2014) admitted that there was a decade-long conflict between the government, experts, and RAS. Considered to be an expert in science policy herself, Dezhina emphasized that research universities according to the Anglo-Saxon model would become the basis for Russian science. Referring to the RAS, she remarked: "The smart way is chosen: that of ignoring the Academy, not scolding it" (Dezhina, 2011). The blatant straightforwardness of this expert in science policy sheds some light on academicians' complaints about the government's indifference to what actual scientists had to say, as Zhores Alfiorov (2013), the physics Nobel Prize Laureate, emphasized.

On the other side of the coin, RECs, research universities, and other governmental initiatives in integrating research and education were given gloomy forecasts: Without stable financial injections and reliable cooperation with the business sector the research centers would hardly function after the end of the program funding (Dezhina, 2007). A research associate at the RAS, Kirill Babaev (2013), also remarked that the educational environment of Russia still vividly expressed antagonism towards entrepreneurial activity, which prevented effective commercialization of the field.

Given the widening communication gap between the policy makers and the RAS, sustainability issues with the newly established RECs, and little advance in commercialization culture, an interesting phenomenon occurred in the fields of education and research in Russia: The brand-new Skolkovo Institute of Science and Technology (Skoltech) was established as an imitation of MIT (Massachusetts Institute of Technology in the United States). Dezhina became Skoltech's expert on scientific and industrial policy, and Alfiorov was assigned to be a scientific supervisor of the Skolkovo Innovation Center.

The attempts at fostering the integration of education and research soon shifted towards establishing brand-new institutions rather than reorganizing the old ones, but what principally new features was this new Western model actually introducing?

## Challenging Principal Novelty: Soviet Freedom Within Limits and Western Limits Within Freedom

The RAS and the Western model of coupling education and research are believed to oppose each other in all qualitative characteristics, as outlined in the following list:

| Russian Academy of Sciences | Research at higher education establishments |
|---|---|
| • Centralized in one institution | • Localized at the universities |
| • State dependent/driven | • Economy driven |
| • Unfavorable for innovation | • Innovation oriented |
| • Ineffective and hard to manage | • Effective and manageable |
| • Elitist and closed science | • Public and "open" science |

The new features listed in the right-hand column assumed a fundamental modernization of research organization in Russia, corresponding to the attributes of the liberal democratic order that Russia pursued. The characteristics of the two models, being principally different at first glance, could be revised through a more thorough consideration of the meanings that stand behind the general terms. As a brief example, we could use the centralization versus localization argument.

Centralization of Russia's science to one particular institution could only be pitied in the West, where the stakes were persistently being put on organizational diversification of research to induce competition and fuel innovation (Vucinich, 1956). A common belief among Western scholars was that flourishing science requires the conditions of cultivated freedom; however, the Soviet experience suggested a different dimension (Graham, 1998, p. xi). In contrast, the decentralization of research and its liberation from state control were supposed to grant this much-needed research freedom; however, it faced a particular kind of individual accounting measures, output assessment, and increased standardization.

In an attempt to understand the principal novelty that the Western model introduces, a striking similarity can be observed: Both the traditional Soviet and the Western democratic model require control and monitoring of the research organization, but while the RAS exercised this control at the meta-level of a single institution, the Western model entered the micro-level of the actual research process. The traces of Russia's Soviet past reflected in the RAS appear to be the reflection of the Western present as well. From a historical perspective, Tröhler (2013) presents a hypothesis about a united world of common attributes on both sides of the Iron Curtain.

## Orthodoxy in Soviet Science

The delicate matter of an internal "logic of its own," comprising the rules and beliefs by which an institution functions, in the RAS is assumed to be related to the Orthodox ethic. Its presence in Soviet science organizations and research hardly resonates with the Western tradition and hence is interesting to consider while talking about the transfer of the Western model of coupling research and education to the Russian environment. In *Orthodox Civilization in a Globalized World* (2002), Aleksandr Panarin, a scholar at the Institute of Philosophy of the RAS and director of the sociology and philosophy research center, analyzes the inner civilizational conflict that Russia is experiencing: the opposition of conciliar nature to individualism, "deaf to the fates of entire mankind" (p. 10): "In the context of Russian civilization, conciliarity is not restricted to communities in a local-regional or patriarchal sense but implies the spiritual unity of entire mankind" (p. 10). This internal conflict, according to Panarin, embodies the very global confrontation between the West and the East.

Soviet science in its concentration at the RAS was permeated with the idea of global importance, which brought its numerous institutes to advanced research in heavy industry, space, and defense, almost never in user-oriented products of comfort. The higher purpose of scientific research that academicians pursued and their self-sacrificing dedication are brilliantly illustrated in the Soviet movie *Nine Days of One Year* (1962). Directed shortly after Yuri Gagarin's journey into outer space, the film relates a story about two nuclear physicists at a remote Siberian institute, one of whom during repetitive experiments is aware of the possibility of dying from radiation. A certain pathos of self-sacrifice for the sake of humankind was an effective propaganda theme in Soviet times that has its roots in the Orthodox ethics of labor and self-abandonment.

Historically, Russia's science has hardly any experience in working for the broader public as the target consumers: In fact, the notion of consumer was immediately associated with the Western bloc, in particular, the United States. In discussions on social modernization, Panarin remarked: "Foreign culture cannot transmit its asceticism to other cultures; only culture's external characteristics such as high-level consumption, comfort, industry of leisure, etc. appear to be the most communicative" (cited in Fedotova, 1997, p. 55).

## Notes

1. To Danilevsky, Russia is the center of Slavic civilization.
2. *Spark* was the name of the revolutionary newspaper (Rus. Искра) printed in Munich and secretly shipped to a growing number of socialist adepts in Russian Empire.
3. The author specifies the title's double meaning: The translation from Russian can be both "Modernization of the *Second* Europe" and "Modernization of the *Other* Europe"; the first refers to Russia as a second world of lagging development, and the second title to Russia as a specific kind of Europe. Here, the first title is used.
4. The "Concept of Modernization" constituted the overall large-scale program for educational transformations for the period of 10 years: In this chapter, however, the time limits for the events considered will not be that explicit. Because the "Concept of Modernization" was elaborated in the 1990s and continues to echo long after 2010, it is preferable to adopt a more inclusive timeframe. The "Concept of Modernization" manifested the overall direction of Russian educational reform.

## References

Alfiorov, Z. (2013, July 3). *Zhores Alfiorov on RAS reform. Pros and cons*. Retrieved from http://www.snob.ru/selected/entry/62238

Babaev, K. (2013, August 7). *Kirill Babaev on the scientist as entrepreneur*. Retrieved from http://postnauka.ru/talks/15423

Chabbott, C. (2003). *Constructing education for development: International organizations and education for all*. New York, NY: Routledge Falmer.

Chistokhvalov, V. N. (2010). *Osobennosti modernizatsii rossijskogo i evropejskogo vysshego obrazovanija v 1991–2005: istoriko-sravnitelnyj analiz* [Peculiarities of modernization in Russian and European higher education, 1991–2005: Historical comparison]. Moscow, Russia: Peoples' Friendship University of Russia (PFUR).

Danilevsky, N. Y. (Ed.). (1995). *Rossija i Evropa: Vzgliad na kulturnye i politicheskie otnoshenija Slavianskogo mira k Romano-Germanskomu* [Russia and Europe: A glance at cultural and political relations of Slavic and Romano-Germanic worlds]. Moscow, Russia: Glagol. (Original work published 1869)

Dezhina, I. G. (2007). Opyt integratsiji obrazovanija i nauki na primere programy "Fundamentalnyje issledovanija i vysshee obrazovanije" [Experience of integration of education and science on the basis of the BRHE program]. *Journal of University Management: Practice and Analysis, 1*, 45–51.

Dezhina, I. G. (2008). Razvitie nauki i innovatsij v federalnykh universitetakh: Rossijskij opyt v mezhdunarodnom kontekste [The development of science and innovation in federal universities: Russian experience in international context]. *Almanac "Science. Innovation. Education," 6*, 48–59.

Dezhina, I. G. (2011, March 31). *Public lecture by Irina Dezhina: "Play with the dolls."* Retrieved from http://polit.ru/article/2011/03/31/dolls/

Dezhina, I. G. (2014, May 29). *Irina Dezhina on RAS reform*. Retrieved from http://www.skoltech.ru/2014/05/irina-dezhina-o-reforme-ran/

Dneprov, E. D. (2002). *Modernizatsija rossijskogo obrazovanija: Dokumenty i materialy* [Modernization of Russian education: Documents and materials]. Moscow, Russia: State University "Higher School of Economics."

Dostoyevsky, F. M. (1986). *Polnoe sobranie sochinenij v tridtsati tomakh* [Full collection of works in thirty volumes]: *Vol. 29*. Leningrad, Russia: Nauka.

Etzkowitz, H., & Leydesdorff, L. (1997). *Universities and the global knowledge economy: A Triple Helix of university-industry-government relations*. London, UK: Pinter.

Etzkowitz, H., Ranga, M., Benner, M., Guaranys, L., Maculan, A. M., & Kneller, R. (2008). Pathways to the entrepreneurial university: Towards a global convergence. *Science and Public Policy, 35*(9), 681–695. doi:10.3152/030234208x389701

Fedotova, V. G. (1997). Modernizatsija "drugoi" Evropy [Modernization of the "second" Europe]. Moscow, Russia: Institut Filisofiji Rossijskoj Akademiji Nauk (IFRAN).

Filippov, V. M. (1989). *Variational principles for nonpotential operators* (Translations of mathematical monographs, Vol. 77). Providence, RI: American Mathematical Society.

Filippov, V. M. (1993). *Prakticheskij opyt organizatsiji i funktsionirovanija vuzov v uslovijakh rynochnoi ekonomiki* [Practical experience in organization and functioning of universities in the conditions of a market economy]. Moscow, Russia: Institute for International Cooperation.

Fukuyama, F. (1992). *The end of history and the last man*. New York, NY: Free Press.

Graham, L. R. (1967). *The Soviet academy of sciences and the communist party: 1927–1932*. Princeton, NJ: Princeton University Press.

Graham, L. R. (1998). *What have we learned about science and technology from the Russian experience?* Stanford, CA: Stanford University Press.

Graham, L. R., & Dezhina, I. (2008). *Science in the new Russia: Crisis, aid, reform.* Bloomington, IN: Indiana University Press.

Huntington, S. P. (1996). *The clash of civilizations and the remaking of world order.* London, UK: Simon & Schuster.

Kontseptsija modernizatsiji rossijskogo obrazovanija na period do 2010 g. [The concept of modernization of Russian education up to 2010]. (2001). In E. D. Dneprov (ed.), *Modernizatsija rossijskogo obrazovanija: Dokumenty i materialy* [Modernization of Russian education: Documents and materials] (pp. 263–282). Moscow, Russia: State University "Higher School of Economics."

Osipov, Y. S. (1999). *Akademija nauk v istoriji Rossijskogo gosudarstva* [The Academy of Sciences in the history of the Russian state]. Moscow, Russia: Nauka.

Panarin, A. S. (2002). *Pravoslavnaja tsivilizatsija v globalnom mire* [Orthodox civilization in a globalized world]. Moscow, Russia: Algoritm.

Tröhler, D. (2013). The OECD and the cold war culture: Thinking historically about PISA. In H.-D. Meyer & A. Benavot (Eds.), *PISA, power, and policy: The emergence of global educational governance* (pp. 141–161). Oxford, UK: Symposium Books.

UNESCO. (1993). *World commission on culture and development.* Retrieved from http://unesdoc.unesco.org/images/0009/000957/095724eo.pdf

UNESCO. (1998). *Final report on World Conference on Higher Education 5–9 October 1998. Higher education in the twenty-first century: Vision and action.* Retrieved from http://unesdoc.unesco.org/images/0011/001163/116345e.pdf

Vucinich, A. (1956). *The Soviet academy of sciences.* Stanford, CA: Stanford University Press.

World Bank. (1994). *Higher education: The lessons of experience.* Washington, DC: World Bank. Retrieved from http://documents.worldbank.org/curated/en/1994/05/437287/higher-education-lessons-experience

World Bank. (2000). *Higher education in developing countries: Peril and promise.* Retrieved from http://siteresources.worldbank.org/EDUCATION/Resources/278200-1099079877269/547664-1099079956815/peril_promise_en.pdf

World Bank. (2002). *Constructing knowledge societies: New challenges for tertiary education.* Retrieved from http://siteresources.worldbank.org/INTAFRREGTOPTEIA/Resources/Constructing_Knowledge_Societies.pdf

World Bank & National Training Foundation. (2006). *Ot znanija k blagosostojaniju: Integratsija nauki i vysshego obrazovanija dlia razvitija Rossiji* [From knowledge to wealth: Integrating science and higher education for the development of Russia]. Moscow, Russia: World Bank & National Training Foundation. Retrieved from http://www-wds.worldbank.org/external/default/WDSContentServer/WDSP/IB/2007/01/31/000020439_20070131113247/Rendered/PDF/385090From0kno10wealth1rus01PUBLIC1.pdf

# 19

# CONTESTING ISOMORPHISM AND DIVERGENCE

## Historicizing the Chinese Educational Encounter With the "West"

*Jinting Wu*

World culture theory offers a compelling—yet contentious—perspective on schooling around the world: the notion that different national educational systems originate from a common source and converge towards similar trajectories over time. This volume critically engages with world culture theory on two fronts: (1) that the harmonization of education policy around the globe may seem isomorphic at the first glance but conceals culturally idiosyncratic adaptations and negotiations; and (2) that the assumed linear progression "from national to global" is misleading, for educational globalization often moves in multiple directions and is deeply intertwined with the cultural history of a nation. Taking up this volume's critical framework, this chapter historicizes the Chinese educational encounter with the "West" to rethink the situated meanings of globalization beyond the conventional lenses of isomorphism and divergence.

The first layer of my analysis examines the concept of the West as a changing notion in Chinese historiography. The Chinese encounter with the West is part of a historical project of Occidentalism, of China's reflective self-understanding through understanding its historical other. In the second step, I explore how the process of Occidentalism is coupled with self-Orientalism to produce the idiosyncrasies of the Chinese educational system. Further, I investigate China's shifting social and educational discourses and, in particular, the oscillating reception of the Confucian classical tradition (from denunciation to revitalization) in the 21st century, which indicates that a hybrid pedagogical landscape in Chinese society is being formed. I conclude with a reflection on the variegated pathways in global education encounters and on the cultural idiosyncrasies in policy transfers that are at once emulative of translocal forces and generative of locally relevant rhetoric. The case of China nuances world culture theory and illustrates that educational globalization necessarily involves simultaneous, multimodal processes, always moving in more than one direction.

## The West as China's Historical Other

Edward Said's (1978) celebrated work *Orientalism* offers a powerful inquiry into coloniality and its modern knowledge structure that has underpinned the relationships between Western and non-Western cultures. Said demonstrates how the modern West constructs its self-identity through binary, imperialist images of the colonial others, and how such images both are at odds with the self-understanding of indigenous cultures and infiltrate the native points of views. Despite its canonical status, *Orientalism* has been challenged for its continual focus on and inadvertent re-centering of the West.

Chinese anthropologist Wang Mingming, for instance, takes issue with such unintended reproduction of Western power in his thought-provoking book *The West as the Other: A Genealogy of Chinese Occidentalism* (Wang, 2014). Wang maintains that Orientalism overemphasizes the Western discourse on the Orient and argues that a simultaneous process of Occidentalism took place in China that employed similar ideological strategies to imagine, construct, and "exoticize" the West. This position maintains that viewing the self in the other, or viewing cultural differences as a means of knowing, is not the privilege of the West. What becomes the objectified colonial historicity includes not only the cultures of the colonies but also those of the colonizers. Thus, this section seeks to sketch a genealogy of China's reflective self-understanding through understanding its historical others in various confrontations and encounters. I will show that the earlier globalization process moved in multiple directions, indicating China's ambivalent, shifting relations to itself and the West.

The concept of the West (*xifang*) is a changing notion in Chinese historiography. Its significations shifted from a periphery, a frontier, a barbarian territory, a sacred origin of religion, and imperialism, to the present-day Euro-American advances in science and modernity. The notion of the West is closely linked with China's understanding of its historical others through imaginary geographies and cosmological representations. For a long time the West carried a derogatory connotation as culturally inferior to the East. In the classical period, between the Zhou and the Han dynasties (the 11th century BC to 24 AD), the cosmological order of self–other began to develop (see Cai, 1926). The Zhou Scripture of Rites (*Zhou Li*), in particular, expressed the classical Chinese worldview of "All Under Heaven" (*tianxia*), which subsumed the entire Earth into ceremonial orders and hierarchical zones "orchestrated toward a high harmony or the 'Great Unity' (*datong*)" (Wang, 2000, p. 6). During the Han dynasty, a Sino-centric cosmological order depicted the West as an outer zone of wilderness, as tributary sources at the imperial fringes.

During the Tang dynasty (618–907 AD), the rising influence of Buddhism enabled a new worldview in which the classical cosmology of "All Under Heaven" was disrupted. Under the auspices of the Tang emperor, Monk Xuanzang undertook a pilgrimage journey to the West (present-day India) and returned after 19 years of adventures with countless sacred books and Buddhist scriptures. Xuanzang subsequently published a travelogue, *Datang Xiyu Ji* [Notes on the Western Territories of the Great Tang], in which the notion of West (*xiyu*, or Western territories) became synonymous with the fountainhead of Buddhist spirituality and the multitudes of city-states, customs, and religiosities encountered along the journey.

The other-centered view of the Tang dynasty was soon replaced by a China-centered tributary system in the Song and Yuan dynasties (10th to 13th centuries AD) as a result of China's maritime trade success. A tributary mode of narrative was utilized in official gazetteers to describe the products and ways of life of "frontier peoples" and foreign merchants in Southeast Asia, India, the Middle East, and as far away as East Africa. A Sino-centric cosmological structure of "All Under Heaven" was reconstituted, bearing great similarity to Said's Orientalism, in which the co-presence of civility and savages is an ultimate self-portrait of Chinese civilizational superiority (Wang, 2000, p. 11). On the other hand, in the ethical and moral bearing of the Confucian doctrine, knowing the others and investigating exterior things are essential to harmonizing the family, ordering the state, and pacifying the world (see Wang, 1995, p. 4).

In the second half of the 16th century, the arrival of Catholic missionaries produced explosive European narratives about China (Spence, 1998, pp. 19–40) and opened China to scientific and religious conquest by the West. Books on Western science and technology brought by Jesuit missionaries at the end of the Ming dynasty also introduced teachings on calendar calculation, medicine, agriculture, and irrigation. The Chinese rulers were exposed to the Western geographical vision of the globe and the arrival of a different world order. The attempt to revitalize Chinese civilization in the face of European scientific-military threats spurred the first generation of Chinese reform-nationalists[1] to search for a synthesis of "All Under Heaven" with Western narratives of progress to remake the Chinese fate.

Throughout the 19th century, political and intellectual discussions in China were dominated by the revision of the Confucian classics, *Book of Rites*, to incorporate a progressive cosmological vision (Wang, 2000, p. 13). China's humiliating defeat in the First Sino-Japanese War (1894–1895) jostled the nation out of its self-congratulatory complacency. The success of Westernization in Japan forced China to reevaluate the long-embraced *Ti-Yong* dichotomy that upheld Chinese learning as the essential core (*Ti*) and denigrated Western learning as mere utility (*Yong*). By 1912 Confucianism was attacked as a drawback to China's modernization, reading of the classics was replaced by vernacular-language literature, and a revolt against Confucian culture led to a call for the creation of democracy and science in Chinese society (Wu, 2011, p. 570). China's political marginality enabled a particular self-critique deemed crucial for the country's survival.

By the second decade of the 20th century, the New Culture Movement, led by a group of influential Chinese intellectuals, had infused a strong dose of self-criticism and a "global" orientation into China's social milieu. Foreign literature was translated into Chinese, and China's first vernacular secondary school textbook, *Model Works of the Vernacular*, was also published, featuring various Western literary figures including English poet Thomas Hood, Russian writer Leo Tolstoy, and Russian author Ivan Sergeyevich Turgenev, among others, to enlighten the young with progressive ideas and an expanded worldview (Liu & Ruan, 2012, p. 36).

The nomenclature of Western knowledge and subject classifications was introduced and absorbed into Chinese intellectual and cultural contexts. Western curriculum theories were translated to facilitate the building of the Chinese educational system. Scholars in the Qing dynasty gradually came to propose the adoption of Western learning as the way of China's self-improvement. Admiration of the principles of calculation and investigation, the techniques of instrument making, and the methods for geographical mapping, and so on, finally led to the establishment of new disciplines in the Chinese university system (Wang, 1995, p. 12). In 1874 the College of Natural Science (Gezhi Shuyuan) was set up in Shanghai. Natural science subjects and foreign languages were subsequently added to the curriculum of many tertiary institutions. Kang Youwei, the Qing reformist, was among the first Chinese intellectuals to popularize the concept of *kexue* (science) in abolishing imperial exams and disseminating Western learning. At the turn of the 20th century, the concepts of "democracy" and "science" were introduced to China and translated as Mr. Virtue (*de xiansheng*) and Mr. Free Competition (*sai xiansheng*), indicating self-critique of internal despotism and authoritarianism and applause for European enlightenment.

Although the Qing reform-nationalists often absorbed Western discourse in their own thinking, their translation of social Darwinism subjected European evolutionism to the Chinese philosophy of "Heaven's change" (*tianyan*) (Zhong, 1989, p. 473; see also Pusey, 1983). The European scientific advancement was interpreted as their optimal utility of the Heaven's Way, and therefore the best model for China was still believed to be the Confucian governance that had flourished in the classical dynasties such as the Zhou dynasty. Thus, such self-critique was in effect also self-exceptionalism. The domestication of the Western concepts of progress into the Chinese "All Under Heaven" resulted in a particular Occidentalism made fit for the nation's revival. The co-presence of Occidentalism and Orientalism infused different stages of Chinese global exchanges and cannot be accounted for by world cultural theory and the dichotomy of divergence or isomorphism. Dynamic cultural self-awareness and the posing of the other against the question of the self have always permeated political debates in China and China's quest for national revitalization.

From the arrival of Buddhism from what was then conceived as the West (*xiyu*) to China's participation in the trade routes linking different parts of Asia, from the heyday of Sino-centric civilization to the collective soul-searching in the late Qing and early Republic periods, from the Maoist antagonism towards the capitalist West[2] to the growing legitimacy of Euro-American products and ideas in the post-reform period, the genealogical accounts of China's encounters with and cultural constructions of the West reveal the arc of change in its global engagements. There was not *one* world culture but a variety of *worlds*, whose images and social perceptions had changing repercussions in the Chinese self-understanding and its charting of the variegated routes to modernity. What is noteworthy is that the local embedding of the world culture(s) invokes not only global borrowing but also internal push and pull, nativism and self-critique, with multiple constructions of "worlds" overlapping and not necessarily in sync with each other.

On the other hand, in recent decades, there is a strong tendency to explain the commonality of cross-national trends, such as the emergence of mass schooling and standardized assessment, through a "world culture" framework. The Stanford school and especially the works of John Meyer and colleagues (Meyer, Ramirez, & Soysal, 1992; Meyer & Ramirez, 2000) take up the neo-institutional lens to grasp the global convergence of educational policy and practice from the perspective of a "world culture" driven by the logic of science, technology, and progress. Despite its explanatory power and widespread appeal among scholars and policymakers, world culture theory has been the subject of heated debates and criticized for using a macro-sociological framework to the neglect of rich local enactments and manifestations, which are not necessarily mimetic of the overarching global tendencies.

The cosmic vision of China as the "Central Kingdom" dominated most of the intellectual and social discourse throughout the 19th century. However, by the end of the century, a series of external pressures, including China's military defeats and economic inferiority and the rise of Japan, began to cast a serious shadow on the Sino-centric cosmology. In attempts to reconstruct a new world order and revive the Confucian ideas of the "turn of civilization" (*liyun*) and the "great unity" (*datong*), Chinese intellectuals including Kang You Wei, Yan Fu, and Liang Qi Chao began to synthesize Western evolutionist doctrines with Chinese cosmological ideals. At this time, world culture presented itself to Chinese society in different shades, offering a range of purchases through social Darwinism, Hegelian linear history and progress, technocratic governance, and more, which were selectively translated into a Chinese worldview to reorient China and renew its centrality (Wang, 2009, p. 255).

## Educational Encounters Then and Now

I will now turn to China's pursuit of educational modernization through various cultural exchanges and global encounters. In the late Qing dynasty (1639–1911), after numerous military defeats by Western imperial powers, the *Ti-Yong* dichotomy of preserving the Chinese essence (*Ti*) while adopting Western means (*Yong*) became a core educational reform principle. In the "Self-Strengthening" campaign, Qing reformers advocated for the learning of Western weaponry, commerce, and modern technology, while upholding Chinese civilization as superior to Western democracy. Western learning was regarded as fragmentary and instrumental *substance*, as application (*Yong*) of professional skills in particular fields of study, which must employ Chinese classics, history, and philosophy as its prerequisites. Thus, an educational system based on Confucian morality while imparting Western scientific means was considered an ideal principle of school reform at the turn of 20th century (Luo, 1998; Cai, 2012). It is the co-presence of Western and Chinese pedagogical modes that marked the *global* aspects of China's earliest educational institutions, such as Tongwen Academy. "Global" in this context is understood not as an emerging homogeneity but as the Western others subsumed in Sino-centric historiography and educational ideals.

The boundary between *Ti* and *Yong*, however, was never definitive or static. What was considered as *Ti* (essence) for a time became dispensable in another period. The Qing imperial political system was overthrown by the nationalists under the leadership of Sun Yat-sen, who based his revolutionary ideals on the Western principles of democracy, liberty, and equality. Previously jettisoned by the Qing reformists as inferior to Confucian values, these principles became the core (*Ti*) of the newly founded Republic of China. When the People's Republic of China was established in the 1949 under the reign of Mao Zedong, the meaning of *Ti* shifted further, defined by a mixture of state Marxism and communism, while Confucian elements—together with the Western *bourgeois culture*, Russian *revisionism*, and Chinese *feudalism*—were revoked and largely wiped out of the political scene. Since the launch of the Reform and Opening Up policy in the late 1970s, the *Ti-Yong* pendulum has swung again. As Deng Xiaoping's developmental pragmatism downplays political ideology, China has adopted a market mechanism as the economic means (*Yong*) and maintains "socialism with Chinese characteristics" as the ideological essence (*Ti*) for realizing modernization.

Education lies at a crossroads of many of these ideological shifts, serving the purpose of political socialization while imparting particular views of the nation's others. For instance, teaching the historical grievance of China's "one hundred years of humiliation" (from the mid-1800s to the mid-1900s) fostered a patriotic outlook and a conception of the Imperial West connected with the deepest threats and fears. Since the early 1980s, however, the prosperity of the West has produced a sense of lack in China's self-image, an admiration of the Global North, and a teleological understanding of development and modernity. Hence, education has been articulated in cultivating national allegiance and, more and more importantly, in imparting technical skills to advance the market economy and the nation's economic future.

As the "international salesman for American pragmatism" (Popkewitz, 2008, p. 6), John Dewey has played a palpable role in China's curriculum reform and practice. In the early 20th century, pragmatism, upheld as the remedy to Chinese educational problems, was widely discussed in educational publications[3] to criticize the traditional dichotomy between school and society and to call for a more child-centered approach in teaching. In 1922 a curriculum reform named *Renxu Xuezhi* was drafted by disciples of Dewey to adopt the American educational model and curriculum guidelines in Chinese universities (Hayhoe, 1996, p. 47). It promoted advanced academic studies of professional skills and popularized pragmatist ideals of social evolution, democracy, individual development, and education for living. One of the Dewey disciples, Hu Shi, linked pragmatism with the superiority of Western science and described Confucian classical learning as irrelevant and "much ado about nothing" (Schulte, 2011, p. 87). Although Dewey himself would never have promoted this view, this cultural self-denial prompted early policy externalization through acute self-reflexivity and the appropriation of global models.

This period of outward-looking and self-critical global encounters did not continue and was later replaced by political climate change, around the founding of the New China, when the communist revolution set out to establish its world order, forming a global alliance against its enemies according to ideological allegiance. From the 1950s to the 1960s, the curriculum reform in China largely followed the Soviet Union's polytechnic curriculum model with emphasis on ideology rather than pragmatism. Internally, Confucianism was denounced as the Four Olds (*si jiu* 四旧), a term coined during the Cultural Revolution to refer to Old Customs, Old Culture, Old Habits, and Old Ideas, denounced for keeping China in the shackles of feudalism. Externally, Dewey and his followers were condemned as reactionary, subversive, and symbolic of capitalism and Western imperialism.

More than three decades after the Reform and Opening, China has largely shed this ideological baggage and once again is beginning to look outward as it is also gazing inward. At the start of the 21st century, "the Chinese language absorbed, or indeed 'devoured,' the nomenclatures of the most diverse branches of Western Knowledge" (Lackner, Amelung, & Kurtz, 2001, p. 2). Leaving the Soviet influences behind, China has largely moved towards the United States in rethinking its curriculum approaches, and Chinese educational discourses have been renormalized and articulated in Western terms (Wu, 2011). Whereas Confucianism has served as "the internal referential system" (see Schriewer, 2000) in Chinese educational systems since 200 BC, its legitimacy is undermined by the language of "crisis" depicting it as a hindrance to Chinese educational innovation. One common concern is that the Confucian educational system engineers book-cramming robots through endless exams, where teachers dictate and students regurgitate without exercising critical thinking.

More recently, the new wave of brain drain has plunged Chinese society into soul-searching over the future of its educational system. Increasing numbers of wealthy citizens send their children abroad at younger and younger ages, seeking greener grass with residency in the developed world and an alternative to the seemingly ineradicable exam meritocracy at home. The reasons behind the alarming rate of exit[4] are certainly complex, yet the anxieties over the looming crisis of the Chinese educational system are cited as a top reason that sends the wealthy in search of an alternative safety net. As the source of both hope and fear, education has become a crucial mechanism for upper middle-class families to tame the unpredictability of the future.

With eroding public confidence in state schools, progressive education has been rehabilitated to insert a strong dose of self-criticism into traditional Confucianism-inspired curricula and pedagogies. In 2001 the Ministry of Education implemented the New Curriculum Reform, one of the most far-reaching curriculum reforms in the history of the People's Republic of China, to further develop a student-centered approach in response to the avalanche of criticisms concerning the centuries-long practices of examination, rote memorization, and teacher authority. The chief academics who drafted the reform guidelines are strong proponents of Dewey and pragmatism. Policy proposals are primarily framed through progressive values and principles featuring homework reduction, constructivist curricular approaches, and, most importantly, child-centered learning and pedagogies. The attempts at implementing whole-person-oriented curriculum reforms as the antidote to the excesses of "teaching to the test" have been ongoing for decades, though with limited success and continual controversies (Wu, 2012).

## Revival of the Classics: While Dewey Returns, Confucius Also Returns

This crisis-reform melodrama and the subsequent provoking of external references at first glance fits the global policy-borrowing paradigm. However, the "borrowing" is not unidirectional, nor does it undermine domestic traditions *tout court*. While Confucian pedagogical practices are continually being challenged, today China is also witnessing a renaissance of classical studies (*guoxue* 国学) and a proliferation of Confucius academies (*shuyuan* 书院) across the nation. The revival of the classical Confucian tradition has spread to different social strata, involving schoolchildren, scholars, businessmen, party officials, and the general public, at a historical moment when China continues to reflect on its past, present, and future at a crossroads of unprecedented social transformation. Embodying a neo-nationalist spirit, the Confucian revival emphasizes going beyond naive imitation of the Global North to reestablish the historical continuity of the Chinese cultural heritage that has previously been rejected or ignored. The revival of Confucianism is part of the discursive new climate as China's economic prowess generates not only global interest in its language and culture but also renewed self-confidence and inward searching for the foundation of its future.

A growing enthusiasm for traditional education has manifested itself in popular television programs featuring the teaching of Chinese history and literature, historical soap operas, Mandarin character competitions, and initiatives to build Confucian academies across the nation. Further, some universities have organized "National Study Classes" to offer training in classical language and literature. In particular, the movement called *ertong dujing yundong* (儿童读经运动), which originated in Taiwan, actively promotes the teaching of Confucian classics to children, as the "most spectacular manifestation of the different appeals for the 'renaissance of tradition'" (Billioud & Thoraval, 2007, p. 8). The dissemination of the Confucian classical tradition takes the form of a burgeoning mass culture in different grassroots environments: extracurricular periods in public schools where children attend classics readings outside their formal curriculum, for-profit private weekend schools, informal neighborhood associations, and even companies where inspired leaders encourage their employees to read the classics. The focus is on acquiring wisdom and existential education rather than obtaining technical knowledge.

While in today's Chinese schools pupils engage in increasingly child-centered, experience-oriented learning processes, they might also be spending time after school reciting and memorizing canonical Confucian texts. Educated parents feel that nothing increases the students' well-being like the ancient wisdom distilled in classics; even if students do not fully understand the meanings of the texts, they will appreciate and benefit from them later in life. Rote memorization and imitation in this sense are not seen as a negative pedagogical feature but as benevolent mnemonics that cultivate the person through silent transformation, or *qianyimohua* (潜移默化) in Chinese, rather than through immediate cognitive gains. Texts are the vehicles of self-transformation, because their chanting and recitation engage the whole person, as explained in 2006 in the newsletter of a Confucian academy:

> Continuing to read the classics in the morning can enable our negative [literally "muddy"] energy to purify itself. This energy (*qi*) and our spiritual dimension (*shen*) reach a state of perception and serenity (*shen qing qi shuang*). . . . From the classics, we become aware of the roots of our culture. . . . Through this daily exercise of reading, we enter into daily exchanges with the sages.[5]

Texts constantly repeated and progressively memorized are believed to have the capacity to serve the children throughout their lives by cultivating rectitude of the heart and enlightening their daily actions. The rhythmic chanting of the classics often involves sentimental display of emotions, as students are encouraged to read with appropriate feelings and facial expressions. The performative aspect of memorization has a certain "properness," such that learning to read "properly" is believed to have a subtle influence on students' personalities, intelligence, and character. The significance of silent transformation needs to be understood in the context of Chinese exemplary society. According to Bakken (2000), a quintessential feature of Confucian governance is through putting forth models for everyone to emulate. The noble, exemplary man (*junzi*), for instance, is one such exemplary persona of social harmony and benevolence. Hence, a process of imitation, repetition, and internalization is at the heart of Confucian learning and social order (Kipnis, 2011). In the past, knowledge of classical Confucian texts legitimated the selection of scholar-officials through imperial exams. Today, the revival of Confucian academies in China indicates the forming of a new pedagogical landscape of governing.

The return of John Dewey and American pragmatism sits within this discursive tradition of learning and governing. In China's striving for educational excellence, one may argue that as much as Dewey has returned, Confucius has also returned. They exist side by side, fulfilling their historical educative functions in a hybrid time. Rather than conflicting with each other, pragmatism and classical Confucian tradition manage to find their own place in co-authoring China's pedagogical projects. Although pragmatism is regarded as an imported concept, I argue that the language of pragmatism is always already part of China's internal cultural struggle as much as it is an example of West–East transfer. After all, China has been one of the most pragmatic nations known to Earth. Imperial education was primarily for the practical purpose of preparing civil servants or scholar-officials. Today, a utilitarian function of education is still widely detectable. Learner-centeredness has already been part of Chinese pedagogical discourse. Even Confucius himself called for *yin cai shi jiao*, which means tailoring pedagogies to the needs of the individual learners. The dichotomous view of traditional China versus America might be less convincing than a diachronic approach that looks at how the educational concerns of today's China are a cross-cultural dialogue as well as having a resonance with China's own past, revisiting what was already nascent through the intellectual lens of the global other.

## Conclusion

From the destructive encounters with the West in the First (1839–1842) and Second (1856–1860) Opium Wars to the *Ti-Yong* dichotomy upholding Chinese cosmology while appropriating Western technology, from the arrival of Deweyan pragmatism to the revival of classic Confucianism, we see a distinctive Chinese response to global influences that cannot be easily explained by either isomorphism or divergence. It is a mutating process intertwined with China's ideological relations with the West and the shifting self–other parameters infusing the nationalist ethos, introspection, self-Orientalism, and changing attitudes towards tradition.

Discourse hybridization is an idiosyncrasy of China's educational globalization. At times, a Confucian emphasis on ritual, imitation, and examination is criticized for stifling the cultivation of China's 21st century talents; at times, it is upheld as ancient wisdom and sensibility that brings prosperity to the Greater China Region. Whether conceived of as a problem or merit, Confucianism often serves as a convenient proxy to explain what is on the Chinese radar yet off the Euro-American screen, and vice versa. Contrary to the assumption that China resisted the pressure of globalization until the Reform and Opening Up in 1978, I argue that Chinese globalization had in fact taken shape long before it was so named. The Open Door policy was preceded by earlier phases of (albeit forced) openings and encounters, and the local and the global have always intertwined in Chinese educational developments (Wang, 2009; Schulte, 2012).

As comparative education scholars often argue, global educational encounters are both emulative of translocal forces and generative of locally relevant practices

(Anderson-Levitt, 2003; Tröhler, 2009; Carney, Rappleye, & Silova, 2012; Steiner-Khamsi, 2012). The conceptual divide of local versus global, divergence versus isomorphism, in world culture theory oversimplifies and obscures the subterranean processes and negotiations behind the scene. More importantly, world culture theory does not adequately account for the frictions when different discourses and paradigms come into contact and when global myths and local myths are intertwined to complicate the directions of either convergence or divergence. Cowen (2009) characterizes global education policies as they travel from one country to the next with the phrase "as it moves, it morphs." Traveling policies "morph" as they enter particular national contexts that have pre-existing ideological, political, and cultural agents of change.

The case of China illustrates that globalization has always moved in more than one direction. Isomorphism and divergence, cultural nativism and self-critique, centripetal and centrifugal forces are sides of the same coin that constitute what is nebulously termed globalization. It is these situated tensions of push and pull, movement and stickiness, that offer a most fruitful lens to examine the heterogeneous process of educational transformation in the new century. As much as it is quick to resort to cultural nativism when confronting Western infiltration, China is equally apt to turn outward and search for international standards and legitimacy. In this chapter, I show that the celebrated globalization of Chinese education today needs to be understood in the context of a historical *longue durée*, that the unique Chinese path to globalization has already been "historically 'contaminated' by cultural and cross-cultural appropriations that belong to the whole of Chinese-Western relationships" (Chen, 1995, p. 4), and that China's conscious pursuit of global membership through educational reform quintessentially reflects its self-imposed Orientalism and its construction of the relationship between itself and others.

## Notes

1. The most influential of the reform-nationalists include Kang Youwei and his disciples, Yan Fu and Liang Qichao.
2. The way in which the West is conceived is also dictated by China's internal social upheavals and the change in the political climate. During the Cultural Revolution, all sorts of derogatory labels were attached to the West: bourgeois, anti-revolutionaries, demons, monsters, exploiters, enemies, traitors, and so on. While the political temperature heated against the West-cum-capitalism, the Occidentalism of previous decades gave way to ideological antagonism constructed through communist texts.
3. A famous essay titled "Discussing About Using Pragmatism in School Education" was published in 1913 by the director of the Educational Office in Jiangsu Province at the time, Huang Yanpei.
4. According to statistics revealed by a recent Bain & Company survey, 60% of Chinese with a net worth of $1.5 million or higher intend to emigrate, and a third of them 'already have investments abroad' (Mishra 2013).
5. *Yidan Xuetang tongxun* [Yidan Xuetang newsletter], No. 9, January 2006, p. 2.

# References

Anderson-Levitt, K. M. (Ed.). (2003). *Local meanings, global schooling: Anthropology and world culture theory.* New York, NY: Palgrave Macmillan.

Bakken, B. (2000). *The exemplary society: Human improvement, social control, and the dangers of modernity in China.* New York, NY: Oxford University Press.

Billioud, S., & Thoraval, J. (2007). Jiaohua: The Confucian revival in China as an educative project. *China Perspectives, 4*, 4–20.

Cai, Y. (1926). Shuo minzuxue [Saying something about ethnology]. In *Yiban* [The general pattern], 1926. Reprinted in *Cai Yuanpei xuanji* [Selected writings of C. Yuanpei]. Zhejiang, China: People's Publishing House, 1993.

Cai, Y. (2012). Traditional reform philosophy and challenges of higher education reform in China. *International Journal of Humanities and Social Science, 2*(6), 60–69.

Carney, S., Rappleye, J., & Silova, I. (2012). Between faith and science: World culture theory and comparative education. *Comparative Education Review, 56*(3), 366–393. doi:10.1086/665708

Chen, X. (1995). *Orientalism: A theory of counter-discourse in post-Mao China.* New York, NY: Oxford University Press.

Cowen, R. (2009). The transfer, translation and transformation of educational processes: And their shape-shifting? *Comparative Education, 45*(3), 315–327. doi:10.1080/03050060903184916

Hayhoe, R. (1996). *China's universities 1895–1995: A century of cultural conflict.* New York, NY: Routledge.

Kipnis, A. (2011). *Governing educational desire: Culture, politics, and schooling in China.* Chicago, IL: University of Chicago Press.

Lackner, M., Amelung, I., & Kurtz, J. (2001). *New terms for new ideas: Western knowledge and lexical change in late Imperial China.* Leiden, the Netherlands: Brill.

Liu, H., & Ruan, J. (2012). Foreign literature education in China's secondary schools from 1919 to 1949. In C. B. Leung & J. Ruan (Eds.), *Perspectives on teaching and learning Chinese literacy in China* (pp. 35–48). Dordrecht, the Netherlands: Springer.

Luo, J. (1998). Jiaoyu gexin nai qiangguo zhiben—jingshi da xuetang chuangban ren, daxueshi sun jianai [Educational innovation as the basis for strengthening the country: The founder of the forerunner of Beijing University, scholar Sun Jianai]. In Y. Tang (Ed.), *Beida xiaozhang yu zhongguo wenhua* [Presidents of Beijing University and Chinese culture] (pp. 15–25). Beijing, China: Beijing University Press.

Meyer, J. W., & Ramirez, F. O. (2000). The world institutionalization of education. In J. Schriewer (Ed.), *Discourse formation in comparative education* (pp. 111–132). Frankfurt, Germany: Peter Lang.

Meyer, J. W., Ramirez, F. O., and Soysal, Y. S. (1992). World expansion of mass education, 1870–1940. *Sociology of Education, 65*(2), 128–149. doi:10.2307/2112679

Mishra, P. (2013, October 24). Brain drain: A headache for India and China. *The Age.* Retrieved from http://www.theage.com.au/comment/brain-drain-a-headache-for-india-and-china-20131023-2w1kg.html

Popkewitz, T. S. (2008). *Inventing the modern self and John Dewey: Modernity and the traveling of pragmatism in education.* New York, NY: Palgrave MacMillan.

Pusey, J. (1983). *China and Charles Darwin.* Cambridge, MA: Harvard University Press.

Said, E. (1978). *Orientalism.* New York, NY: Random House.

Schriewer, J. (2000). World system and interrelationship networks. In T. Popkewitz (Ed.), *Educational knowledge: Changing relationships between the state, civil society, and the educational community* (pp. 305–344). Albany, NY: State University of New York Press.

Schulte, B. (2011). The Chinese Dewey: Friend, fiend, and flagship. In R. Bruno-Jofre & J. Schreiwer (Eds.), *The global reception of John Dewey's thought: Multiple refractions through time and space* (pp. 83–115). London: Routledge.

Schulte, B. (2012). World culture with Chinese characteristics: When global models go native. *Comparative Education, 48*(4), 473–486. doi:10.1080/03050068.2012.726064

Spence, J. (1998). *The Chan's great continent: China in Western minds.* New York, NY: Norton.

Steiner-Khamsi, G. (2012). The global/local nexus in comparative policy studies: Analyzing the triple bonus system in Mongolia over time. *Comparative Education, 48*(4), 455–471. doi:10.1080/03050068.2012.681120

Tröhler, D. (2009). Globalizing globalization: The neo-institutional concept of a world culture. In T. S. Popkewitz & F. Rizvi (Eds.), *Globalization and the study of education: Yearbook of the National Society for the Study of Education: Vol. 108, Issue 2* (pp. 29–48). New York, NY: Wiley.

Wang, H. (1995). The fate of "Mr. Science" in China: The concept of science and its application in modern Chinese thought. *Positions, 3*(1), 1–68. doi:10.1215/10679847-3-1-1

Wang, M. (2000, December). *Empire to nation, and the relevance of reciprocal understanding to China.* Paper presented at the International Conference on Reciprocal Knowledge, Bologna, Italy.

Wang, M. (2009). *Empires and local worlds: A Chinese model of long-term historical anthropology.* Walnut Creek, CA: Left Coast Press.

Wang, M. (2014). *The West as the other: A genealogy of Chinese Occidentalism.* Hong Kong, Hong Kong: The Chinese University Press.

Wu, J. (2012). Governing suzhi and curriculum reform in rural ethnic China: Viewpoints from the Miao and Dong communities in Qiandongnan. *Curriculum Inquiry, 42*(5), 652–681. doi:10.1111/j.1467-873x.2012.00611.x

Wu, Z. (2011). Interpretation, autonomy, and transformation: Chinese pedagogic discourse in a cross-cultural perspective. *Journal of Curriculum Studies, 43*(5), 569–590. doi:10.1080/00220272.2011.577812

Yanpei, Huang. (1913). Discussing about using pragmatism in school education. *Jiaoyu Zazhi* [Educational Magazine], *5*(7), 55–82.

Zhong, S. (1989). *Cong Dongfang dao Xifang: Zouxiang Shijie Congshu Xulun* [From East to West: Prefaces to the Series of Going to the World]. Shanghai, China: People's Publishing House.

# CONTRIBUTORS

**Ragnhild Barbu** is a scientific assistant at the Institute of Education and Society at the University of Luxembourg. She was assisting with the research priority Education and Learning in Multilingual and Multicultural Contexts (2010–2013) and strongly engaged with the creation and development of the Doctoral School of Educational Sciences. Currently she is a member of the research team of the INTER research project: Educating the Future Citizens: Curriculum and the Formation of Multilingual Societies in Luxembourg and Switzerland, Funded by the Fonds National de la Recherche and the Swiss National Science Foundation.
ragnhild.barbu@uni.lu

**Viktoria Boretska** is a PhD candidate at the Institute of Education and Society at the University of Luxembourg. Her PhD thesis is titled *A Divided World with Common Educational Technology: Programmed Instruction and the Race for Global Supremacy in the Cold War.*
viktoria.boretska@uni.lu

**Lukas Boser** is a senior researcher at the University of Lausanne, Switzerland. He holds a master's degree in history and a PhD in the history of education from the University of Berne. He was a guest lecturer at the Humboldt University of Berlin and at the University of Education in Ludwigsburg, and he was a visiting scholar at the University of Wisconsin–Madison. His latest publications include *Lehrbuch Pädagogik. Eine Einführung in grundlegende Themenfelder* (hep, 2015) and "Learning to See the Nation-State" (*IJHE*, 1/2015).
Lukas.BoserHofmann@unil.ch

**Regula Bürgi** is a PhD candidate at the University of Luxembourg. She studied German literature, linguistics, and educational science in Zurich and Heidelberg.

In 2011 she graduated with a degree in educational science from the University of Zurich with a focus on the Organization for Economic Co-operation and Development (OECD) as an actor in Switzerland's educational policy. In her PhD research, she is analyzing the emergence of the OECD as an expert in education, particularly the creation of the Center for Educational Research and Innovation (CERI).
regula.buergi@uni.lu

**Peer Daugbjerg** is a senior lecturer in teacher education in Nørre Nissum, VIA University College in Denmark. His main interest is science education, teacher education and development, and research on the teacher profession. His PhD research at the Department for Learning, Aalborg University, focused on the relation between science teachers' lives and work, inspired by life history and sociocultural studies.
pd@via.dk

**Philipp Eigenmann** is a research and teaching assistant at the Institute of Education, Department of Vocational Education and Training, University of Zurich. In his PhD project, he is studying Italian labor immigrants in Switzerland between 1950 and 1990 regarding their vocational training, their further education, and the schooling for their children. Eigenmann studied educational sciences, sociology, and philosophy at the University of Zurich. His research interests are education, training, and migration in historical perspective; the history of apprenticeship; and educational reforms.
peigenmann@ife.uzh.ch

**Matias Gardin** is a research associate at the University of Luxembourg. He studied European studies at King's College London, where he obtained his PhD in 2013, supported by the Finnish Cultural Foundation. In 2012 he held a residential grant in Wiepersdorf Castle (Brandenburg). He holds a BA (2006) and an MA (2008) from the University of Manchester. Before coming to Luxembourg, he worked as a graduate teaching assistant at King's College London in comparative politics, political economy, and European history. He is currently involved in the project Educating the Future Citizens: Curriculum and the Formation of Multilingual Societies in Luxembourg and Switzerland.
matias.gardin@uni.lu

**Lukas Graf** is a postdoctoral researcher at the Institute of Education and Society of the University of Luxembourg. From 2008 to 2013 he worked at the Berlin Social Science Center. His research combines comparative and historical institutional analysis as well as sociology of education and political economy of skills. His book *The Hybridization of Vocational Training and Higher Education in Austria, Germany, and Switzerland* (Budrich, 2013) won the Best Dissertation Award from the

Higher Education Section of the Comparative and International Education Society and the Ulrich-Teichler-Prize of the German Association for Higher Education Research.
lukas.graf@uni.lu

**Norbert Grube** is a lecturer at the Centre for School History at the Zurich University of Teacher Education (PH Zurich). His research interests are the history of education and contemporary history. His recent articles include "Debates About Propaganda and Education in the USA in the 20th Century," in Aubry, C., Geiss, M., Magyar-Haas, V., & Oelkers, J. (Eds.), *Education and the State* (pp. 178–195, Routledge, 2014) and "Targeting and Educating Consumers in West Germany: Market Research by the Allensbach Institute up to the 1970s," in Brückweh, K. (Ed.), *The Voice of the Citizen Consumer* (pp. 75–95, Oxford University Press, 2011).
norbert.grube@phzh.ch

**Michèle Hofmann** is a research associate and lecturer at the University of Applied Sciences and Arts Northwestern Switzerland, School of Education. She holds a master's degree in history and a PhD in the history of education from the University of Bern. She was a guest lecturer at the Humboldt University of Berlin and at the University of Education in Ludwigsburg, and a visiting scholar at the University of Wisconsin–Madison. Her academic interests include the medicalization of education, the history of (special) education in Switzerland, and research methodology in history and the history of education.
michele.hofmann@fhnw.ch

**Rebekka Horlacher** is a research fellow in educational sciences at the University of Zurich and lecturer at the Zurich University of Teacher Education. Her latest publications include *Bildung or the Cultural Conceptualizing of Education: German Origins and International Misunderstandings* (Routledge, 2015), a six-volume edition of the letters written to Johann Heinrich Pestalozzi, and she is member of the editorial board of the journal *Bildungsgeschichte: International Journal for the Historiography of Education*.
rhorlach@ife.uzh.ch

**Malin Ideland** is a professor of educational sciences with a specialization in ethnology at Malmö University, Sweden. Her research interest is how discourses fabricate desirable subjects inside education, with a focus on environmental and sustainability education. She is the project leader for a Nordic network on cultural and political perspectives on science education, and her latest publications include the articles "'Our Common World' Belongs to 'Us': Constructions of Otherness in Education for Sustainable Development (*Critical Studies in Education*) and "Governing 'Eco-certified Children' Through Pastoral Power: Critical Perspectives on

Education for Sustainable Development (*Environmental Education Research Journal*; both articles are co-authored with Claes Malmberg).
malin.ideland@mah.se

**Thomas Lenz** is a research associate at the Institute for Education and Society at the University of Luxembourg. Currently he is working on the first national Education Report for Luxembourg. Before that, he elaborated a research project on school history and institutional change. He obtained his PhD in sociology at the University of Trier, Germany. In addition, he has been working as a scientific collaborator at the University of Trier and has given courses at Hamline University, Minneapolis, United States, and at the Babes-Bolyai University, Cluj-Napoca, Romania. His latest publications include *Konsum und Modernisierung: Die Debatte um das Warenhaus als Diskurs um die Moderne* (transcript, 2011) and *Tomorrow Never Dies: A Socio-Historical Analysis of the Luxembourgish Curriculum* (with C. Schreiber and A. Rohstock, Routledge, 2013).
thomas.lenz@uni.lu

**Catarina Silva Martins** is a professor in the Faculty of Fine Arts, Oporto University, and researcher at i2ADS-Institute of Research in Art, Design, and Society, University of Oporto, in which she coordinates the Research Group in Arts Education. She is the link convenor of Network 29: Research on Arts Education at the European Educational Research Association, as well as editor of the journal *Derivas: Research on Arts Education*. Her research interest lies in rethinking arts education curriculum studies in the present from a historical approach, focusing on the systems of reason that govern policy and research.
catarina-martins@campus.ul.pt

**Thomas S. Popkewitz** is a professor in the Department of Curriculum and Instruction at the University of Wisconsin–Madison, United States. His studies focus on social epistemologies, that is, the systems of reason that govern educational reforms, teacher education, and the education sciences. Central are the paradoxes of efforts for social equity that exclude and abject in the impulse to include; and the inscriptions of principles of stability in research about educational change. His recent books include *Políticas Educativas e Curriculares. Abordagens Sociológicas Críticas* (2011, Lisboa), *Cosmopolitanism and the Age of Reform* (2008), *Rethinking the History of Education* (ed., 2013), and *The "Reason" of Schooling* (ed., 2014). Currently he is writing a book about the impracticality of "practical" and "useful knowledge" in the education sciences.
popkewitz@education.wisc.edu

**Thomas Ruoss** is a historian and educational scientist at the University of Zurich's Institute of Education. He is working on the history of statistics and the history of education systems, administration, and politics. As a research assistant for the project "Education by Numbers," he is reconstructing educational statistical data to

publish them on www.bildungsgeschichte.uzh.ch and to provide an empirical basis for further research on the history of education in Switzerland.
truoss@ife.uzh.ch

**Jette Schmidt** is a senior lecturer of science education at University College Nordjylland in Denmark. Her main interest is science education, in particular geography education, in the context of the initial education of teachers. She has researched the recent changes in science teacher education policies in Denmark and their impact in transforming notions of the utility of teachers and education in society. Her research provides a critical and political reading of the work of science teachers in the context of a changing Danish welfare state.
jrs@ucn.dk

**Catherina Schreiber** works as a historian of education at the University of Luxembourg. In 2010 she received her master's degree in modern and contemporary history, modern and contemporary German literature, and information sciences from Saarland University (Germany). From October 2010 to October 2014 she worked as a PhD student at the University of Luxembourg. Her research focus was on constructions of citizenship in the Luxembourgian curriculum (her dissertation was titled *Curricula and the Making of the Citizens: Trajectories From 19th and 20th Century Luxembourg*). Her postdoctoral research focuses on science education, innovation, and policy in modern Luxembourg.
catherina.schreiber@googlemail.com

**Martin Sillasen** is an associate professor of science education and leader of the Center for Math- and Sciencedidactics at the School of Teacher Training, VIA University College, Denmark. His latest articles include "Science Teachers' Individual and Social Learning Related to IBSE in a Large-Scale, Longitudinal, Collaborative TPD Project" (*Proceedings of the ESERA*, Cyprus, 2013) and "Municipal Science Consultants' Participation in Building Networks to Support Science Teachers' Work" (Cultural Studies of Science Education, 2012).
msil@via.dk

**Daniel Tröhler** is a professor of education and director of the Doctoral School in Educational Sciences at the University of Luxembourg and visiting professor of comparative education at the University of Granada, Spain. His latest publications include *Languages of Education: Protestant Legacies, National Identities, and Global Aspirations* (Routledge, 2011; AERA Outstanding Book of the Year Award) and *Pestalozzi and the Educationalization of the World* (Palgrave, 2013). In 2014 he served as co-guest editor for the *Teachers College Record* special issue "Accountability in Education Governance: Antecedents, Power, and Processes." Several of his publications have been translated into different languages.
daniel.troehler@uni.lu

**Paola Valero** is a professor of education in mathematics and science, director of the Science and Mathematics Education Research Group, and director of the Doctoral Program in Technology and Science at the Faculty of Science and Engineering at Aalborg University, Denmark. She studies the significance of mathematics and science in the school curriculum as fields where power relations are actualized in producing subjectivities and generating inclusion/exclusion of different types of students. Her research is part of the Nordic Center of Excellence "Justice Through Education in the Nordic Countries."
paola@learning.aau.dk

**Peter Voss** is an assistant researcher at the Institute for Education and Society at the University of Luxembourg. His research fields encompass the history of the development of the primary school system in the 19th and 20th centuries and of the New Education movement in Luxembourg.
peter.voss@uni.lu

**Jinting Wu** is an assistant professor of education policy at the University of Macau. She received her PhD in educational policy studies and curriculum and instruction from the University of Wisconsin–Madison. She was postdoctoral fellow of educational sciences at the University of Luxembourg, also a recipient of the 2013 Gail P. Kelly Outstanding Dissertation Award in Comparative Education. She is the author of *Fabricating an Educational Miracle: Compulsory Schooling Meets Ethnic Rural Development in Southwest China*, forthcoming with the State University of New York Press (SUNY). Her research interests include comparative education, anthropology of education, educational philosophy, immigrant education, and the Chinese diaspora.
wujinting@umac.mo

**Yanmei Wu,** Minzu University of China, studies questions of social epistemology as it relates to minority education in China. She is doing research on Chinese textbooks in primary schools in inner Mongolia to explore how the knowledge of Chinese textbooks constructs the child, what the character of the knowledge in the textbook is, and how the knowledge of the textbook is reconstructed when used in the school practice.
meizimail@126.com

# INDEX

Note: Page numbers with *f* indicate figures; those with *t* indicate tables.

abstinence movement *see* temperance movement, Swiss schools and
abstinent teachers, in Swiss schools 99–101
accountability: described 215; neoliberalization and developing 220–2
achievement gap 17–18
*Action Program to Combat the Teacher Shortage* (Baden-Württemberg ministry of education) 140
actions 14
Adorno, T. W. 130
Advisory Committee of the Special Representative for National Refugees and Over-Population 147
Agenda 21, United Nations (UN) 200
Ahmed, S. 208, 209
aide à la presse law 177
alcoholism 98; *see also* temperance movement, Swiss schools and
Alfiorov, Z. 251
Allensbach Institute of Public Opinion Research 129, 130; archives of 141–2; Ettlinger circle and 130–1; Hahn and 132–3; teacher shortages and 139–40; *see also* Baden-Württemberg ministry of education case study; polls, educational policy and
*Amtliches Schulblatt* 92
anti-alcohol movement, international: abstinent faction of 100; moderate faction of 99–100

assimilation 149
*ausbildungsintegrierende* programs 232

Babaev, K. 251
Baden-Württemberg ministry of education case study 129; Allensbach polls and, overview of 128–9; Hahn and 131–2; national coherence presentation of 132–6, 134–5*t*, 136*t*; school reforms and, legitimation of 137–8; teacher shortage and, role in combating 138–40; West German government's use of 129–32
Baethge, M. 227
Bähler, E. L. 86
Bakken, B. 264
Barbu, R. 46–55
Basic Research in Higher Education (BRHE) 247–8; Dezhina and 249; program funding for 248*f*
Becker, K. S. 132
Bell, A. 113
BHS programs, Austria 230–1; location of, and impact of 235; loose coupling and, scope for 236, 238; universities of applied sciences and 234
Bitzius, A. 98
Blue Cross 99
Blumler, J. 175
Bologna Declaration 228–9
*Book of Rites* (Confucias) 258
Borda, J.-C. 75

## Index

Boretska, V. 241–53
Boser, L. 73–82
Bourdieu, P. 209
Brandt, W. 190–1
Bürgi, R. 144–53

Canton of Zurich, education statistics and: administrative bodies and 85; diffusion and institutionalization of 87–9; domestic school reforms and 91–2; homogenization of 89–91; nationalizing schooling through 86–7; overview of 85–6; as standardized language 85
Canton of Zurich, programmed learning in: American model and 118; computer-supported teaching and 120–2; conference to establish 118; critics and proponents of 118–19; implementation of 116–18; Stadlin and 118–19; teaching materials and, lack of 120; *see also* Department of Programmed Learning, Pestalozzianum
Canton of Zurich, school law of: central *versus* local governance and 30–1; Christian citizen ideals and 53–5, 54*f*; communicative practices and 32, 33, 34–5*f*; cultural sustainability and 40–1, 42–3; enrollments and 36*f*; school synod and 40; teacher reaction and organization in 39–40; treatment of teachers and 36–7
cantons, defined 30, 115
Carr, D. 46
catching-up modernization model 242
Catholic citizen, educating 46–55; Luxembourgish secularization process and 47–50; neutrality principle and 49–50; teacher education/employment and 52; textbook religious themes and 51; *see also* Luxembourg, institutionalization of primary education in
Catholic Deutsche Bischofskonferenz (German Bishops' Conference) 132
Catholic school regulations, introduction of 51
Central Science Council 186
*Check for Yourself!* (Association of Abstinent Teachers) 101
China, world culture theory and 256–66; Confucian practices and, return of 263–5; Deweyan pragmatism and 265; educational modernization and 260–3; New Culture Movement and 258–9; Occidentalism and 257, 259; Orientalism and 257, 259; overview of 256; West (xifang) concept and 257–60
Chinese, teachers' practice research 12
Chinese educational modernization 260–3
Chomsky, N. 161
Christian citizen ideals, schooling and 53–5, 54*f*
Christian Democratic Party 130
Christian Social People's Party (CSV) 175, 176–7
Civilian Research and Development Foundation (CRDF) 247
*Clash of Civilizations, The* (Huntington) 242
College of Natural Science 259
Common Aims: competence-based learning and 219–20; introduction of 222
competence-based learning: Common Aims and 219–20; described 215; neoliberalization and 218–20
computer-supported teaching, from programmed learning to 120–2
Conant, J. B. 113–14
"Concept of Modernization of Russian Education, The" 242–6
Condorcet, N. 75
Confucian practices/teaching 263–5
constituency grammar theory 161
*Constructing Knowledge Societies: New Challenges for Tertiary Education* (World Bank) 249
Council for Cultural Cooperation 147
Council of Europe: establishment of 146; Resolution 35 of 146–7; Social Charter 146–7; social policy function of 147
Council of Europe, migrant children schooling policies of 144–53; committee representatives selected for 147–50; historical context of 146–7; Malenfant and 147–8; overview of 144–5; qualitative information gathering for 149–50; quantitative information gathering for 148–9; Resolution 35 and 145–6, 150–2; world-cultural mission of 152–3
Cowen, R. 266
cybernetic concepts 158, 162–3

Dahrendorf, R. 131
Danilevsky, N. 241, 242
Danish science education reform, neoliberalization of 213–23;

accountability and 220–2; competence-based learning and 218–20; curriculum changes, overview of 215–16t; described 214–16; individualism and 217–18; overview of 213–14
*Das fleissige Hausmütterchen* (Müller) 80
*Das Tier* (magazine) 202
*Datang Xiyu Ji* (Xuanzang) 257–8
Daugbjerg, P. 213–23
*Definition and Selection of Key Competences* (DeSeCo) 219
Delambre, J.B.J. 75
Deng Xiaoping 261
Department of Comparative Educational Policy 244
Department of Computer Science, Pestalozzianum 115, 122
Department of Programmed Learning, Pestalozzianum 115; computer science and 121–2; establishment of 118–20; history of 116–17; Media as a Partner conference and 120–1; reciprocal knowledge exchange bulletin of 120; Stadlin and 117–18; teaching machines and 117
*Der Spiegel* (magazine) 140
Develey, E. 77
dewesternizing 242, 243
Dewey, J. 261–2, 265
Dezhina, I. 248, 249, 251
domestic school reforms, advancement of 91–2
Dostert, L. 160
Dostoyevsky, F. 241
dual study programs, Germany 231–2; academic drift and 236–7; dual apprenticeship training and 234–5; location of, and impact of 235–6
Dufour, G.-H. 80
*Dursli the Liquor Drunkard* (Gotthelf) 98
Dutch school law of 1806 29

Earth Hour 204, 205f
Earth Summit 201
Echternach case study 62–70; allegations against primary school 63–4; classical *versus* vocational education 67–70; course of proceedings 63; discussion of allegations 64–5; overcrowding and 65; pedagogical research 65–6; prelude 62; school location 67
*École Normale* (teacher education school) 52, 75

Editpress 176
educating methods 113
education, contesting 174–81; Luxembourgish media and 176–8; overview of 174; PISA results example of 180–1; Sputnik crisis example of 178–80; theoretical framework for 174–6
educational catastrophe 184
educational expansion: in Finland see Finland, educational expansion in; rationale for 184–8
educationalization: described 199; examples of 199–200; see also WWF International
educational modernization, Chinese 260–3
educational policy and polls see polls, educational policy and
educational research, defined 43
educational schism 227
education and research, coupling 245–6
*Education and the Economy in a Changing Society* (OECD) 217
Education and Training Assistance Act, West Germany 188, 189
Education Council (Germany) 186
education for sustainable development (ESD) 200–1; environmental non-governmental organizations and 200; see also WWF International
education reforms 188–91; neoliberalization of 214–16
education statistics, Canton of Zurich see Canton of Zurich, education statistics and
Education System Act, Finland 188-9
Egger, E. 148, 149–50
Eigenmann, P. 144–53
E-learning 113
elementarizing concept 119
environmental citizenship, changes in 202
environmental non-governmental organizations (NGOs): as educational agents 200; rise of 201–4; waves of increase in 201
Erhard, L. 185–6
Erler, F. 186
*ertong dujing yundong* movement 263–4
*Ettlinger Kreis* (Ettlinger circle) 130–1, 139
European Credit Transfer and Accumulation System 229
European Economic Community 145
European educational model 227–38; Bologna Process and 236–7; European

integration and 235–8; hybrid organizational forms of 230–5; impact of 235–6; institutional permeability and 237–8; overview of 227–9; research methods and data used 229–30
European Qualification Framework (EQF) 229
European teacher educators, described 10–11
European Union 144
Evers, C.-H. 113
Excellent Teacher 14–15, 19
exceptionalism, in Russia 241
expert teachers 13–16

Federal Institute for Population Research 141
Federal Ministry of Education and Science 186
Federal Ministry of Scientific Research 186
Fedotova, V. G. 242
Filippov, V. 243–5
Finland, educational expansion in: educational bodies of 186; educational expenditures and 185; law frames of 188, 189–90; overview of 183–4; policy trends in, 1960–1970 185; political transformation of 184–8; reforms introduced for 188–91
Finnish Study Allowance Act 191
First International Conference on Programmed Learning and Teaching Machines 113
Flitner, A. 131
*Fountain of Youth* (Association of Abstinent Teachers) 101
Four Olds 262
*Framework for Priority Action for Change and Development in Higher Education* (UNESCO) 245
French Academy of Sciences 75
Frieden, P. 179
*From a Fresh Spring* (Association of Abstinent Teachers) 101
*From Care to Action: Making a Sustainable World* (Holdgate) 203
*From Knowledge to Wealth: Integrating Science and Higher Education for the Development of Russia* (World Bank and NTF)
*From Vision to Lesson: Education for Sustainable Development in Practice* (Östman, Svanberg, and Aaro-Östman) 205–6

fruit and milk schoolbooks 101–7; as anti-alcohol education 102–4; economic reasons for 101–2; school subjects involved in 104–5; worldwide economic crisis and 102
Fukuyama, F. 242

Gagarin, Y. 253
Gallup Institute 130
Galperin, P. J. 114
Gardin, M. 183–92
genius loci 29
German Science Council 131
German tripartite school system 137
*Geschichtslosigkeit* 160
ghettoization 150
Gorbachev, M. 242
Gotthelf, J. 98
Graf, L. 227–38
Graham, L. 247
grammar of schooling concept 47
*Graphical Tables With Accompanying Text on the Alcohol Issue* (Stump and Willenegger) 100, 101, 108
Grob, J. C. 87
Grossman, P. 14
Grube, N. 128–41
Grzimek, B. 202
Gubler, M. 118
Gurevitch, M. 175
*Gymnasium* schools 61, 131, 227, 230; *see also* European educational model

Haarder, B. 217
Habermas, J. 174
Hadjar, A. 185
Hahn, C. 43
Hahn, W. 131; Allensbach polls and 132–3, 140; education policy beliefs of 131–2; national prosperity and, increasing 137; Social Democrat reforms and 133–5; teacher shortages and 139–40, 141; *see also* Baden-Württemberg ministry of education case study; polls, educational policy and
Hamburg Agreement, West Germany 188–9
harmonization aspects of schooling 5–6
Hartmann, A. 103–4
Hartmann, H. 86
Hartz, M. 39
Hauser, J. 107
*Haus und Schule* (monthly journal) 53, 54f

*Healthy Youth* (Association of Abstinent Teachers) 101
higher education (HE) 227
higher education and research model, integration of 246–50, 246f, 248f
*Higher Education in Developing Countries: Peril and Promise* (World Bank) 249
*Higher Education: The Lessons of Experience* (World Bank) 247
high leverage practices 17
historicity, absence of 160, 166–7
Hofmann, M. 98–108
Holkenbrink, H. 188
homogenization: of education statistics 89–90; of education structures 90–1
Honkonen, K. 186
Hood, T. 259
Horlacher, R. 113–23
Hosjöskolan (Hosjö school), Falun 207–8
*How Five Girls Perish Pitifully From Liquor* (Gotthelf) 98
Huber, A. 86–7, 88
Hug, J. C. 79
human capital century 191
Huntington, S. P. 242
Hu Shi 262
hybrid educational organizational forms 230–5; BHS in Austria and 230–1, 234; dual study programs in Germany and 231–2, 234–5; impact of Europeanization on 237–8; precarious status of 233–5; survival of 233–4

Ideland, M. 199–210
individualism: defined 215; neoliberalization and 217–18
intercultural education 152

James, W. 115, 119
Javet, M. 106
Johansen, G. 208
*Journal for Healthcare* 102
*Journal for Hygiene* 103
Jungo, M. 149, 150
Jürgens, H.-W. 141

Kang You Wei 259, 260
Keller, A. 105
*Key Competencies for a Successful Life and a Well-Functioning Society* (Rychen and Salganik) 219
king's foot 74
Kirpach, H. 49

Kohl, H. 138
Kollerics, F. 117
Koppes, J. J. 51
Kull, M. 187

Lancaster, J. 113
language education 157–70; competing perceptions of 160–2; to construct coherence 165; current multilingualism policies in 169–70; Luxembourgian 162–9; overview of 157–60; Sputnik launch and 160; in United States 160
Laplace, P.-S. 75
Laurent, J.-T. 47, 48, 51
Lavoisier, A. 74, 75
learning through insight 118–19
*Le Monde* (newspaper) 179
Lenz, T. 3–8, 174–81
Leontjew, A. N. 114
Lerf, R. 118
Liang Qi Chao 260
liberal democracy 242
Linnaeus, C. 74
Livanov, D. 251
loose coupling model 3–5, 233–4, 235, 236, 238; *see also* European educational model
Luhmann, N. 174–5
Luxembourg, early school evaluation and competency conflicts in 60–70; *see also* Echternach case study
Luxembourg, institutionalization of primary education in 46–55; Christian citizen ideals and 53–5, 54f; first school law of 1843 and 48; overview of 46–7; religious foundation and, teacher education 52; sacralization of teaching and 50–2; school law of 1881 and 49; secularization process and 47–50; separation of church and state and 49–50; textbook religious themes and 51
Luxembourg, school law of: central *versus* local governance and 31–2, 31f; communicative practices and 32–3, 33f; cultural sustainability and 41–3, 41f; secularization process and 47–50; teacher reaction and organization in 39; treatment of teachers and 36, 37–8f, 37–9
Luxembourgian language education 162–9; adaptations in 162–5; coherence construction and 165; current multilingualism and 169–70; cybernetics and 162–3; historicity and, absence of 166–7; intranational hierarchies and

167–9; Luxembourgish as informal language and 166
Luxembourgish media: PISA results and education contesting in 180–1; Sputnik crisis and education contesting in 178–80; structure of 176–8
*Luxembourg School Herald* 32–3, 33*f*, 37–9, 41
Luxembourg Socialist Workers' Party (LSAP) 175, 176–7
*Luxemburger Journal* 176
*Luxemburger Schulbote (Luxembourg School Herald)* 32–3, 33*f*, 37–9
*Luxemburger Schulfreund* (Catholic teacher journal) 51
*Luxemburger Wort* (newspaper) 48, 50, 175, 176–7; PISA results and 180–1; Sputnik crisis and 178–9
*Lycée* school 61

MacArthur Foundation 247
maintenance teaching 150
Malenfant, P. 147–8
Mao Zedong 261
Martin, B. 186–7, 190
Martin-Nielsen, J. 161–2
Martins, C. S. 7–8, 10–21
mathematical information theory 158
measurement and weights: Bible and 74; metric system in Switzerland and 73–82; metrology reforms for 75; natural scientists and 74–5; overview of 73–4; properties of 74; standardization of 74–6
Méchain, P. 75
Media as a Partner (conference) 120–1
media education, from programmed learning to 120–2
Mergel, T. 184
messy public idea 175
metric system in Switzerland 73–82; beginnings of, standardization of measurements and 74–6; constitutional amendment for 81–2; measurement and weights overview 73–4; national integration of 79–81; politics of introducing 76–9; Tralles and 75–6
metrology reforms 75
Metz, N. 61, 70
Meyer, J. 260
*Milk* (Schuler) 104
*Model Works of the Vernacular* (Chinese textbook) 258–9

*Modernization of the "Second" Europe* (Fedotova) 242
Monitorial System 113
Müller, S. 80
multilingual nation-states 158, 159, 169–70

*Nachbarschaftsschulen* (neighborhood schools) 135
National Danish School Act 217
National Defense Education Act 199
national qualification framework (NQF) 229
National Research Fund, Luxembourg 7, 8
*Nation at Risk, A* (National Commission on Excellence in Education) 199
nation-states, Europe's 28*f*; categories of 28; school system development in 29–30
*Nature* (science journal) 82
neo-institutionalism 3; loose coupling model 3–5; world culture theory of 144; world polity thesis of 4
neo-institutional sociology 29
neutrality principle 49–50
New Culture Movement, China 258–9
New Curriculum Reform, China 263
New Mathematics in Europe 6
*Nine Days of One Year* (movie) 253
Noelle-Neumann, E. 129, 130, 131
non-expert teachers 13
Normal School (teacher education school) 52
notion of the public 174–5

Occidentalism 256, 257, 259
Oettli, M. 104
opinion polls 128
Organization for Economic Co-operation and Development (OECD) 6, 28–9, 177; competence concept and 219; Danish educational policy *see* Danish science education reform, neoliberalization of; harmonization and 4; neo-institutionalism theory and 144; Programme for International Student Assessment and 19, 174, 200, 217–18
Organization for European Economic Co-operation (OEEC) 6
Orientalism 257, 259
*Orientalism* (Said) 257
Orthodox ethic, Soviet science and 252–3
*Orthodox Civilization in a Globalized World* (Panarin) 253

Orton, J. D. 233
Osipov, Y. 250
Östman, L. 205–6
*Our Country: A Heimatbuch for Adults and Children* 51
*Our Creative Diversity* (World Commission on Culture and Development) 244

Panarin, A. 253
Parsons, T. 174
*PcU-Bulletin* 121, 122
Pedagogical Institute 52
Peoples' Friendship University of Russia (PFUR) 243
Pestalozzi, J. H. 60, 119
Pestalozzi Method 113
Piaget, J. 139
Piazolo, P. H. 131
Picht, G. 130, 131, 184
Pinar, W. 7, 8
PISA *see* Programme for International Student Assessment (PISA)
polls, educational policy and 128–41; Hahn, Wilhelm; Hahn and 131–2; overview of 128–9; public opinion, in 1950s West Germany 129–32; questioning techniques used 134–5*t*; school reforms and, legitimation of 137–8; support for, monitoring 132–6, 136*t*; teacher shortages/images and 138–40; *see also* Baden-Württemberg ministry of education case study
Pongratz, L. 160
Popkewitz, T. S. 7, 10–21, 223
Posch, P. 139, 141
*Practical Experience in Organization and Functioning of Universities in the Conditions of a Market Economy* (Filippov) 244
Prieur, C. A. 75
Prigogine, I. 244
primary education in Luxembourg, institutionalization of *see* Luxembourg, institutionalization of primary education in
*Proceedings of the School Synod* 40
professional teacher, elements of 14
programmed learning: critics and proponents of 118–19; department of 118–20; as educational reform example 122–3; implementation of, in Canton of Zurich 116–18; media education and 120–2; overview of 113–16; Skinner and 114–15; teaching materials and, lack of 120

programmed learning, Canton of Zurich *see* Canton of Zurich, programmed learning in
Programme for International Student Assessment (PISA) 19, 174; individualization in Danish schools and 217–18; Luxembourg media and 180–1
Prohibition, United States 101
Pro Juventute fruit donation 106
promentaboy 116–17
protective book covers, abstinent teachers and 105–6
psycholinguistic theory 161
*PU-Bulletin* 120, 121
Putin, V. 243

Rancière, J. 20
Ranson, S. 222
Rasmussen, A. F. 222
Read, J. 214
readability of qualifications 228
Reagan, R. 199
reception and integration teaching 150
reflective practitioners 13, 14
reform-oriented teacher practices, research on 12–13
*Renxu Xuezhi* reform 261–2
Republic of Letters 75
research, teacher practice *see* teacher practices, research on
Resolution 35, Council of Europe's 145–6; *see also* Council of Europe, migrant children schooling policies of; information gathering for 148–50; meanings of 150–2; overview of 144–5; recommendations made in 151; special classes and 145
Rio Conference on Environment and Development (Earth Summit) 201
Rochat, L.-L. 99
Rohrbach, C. 121
Rose, N. 214
Royaumont seminar 6
RTL group 176
Ruoss, T. 85–93
Russia, Westernization in post-Soviet 241–53; Basic Research in Higher Education and 247–8, 248*f*; Concept of Modernization of Russian Education and 243–6; education and research coupling and 245–6; Filippov and 243–5; higher education and research model, integration of 246–50, 246*f*; Orthodox ethic and 252–3; overview of

241–3; policy *versus* public discussion and 251; Russian Academy of Sciences and 252; Russian history/reality and 250–3
*Russia and Europe* (Danilevsky) 241
Russian Academy of Sciences (RAS) 247; Soviet science at 253; Western model and 250–1, 252
Russian Institute of Economy in Transition 248
Russon, E. 8
"Ruthli" (small-format illustration) 105

Said, E. 257
Saint-Paul 176
Schlapbach, F. 185
Schmidt, J. 213–23
school campaigns, abstinent teachers and 106
school concordat 48
schooling, development of modern 3–8; harmonization aspects of 5–6; internationalization of 6–7; neo-institutionalism and 3–5; transnational beliefs and 6
school law *see* Canton of Zurich, school law of; Luxembourg, school law of
school reform, practical knowledge and 10–21; exclusion and 19–20; overview of 10–11; systems analysis and 16–19; teacher practices and 11–16
school reforms, legitimation of 137–8
Schreiber, C. 157–70
Schuler, F. 102–3
*Schweizerisches Kaufmännisches Zentralblatt* (Stadlin) 118
*Science Education in the Future* (Andersen) 219
"Science of Learning and the Art of Teaching, The" (Skinner) 114–15
separation of church and state 49–50
*Serengeti Shall Not Die* (Grzimek) 202
*Silent Spring* (Carson) 203
Sillasen, M. 213–23
Skinner, B. F. 114–15, 160–1
Skolkovo Institute of Science and Technology (Skoltech) 251
Social Darwinism 141
social epistemology 11
Social Question 13–16
Society for Programmed Instruction 120
Society for Teaching and Learning Methods 120
special classes: immigration countries and 146; relevance of 149–50; Resolution 35 and 145
specialist teachers 146
Sputnik crisis, Luxembourg media and 174, 178–80
Stadlin, A. 117–19
Stammer, H. 60
standardization of measurements 74–6
Standing Conference of the Ministers of Culture 186
statistics, use of 128
Steiger, H. 100
Steiner-Khamsi, G. 92
Stevenson, P. 158
stratificational grammar theory 161
structural functionalism 174
Study Allowance Act, Finland 188, 189–90
Stump, J. 100, 108
*Stuttgarter Zeitung* (newspaper) 131–2
Sulzberger, J. J. 80
Sun Yat-sen 261
*Supporting Teacher Educators for Better Learning Outcomes* (European Commission) 12
Swedish exceptionalism 206–9
Swiss Association of Abstinent Teachers 99, 100, 105–6
Swiss cartography 80
Swiss Central Office for the Fight Against Alcoholism 104, 105
Swiss Conference of Cantonal Ministers of Education (EDK) 87–8, 89
Swiss Information Centre for Teaching and Education (CESDOC) 148, 149–50
Swiss International Bureau of Education 139
*Swiss School* (journal) 107
Swiss school temperance movement *see* temperance movement, Swiss schools and
*Swiss Teachers' Journal* 100, 104, 105, 107
Switzerland: Council of Europe and 145; Italians in 149–50; qualitative information gathering and 149–50; quantitative information gathering and 148–9
Switzerland metric system 73–82; beginnings of, standardization of measurements and 74–6; constitutional amendment for 81–2; measurement and weights overview 73–4; national integration of 79–81; politics of introducing 76–9; Tralles and 75–6

systems analysis 16–19
system theory 174

*Tageblatt* (newspaper) 175, 176; PISA results and 180–1; Sputnik crisis and 179–80
*Tages-Anzeiger* (newspaper) 118
*Talks to Teachers on Psychology* (James) 115
Talleyrand, C. M. 75
teacher education: Catholic influence in 52; as human improvement 13; social improvement and 14; three activities of 14
teacher practices, research on 11–16; definition of 18; impracticalities of local knowledge and 20–1; overview of 11–12; reform-oriented 12–13; Social Question and 13–16
teachers, nation-states in Europe: educational policy participation of 39–43; primary, in Luxembourg 41*f*; professional/social-moral behavior of 36–9
Teach for America (TFA) 14; core practices and 15–16; Excellent Teacher standards of 14, 15; teacher portfolios and 16; transformation and 15
teaching, practical knowledge of 19
temperance movement, Swiss schools and 98–108; abstinent teachers and 99–101; fruit and milk schoolbooks and 101–7; overview of 98–9; protective book covers and 105–6; school campaigns and 106; visual material and 105
temperance societies, for children 98
Tenth International Anti-Alcohol Congress 100
textbook religious themes 51
*Times, The* 191
*Ti-Yong* dichotomy 260–1
Tolstoy, L. 259
Tørnæs, U. 221
Tralles, J. G. 75–6
transformational grammar theory 161
Triple Helix concept 245–6
Tröhler, D. 3–8, 27–43, 199–210, 252
Tuomioja, E. 186
Turgenev, I. S. 259

UNESCO 29, 139, 144, 162, 169, 183; educational initiatives 200; Education for All 4; International Institute for Educational Planning 6; World Bank joint projects with 249;
World Commission on Culture and Development 244; World Conference on Higher Education 245
United Nations (UN): Agenda 21 200; Environment Program 201
United States: desired teacher in 12–13; teacher education reforms, focus of 10
universal language structures, search for 160–2
University Development Act, Finland 188, 189, 190
University of Luxembourg 7, 8
U.S. National Council for Research 12
USSR Academy of Sciences 160

Valero, P. 213–23
*Verbal Behavior* (Skinner) 160–1
*Verhandlungen der Schulsynode (Proceedings of the School Synod)* 40
Vestager, M. 219
Virolainen, J. 190
visual material, abstinent teachers and 105
vocational education and training (VET) 227
Volkart, H. 100
von Friedeburg, L. 140
von Humboldt, A. 245
Voss, P. 60–70

Wang Mingming 257
von Wartburg, W. von 119
Weber, J.-J. 170
Weick, E. K. 233
weights and measurement: Bible and 74; metric system in Switzerland and 73–82; metrology reforms for 75; natural scientists and 74–5; overview of 73–4; properties of 74; standardization of 74–6
Werner, M. G. Z. 63, 64, 65–7
*West as the Other: A Genealogy of Chinese Occidentalism, The* (Wang) 257
West *(xifang)* concept, China and 257–60
Western Europe, modern school system development in; Luxembourg, school law of: central *versus* local governance and 30–2; Cold War and expansion of 29; communication practices and 32–6; neo-institutional approach to 29; origins of 27; overview of 27–30; school laws and syllabi established for 29–30, 42; teacher reaction and organization to 39–43; treatment of teachers and 36–9; *see also* Canton of Zurich, school law of

Westernization: characteristics of 252; defined 242; Filippov and 243–5; Modernization as 242; in post-Soviet Russia *see* Russia, Westernization in post-Soviet

West Germany: educational policy monitoring by, public polls and 129–32; *Ettlinger Kreis* (Ettlinger circle) creation in 130–1; teacher shortages/images and 138–40; tripartite school system 137; *see also* Hahn, W.

West Germany, educational expansion in: educational bodies of 186; expenditures and 185; law frames of 188–9; overview of 183–4; policy trends in, 1960–1970 185; political transformation of 184–8; reforms introduced for 188–91

Willenegger, R. 100, 108

Wilson, W. 129

World Bank 4, 6, 247–8, 249

world culture theory 153, 256; advocates of 144; of neo-institutionalism 144; proponents of 144; *see also* Council of Europe, migrant children schooling policies of

*World Declaration on Higher Education for the 21st Century* (UNESCO) 245

world polity thesis 4

world society 4

World Wide Fund for Nature (WWF) 200; *see also* WWF International

Wu, J. 256–66

Wu, Y. 7, 10–21

WWF International 201; branding of 204; Earth Hour 204, 205f; educational programs of, as Swedish exceptionalism 207–9; education for sustainable development and 200–1; growth of 201–2; Hosjöskolan school, Falun 207–8; inclusion/exclusion, double gesture of 204–5; internationalization of ESD and 204–7; overview of 199–201; role of 203–4

WWF Sweden 200

Wymann, H. 118

Xuanzang, M. 257–8

Yan Fu 260

*Yearbook of the Education System in Switzerland (Jahrbuch des Unterrichtswesen in der Schweiz)* 86, 87, 89

*Zarya* (journal) 241

Zehnder, H. U. 37

*Zeidung vom letzeburger Vollek* (newspaper) 176

Zhou Scripture of Rites 257

Zollinger, F. 88

Zurich *see* Canton of Zurich, education statistics and; Canton of Zurich, programmed learning in; Canton of Zurich, school law of

Zurich, Switzerland, Republic of 53

Zurich Education Council 116, 118

Zurich school synod 40

Zurich Teachers' Training College 118